East Asian Sign Linguistics

Sign Language Typology

Editors
Marie Coppola, Onno Crasborn, Ulrike Zeshan
and Susanne Maria Michaelis

Editorial board
Sam Lutalo-Kiingi, Ronice Müller de Quadros,
Nick Palfreyman, Roland Pfau, Adam Schembri,
Gladys Tang, Erin Wilkinson, JunHui Yang

Volume 10

East Asian Sign Linguistics

Edited by
Kazumi Matsuoka, Onno Crasborn and Marie Coppola

ISBN 978-1-5015-2388-5
e-ISBN (PDF) 978-1-5015-1024-3
e-ISBN (EPUB) 978-1-5015-1016-8
ISSN 2192-5186

Library of Congress Control Number: 2022938178

Bibliographic information published by the Deutsche Nationalbibliothek
The Deutsche Nationalbibliothek lists this publication in the Deutsche Nationalbibliografie;
detailed bibliographic data are available on the internet at http://dnb.dnb.de.

Chapter "Time and timelines in Tibetan Sign Language (TSL) interactions in Lhasa"
© the author

This chapter is licensed under the Creative Commons Attribution-NonCommercial-NoDerivatives 4.0
International License. For details go to http://creativecommons.org/licenses/by-nc-nd/4.0/.

© 2024 Walter de Gruyter Inc., Boston/Berlin and Ishara Press, Lancaster, UK
This volume is text- and page-identical with the hardback published in 2023.
Typesetting: Integra Software Services Pvt. Ltd.

www.degruyter.com

Contents

Kazumi Matsuoka, Onno Crasborn and Marie Coppola
Introduction —— 1

Part 1: **Manuals: Numerals, classifiers, modal verbs**

Keiko Sagara
Historical relationships between numeral signs in Japanese Sign Language, South Korean Sign Language and Taiwan Sign Language —— 7

Shengyun Gu
Phonological processes in complex word formation in Shanghai Sign Language —— 37

Ki-Hyun Nam and Kang-Suk Byun
Classifiers and gender in Korean Sign Language —— 71

Jia He and Gladys Tang
Causative alternation in Tianjin Sign Language —— 101

Kazumi Matsuoka, Uiko Yano and Kazumi Maegawa
Epistemic modal verbs and negation in Japanese Sign Language —— 137

Part 2: **Non-manuals and space**

Sung-Eun Hong, Seong Ok Won, Hyunhwa Lee, Kang-Suk Byun and Eun-Young Lee
The Korean Sign Language (KSL) corpus and its first application on a study about mouth actions —— 171

Felix Sze and Helen Lee
Negative polar questions in Hong Kong Sign Language —— 203

Natsuko Shimotani
Analyzing head nod expressions by L2 learners of Japanese Sign Language: A comparison with native Japanese Sign Language signers —— 241

Shiou-fen Su
Composite utterances in Taiwan Sign Language — 263

Theresia Hofer
Time and timelines in Tibetan Sign Language (TSL) interactions in Lhasa — 311

Index — 347

Kazumi Matsuoka, Onno Crasborn and Marie Coppola
Introduction

The purpose of this volume is to provide research results of sign languages in East Asian communities, which have often been considered as underrepresented varieties of sign languages in the world. It does not mean, however, that sign languages in Asian countries do not have a long history. For instance, Japanese Sign Language is at least 140 years old, counting from the foundation of the first school for the deaf in 1878. Further, Ito (1998) noted that written and illustrated documents indicate that there were deaf Japanese who might have been signing before that time. Similarly, it is very likely that sign languages used by deaf communities existed in other parts of Asia. It has been reported that some sign languages in Asia are historically related: Hong Kong Sign Language has developed from Shanghai Sign Language, for instance (Sze et al. 2013). In modern days, the occupation of South Korea and Taiwan by Japan is considered a decisive factor in the development of Korean Sign Language and Taiwan Sign Language (cf. Sagara, this volume).

The scarcity of information about sign languages in Asia, written in English, has significantly affected the field of sign language research in the West. In particular, sign linguists who are interested in a comparative approach are faced with the lack of materials written in English for them to refer to. Though there are some exceptions, such as Smith (1989), Fischer (1996), Fischer and Gong (2010), as well as chapters in edited volumes such as Zeshan (2006) and Bakken Jepsen et al. (2015), these show variation in the range and the systematicity of the observations reported in those works, due to the limited availability of local informants. Another prominent exception is the rich work on Hong Kong Sign Language (e.g. Tang 2003; Sze 2011), where English is one of its official languages.

Indeed, 'language barrier' is a serious issue in the consideration of the development of sign language research in Asia. Unlike in many Western countries, English is not an official or a common language in East Asia. In general, it is not usually the case, particularly in fields outside natural science, that researchers are expected to publish their works in English. Sign language researchers in those countries often are under social pressure to share their research results in the language accessible to families of deaf individuals, educators, as well as among the general public. It is particularly important to note that information provided in English is considered inaccessible by members of the local deaf community. In such an environment, it is understandable that the authors' focus is not always on publishing their research in English. However, this situation is gradually changing, as more deaf and hearing researchers have been receiving academic training in graduate programs in English-speaking countries. Furthermore, interactions with colleagues in different countries has become easier with the remarkable development of digital technology. We truly hope that the present volume contributes to comparative studies of sign language linguistics in various frameworks.

We are delighted to compile this volume on East Asian Sign Linguistics, in the Sign Language Typology series. The book contains ten chapters covering a variety of sign languages in East Asia, including ones which have not been widely discussed in the field (e.g., Tibetan Sign Language, Tianjin Sign Language). The chapters in the first part (chapters 1–5) mostly deal with manual articulations, and the chapters in the second part (6–10) are mostly focused on non-manual properties and the use of space.

In the first chapter, Sagara elucidates historical relationships among three Asian sign languages (Japanese, South Korean, and Taiwanese) by considering diachronic changes in numerical signs. In the following chapter, Gu considers phonological processes seen in compounding and affixation in Chinese Sign Language (Shanghai variety), and how the shapes of Chinese characters may interfere with phonological patterns. Nam and Byun, in Chapter 3, discuss word formation in Korean Sign Language: how handshapes in Korean Sign Language, associated with sociological gender, are incorporated in lexical signs, classifiers, and agreement verbs. Next, in Chapter 4, He and Tang provide a typological analysis of causative alternations in Tianjin Sign Language. At the end of the first part, in Chapter 5, Matsuoka, Yano, and Maegawa demonstrate how multiple categories of modals and negation are aligned in a cartographic paradigm in Japanese Sign Language.

The chapters in the second part focus on non-manual aspects of the sign language(s) under study. In Chapter 6, Hong, Won, Lee, Byun, and Lee provide a detailed description of their large-scale Korean Sign Language corpus project, which is followed by comparative discussions of mouth actions. Next, in Chapter 7, Sze and Lee investigate syntactic and semantic properties of negative polar questions in Hong Kong Sign Language, which led to the discussion of grammaticalization of multiple non-manual expressions. In her systematic comparison of head nods of native signers and hearing learners of Japanese Sign Language, Shimotani distinguishes what can be learned with or without explicit instructions. The remaining two chapters deal with the use of space. In Chapter 9, Su provides detailed analysis of narratives of native and non-native signers of Taiwanese Sign Language, and how three methods of signaling are materialized in signers' expressions. Finally, in Chapter 10, Hofer describes several types of timelines in Tibetan Sign Language (TSL) Interactions in Lhasa.

The following map of the countries where those sign languages are used is provided to orient readers.

- Sagara (Chapter 1): Japanese Sign Language, South Korean Sign Language, Taiwan Sign Language
- Gu (Chapter 2): Shanghai Sign Language
- Nam and Byun (Chapter 3) / Hong, Won, Lee, Byun, and Lee (Chapter 6): Korean Sign Language
- He and Tang (Chapter 4): Tianjin Sign Language.
- Matsuoka, Yano, and Maegawa (Chapter 5) / Shimotani (Chapter 8): Japanese Sign Language
- Sze and Lee (Chapter 7): Hong Kong Sign Language
- Su (Chapter 9): Taiwan Sign Language
- Hofer (Chapter 10): Tibetan Sign Language in Lhasa

In conclusion, this book project became possible with support from various sources. We would like to express our gratitude to the many anonymous reviewers. Michaela Gobels (of De Gruyter Press) and Suruthi Manogaran (Integra Software Services) has provided continuous support to the project. We are grateful to Asako Uchibori, who temporarily stepped in to assist with editorial duties. The editing was further supported by JSPS KAKENHI Grant 19H01259, awarded to Kazumi Matsuoka, grants no. 360-70-500 and 277-70-014 from the Netherlands Organization for Scientific Research, awarded to Onno Crasborn, and United States National Science Foundation grant no.1553589 awarded to Marie Coppola.

References

Bakken Jepsen, Julie, Goedele De Clerck, Sam Lutalo-Kiingi, & William B. McGregor (eds.). 2015. *Sign Languages of the World: A Comparative Handbook*. Berlin: De Gruyter Mouton.
Fischer, Susan. 1996. The role of agreement and auxiliaries in sign language. *Lingua* 98(1–3). 103–119.
Fischer, Susan & Qunhu Gong. 2010. Variation in East Asian sign language structures. In Diane Brentari (ed.) *Sign Languages*. 499–518. Cambridge: Cambridge University Press.
Ito, Masao.1998. *Rekishi no naka no roasha* [The deaf and mute in the history]. Tokyo: Kindai Shuppan.
Sze, Felix. 2011. Nonmanual markings for topic constructions in Hong Kong Sign Language. *Sign Language & Linguistics* 14(1). 115–147. https://doi.org/10.1075/sll.14.1.07sze
Sze, Felix, Connie Lo, Lisa Lo, & Kenny Chu. 2013. Historical development of Hong Kong Sign Language. Sign Language Studies 13(2). 155–185.
Smith, Wayne Henry. 1989. The morphological characteristics of verbs in Taiwan Sign Language. Doctoral dissertation, Indiana University.
Tang, Gladys. 2003. Classifiers of Hong Kong Sign Language: Conflation and lexicalization. In Karen Emmorey (ed.) *Perspectives on classifier constructions in sign languages*. 143–166. Lawrence Erlbaum Associates.
Zeshan, Ulrike (ed.) 2006. *Interrogative and negative constructions in sign languages*. Nijmegen: Ishara Press.

Part 1: **Manuals: Numerals, classifiers, modal verbs**

Keiko Sagara
Historical relationships between numeral signs in Japanese Sign Language, South Korean Sign Language and Taiwan Sign Language

Abstract: How do numeral expressions in sign languages change over time? Three sign languages used in East Asia – namely Japanese Sign Language, South Korean Sign Language and Taiwan Sign Language – offer an excellent opportunity to address this question, because of historic links between them. Two dialects of Japanese Sign Language were introduced to Taiwan and South Korea in the first half of the twentieth century, and remnants of these dialects can still be detected in the modern-day sign languages used in these respective countries. Using the literature, historical sources, and data collected from users of each sign language, this chapter examines changes in numeral expressions with a view to studying language change and relationships between sign languages. These expressions are often motivated by iconicity, but frequently contain abstract and systematic elements, providing a window to understand processes of language change more fully. I compare expressions for '10', '100' and '1,000' and the structure of numbers based on them, and find that, while some similar changes can be observed in the sign languages of Taiwan and South Korea, not all changes have occurred in parallel. Additionally, the expression of numerals in Taiwan Sign Language has been influenced by regional differences.

Keywords: Japanese Sign Language, South Korean Sign Language, Taiwan Sign Language, numeral expressions, historical linguistics

Acknowledgements: This research would not have been possible without the input of the research participants, to whom I express my heartfelt thanks, along with Mayumi Arata and Kim Bo Seok for introducing me to participants in South Korea and Taiwan. I would like to express my gratitude to Masumi Ikeda and Kang-Suk Byun for assisting with photographs for this chapter, and to Carl Börstell for creating the map. The text has benefited considerably from comments by two anonymous reviewers, and through discussion with my peer Nick Palfreyman. This research was funded by JSPS KAKENHI Grant Number JP16K13229.

https://doi.org/10.1515/9781501510243-002

In this chapter, I investigate diachronic lexical changes with specific examples from numeral expressions in Japanese Sign Language (JSL), South Korean Sign Language (SKSL) and Taiwan Sign Language (TSL). I compare data of numerals described in the literature and historical sources with data collected from users of each sign language. Such a method has rarely been used in the field of historical linguistic research of sign languages. Examining changes in numeral expressions is a useful way to study language change and relationships between sign languages because even though these expressions are often motivated by iconicity, they frequently contain abstract and systematic elements, making it easier to analyse changes. The numeral expressions in these three languages are investigated by comparing forms for '10', '100' and '1,000' and the structure of numbers based on them.

Previous research seeking to establish relationships between sign languages has often used methods informed by lexicostatistics, which were used by spoken language linguists to identify phylogenetic relationships in spoken languages. This method is based on the rate of lexical sharing found in the target language, but it is not used as a basis for phylogenetic relationships in current historical linguistics (Crowley & Bowern 2010: 149). On the other hand, much of the research on historical relationships between sign languages is based on the rate of lexical sharing between languages (Woodward 1993, Parkhurst & Parkhurst 2003, etc.). Sasaki (2007) applied the same method to JSL and TSL to investigate the similarities between the two languages. Similar methods were applied to JSL and TSL in Sasaki (2007), and Xu (2006) for TSL and Chinese Sign Language. The application of lexicostatistical methods to sign languages has been controversial (see Palfreyman & Schembri, 2022, for a summary of these criticisms).

In the first half of the twentieth century, the Tokyo dialect of JSL was introduced to the Korean Peninsula and Taipei, the Taiwanese capital; while the Osaka JSL dialect was brought to Tainan, in south Taiwan. This chapter demonstrates the extent to which the historic Tokyo and Osaka numeral systems are reflected in modern SKSL and TSL. The process of change in each language is traced by comparing the forms and structures for these two systems. The methodology employed in this research might be harnessed to explore historical changes in other sign languages and shed light more generally on how signed languages develop over time, which is an under-researched area.

1 Background and history of JSL, SKSL and TSL

Several sign language linguists refer to a 'Japanese Sign Language family' (Smith 2005; Sasaki 2007; Fischer & Gong 2010), comprising Japanese Sign Language

(JSL), South Korean Sign Language (SKSL) and Taiwan Sign Language (TSL). This is based on language contact during the Japanese colonial era (1895–1945), and the legacy of this contact. This chapter aims to ascertain how numeral signs in JSL, SKSL and TSL have changed over time, and what this tells us about the historical relationships between these three sign languages.

The two numeral systems are introduced in section 2, followed by the data used to analyse language change (section 3). Examples of language change found for the semantic domain of numerals are analysed in section 4, and I conclude with a discussion about the significance of these findings for variation and change in sign languages more generally. In the remainder of this section, I introduce each sign language in turn and present details of known language contact, which enables a better understanding of the language variation and change analysed in later sections. Figure 1 shows a map indicating the locations of cities referred to in the text, and the year when contact between varieties is first attested in the historical record.

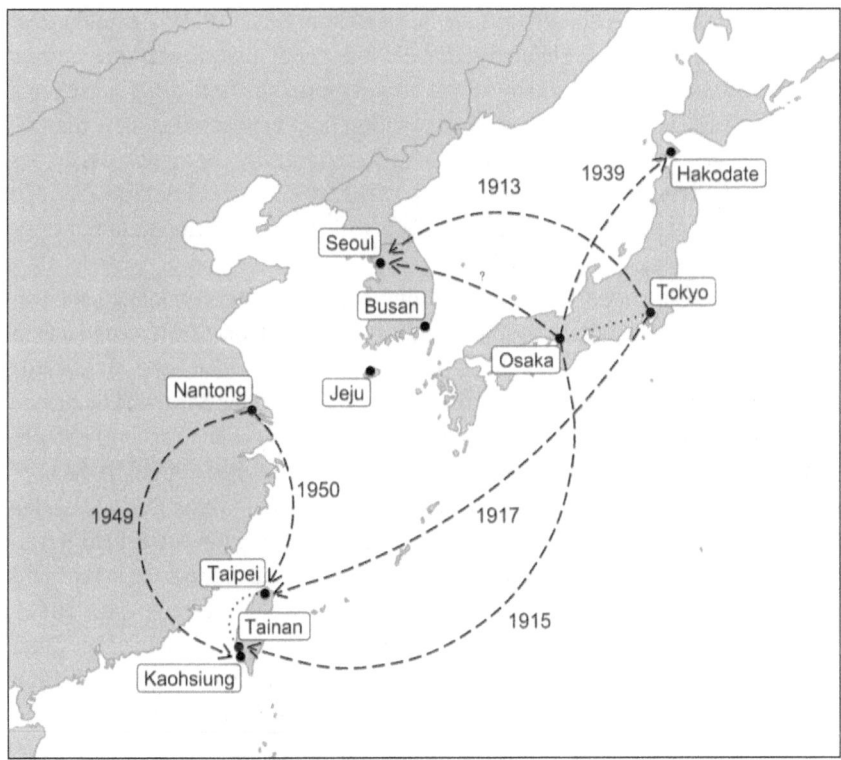

Figure 1: Map showing Japan, South Korea and Taiwan, and directions of influence affecting the locations mentioned in this chapter (with thanks to Carl Börstell).

1.1 Japanese Sign Language

The first deaf school in Japan was established in the city of Kyoto in 1878, followed by schools in Tokyo (1880) and Osaka (1890). The Milan conference of 1880 promoted oral teaching methods (Ueno 2001), but it is clear from the recollections of older signers in their 80s and 90s that teachers in Japan's early deaf schools were teaching using sign language (even though it is not possible to determine their proficiency or what their sign language might have looked like). The government's education policy changed in 1933, and by 1936 oral methods had become widespread in Japan, with only eight out of 70 deaf schools from elementary to high school level teaching in sign language (Seino 2002). One of those eight schools is the Osaka deaf school, in the Kansai region, which has continued to support the use of sign language in education throughout its existence (Kajimoto 2012).

Many other schools were set up over the years that followed, but it is the schools in Osaka, and Tokyo, in the Kanto region, that are known to have had an impact on deaf education overseas (see sections 1.2 and 1.3). The early deaf schools appear to have developed relatively independently of each other; there is some evidence of occasional meetings between teachers from different schools (Matsunobu & Shintani 2018), but lexical differences between the signs that we know of suggest that no attempts were made to standardise the signs used across schools. For example, the numerals used by the Kyoto deaf school in the 1900s are based on characters from the Kanji script, which is quite different to the signs used in Osaka at the time (Shintani 2011).

It is well-attested that the domain of numerals can display sociolinguistic variation, which is often linked in the literature to the social factors of school and region (e.g. Quinn 2010 & Stamp et al. 2015 for British Sign Language; McKee & McKee 2011 for New Zealand Sign Language and Palfreyman 2019 for Indonesian Sign Language). As with these languages, differences between sign varieties used in schools contributed to the development of dialects in JSL. Over time, the varieties used in the populous regions of the Kanto (around Tokyo) and the Kansai (around Osaka) became key dialects in terms of their influence over other JSL dialects (Sagara & Palfreyman 2020). This can be seen with respect to the distribution of variants for 'name' and 'water' (Tsay et al. 2019; see also Fischer 2014 and Sagara 2017 on regional variation).

Since the 1970s, the Tokyo dialect has had much more influence over other dialects, due to factors such as the prestige of the capital city, and the publication of the first short dictionary of JSL by the Japanese Federation of the Deaf (JFD) in 1969 (Sagara & Palfreyman 2020), which seems to have included more Tokyo variants than variants from other cities. However, at least one other region of Japan is known to have had contact with the Osaka dialect. Hakodate is situated around 1,300km to the north of Osaka on the island of Hokkaido. The Hakodate dialect is historically related to the Osaka dialect due to a series of interactions between the Municipal Deaf School in Osaka and the Hakodate Blind House, founded in 1900, which also accepted deaf pupils. Between 1939 and 1955, there were particularly strong links between the directors of the schools, Sato Zaikan in Hakodate, and Kiyoshi Takahashi in Osaka, who were both advocates of teaching using sign language in an era where oralism was the favoured practice (Seino, 2002). It is likely that the influence of the Osaka dialect in Hakodate began to wane from 1969 onwards, due to the JFD publication mentioned above.

1.2 South Korean Sign Language (SKSL)

A school for blind children, established in Pyongyang in 1898 by a US missionary, began to accept deaf children from 1909, and taught using oralist methods (Kim Chilkwan 1998: 22). In some other situations where oralist policies are used, it is attested that deaf children continue to use gestures and sign language informally outside of the classroom (Schembri 2012), and it is possible that this happened in Pyongyang as well. During the period of Japanese rule (1910–1945), Japan exerted considerable influence over deaf education, and sign language was used with the aim of teaching spoken language in the classroom (Kim Chilkwan 1998). In 1911, the Governor-General of Korea founded a charity in Seoul for orphans and other children called the Saisei In Deaf Institute, and in April 1913 deaf education was established as part of its remit (Suemori 2016). In 2015, I interviewed Aki Takayama, an alumnus of Saisei In, who entered the school in 1941. In her 80s at the time of the interview, she recalled separate classes of children taught orally and using sign language – her deaf sister was in the oral class, while she was taught using sign language, but they had physical education together. This shows that, while oral education methods had taken hold in Japan, education in sign language continued to be available for at least some deaf children in Korea.

Japanese hearing teachers such as Beizô Otsuka were dispatched from the Tokyo deaf school to Saisei In, and Otsuka himself became chief executive of the department of education for deaf and blind children (Suemori 2016). According to Takayama, in 1944 a teacher from the Osaka school joined Saisei In, which might explain how Osaka variants can still be observed in SKSL alongside Tokyo variants.

Much remains unknown about the origins of what is now referred to as SKSL, but it is clear that the Saisei In Institute in Seoul had a prominent role in its early development. Deaf schools were established in each of South Korea's states (Suemori 2016), including Jeju Island (1951) and Busan (1955), but these did not include high schools until 1999 and 1974, respectively, while Saisei In taught at high school grades from 1964 onwards. This meant that, for many years, pupils had to move to Seoul to continue their education, providing a means by which the variants used in Saisei In became dispersed around South Korea. In discussing the Korean peninsula, the remainder of this article refers only to the sign language of South Korea (South Korea Sign Language), because too little is currently known of how sign language has developed in North Korea since 1945.

1.3 Taiwan Sign Language

TSL is said to have two main regional variants which, as with JSL, are linked to the history of deaf education (Smith 2005: 188). Deaf schools were established in Taiwan during the period of Japanese rule (1895–1945), first in Tainan (1915) and then in Taipei (1917). Prior to this, next to nothing has been published about the sign language used on the island (Smith 2005: 188). Teachers from deaf schools in Japan were invited to move to Taiwan and teach there, bringing with them some of the signs that they used. For reasons that are unclear, many of the teachers who moved to Tainan came from the Osaka deaf school, while teachers from the Tokyo area went to the school in Taipei (Smith 2005; Su and Tai 2009).

After 1945, any remaining Japanese teachers returned to their homeland, but Lin Wensheng, a deaf man who had been educated in Tokyo, became headteacher of the Taipei deaf school. There followed some influence from sign language varieties on mainland China as a result of the exodus to Taiwan in 1949, which included teachers from Chinese deaf schools (Smith 2005: 189). For example, in Tainan, Chen Tiantian trained local teachers in using signs that his school had used in China.

2 Previous research on numeral signs

Signs for numerals have long attracted the attention of sign language researchers (Woodward 1972, Liddell 1996, Skinner 2007). Zeshan and Sagara (2016) provide a typological overview of 21 sign languages in the domain of numerals, and identify several strategies for expressing numerals: lexical, digital, additive, multiplicative, subtractive, spatial and numeral incorporation. They also consider the motivations of numerals from 0–9 cross-linguistically. For example, in Ugandan Sign Language and Turkish Sign Language, numerals from 6–9 are based on orthographic iconicity, while several strategies are used in sign languages around the world to express 'zero' (Sagara and Zeshan 2016: 28).

For JSL, Ichida (2005) describes the phonological structure of numerals, while Mori (2005) studies the structure of cardinal numerals from 1–99, including variants for numerals 1–4. Relying chiefly on introspection, he describes the phonological structure of these numerals, including signs such as TWO-WEEK and THREE-MONTH, which use numeral incorporation. Fischer, Hung & Shih-Kai (2011) focus on numeral incorporation in TSL, while making comparisons with JSL, SKSL and ASL. They contend that TSL bypasses a phonological constraint on the use of internal movement in numeral incorporation, which means that numerals can be incorporated in contexts that would not be permitted in other sign languages.

Ktejik's (2013) recent study of numeral incorporation in JSL provides an analysis of the numeral morphemes which are bound to root morphemes. She presents 14 paradigms in JSL that use numeral incorporation, such as weeks, age, floors of a building and places in a race (Ktejik 2013: 186). Sagara and Zeshan (2016: 32) investigate numeral signs from a typological perspective, and find that JSL matches an implicational hierarchy whereby if a sign language allows numeral incorporation with signs for money or school grade, it will allow numeral incorporation for time units.

Sociolinguistic concerns have also attracted attention. To examine synchronic and diachronic variation in JSL, Osugi (2010) created a database based on lexical items used by Sadobaru (1902), the oldest known source to include numeral signs in Japan.[1] The database comprises signs elicited from two respondents, one in their 70s and one in their 30s, in each of Japan's 47 prefectures. Sagara and Palfreyman (2020: 129) note that, for the numerals included in Osugi's survey, more variants occur across older respondents compared with younger ones. This might be taken to suggest that dialect levelling is taking place in JSL, although analysis of a more substantial dataset is needed in order to establish this more conclusively.

Sagara (2016) investigates numeral signs from a typological perspective, and identifies variants used in Osaka and the surrounding Kansai region, and in Tokyo and the Kanto region.[2] These variants, which are used to express multiples of 10, 100 and 1,000, occur in SKSL and TSL as well as JSL. They play an important role in realising the aim of this chapter, because they shed light on contact between these languages, and changes that have happened subsequently. The variants are introduced in sections 2.1 and 2.2 below as the Z system (for Osaka variants) and the NI system (for Tokyo variants).

---

1 An English language version of the database can be found at www.deafstudies.jp/osugi/jsl-mapen/map.html (accessed 6 August 2020).
2 In this chapter, I refer to 'the Osaka variety' and 'the Tokyo variety' because these varieties are based on schools in those cities. It should be noted that these varieties are used across an entire region – both the Kansai region around Osaka and the Kanto region around Tokyo comprise seven prefectures each.

2.1 Z variants

The Z variants are so named because they make use of a 'zero paradigm', where powers of 10 are based on a representation of the number of zeroes present in the written form of the numeral (see Figure 2). This is indicated in the glosses below with a 'z' suffix (NUMERAL:**z**).

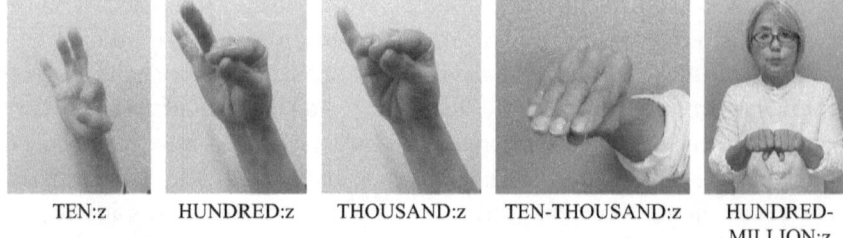

TEN:z   HUNDRED:z   THOUSAND:z   TEN-THOUSAND:z   HUNDRED-MILLION:z

Figure 2: Z variants for the numerals '10', '100', '1,000', '10,000' and '100,000,000'.

The number of fingers touching the thumb indicates how many powers of ten there are in the numeral, e.g. the index finger alone for '10', index and middle finger for '100', and so on, up to four selected fingers for '10,000'. There is an additional sign, articulated with both hands (eight selected fingers) for 100 million. To articulate multiples of these forms, compounding is used, with the form shown after another cardinal numeral sign. For example, '3,000' would be shown as THREE THOUSAND:z (see Figure 3). Historically, this strategy could be used in JSL to show multiples of 100, 1,000 and 10,000, but not multiples of 10 (Sagara & Palfreyman 2020).

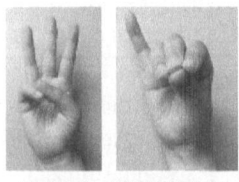

THREE   THOUSAND:z

Figure 3: '3,000' expressed using the Z system.

2.2 NI variants

The NI variants are so called because they use numeral incorporation (Liddell 1997), with movements indicating the base. The suffix 'ni' is used for numeral glosses to show this (NUMERAL:**ni**). Kanji characters have been highly influential in Japan for centuries, and there has been further contact between kanji characters and JSL: for the numeral 1,000, the index finger traces a Chinese kanji character meaning 'thousand' (see Figure 4). The handshape for this sign can be any numeral from 1 to 9, creating the multiples 1,000 to 9,000. These and other NI variants are regarded as outcomes of numeral incorporation on morphological grounds, with the movement as the stem, and the multiplier as an affix.

THOUSAND:ni

Figure 4: The NI variant for '1,000'.

For '100', the hand makes a short, sharp upwards movement to mean '100', as per Figure 5. Again, the handshape can change to create multiples up to 900. For example, in the expression of '200', in the Tokyo variant of JSL, the '2' handshape is incorporated with a movement meaning 'hundred' (see Figure 5).

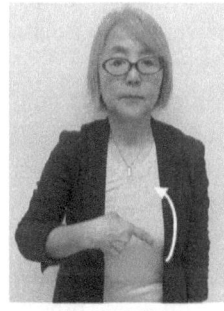 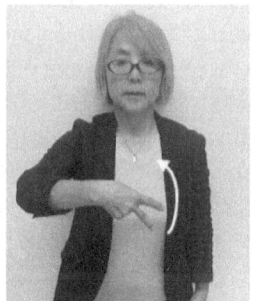

HUNDRED:ni   TWO-HUNDRED:ni

Figure 5: NI variants for '100' and '200'.

Signs for 10 and its multiples, from 20 to 90, are expressed by adding an internal movement to the basic form, whereby selected digits are bent, e.g. four fingers are bent to mean '40' (see Figure 6).

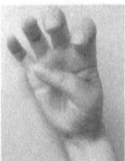

FORTY

Figure 6: The numeral '40'.

3 Data collection

The analysis in this chapter uses two types of sign language data, collected from living participants, and from historical sources.

3.1 Sign language data from living participants

The data on the Osaka and Tokyo varieties of JSL were gathered from 18 participants in Osaka and 18 in Tokyo during a three-month period from November 2015 to January 2016. The data collection targeted signers who had remained in the same place throughout their lives, so as to minimise the influence of variants from other regions on their signing. This enabled the researcher to isolate changes in numeral expressions that are based on regional variation.

Data from the Taipei and Tainan varieties of TSL were collected from mid-October to mid-November 2016, and involved collecting data from 20 users of each variety. The researcher targeted signers who currently live in these respective areas, but as with the JSL data, only those participants who had remained in that area for their whole lives were included in the analysis. Therefore, for example, data from signers who had moved from Taipei to Tainan were excluded. As a result, out of the 20 participants for each region, only the data of nine people in Tainan and nine in Taipei were ultimately analysed. For JSL and TSL signers, data were collected from as many different age groups as possible, and the sample was broadly balanced for gender. The sample stratification is not relevant to the discussion in this chapter, but further details can be found in Sagara and Palfreyman (2020: 129, 135).

The SKSL data were gathered from three groups of signers ranging in age from their 20s to their 80s: six people in Seoul, in March 2017; four from Jeju Island, in June 2018; and six from Busan in July 2018 (see Figure 1). The latter two cities were chosen because they have a large deaf community, and historic links with the capital city (in section 1.2 it was noted that one of these links is education). The historical record shows that teachers from Japan worked only in Seoul, but given the movement outlined in section 1.2, it was useful to establish the degree of homogeneity in SKSL in terms of numeral variation. Data were collected from signers who had always lived in the Seoul area, while signers from Busan and Jeju Island had lived in their respective city for more than 20 years.

Two methods were used to elicit expressions of numerals featuring 10, 100 and 1,000 and their multiples. Pairs of participants played a matching game, where they were each given cards. For each round, one player (Player A) had a card containing two numbers, while Player B had only one of these numbers. Player B had to sign this number to Player A, who would identify the card and tell them what the 'missing' number is. Player B would then write this number down. and were asked to demonstrate the form they use for these numbers. The list of numerals used is shown in the Appendix. By giving participants this task, the aim is to elicit numerals in a more natural way, and prevent them from focusing too much on how they sign the numeral. Another aim is to elicit comparable numerals from different participants.

For the second method, pairs of participants were asked to play a bargaining game where they had to negotiate or haggle over the price of different items, such as some apples, a motorbike or a house. This game has been used around the world (Zeshan & Sagara 2016), and although it was new to participants, they found it easy to assume a role as 'buyer' or 'seller'. The game is not intended to elicit specific numbers, but rather to elicit examples of numerals in natural conversation: altogether, these comprised 35 contexts, including three monetary contexts (how much?).

In addition, participants were interviewed and asked for metadata, including their age, family background, schooling and so on. They were also explicitly asked about which older variants they were aware of for 10, 100 and 1,000, and multiples based on them. These data were compared with signs that occur in historical documents.

3.2 Sign language data from historical sources

The historical sources consulted for the research underpinning this chapter comprise drawings, photos and descriptions of signs, which appear in lists, short dictionaries, and transcripts or reports of presentations, and many are linked with deaf associations. These documents, which are all in the public domains, are presented in Table 1, along with an indication of whether the documents show signs used in Osaka or Tokyo (or both).

Table 1: Historical documents that show JSL signs.

Name	Year of publication	Place of publication	Z system represented?	NI system represented?
Sadobaru	1902	Kagoshima	−	+
Matsunaga	1937	Osaka	+	−
Mishima & Kaneda	1963	Tokyo	+	+
Matsunaga	1963	Tokyo	+	+
JFD	1969	Tokyo	+	+
Fukushima	1982	Kyoto	+	−
JFD	2011	Kyoto	+	+

Most of the documents were created by hearing men who were neither linguists nor sociolinguists, and most are teachers in deaf schools. None of the documents are based on systemic and rigorous research. Although some present more than one variant for a given concept, they may all be regarded as containing elements of language planning in one way or another. It is not possible to determine how exhaustive these documents are, which is a significant limitation for the historical linguist, and when using documents (Crowley & Bowern, 2010). One can only note that a particular sign or variant is presented, as no information is given about which signers were using the sign, or whether they knew any other variants. When used in combination with data from living participants and elicited data, it usually becomes possible to attain a greater level of certainty about where and when variants were used. However, there are challenges. For example, a teacher at the deaf school in Tokyo called Sadobaru moved to teach at a school in Kagoshima, in the south of Japan (established in 1900). In 1902, Sadobaru published a collection of signs that include early forms of NI variants for 100 and 1,000, and it is assumed that this collection shows the Tokyo variants that he brought to the Kagoshima school. This tallies with the predominance of the NI system in Tokyo (Sagara & Palfreyman, 2020), and its prevalence there led to the introduction of the NI system to Seoul and Taipei, by teachers from the Tokyo deaf school.

But the Z system was also introduced to Tokyo at some point, and the historical record does not make it easy to ascertain how this happened. Another collection published in Tokyo (Mishima & Kaneda, 1963) features only the Z variants for 100 and 1,000, and some older Tokyo signers born in the 1930s also still use the Z system, which corroborates this. Conversely, the JFD volume (1969) features both variants side by side. These indications are summarised in Table 2 below.

Table 2: The presence of different systems in documents representing signs from the Tokyo dialect.

	Z system	NI system
Sadobaru (1902)	–	+
Mishima & Kaneda (1963)	+	–
JFD (1969)	+	+

From this evidence, it is difficult to deduce when the Z system was first introduced to Tokyo – the complicating factor is the non-appearance of the NI system in the 1963 publication, and it is not clear why this is.

4 Changes of numeral expressions of JSL, TSL and SKSL

The data collected for this study point to several changes in the expression of numerals in JSL, TSL and SKSL. These include changes to expressions for '10' (section 4.1), while expressions for '100' and '1,000' have shifted in Tokyo, Seoul and Taipei from two-handed to one-handed forms (section 4.2). Section 4.3 presents evidence for an ongoing shift in Osaka and Tainan from the Z system to the NI system, and then focuses on changes in the expression of multiples. Not all changes have happened in parallel, and section 4.4 presents a compounding system that has developed only in the Tainan variety of TSL. Finally, section 4.5 discusses the distribution and articulation of numeral variants according to the semantic domain involved.

4.1 Changes to variants for '10' in JSL

The expression of multiples of 10 using bending digits has been used since at least the 1930s, as it appears in Matsunaga (1937). Fukushima (1982), a hearing man with deaf parents, shared his observations about where certain signs had come from. He noted that, in Osaka, the bent finger variants of the NI system were only used for multiples of 10 (20, 30, and so on) and not for '10' itself. Instead, to express '10' signers would hold up the ten digits of both hands, or use TEN:z. If

Fukushima's observations are correct, it would seem that TEN:ni was added to the NI system as a result of assimilation and analogical reasoning.

It is unclear whether this development first occurred in Osaka, Tokyo, or elsewhere. What *is* clear is that, although TEN:z is still used in some of the regions under study to express '10', *multiples* of 10 are in all regions of JSL, SKSL and TSL are expressed in the data using only the NI system. For example, no signer has been observed to express '30' using THREE TEN:z. As a result, if a signer expresses a numeral such as 3,340 beginning with the Z system, there is a natural switch at the end to the NI system to show '40', as per Figure 7.

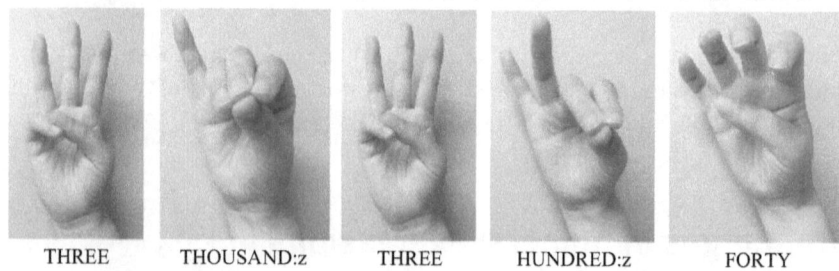

| THREE | THOUSAND:z | THREE | HUNDRED:z | FORTY |

Figure 7: The number '3,340' expressed using Z variants and a switch to the NI variant for the last component.

4.2 Handedness and phonological reduction in the NI system

Older forms of signs for 100 and 1,000 used both hands, and in the case of 100, the iconic origins of the sign are clearer in that form (the iconicity has become lost over time). The non-dominant hand makes a shape that signifies a wallet, while the dominant hand moves upwards from the wallet, reflecting the removal of banknotes (Figure 8a). With time, the non-dominant hand has been dropped, and the monetary context has been lost through semantic bleaching (Aitchison 2001), so that the sign can be used for any kind of numeral. This leaves only the orientation and movement of the dominant hand to signify the meaning '(x) hundred' (Figure 8b).

The older form for '1,000' is still based on the Kanji character, which is traced using a selected index finger in the dominant hand, while the non-dominant hand shows the multiplier as a handshape (Figure 9a). For the one-handed form, the entire numeral handshape adopts a similar path movement (Figure 9b), although the movement itself can be reduced to a considerable extent (Figure 9c). For comparison, Figures 10a and 10b show equivalent signs for '6,000'.

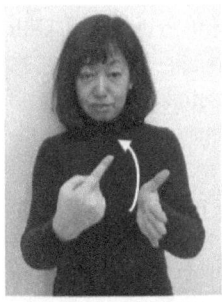 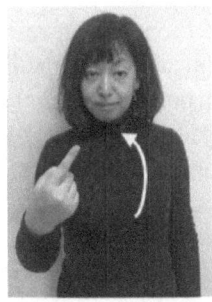

Figure 8a: HUNDRED:ni (two-handed). The left hand can also be produced with a pinched hand and an 'O' handshape.

Figure 8b: HUNDRED:ni (one-handed).

Figure 9a: THOUSAND:ni (two-handed).

Figure 9b: THOUSAND:ni (one-handed).

Figure 9c: THOUSAND:ni (one-handed, reduced).

Figure 10a: SIX-THOUSAND:ni (two-handed).

Figure 10b: SIX-THOUSAND:ni (one-handed).

When a word or sign changes from one form to another due to language shift or other changes, there is often a point at which both forms are used (Heine 2002). The change from an expression with both hands to an expression with one hand is well known in sign language linguistics (Frishberg 1975; Battison 1978) and is considered to be due to the economics of articulation.

A Tokyo signer (born in 1935), a Taipei signer (b. 1934) and a Seoul signer (b. 1938) all say that these mostly one-handed signs used now were all, in their respective cities, originally two-handed. Furthermore, the JFD (1969) sign list still shows '100' with two hands, suggesting that the transition period spanned several decades. Indeed, although the data collected for this study do not feature the older forms, the shift to one-handed forms does not yet seem to be complete. In Japan, at least, there are still a few older JSL signers who use the two-handed form. In Tokyo, two Japanese signers who were in their 80s in 2016 still express 1,000 with both hands. According to the dialect map created by Osugi, the two-handed form also occurs in various other prefectures of Japan (2010). In addition, signers of a similar age in the South Korean cities and in Taipei stated in interviews that they used the older two-handed forms for '1,000'. Some South Korean signers who use the one-handed forms on a daily basis said in a 2017 interview that they were aware of the two-handed variants through contact in their youth with older signers.

While two-handed forms are attested by older signers in Tokyo and Taipei, older signers in Osaka and Tainan do not recall these forms, which might be taken to suggest that the NI system spread to Osaka and Tainan only after the one-handed forms had emerged. In other words, this timeline can help us to understand the duration of language change given the language contact situation in the Korean peninsula and Taiwan, and to estimate when the NI system spread to Osaka and Tainan: it seems that the NI system spread from Tokyo to Seoul and Taipei before the one-handed forms had emerged, and to Osaka (from Tokyo) and Tainan (from Taipei) after these one-handed forms emerged.

However, there is an alternative scenario, whereby the shift from two- to one-handed forms occurred in Seoul and in Taipei independently of the development in Tokyo. These developments are all shown in Figure 11. A double line is used to represent two-handed forms of the NI system, and a single line refers to one-handed forms. Uncertainty regarding whether the shift from two- to one-handed forms occurred in Taipei and Seoul independently of, or through contact with, a similar shift in Tokyo, are indicated by black squares.

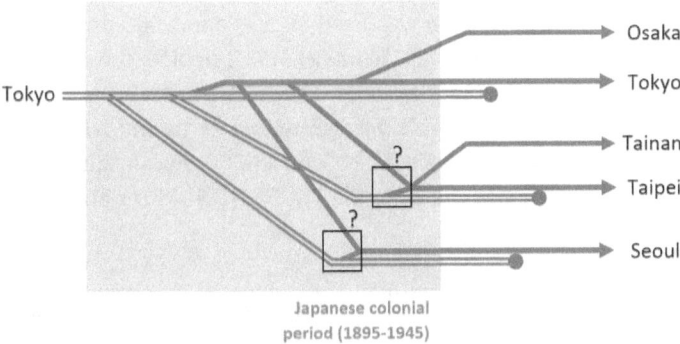

Figure 11: Origins and changes to the handedness of NI variants for multiples of 100 and 1,000.

4.3 The shift from the Z system to the NI system

The Z system has long been associated with Osaka, and appears in Matsunaga (1937), but contact with the Tokyo variety of JSL has led to the use of the NI system in Osaka co-existing with the Z system. According to Sagara (2014), older signers from Osaka are also found to favour Z variants over NI variants: 75% of tokens produced for '10' and '100' by signers aged 46 or older use the Z system (n = 116), but only 22% of equivalent tokens produced by signers aged 45 or younger use the Z system (n = 55). Sagara and Palfreyman (2020) find that region and age are statistically significant factors in predicting the choice of variant, and according to the apparent time hypothesis (Bailey, Wikle, Tillery & Sand 1991) the relevance of the age of the signer provides evidence of a shift from the Z system to the NI system in Osaka. There are several possible reasons for this shift, including the promotion of the NI variants in schools, and the association of NI variants with Tokyo and the national standard (Sagara & Palfreyman 2020: 133).

However, while TEN:z and HUNDRED:z are not produced by Tokyo signers, use of THOUSAND:z has been maintained, so that both variants (THOUSAND:z and THOUSAND:ni) are used by Tokyo signers. A strikingly similar pattern occurs in TSL, albeit for '100' rather than '1,000'. In Taipei, the Z system is strongly favoured for '100' but strongly disfavoured for '10' and '1,000'. Frequency might be a factor in the retention of THOUSAND:z in Tokyo and HUNDRED:z in Taipei – Sagara and Palfreyman observe that ¥1000 and TS$100 are the lowest denomination of banknotes in the respective currency of these countries, while Z variants are also able to inflect in the sign space, making them useful for example when talking about how much money each person should contribute to a meal (Sagara & Palfreyman 2020).

In Osaka in the 1930s, the Z system was used for 100 and 1,000 and multiples thereof. To sign the numeral 6,537, Matsunaga (1937) depicts the multiple forms 6,000 and 500 expressed using Z variants, as SIX THOUSAND:z and FIVE HUNDRED:z (as shown in Figure 12). This was confirmed by an interviewee in Osaka, who told me that numerals such as 300 or 4,000 could originally be shown using Z variants in sequence (for example THREE HUNDRED:z and FOUR THOUSAND:z).

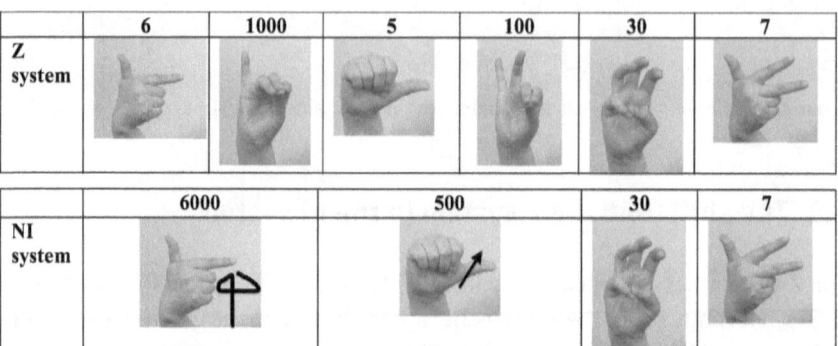

Figure 12: The numeral 6,537 articulated using the Z system (first row), as it is shown in Matsunaga (1937). The NI system is shown on the second row, in the interests of comparison.

In the Tainan variant of TSL, this sequential method continues to be used with HUNDRED:z and THOUSAND:z. However, every JSL signer in the data, and all JSL signers the author has observed, apart from the very oldest signers, do not use the sequential method anymore, and the data collected in Osaka contain no such examples. Instead, HUNDRED:z and THOUSAND:z are only used in JSL to show the numerals 100 and 1,000: for any multiples, JSL signers automatically use the NI system (the numeral shown in Figure 12 would now be expressed as SIX-THOUSAND:ni FIVE-HUNDRED:ni THIRTY SEVEN).

In order to understand the extent of the shift from the Z system to the NI system, 15 signers from Osaka and the surrounding region aged from their 30s to their 90s were asked to sign 20 numerals, shown on cards, that require multiples of 100 and 1,000. Fourteen of these participants used only the NI system for these kinds of numerals, and only one signer, aged 90, used the Z system. This confirms the researcher's own observations that only elderly signers still use the Z system with multipliers, and most Osaka signers prefer to use the NI system rather than compounds. Indeed, Sagara & Palfreyman (2020) note that this constraint may work against the popularity of the Z system, and provides another likely explanation for the shift from the Z system to the NI system.

Given that only a few signers in Osaka continue to use the Z system for multiples, it is useful to investigate the extent to which signers use this method in the two other places where the Osaka dialect is known to have had influence: Hakodate (Hokkaido), and Tainan (Taiwan). In 2017, data were collected from ten signers in Hakodate, using the same 20 cards previously used in Osaka. None of the four younger signers, in their 30s and 40s, used the Z variant to express the target numerals, but were aware that the Z system was used in Hakodate historically. Conversely, all of the six speakers over the age of 70 used the Z system with multiples. This confirms the hypothesis that, in Hakodate, there has been a shift from the Z system to the NI system for expressing multiples.

Since all of the elderly signers surveyed in Hakodate continue to use the Z system, compared with only one in Osaka, it may be presumed that the change is slower in areas that have less contact with other variants. The difference in the rate of change between Osaka and Hakodate could be linked to their respective geographical locations, and the comparative isolation of Hakodate. Osaka, situated on Japan's largest island, Honshu, is much better connected than Hakodate. Even on Hokkaido island, notable differences have been reported by signers and observed by the researcher between the dialects in Hakodate and the island's largest city, Sapporo, suggesting that there has been less contact between Hakodate and other dialects.

In Tainan, Sagara and Palfreyman (2020: 137) report that 72% of multiple tokens for '100' (n=83) are expressed using the Z system, while for multiple tokens of '1,000', the split between the two systems is 50–50 (n=20). This shows that the use of the Z system for multiple tokens is still dominant, especially for multiples of '100'. However, a statistical analysis shows that younger signers in Tainan prefer the NI system, suggesting that the use of the Z system for multiples is still diminishing, if at a much slower rate than for Osaka and Hakodate. It is not clear why the Tainan variety is changing at a slower rate compared with the Japanese varieties, although one must bear in mind that there has been no notable contact between JSL and TSL since 1945, and so it cannot be assumed that patterns of change in Taiwan will mimic those observed in Japan.

Figure 13 shows the shift from the Z system to the NI system, according to the analyses presented in this sub-section. Red lines indicate the Z system, while blue lines indicate the NI system. The thickness of the line is intended to give an indication of the relative dominance of each system.

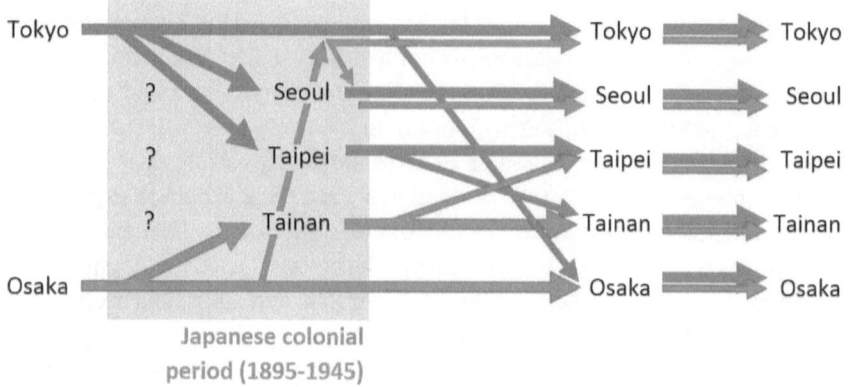

Figure 13: A diagram showing the likely development of the NI system and the Z system across the five cities analysed in this chapter.

4.4 Post-colonial developments in numeral systems: The lexicalisation of numeral forms in TSL

Since contact with JSL ended, further developments have been observed in TSL and SKSL. In some cases, these are isolated developments but, interestingly, other changes seem to be occurring in parallel, with at least one similar development identified in TSL (Tainan), SKSL and JSL (Hakodate).

In Tainan, a series of lexicalised forms have emerged for the numerals 100, 1,000 and 2,000, whereby the component numerals have become fused and are articulated simultaneously. These lexical forms are articulated by certain fingers retaining contact with the thumb, while (an)other index finger(s) move(s) up and down:

- for 100, the middle finger is held while the index finger moves (Figure 14a);
- for 1,000, the middle and ring fingers are held while the index finger moves (Figure 14b);
- for 2,000, the ring finger is held while the index and middle fingers move (Figure 14c).

These are different from the numeral incorporation examples in two respects. Rather than combining handshape and movement (as with numeral incorporation), here it is two numeral handshapes that have become fused together. The outcomes are lexical, with only three known fused forms for multiples of hundred and thousand; crucially, the process is not productive, unlike numeral incorporation, which can take any numeral between 1 and 9.

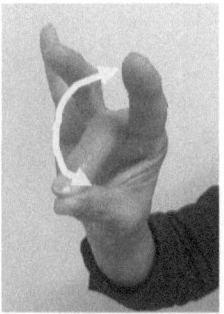 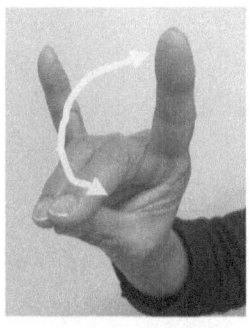 

Figure 14a: Fused form for '100' in Tainan.

Figure 14b: Fused form for '1000' in Tainan.

Figure 14c: Fused form for '2000' in Tainan.

Other examples of lexicalisation processes for numerals have been attested cross-linguistically (Sagara & Zeshan, 2016). In ASL in particular, the numeral '25' can be articulated either as two separate handshapes, or as a fully lexicalised sign, where the middle finger moved rapidly as a proxy for the movement of the middle, ring and pinky fingers (Sagara & Zeshan, 2016: 33), which is a very similar kind of lexicalisation to that discussed above, because allomorphs are created for the numerals '2' in ASL, and '1' and '2' in TSL.

Unfortunately, the participants could not remember when these forms first appeared, which might otherwise have given an indication of when this divergence began. In Tainan, these fused forms were still being used in 2017 by all of the age groups in the sample, including signers in their 70s. Sagara and Palfreyman (2020) note the importance of monetary currency as a factor that might explain the frequency of certain signs, and it is worth pointing out that Taiwan has banknotes of values NT$100, NT$1000, and NT$2000. However, this development appears to have occurred only in TSL. It is not possible to detect when this development began: in particular, there are no known examples of reciprocal influence, whereby TSL has influenced JSL, so one cannot detect whether, for example, this development has occurred since 1945.

This variant seen in Tainan is not known to occur in other JSL family languages, so it is considered to be unique to TSL and used in Tainan (Figure 15).

 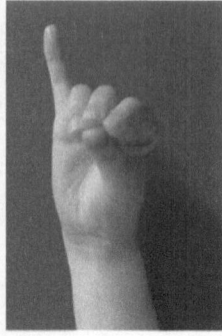 

Figure 15a: '2000' in Tainan – sequential compound.

Figure 15b: '2000' in Tainan – simultaneous compound.

4.5 Distribution and articulation of numeral variants according to semantic domain

In addition to changes in forms and strategies for expressing multiples, there have also been changes to the particular semantic domains in which numeral variants are used. One change is seen among Taiwan signers, who have added a side-to-side movement to NI signs for TEN and its multiples, and to THOUSAND:z when monetary amounts are referred to. Another change reported by South Korean signers is that the Z system was formerly used to refer to sums of money, but that they now use the NI system for money.

In SKSL and in the Osaka dialect of JSL, the Z system has become part of lexical signs related to time, such as the signs DECADE, CENTURY and MILLENNIUM, and the use of Z variants in lexical signs is also reported for TSL (Sagara & Palfreyman 2020: 144).

For some contexts, signers seem to have developed a preference for which system is used, while for other contexts, values may be expressed by either system. Table 3 gives examples of how the Z and NI systems are distributed across different contexts, according to deaf SKSL informants and details given in Lee et al. (2015: 118–119).

Table 3: The distribution of Z and NI variants for '10' across different contexts in SKSL.

Context (and example)	Z system	NI system
age (10 years old)	+	
October (10th month)	+	

Table 3 (continued)

Context (and example)	Z system	NI system
o'clock (10:00am)	+	
hours (10 hours)	+	+
decade (10 years)	+	+
fractions (one tenth)	+	+
minutes (10 minutes)		+
test marks (10 out of 100)		+
money (10₩)		+
10,000s (10 x 10,000)		+

The distribution between systems does not appear to be linked to the spoken language with which signers are in contact, and the reasons remain, for the most part, elusive. However, it is attested that signers sometimes exploit the two different systems by juxtaposing them to refer to different units. According to Lee et.al. (2015), SKSL uses the Z variant for 'ten hours' and the NI variant for 'ten minutes', as in the interlinear gloss below, and Figure 16:

TEN:z   TEN:ni   (South Korean Sign Language)
10 hours   10 minutes
'Ten minutes past ten'

Figure 16: SKSL structure meaning 'ten minutes past ten'.

Isolating the hours and minutes in this way would seem to establish a clearer division between different types of units. Similar exploitation has been noted for TSL (Sagara & Palfreyman, 2020: 144), where a signer uses the NI system on his left hand to refer to quantity (10 apples) and the Z system on his right hand for the cost of each apple (NT$100).

Preliminary data suggest that SKSL signers might use the Z variant for counting, and either system in some other contexts, but further research is needed to establish how far signers apply a consistent approach, and if so, whether such an approach occurs across the entire language, or depends on the individual signer.

5 Discussion and conclusion

In this study, two systems have been analysed in the numeral expressions of JSL, SKSL and TSL: these are referred to as the Z system, which is zero-based, and the NI system, which uses numeral incorporation. In each language, expressions for numerals of between two and four digits have changed from the era of Japanese rule when the JSL variants from Osaka and Tokyo were dispersed to Taiwan and South Korea.

The analysis used data from both historical sources and from users of each sign language. As a result, different developmental histories have been uncovered for signs meaning '10' and '100' and '1000', and multiples thereof. More specifically, '10' in the Tokyo variant changed from the Z system to the NI system, and then transferred to Taipei and South Korea. In the Osaka variety, the Z system was used, and transmitted to Tainan, although ultimately both systems came to be used in Osaka and Tainan as a result of contact with signers in their respective capital cities, Tokyo and Taipei.

Evidence from historical documents and from older signers show that NI variants for 100 and 1,000 and their multiples were originally expressed with both hands in Tokyo. Once the NI system for 100 and 1,000 and their multiples had been transmitted to South Korea and Taipei, and signers each region either made an independent change from two- to one-handed forms, or were influenced by contact with the latest one-handed forms used in Tokyo. As for the expression of multiples, for two-digit multiples, the NI system was used historically in both Osaka and Tokyo. For the three- and four-digit numbers, the sequential method of representing multiples (such as THREE HUNDRED:z) was replaced by numeral-incorporated expressions that simultaneously represent numbers and places of digits.

Statistical evidence points to a shift from the Z system to the NI system in JSL, with TEN:z and HUNDRED:z used much less by younger signers, and only THOUSAND:z still in common use by signers in Osaka and Tokyo. This seems to be echoed in TSL, where younger signers in Tainan are joining Taipei signers in using NI variants more often. However, HUNDRED:z is still very common, and unlike in Osaka, the Z system is still used as part of a sequential method to express multiples. These developments in JSL and TSL since 1945 seem to have happened independently of each other, but the underlying reasons may be very similar.

However, not all changes have occured in parallel. In Tainan, for example, a series of lexicalised forms have emerged for the numerals 100, 1,000 and 2,000, whereby the component numerals have become fused and are articulated simultaneously. This is not a productive process, but it is noted that all three numerals are also values of Taiwanese banknotes, and the frequency with which the numerals are produced may have contributed to phonological change. In SKSL, the two variants for 10 have become linked with different semantic domains. It seems that, in some cases, SKSL and TSL signers exploit the co-existence of variants to establish a clearer division between different types of units, such as hours on one hand with one variant, and minutes on the other hand with a different variant.

This is the first time that these kinds of changes have been shown for the sign languages that have developed in historic contact with JSL, but similar development paths have been reported for these properties in other sign languages. For example, the change from an expression with both hands to an expression with one hand has also been reported in a comparative study of American Sign Language and French Sign Language (Woodward 1977) and in the study of the African-American variant of ASL (Woodward 1978). It is known as a common change in sign languages (for example, see Frishberg 1975 & Battison 1978 for ASL; van der Kooij (2001) for NGT; Paligot, 2017 for LSFB) and is considered to be due to the economics of articulation and ease of perception. Also, changes from sequential compounding to number conjugation in the representation of numbers have been found, e.g. in the New Zealand Sign Language expressions for multiples of '10', older signers express the two-digit numbers side by side, while younger signers use only the dominant hand. It is said that these expressions have become numeral-incorporated and now use a number handshape combined with a meaningful movement (McKee 2016: 357). Future research should target specific semantic domains related to numerals such as time and money, to see how these meanings may be incorporated into numeral expressions.

The domain of numerals can be an ideal one to examine in order to shed light on diachronic change in languages, because although the forms in this domain tend to be motivated by iconicity, as are many forms in sign languages, they are also part of larger systems (cf. Palfreyman 2016 on paradigms and lexical sets in BISINDO). This means that it is possible to make assertions about historical relationships, because similarities between numeral systems can be identified with a certain amount of confidence that these are not only due to universal similarities in iconic motivation as may often be the case in other semantic domains.

Few studies have contributed convincing evidence for historical relationships between sign languages, in part because of the possibility that iconicity led to the emergence of similar lexical forms independently. With numerals, there are other pressures involved in addition to iconicity, such as the integrity of the counting system. Moreover, few historical studies comparing lexical items have contributed such detailed historical evidence of historical relations between individual cities.

Studies on the historical development of sign languages are often limited in terms of the data they can draw on, but the present research has been able to utilise a relatively extensive set of data comprising a variety of numeral expressions, and analyse them both qualitatively and quantitatively. More investigation is needed on how changes in the expression of numerals might apply more broadly to diachronic aspects of phonology, form, semantics and grammar. In particular, to advance our knowledge about historical changes to sign languages, further comparison of different age groups will be needed, and the current rise of corpus-based methods will surely make a strong contribution to this.

Appendix

1. matching game

Cards with numbers on both sides

8	2	40	4
150	10	20	30

front

2	15	4	1580
5	470	75	30

back

Cards with numbers on one side

8	2	40	4
5	10	20	30

front

back

2. bargaining game (example: pictures of apples and house)

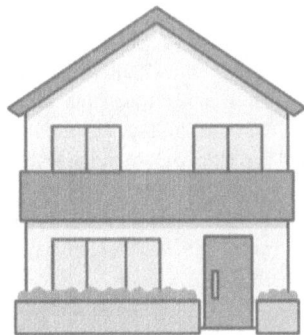

References

Aitchison, Jean. 2001. *Language Change: Progress or Decay?* Cambridge: Cambridge University Press.
Battison, Robbin. 1978. *Lexical Borrowing in ASL*. Maryland: Linstok Press.
Bailey, Guy, Tom Wikle, Jan Tillery & Lori Sand. 1991. The apparent time construct. *Language Variation and Change* 3(3). 241–264.
Crowley, Terry & Claire Bowern. 2010. *An Introduction to Historical Linguistics*. Oxford: Oxford University Press.
Fischer, Susan & Qunhu Gong. 2010. Variation in East Asian sign language structures. In Dian, Brentari (ed.), *Sign Languages*, 499–518. Cambridge: Cambridge University Press.
Fischer, Susan, Yu Hung & Shih-Kai Liu. 2011. Numeral incorporation in Taiwan Sign Language. In Jung-hsing Chang and Jenny Yichun Kuo (eds.), *Language and Cognition: Festschrift in Honor of James H-Y. Tai on His 70th Birthday*, 147–170. Taipei: The Crane Publishing.
Fischer, Susan. 2014. Sign languages in their historical context. In Claire Bowern and Bethwyn Evans (eds.), *The Routledge Handbook of Historical Linguistics*, 442–465. London: Routledge.
Frishberg, Nancy. 1975. Arbitrariness and iconicity: historical change in American Sign Language. *Language* 51(3). 696–719.
Fukushima, Tadashi. 1982. *Shuwa no gogen to sono miryoku*. [Etymology and its Appeal in Sign Language: Beginner's Guide to Sign Language Interpreting]. Kyoto: Society for Sign Language Interpreters.
Heine, Bernd. 2002. On the role of context in grammaticalization. In: Ilse Wischer and Gabriele Diewald (eds.), *New Reflections on Grammaticalization*, 83–101. Amsterdam: John Benjamins.
Ichida, Yasuhiro. 2005. Nihonshuwa no oninron to Suushikatei [Phonology of the number system in Japanese Sign Language]. *Sign Language Communication Research* 57. 9–17.
Japanese Federation of the Deaf. 1969. *Watashitachi no shuwa*. [Our Sign Language]. Vol 1. Kyoto: Japan Federation of the Deaf.

Japanese Federation of the Deaf. 2011. *Nihongo- syuwa jiten*. [Japanese-Japanese Sign Language Dictionary]. Kyoto: Japanese Federation of the Deaf.

Kajimoto, Katsushi. 2012. Survey about signs for particles of the sign language at Shiritsu Hamamatsu deaf school, Kyoto. *Deaf Historical Report* (2). 131–164.

Kim, Chilkwan. 1998. Kankoku no roukyouiku to shuwa: Rougakkoukyouiku no hensen wo chushin ni [Korean deaf education and sign language: Focus on the change of the school curriculum]. *Sign Language Communication Research* 28. 21–29.

Ktejik, Mish. 2013. Numeral Incorporation in Japanese Sign Language. *Sign Language Studies* 13(2). 186–209.

Lee, Yul-Ha, Huh In Young and Hakkyu Kim. 2015. 한국수어: 또 하나의 언어 [Korean Sign Language: Another language]. Seoul: Sign Books.

Liddell, K. Scott. 1996. Numeral incorporating roots & non-incorporating prefixes in American Sign Language. *Sign Language Studies* 1092(1). 201–226.

Liddell, K. Scott. 1997. Numeral Incorporating roots and non-incorporating prefixes in American Sign Language. *Sign Language Studies* 92. 201–226.

Matsunaga, Tan. 1937. *Roua kai* [The deaf-mute world]. *cyclopedia of deaf-mute temane* 78. 123–126.

Matsunaga, Tan. 1963. Shuwa jiten [Sign Language dictionary]. Tokyo: Association for Special Education in Japan.

Matsunobu, Shuichi & Yoshihiro Shintani. 2018. Roua kyouiku kouenkai/ Daiikkai zenkokurouataikai houkoku [Lecture on deaf education/ the report on the 1st Deaf people conference]. Osaka: Kinki Deaf History Research Group.

McKee, Rachel & David McKee. 2011. Old signs, new signs, whose signs? Sociolinguistic Variation in the NZSL Lexicon. *Sign Language Studies* 11(4). 485–527.

McKee, Rachel. 2016. Number, colour and kinship in New Zealand Sign Language. In Ulrike Zeshan & Keiko Sagara (eds.), *Semantic Fields in Sign Languages: Colour, Kinship and Quantification*, 351–384. Berlin and Lancaster: Mouton De Gruyter and Ishara Press.

Mishima, Jiro & Fumi Kaneda. 1963. *Nihonshuwa zue: temane no tebiki* [Figures and pictures of sign language: Guidance of the Sign] Tokyo: Waseda University of Educational Psychology Laboratory.

Mori, Soya. 2005. Nihonshuwa no 1 kara 2 ketano kazumadeno suusi [Japanese Sign Language numerals from 1 to 99]. *Sign Language Communication Research* 57. 3–7.

Osugi, Yutaka. 2010. Japanese Sign Language Map (experimental production) (online). Available from: http://www.a.tsukuba-tech.ac.jp/ge/~osugi/jslmap/map.html (accessed 29 April 2019)

Palfreyman, Nick. 2016. Variation and change in the expression of numerals across urban sign language varieties in Indonesia. In Ulrike Zeshan & Keiko Sagara (eds.), *Semantic Fields in Sign Languages: Colour, Kinship and Quantification*, 351–384. Berlin and Lancaster: Mouton De Gruyter and Ishara Press.

Palfreyman, Nick. 2019. *Variation in Indonesian Sign Language: A Typological and Sociolinguistic Analysis*. Boston/Berlin, and Lancaster: Walter de Gruyter Inc. and Ishara Press.

Palfreyman, Nick & Adam Schembri. 2022. Lumping and splitting: Sign language delineation and ideologies of linguistic differentiation. *Journal of Sociolinguistics* 26(1). 105–112.

Paligot, Aurope. 2017. *Vers une description des registres de la langue des signes de Belgique francophone (LSFB)*[Towards a description of the registers of sign language in French-Belgium Sign Language (LSFB)] PhD Thesis. Université de Namur.

Parkhurst, Stephen & Dianne Parkhurst. 2003. Lexical Comparisons of Signed Languages and the Effects of Iconicity. Working Papers of the Summer Institute of Linguistics, University of North Dakota Session, 47. https://commons.und.edu/sil-work-papers/vol47/iss1/2/ (accessed on 20 November 2021)

Quinn, Gary. 2010. Schoolization: An account of the origins of regional variation in British Sign Language. *Sign Language Studies* 10(4). 476–501.

Sadobaru, Sue. 1902. *Roua shuwa kyoujyu hou*. [Method of Teaching Sign language to Deaf-people] Kagoshima: Kagoshima Deaf-blind School.

Sagara, Keiko. 2014. *The numeral system of Japanese Sign Language from a cross-linguistic perspective*. Preston: Central Lancashire of University.

Sagara, Keiko. 2017. Investigation of lexical change in Japanese Sign Language and Taiwan Sign Language: Focus on numeral signs. *Historical Linguistics in Japan* 6. 13–40.

Sagara, Keiko & Nick Palfreyman. 2020. Variation in the numeral system of Japanese Sign Language and Taiwan Sign Language: A comparative sociolinguistics study In Nick Palfreyman (ed.), *Macro and micro-social variation in Asia-Pacific sign languages* (special issue). *Asia-Pacific Language Variation* 6(1). 119–150. Amsterdam: John Benjamins.

Sagara, Keiko & Ulrik. Zeshan. 2016. A Comparative Typological Study. In Ulrike Zeshan & Keiko Sagara (eds.), *Semantic Fields in Sign Languages: Colour, Kinship and Quantification*, 3–37. Berlin and Lancaster: Mouton De Gruyter and Ishara Press.

Sasaki, Daisuke. 2007. *Lexical Comparisons: Comparing the Lexicons Japanese Sign Language and Taiwan Sign Language. A Preliminary Study Focusing on the Difference in the Handshape Parameter. Part Two*. Washington D.C.: Gallaudet University Press.

Schembri, Adam. 2012. Deaf education and bilingualism. In: Roland Pfau et.al. (eds), *Sign Language: An International Handbook*, 949–979. Berlin/Boston: Hubert & Co.

Schembri, Adam & Trevor Johnston. 2012 Variation and Change: Sociolinguistic aspect of variation and change. In Roland Pfau, Markus Steinbach & Bencie Woll (eds.), *Sign Language: An International Handbook*, 788–816. Berlin/Boston: Mouton De Gruyter.

Seino, Shigeru. 2002. *Shuwa, kouwa ronsou no jidai to shuwawo houyou sita hitobito* [An era of controversy of sign language and the oral method, and people who embraced sign language] Nayoro: Municipality of Nayoro Junior College, Seino Lab.

Shintani, Yoshihiro. 2011. Roushi tanpou [Deaf history across Japan]. Kyoto Deaf News No. 448. Kyoto Deaf Association.

Skinner, Robert. 2007. *What Counts? A Typological and descriptive analysis of British Sign Language Number Variations*. Birbeck College, University of London dissertation.

Smith, H. Wayne. 2005. Taiwan Sign Language research: An historical overview. *Language & Linguistics* 6(2). 187–215.

Stamp, Rose, Adam Schembri, Jordan Fenlon & Ramas Rentelis. 2015. Sociolinguistic variation and change in British Sign Language number signs: Evidence of leveling? *Sign Language Studies* 15(2). 151–181.

Stamp, Rose, Adam Schembri, Bronwen G. Evans & Kearsy Cormier. 2016. Regional sign language varieties in contact: Investigating patterns of accommodation. *Journal of Deaf Studies and Deaf Education* 21(1). 70–82.

Suemori, Akio. 2016. Deaf History: Eastern Asia. In Genie Gertz & Patrick Boudreault (eds.) *The SAGE Deaf Studies Encyclopedia*. London: SAGE Publications.

Su, Shiou-fen & James H-Y Tai. 2009. Lexical Comparison of Signs from Taiwan, Chinese, Japanese, and American Sign Languages: *Taking Iconicity into Account*. Chiayi: National Chung Cheng University.

Tsay, Jean. Keiko Sagara & Ritsuko Kikusawa. 2019. Arbitrary Signs Are More Stable Than Iconic Signs: Evidence from Taiwan Sign Language and Japanese Sign Language. Paper given at the 8th Meeting of Signed and Spoken Language Linguistics, National Museum of Ethnology, Osaka, 6–7 December.

Ueno, Masuo. 2001. *Roukyouiku mondaishi: rekishi ni manabu.* [History of the debatable points for deaf education: Learning from history.] Tokyo: Centre for Nippon Library.

van der Kooij, E. 2001. Weak Drop in Sign Language of the Netherlands. In Valerie Dively, Melanie Metzger & Sarah Taub (eds.), *Signed languages – Discoveries from international research.* 27–42. Washington DC.: Gallaudet University Press.

Woodward, James. 1972. Implications for sociolinguistic research among the deaf. *Sign Language Studies* (1). 1–7.

Woodward, James. 1977. Two to one it happens: Dynamic phonology in two sign languages. *Sign Language Studies* 17. 329–346.

Woodward, James. 1978. Historical bases of American Sign Language. In Patricia Siple (ed.), *Understanding Language through Sign Language Research*, 333–348. New York: Academic Press.

Woodward, James. 1993. Lexical Evidence for the Existence of South Asian and East Asian Sign Language Families. *Journal of Asian Pacific Communication* 4. 91–106.

Xu, Wang. 2006. *A Comparison of Chinese and Taiwan Sign Language: Towards a New Model for Sign Language Comparison.* Columbus: The Ohio State University.

Zeshan, Ulrike & Keiko Sagara. 2016. *Semantic Fields in Sign Languages: Colour, Kinship and Quantification.* Boston/Berlin and Lancaster: Mouton De Gruyter and Ishara Press.

Shengyun Gu
Phonological processes in complex word formation in Shanghai Sign Language

Abstract: This study investigated phonological processes in complex word formation through the lens of Shanghai Sign Language (SHSL), the southern variety of Chinese Sign Language. Concatenative and nonconcatenative morphology were used for the search of complex word formations in this language. In the concatenative morphology, I analyzed compounding and affixation, both undergoing phonological restructurings by means of assimilation and deletion, exhibiting a strong tendency towards a monosyllabic unit. In the nonconcatenative morphology, I examined initialization and numeral incorporation, both of which are realized by handshape substitution. Despite the regularity of phonological processes in complex word formation, some exceptional instances were identified on number signs, iconic signs, and character signs. The former one is not uncommon among languages, and the latter two are more prevalent in sign languages. Some number signs exhibit idiosyncratic variations that are not predictable by the phonological restructuring rules in word formation. Signs that contain a highly iconic handshape resist numeral incorporation and therefore block handshape substitution. Finally, some character signs were found to resist numeral incorporation. The non-conformity to phonological rules in a character sign offers a unique dimension to examine the relationships between orthography, iconicity, and phonology in sign language.

Keywords: phonological processes, compound, numeral incorporation, iconicity, Shanghai Sign Language (SHSL)

1 Introduction

Phonological processes refer to the result of applying a set of rules (usually to satisfy some constraints), which manipulate the phonological shape of underlying forms to obtain surface forms. Phonological processes occur when the affected unit appears in a certain context. In spoken language phonology, typical processes include assimilation, dissimilation, insertion, deletion, reduction, coalescence, and metathesis.

Shengyun Gu, Department of Linguistics, University of Connecticut

https://doi.org/10.1515/9781501510243-003

A phonological process may operate at the lexical and post-lexical levels. Phonological processes at the lexical level refer to the modifications of units in the formation of morphologically complex words. Phonological processes above the lexical (i.e., post-lexical) level concern the adaptation of units in the context of a running stream of speech or signs. The phonological behavior at the two levels exhibits distinct patterns (Kiparsky 1982, Mohanan 1986). The studies on sign languages lend support to the existence of processes in which the form of sub-lexical units, i.e., handshape, location, movement, orientation, and the weak hand, undergo alternations (Battison 1974, 1978, Kegl and Wilbur 1976, Klima and Bellugi 1979, Liddell and Johnson 1986, Padden and Perlmutter 1987, Sandler 1987, Cheek 2001, Mauk 2003, Sandler and Lillo-Martin 2006, Mak and Tang 2011, Russell, Wilkinson, and Janzen 2011, Grosvald and Corina 2012, Ormel, Crasborn, and van der Kooij 2013, Ormel et al. 2017, Brentari 2019). These processes are comparable to the phonological or coarticulatory processes in spoken languages, which corroborates the universality of phonological processes in a language, be it signed or spoken. Based on literature, it seems to be the case that Shanghai Sign Language (henceforth SHSL) is very rich in compounds, and this lends itself well to a closer look into phonological processes in the formation of a morphologically complex word in a sign language.

1.1 Shanghai Sign Language (SHSL)

The earliest systematic form of Chinese Sign Language (CSL) was associated with school settings (Gong 2005) with contributions from missionaries from America, France, and Britain when they taught deaf children in China between 1880 and 1930 (Yang 2006). In general, there are two major CSL dialect groups, namely, the Northern (Beijing) one and the Southern (Shanghai) one (Fischer and Gong 2010, Chen and Gong 2020, Ma 2020). The two major CSL dialects arguably differ primarily at a lexical level rather than in their grammatical system (Yau 1977, Yang and Fischer 2002, Yang 2016).

Shanghai has been a pioneer in deaf education and deaf culture in China. The first deaf school in Shanghai, which was also the second deaf school in China, was established in 1897 by the French Catholic church (Lytle, Johnson, and Yang 2005). In addition to the work by foreign missionaries, an increase in deaf teachers and sign language as the major means of instruction and communication are arguably the two key factors that facilitated the early development of SHSL before 1949 (Lin 2021). In 1937, a deaf association was initiated in Shanghai (Fu and Mei 1986), aimed at promoting the deaf community's well-being and later their right to use natural sign language. Despite attempts to promote oralism between 1954 to

1956, sign language was allowed to supplement language teaching in deaf schools in Shanghai from the 1960s (Gu, Liu, and He 2019). Shanghai, among the largest cities in Mainland China, has a considerable size of deaf community with established signs and offers opportunities for more social interaction (Lin, de García, and Chen Pichler 2009). SHSL is less influenced by the ambient spoken languages than its northern counterpart (Fischer and Gong 2010). SHSL is very similar to signs used in Zhejiang province and Jiangsu province due to geographical vicinity and robust exchanges, and it also radiates inland, showing an affinity to signs used in Southwestern China (Chen and Gong 2020). Historically, SHSL is closely related to Hong Kong Sign Language (HKSL) (Sze et al. 2013), sharing about two thirds of its basic vocabulary (Woodward 1993, Tang 2007). It also exhibits impacts on Singaporean Sign Language and Thai Sign Language (Fischer and Gong 2010).

By the end of 2019, Shanghai's population reached 24.3 million residents (Shanghai Municipal Statistics Bureau 2020), and the number of registered residents with hearing loss in Shanghai was 75,520 (Shanghai Disabled Persons' Federation 2020). Another estimate (Yi 2008) put this number at about 170, 000 deaf people in this city in 2008.

1.2 Participants, methodology, data analysis

Three signers participated in this study by providing citation forms of the SHSL lexical words. Table 1 gives the self-reported background information of these three signers in 2016. The citation form was elicited by picture prompts from the SIGNTYP database,[1] or extracted from video clips of deaf signers' naturalistic signing, re-recorded in isolation.

Table 1: Background of the three deaf signers.[2]

Signer	Gender	Age	Age of hearing loss	Age of sign language acquisition	Parents
A	male	64	2	8	hearing
B	male	49	3	9	hearing
C	male	32	born deaf	from birth	deaf

---

1 http://signtyp.uconn.edu/Prompt/promptindex
2 Not all signers who participated in the study were born into deaf families. The citation forms of complex words are nonetheless conventionalized with a confirmation among more deaf signers in Shanghai. Since this study concerns phonological operations at the lexical level, which is frozen and varies little among signers except for some sociolinguistic factors such as age on a few signs (see section 2.1 below), I regard age of acquisition as having a minimal impact on the results.

The video clips were transcribed and annotated in the software ELAN (Crasborn and Sloetjes 2008).[3] The gloss and sentence translation were transcribed by a deaf signer. The types of phonological processes (insertion, assimilation, deletion) and the modulated sub-lexical units (handshape, location, orientation, movement, and weak hand) were annotated by the author.

1.3 Phonological processes in SHSL complex word formation

Spoken languages exhibit two major types of complex word formation approaches: concatenative morphology and nonconcatenative morphology. Concatenative morphology refers to sequential and contiguous combinations of morphemic units whereas nonconcatenative morphology involves combinations of morphemes that are not linearly ordered. Studies of complex word formation in other sign languages attest to both types, with concatenative morphology being manifested in processes such as compounding, affixation, and reduplication, and nonconcatenative morphology being exemplified by processes such as aspectual marking, numeral incorporation, initialization, and verb agreement (Sandler and Lillo-Martin 2006, Napoli 2018).

SHSL word formation was attested with both approaches. For concatenative morphology, compounding and affixation were found. For nonconcatenative morphology, initialization, numeral incorporation, and verb agreement were attested. There is a paucity of reduplication and aspectual marking as systematic morphological processes in SHSL except for the distributive aspectual marking, which is realized by reduplicated movement horizontally in neutral space. Since the morphophonological realizations of verb agreement are very different from those in initialization and numeral incorporation, which boil down to handshape modulation, I will focus on the latter two in this paper. The discussions of word-level phonological processes in SHSL are as follows: Section 2 is about phonological processes in compounding. A distinction between productive compounds and lexical compounds is made, and their connections in historical development are illustrated. The regularity regarding assimilation, deletion, and insertion in lexical compounds are demonstrated. Further, I will show some idiosyncratic processes in number signs. In Section 3, the phonological restructuring pattern in affixation is scrutinized with respect to the phenomenon of negative incorporation. In Section 4, two processes in nonconcatenative morphology, namely, ini-

---

[3] ELAN (https://archive.mpi.nl/tla/elan) was developed by the Language Archive of the Max Planck Institute for Psycholinguistics, Nijmegen, the Netherlands.

tialization and numeral incorporation, are analyzed. I will also show that in addition to phonological restrictions, certain phonological processes are disallowed on some signs due to the pressure to preserve the iconicity in the sign structure. Section 5 concludes.

2 Phonological processes in concatenative morphology: Compounding

A compound contains at least two bases which are root morphemes or free words (Katamba 1993). Compounding is a fundamental process of word formation in spoken languages and there is rarely a language without compounding (Greenberg 1963: 92). It has also been identified as a productive word formation device across sign languages (Bellugi and Newkirk 1981, Wallin 1983, Sandler and Lillo-Martin 2006, Lepic 2016, Quer et al. 2017), including emerging sign languages (Tkachman and Meir 2018). Depending on the way the constituting elements are put together, compounding is classified into two types – sequential compounding and simultaneous compounding, both of which are attested in sign languages (Brennan 1992, Hendriks 2008, Meir et al. 2010, Santoro 2018). I report the sequential realization of SHSL compounds in this study.

To identify a compound in SHSL, I use semantic opacity and phonological simplification (Klima and Bellugi 1979, Liddell and Johnson 1986) as the two criteria. If the overall meaning of the concatenations of signs are not fully predictable from the simple addition of constituting signs, these signs are regarded as a compound rather than a phrase. Based on the phonological criteria (Liddell and Johnson 1986), sequential compounds are divisible into lexical compounds and productive compounds.

2.1 Productive compounds and lexical compounds

Productive compounds, according to Liddell and Johnson (1986), preserve identifiable signs. That is, members of a compound are clearly visible on their own with respect to the phonological form. Productive compounds tend to follow a certain template. LIBRARY, as constituted by READ and HOUSE, is a typical productive compound in SHSL. HOUSE is productive in combining with other signs to create compounds like SCHOOL (STUDY^HOUSE), and HOSPITAL (MEDICINE^HOUSE). These three compounds conform to a single morphological template [X^HOUSE].

Within each compound, the constituting signs maintain their phonological form in isolation and no substantial phonological processes occur.

Although productive compounds such as the [X^HOUSE] group retain the constituting units in isolation, this does not mean that phonological adjustment is untenable. In fact, it is obligatory for a compound to delete the [repeated] feature to surface as a well-formed lexical item. For example, the SHSL sign PARENTS is a coordinate compound of DAD and MOM. DAD is produced with an 'A' handshape (i.e., extended thumb) and MOM with a '1' handshape (i.e., extended index finger). Both DAD (Figure 1) and MOM (Figure 2) involve a movement that ends with a contact on the lips twice or multiple times in citation form.

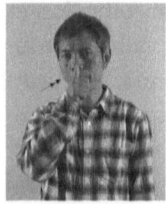 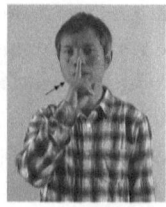 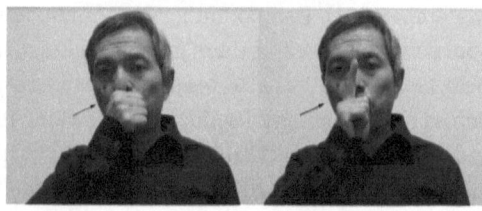

Figure 1: DAD.   **Figure 2:** MOM.   **Figure 3:** PARENTS formed by DAD and MOM.

As indicated by the double arrows in Figures 1, 2, canonically two consecutive contacts with the lips are produced in DAD and MOM. When they are combined to form a single word PARENTS in Figure 3, the multiple contact is reduced to one brief contact, a loss of repetition in each sign. Loss of repetition in the compound PARENTS can probably be seen as a result of spoken language interference, given that the counterpart *parents* [pa.ma] in Mandarin undergoes a similar reduction in each word whereas the canonical forms for *dad* and *mom* in Mandarin are disyllabic [pa.pa] and [ma.ma] respectively. There is undeniably a tendency for signers to align the time span of the manual sign PARENTS with the spoken word *parents*[pa.ma] among some signers who adopt mouthing, i.e., the silent articulation of a spoken word in sign production. I propose that loss of repetition in PARENTS is mainly triggered by the intrinsic compound formation rules in SHSL based on the following four arguments. First, the signing of DAD and MOM can involve multiple contact, which is not found in the pronunciation of these words in Mandarin. Second, loss of repetition is attested in other SHSL productive compounds that lack evidence of spoken language interference. For instance, the sign MALE involves repetition in citation form regardless of the monosyllabicity of the counterpart *male*[næn] in Mandarin. When MALE appears in the productive compound of HUSBAND (MARRY^MALE), the repetition is nonetheless deleted. Third, regardless of morphological complexity, a sign is biased towards a monosyllabic form and does not exceed a length of disyllabicity (Coulter 1982, Johnson and Liddell 1986, Wilbur 1993). This constraint on the maximal length of a sign is robust in SHSL and better accounts for the repetition loss in PARENTS, which yields a well-formed disyllabic form. Lastly, loss of repetition is observed as an obligatory process in lexical compounds as well.

Productive compounds are not distinguished from lexical compounds by a clear-cut boundary (Liddell and Johnson 1986, Lepic 2019). They are arguably two extremes on a continuum. The identifiable concatenative units in a productive compound would gradually be compressed into a single unit (Liddell and Johnson 1986, Yau 1988). A SHSL example is YOUNGER-SISTER, which has gone through a three-stage change with a decaying trace to its identifiable constituents. The form of YOUNGER-SISTER that is used by Signer A (age group above 60), is a typical productive compound that preserves the two combining signs – YOUNGER-SIBLING and FEMALE, as shown in Figure 4.

a. YOUNGER-SIBLING   b. FEMALE

Figure 4: YOUNGER-SISTER as formed by YOUNGER-SIBLING and FEMALE.

In Figure 4, YOUNGER-SIBLING is articulated with an 'I' handshape (extended pinky finger) in contact with the area near the lower lip. FEMALE is produced with the thumb and the index finger, which form a curved closed aperture at the earlobe. With time, handshape assimilation occurs at the juncture between the two signs, as shown in Figure 5 by Signer B (40–59 age group). The thumb in the second sign FEMALE (Figure 5b) regressively spreads to the first sign YOUNGER-SIBLING (Figure 5a).

The handshape assimilation acts as a transition from the productive compound that maintains the two constituting units into a lexical compound that merely encompasses a single unit. The drastic change is attested in the young SHSL signers. In Figure 6 with Signer C (age group of 20–39), YOUNGER-SISTER has become a sign with a single set of selected fingers.

a. YOUNGER-SIBLING   b. FEMALE

Figure 5: YOUNGER-SISTER as formed by YOUNGER-SIBLING and FEMALE.

Figure 6: YOUNGER-SISTER.

The first sign YOUNGER-SIBLING, on the left part of Figure 6, is identical to that in Figure 5, a result of regressive thumb assimilation. Total handshape assimilation occurs in the second sign, resulting in a loss of the original handshape in FEMALE. In addition to handshape assimilation, the two constituting signs have been fused into a single unit by reducing the two contacting movements into an orientation change. Apart from the transitional movement arising as the movement in the resulting compound, the sonority is reduced by a distalization in the activated joints from shoulder/elbow joints to elbow/wrist joints. Moreover, this distalized orientation change is produced repetitively.

The three variants of the same compound YOUNGER-SISTER by age in Figures 4–6 show a trajectory of how a productive compound diachronically develops into a lexical compound through ordered phonological changes. More phonological modifications occur in lexical compounds since the constituting signs are hardly identifiable. The next subsection describes types of phonological processes and generalizes the pattern of lexical compounding in SHSL.

2.2 Regular phonological processes in a lexical compound

A lexical compound is characteristic of phonological simplification (Liddell and Johnson 1986, Sandler 1989). The length of time it takes to sign a compound is about the same as the average of a single sign (Klima and Bellugi 1979). The phonological processes such as assimilation and deletion are particularly frequent in the first sign (Liddell and Johnson 1986, Brentari 1990a, 1990b). The SHSL data reveal a similar pattern. A variety of phonological processes are attested in the formation of the SHSL lexical compounds, including syllable reanalysis, loss of repetition, handshape assimilation, location assimilation, deletion of the weak hand, and insertion of the weak hand. I explicate each process with examples and draw a generalization on the phonological processes occurring in SHSL lexical compounds.

2.2.1 Assimilation

Assimilation refers to the impact of a certain unit on the articulation of another unit. The assimilation observed in the SHSL lexical compound involves the effects on handshape and location. For example, the compound SUPERFICIAL is formed by the concatenation of two free signs HEAD and FEW. In Figure 7a, HEAD is produced by pointing to the central location on the forehead with a '1' handshape. In Figure 7b, FEW is articulated in neutral space with the thumb and the index finger forming a curved closed aperture. In Figure 7c, when the two signs are put together to form SUPERFICIAL, the handshape of HEAD anticipates that of FEW. That is, the first sign HEAD loses its handshape and takes the handshape of the second sign FEW. Under the influence of the first sign HEAD, the location of FEW is raised to a high position in front of the head. In addition to handshape and location assimilations, the two signs are fused into a single unit by having the transitional movement as the only movement of the resulting compound.

a. HEAD   b. FEW   c. SUPERFICIAL

Figure 7: SUPERFICIAL as compounded by HEAD and FEW.

2.2.2 Deletion

Deletion refers to the phonological process where an element is omitted. Syllable reanalysis, as shown in the compounds SUPERFICIAL and YOUNGER-SISTER (the young age signer), is one type of deletion that pertains to movement. Other deletion processes such as loss of repetition and deletion of the weak hand, are attested in SHSL compounds, with the former affecting the movement property and the latter the entire weak hand.

For deletion of repetition, iteration in movement is omitted. For deletion of the hand, the weak hand is omitted in the articulation of a compound. The compound PARADE-WEALTH is attested with both repetition loss and weak hand deletion.[4] PARADE-WEALTH is a combination of MONEY and NUMEROUS. In Figure 8a, MONEY is a one-handed sign and has a static handshape with the thumb and index finger forming a curved open aperture. Although there is no lexical movement in MONEY, the movement constraint, which mandates movement for a sign to surface as a well-formed syllable (Brentari 1998, Geraci 2009), triggers an epenthesis of a default slightly forward movement at the implementation of MONEY. In Figure 8b, NUMEROUS is a two-handed sign and has a static handshape with the thumb and all fingers forming a curved open position. NUMEROUS contains two simultaneous movement types, i.e., repetitive orientation change and path movement, the former superimposed onto the latter. When the two signs are combined to form PARADE-WEALTH in Figure 8c, weak hand deletion and repetition loss occur on NUMEROUS. Also, syllable reanalysis is seen so that only one sequential movement is retained in the compound. The movements are reduced into one by recombining the location of the first sign MONEY and the end point of the second sign NUMEROUS. Meanwhile, the handshapes of both signs are preserved and aligned with the starting and ending points of the path movement in PARADE-WEALTH.

---

[4] Another relevant compound is CLASS-OVER (composed of CLASS and FINISH). CLASS is one-handed and involves a repetitive straight movement and FINISH is two-handed. Like PARADE-WEALTH, the compound CLASS-OVER is produced with one hand only and the repetition is lost. Loss of repetition thus applies to both the first sign and the second sign in the lexical compound.

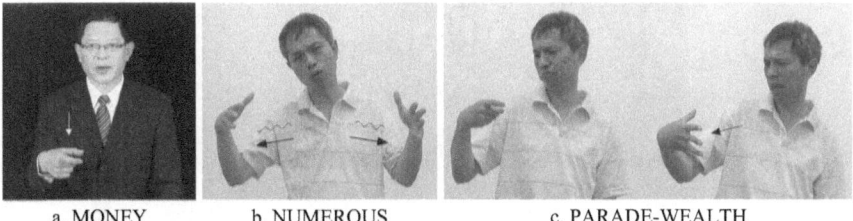

a. MONEY   b. NUMEROUS   c. PARADE-WEALTH

Figure 8: PARADE-WEALTH as compounded by MONEY and NUMEROUS.

Only one contrastive handshape is allowed per syllable (Brentari 1990b, Perlmutter 1993) except for certain morphological contexts where maximally two contrastive handshapes can occur within a single syllable (Sandler 1993, Brentari 1998). The preservation of two handshapes in the compound PARADE-WEALTH suggests that by having two contrastive handshapes, a morphologically complex word eases the one-handshape restriction. We nonetheless see that a maximum of two contrastive handshapes are allowed in each syllable structure regardless of morphological complexity of the sign.

2.2.3 Insertion

The last type of phonological modulation concerning lexical compounding in SHSL is insertion, a phenomenon of epenthesis of a phonological element. Insertion is mainly manifested in addition of the weak hand. The compound CLASSMATE is a fused form of two signs – STUDY and GROW-UP. In Figure 9a, 9b, STUDY is two-handed while GROW-UP is one-handed. In Figure 9c, the concatenation of the two signs results in the weak hand insertion in GROW-UP, which copies the articulation of its strong hand counterpart. The two signs also undergo a syllable reanalysis in which the location of STUDY and the ending point in GROW-UP are recombined into a path movement. The orientations of the two constituting signs are also recombined to form an orientation change that aligns with the starting and ending points of the path movement.

This example also illuminates the representation of the weak hand. What undergoes assimilation across the compound CLASSMATE is not the specific phonological features of the weak hand in the triggering sign STUDY, but the sheer fact of being two-handed, lending support to the phonological representation of the weak hand in a high position of the hierarchical structure of a sign (van der Hulst 1996, Brentari 1998).

a. STUDY   b. GROW-UP   c. CLASSMATE

Figure 9: CLASSMATE as compounded by STUDY and GROW-UP.

2.2.4 Summary: Phonological processes in lexical compounds

The SHSL lexical compounds undergo syllable reanalysis in which two independent signs are blended into a single unit. Syllable reduction is a diagnostic to distinguish lexical compounds from productive compounds, which preserve the constituting signs in a sequence. Accompanying the syllable reduction, other phonological processes of assimilation, insertion, and deletion were found to obey patterned modifications in the creation of a morphologically complex word. The two adjectives GOOD and BAD exhibit regular phonological processes as well. GOOD (Figure 10) and BAD (Figure 11) are free words that can appear independently.

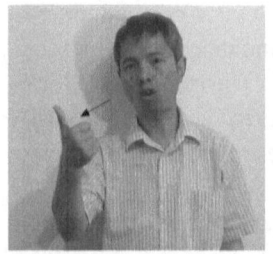

Figure 10: GOOD.   **Figure 11:** BAD.

GOOD uses an 'A' handshape in front of the chest. BAD is produced with an 'I' handshape that undergoes orientation change and downward path movement in neutral space. The two signs have differing phonological structure, with BAD containing lexical movements and GOOD having no lexical movement other than an epenthetic one in the surface representation. Both GOOD and BAD are productive in lexical compounding. When the two antonyms paradigmatically occur with a base sign, they appeal to the same adjustment rules. Three such example pairs of SHSL compounds are provided in Figures 12–14. The (UN)LUCKY pair is composed of FORTUNE and GOOD/BAD. The (UN)CLEAN pair is composed of WIPE and GOOD/BAD, and the (UN)SMOOTH pair of SAILBOAT and GOOD/BAD.

a. FORTUNE   b. LUCKY (FORTUNE ^ GOOD)   c. UNLUCKY (FORTUNE ^ BAD)

Figure 12: FORTUNE, LUCKY, and UNLUCKY.

In Figure 12a, the sign FORTUNE is articulated with a 'B' handshape, i.e., an open palm. Although there is no lexical movement in FORTUNE, an epenthetic movement is inserted to realize a movement towards the forehead. The morphologically complex words LUCKY (Figure 12b) and UNLUCKY (Figure 12c) are formed through syllable reanalysis in which the transitional movement arises as the sole path movement in the compound. Meanwhile, coalescence of the handshapes of FORTUNE and GOOD/BAD occur and they align with the starting and ending points of LUCKY/UNLUCKY respectively. Like SUPERFICIAL (Figure 7c), progressive location assimilation leads to location raising to the head level.

a. WIPE   b. CLEAN (WIPE^GOOD)   c. UNCLEAN (WIPE^BAD)

Figure 13: WIPE, CLEAN and UNCLEAN.

a. SAILBOAT   b. SMOOTH (SAILBOAT^GOOD)   c. UNSMOOTH (SAILBOAT^BAD)

Figure 14: SAILBOAT, SMOOTH and UNSMOOTH.

WIPE in Figure 13a involves the strong hand brushing the palm of the weak hand. SAILBOAT in Figure 14a involves a forward path movement in neutral space. Both signs contain a lexical path movement. In Figures 13c, 14c, UNCLEAN and UNSMOOTH undergo syllable reanalysis, deleting the movement of BAD. Also, the handshape of the first sign and that of BAD are combined into one syllable.

The formational processes in SHSL lexical compounds are summarized in Table 2:

Table 2: Phonological processes in lexical compounding in SHSL.

	First sign	Second sign
	syllable reanalysis	
Deletion	loss of repetition	loss of repetition
		weak hand deletion
Insertion		weak hand insertion
Assimilation	handshape assimilation	n.a.
	n.a.	location assimilation

In Table 2, the gray cell indicates an accidental gap, i.e., an unattested phonological form. The insertion and deletion of the weak hand on the first sign were not found in my SHSL data but not necessarily ungrammatical. The cell with n.a. indicates that handshape assimilation is exclusively attested in the first sign (i.e., regressive direction) whereas location assimilation is only applied on the second sign (i.e., progressive direction). I make the generalizations of phonological processes that occur in SHSL lexical compounding in (1):

(1) Generalizations on processes in SHSL lexical compounding:
(1a) Deletion: Syllable reanalysis is automatically applied to fuse the two signs into one; Loss of repetition is obligatorily applied to both signs; Whether weak hand deletion occurs in the first or second sign is not fully predictable from phonology.
(1b) Insertion: The insertion of the weak hand is not fully predictable from phonology.
(1c) Assimilation: Handshape assimilation regressively affects the first sign; Location assimilation progressively affects the second sign.

2.3 Idiosyncratic variations

I have demonstrated the patterns of a SHSL lexical compound in terms of the formational modulations of the constituting signs. Despite the regularity in the phonological processes ascertained above, less predictable phonological processes were observed. The representation of the numeral system illustrates such idiosyncratic variations. The signs for two-digit cardinal numbers are created as a constellation of two number signs in SHSL, among which some obey the phonological generalizations in (1) while some exhibit variations that require separate specifications.

The SHSL sign SIXTEEN is composed of ONE (Figure 15a) and SIX (Figure 15b). Since there is no lexical movement in either ONE or SIX, a default slight forward movement is inserted in the surface representation. When the two number signs come together, the transition between the two handshapes becomes the sole movement in SIXTEEN. This form of SIXTEEN in Figure 15c is predictable and conforms to the generalizations in (1).

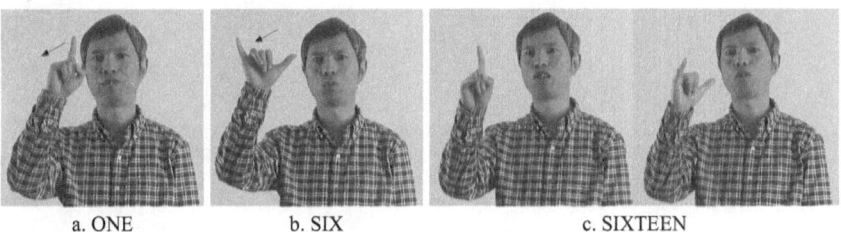

a. ONE   b. SIX   c. SIXTEEN

Figure 15: SIXTEEN as compounded by ONE and SIX.

While the form of SIXTEEN in Figure 15c involves predictable formational modulations, an alternative form of SIXTEEN, as shown in Figure 16, involves unpredictable modulations.

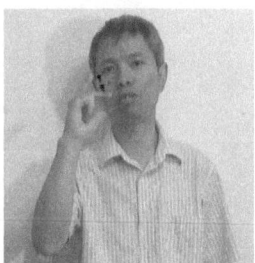

Figure 16: SIXTEEN involves idiosyncratic processes.

In this alternative form of SIXTEEN in Figure 16, the first sign ONE anticipates the handshape of the following sign SIX by adding the extended thumb and the pinky finger in articulation. The prominent movement of this compound is no longer the handshape contrast which is formed by a transitional motion from the handshape of the first sign to that of the second one. Rather, the index finger, the selected finger in ONE, undergoes a flattening joint position change. Moreover, this flattening is repetitive. The generalizations of lexical compounding in (1) fail to capture these modulations. Such phonological variations in SIXTEEN are stored in the SHSL lexicon. The idiosyncrasies in the representation of numeral systems are also found in other sign languages. The American Sign Language (ASL) TWENTY-FIVE, for instance, is composed of TWENTY (Figure 17a) and FIVE (Figure 17b). The number sign TWENTY-FIVE in Figure 17c involves a transition between the handshape of TWENTY and that of FIVE.

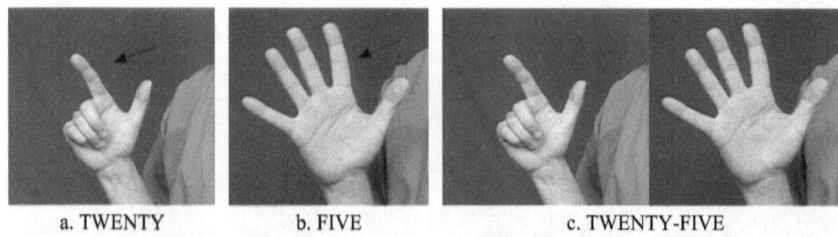

a. TWENTY   b. FIVE   c. TWENTY-FIVE

Figure 17: The ASL TWENTY-FIVE composed of TWENTY and FIVE ©www.Lifeprint.com.

In addition to the regular form, one variant of the ASL TWENTY-FIVE (Figure 18) involves the middle finger as the selected finger, assuming a repeated flattening. Such formational modulations are unpredictable by the general lexical compounding pattern in ASL (Liddell and Johnson 1986). It requires memorizing and independent specification in the ASL lexicon.

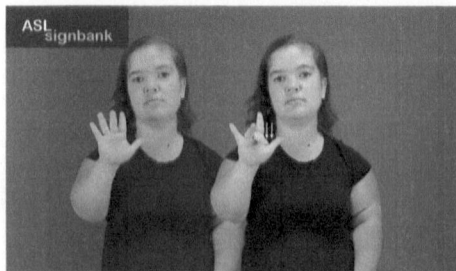

Figure 18: The ASL TWENTY-FIVE with idiosyncratic processes Hochgesang et al. (2021).

In spoken languages, some lexicalized compounds also tend to exhibit certain phonological phenomena that are not observed in more typical types of compounds (Vogel 2010:149). While the numeral system is integrated into the language, it nonetheless shows various irregularities in spoken languages (Hurford 2011). The idiosyncratic processes in number representation are common among spoken and signed languages.

3 Phonological processes in concatenative morphology: Affixation

In addition to compounding, affixation is another device in creating new words in concatenative morphology. While compounding involves independent words, affixation refers to the process in which a bound morpheme is attached to a base. In sign languages, concatenative morphology tends to be expressed through compounding rather than affixation (Meir 2012). Sequential affixation is rare across sign languages.[5] Simultaneity arguably accounts for the paucity of linear affixation in sign languages (Emmorey 2002, Meier 2002). The young age of most sign languages is another factor since an affix usually develops as a result of the grammaticalization of a free word (Aronoff, Meir, and Sandler 2005). Provided that grammaticalization requires a series of diachronic changes in phonology and semantics, sign languages do not display a richness in affixes.

Despite the sparse number of productive affixes in sign languages due to modality and age effects, sequential affixation was attested in ASL (Sandler 1996, Sandler and Lillo-Martin 2006) and Israeli Sign Language (ISL) (Aronoff, Meir, and Sandler 2005). My data confirmed one type of affix in SHSL that bears on the negative. Following Woodward (1973, 1974), I call this affixation process negative incorporation. Negative incorporation occurs when "a verb is negated by a bound outward movement of the moving hand(s) from the place where the sign is made" (Woodward 1974:22). The negative morpheme means 'not' or 'no'. Negative incorporation was also attested in other sign languages such as French Sign Language (*langue des signes française:* LSF) (Woodward and De Santis 1977) and British Sign Language (BSL: Deuchar 1984). The negated signs are primarily about experience or sensation (Sutton-Spence and Woll 1999).

---

5 Pfau (2008) analyzed one type of negative in DGS as a featural affix. It is expressed by headshake and hence simultaneously layered onto the manual predicate that it attaches to.

In SHSL, the negative, which is articulated with an open palm in an outward movement, cannot appear as a free word. It is therefore a bound morpheme and must combine with a base. This negative morpheme is a suffix by consistently occurring after but never before the base. My data revealed at least nine SHSL signs that involve negative incorporation. Table 3 lists these signs with the left column marking the item number, the middle one illustrating the base, and the right one illustrating the lexical signs with negative incorporation.

Table 3: The SHSL signs with negative incorporation.

Item	Base	Negative incorporation
1	a. BELIEVE	b. DISBELIEVE
2	a. SATISFIED	b. UNSATISFIED
3	a. USE	b. NOT-USE
4	a. ENOUGH	b. NOT-ENOUGH

Table 3 (continued)

Item	Base	Negative incorporation
5	a. KNOW	b. NOT-KNOW
6	a. MONEY	b. NOT-HAVE-MONEY
7	a. RELATE	b. NOT-RELATE
8	a. MATCH[6]	b. NOT-MATCH
9	a. DREAM	b. NOT-THINK-OF

---

6 RELATE and MATCH involve two hands in symmetrical articulation. The weak hand undergoes negative incorporation in RELATE, but not in MATCH. Whether negative incorporation affects

With respect to word category of the base signs, Table 3 indicates that in SHSL the base for negative incorporation can be verbs, nouns (e.g., MONEY in item 6), and predicative adjectives (e.g., SATISFIED in item 2, ENOUGH in item 4). Besides a variety of word categories of the base sign, the selection of the base sign's meaning, which is confined to mental activities in BSL (Sutton-Spence and Woll 1999), is less restricted in SHSL. As shown in Table 3, although bases like BELIEVE, SATISFIED, and DREAM are sensation/experience-related, other bases such as USE, RELATE and MATCH are not. SHSL is more permissive on the selection of the base with respect to its word categories and meaning.

Regarding phonological modulations, negative incorporation resembles lexical compounding by having an obligatory syllable reanalysis. The base and the negative are compressed into a compact unit. Location assimilation is also exclusively found on affecting the second constituent, i.e., negative affix. The slight difference from lexical compounding resides in movement deletion and handshape assimilation. First, while the movement of the negative affix in negative incorporation is always preserved, the movement in a lexical compound is sensitive to the underlying movement of the constituting signs and which movement is preserved is not predictable from phonology alone. Second, in negative incorporation, no handshape assimilation occurs and both handshapes from the base and negative affix are preserved. In some lexical compounds, hand assimilation occurs and exclusively targets the first sign. The pattern of phonological processes in negative incorporation in SHSL is provided in Table 4 and summarized in (2):

Table 4: Phonological processes in negative incorporation (affixation) in SHSL.

	Base sign	Negative affix
Deletion	deletion of movement	n.a.
Handshape Assimilation	Recombination of handshapes	
	n.a.	location assimilation

(2) Generalizations on phonological processes in negative incorporation in SHSL:
(2a) Movement: The outward movement of the negative affix becomes the sole movement of the resulting sign no matter whether there is an underlying lexical movement in the base sign or not.

---

one hand or two and how two-handed motivations impact the preservation of two-handed form is left for future research.

(2b) Handshape: The handshape of the negative affix combines with the underlying handshape of the base sign to form a handshape contrast unless the two handshapes are both in 'B' handshape.
(2c) Location: The location of the base assimilates the negative affix.

While the phonological processes that occur in negative incorporation in SHSL concur with the patterns in other sign languages and conform to the generalizations in (2), there is one exception. NOT-THINK-OF seems to violate the movement pattern in (2a). This complex sign (item 9 in Table 3) undergoes an outward path movement from the ipsilateral temple to neutral space and a handshape contrast from a 'Y' handshape to a 'B' handshape. By (2a), NOT-THINK-OF would contain a path movement that starts from the final setting in neutral space of its base sign DREAM, contrary to the actual form which starts at the initial setting in DREAM. Here I account for the violation of NOT-THINK-OF from two aspects. First, the underlying lexical movement of the base sign DREAM is identical to that of the negative affix. The form with negative incorporation directly takes on the underlying outward movement of the base and conflates the two outward movements into one. This reduction of movement is ascribable to monosyllabicity of a sign (Coulter 1982) so that only one movement is preserved. Second, the lexical movement in DREAM starts at the temple, a location that is associated with mental activities across sign languages (Brennan 1992, Östling, Börstell, and Courtaux 2018). Retaining this iconic location is arguably another factor that causes the violation of (2a). Modulations of locations, which may lead to a loss of iconic mapping, may be prohibited in a sign language (Meir et al. 2013). A modification of the location in NOT-THINK-OF is therefore disfavored in SHSL negative incorporation by virtue of a pressure to preserve an iconic mapping from the temple location to the relevant mental activity.

4 Phonological processes in nonconcatenative morphology

In the previous section, I have discussed phonological processes in concatenative morphology, focusing on phonological restructurings in compounding and affixation. In this section, I zoom in on phonological processes in nonconcatenative morphology, which is favored over concatenative ones in sign languages (Fernald and Napoli 2000, Aronoff, Meir, and Sandler 2005). Two non-concatenative processes, namely, initialization and numeral incorporation, will be analyzed.

4.1 Initialization

Initialization is a combination of movement, location, and orientation from a sign and handshape from a spoken word (Stokoe, Casterline, and Croneberg 1965, Brentari and Padden 2001). The handshape of an initialized sign stands for a manual alphabetical letter, which corresponds to the first letter in the written form of that word in the spoken language. Initialization is a common device for word formation in western sign languages. For instance, the ASL signs GROUP, TEAM, FAMILY, and CLASS involve the same phonological specification of movement, location, and orientation in Figure 19. GROUP, TEAM, FAMILY, and CLASS are formed with the incorporation of distinct handshapes in the manual letters G, T, F, and C.

a. GROUP b. TEAM

c. FAMILY d. CLASS

Figure 19: The ASL initialized signs GROUP, TEAM, FAMILY, CLASS (ASL Signbank 2021).

Initialization is not a common method in creating new words in SHSL because the Chinese written system mainly consists of Chinese characters instead of *pinyin*, the Romanized system for Mandarin. Although there is a set of Chinese manual alphabetical letters promoted at the national level, its actual use in SHSL is very limited and some of them do not enter the handshape inventory of SHSL (Gu 2018, Zhang 2019). My data only identified one instance of initialization in the SHSL lexicon. The sign COFFEE in Figure 20a has clear evidence of incorporating the manual letter K, which stands for the first letter in *kafei*, the *pinyin* for the

a. COFFEE   b. STIR

Figure 20: Initialized sign COFFEE in comparison to STIR.

word 'coffee' in Mandarin. COFFEE is minimally distinctive from another SHSL sign STIR, which uses a '1' handshape in Figure 20b.

In Figure 20, STIR and COFFEE form a minimal pair in that they are identical in the phonological representation except for handshape. COFFEE is created on the basis of STIR by replacing the 'K' handshape for the '1' handshape, thus lending STIR an addition of a specific meaning, i.e., manual K as the initial letter of *kafei* ('coffee') in Mandarin.

4.2 Numeral incorporation

Numeral incorporation resembles initialization in that both processes involve a simultaneous combination of the phonological specification from two sources: movement, location, and orientation from the base and handshape from a manual alphabetical letter (initialization) or a number sign (numeral incorporation). Numeral incorporation is produced by including a numeral marker into a free or bound root (Liddell 1996). Like initialization, the phonological process in numeral incorporation substitutes the existing handshape of the base form, which is usually the '1' handshape, with a handshape that stands for a number. On par with Liddell's (1996, 2003) ASL studies, numeral incorporation in SHSL was primarily found in signs that denote notions like time periods, age, and money. Table 5 provides the attested numeral incorporations in SHSL, with the left column on types of bases, the middle one on the values allowed for incorporation, and the right one on the meaning of the numeral incorporated signs.

Table 5: Numeral incorporation in SHSL.

Numeral incorporating bases	Values	Meaning
1. Free roots (dual meaning)		
MONTH	1–10	number of months
DAY	1–10	number of days
WEEK	1–10	number of weeks
HOUR	1–10	number of hours
MINUTE	1–10	number of minutes
SECOND	1–10	number of seconds
TEN-THOUSAND	1–10	number of ten-thousands
THOUSAND	1–9	number of thousands
HUNDRED	1–9	number of hundreds
TIME	1–10	number of times
GRADE	1–10	the ordinal number of grades
RANKING	1–10	the ordinal number of rankings
ORDINAL	1–10	the ordinal number
2. Free roots (single meaning)		
HALF-KILOGRAM	1–10	number of half kilograms
TEN-CENTS	1–9	number of RMB ten cents
YEAR	1–10	number of years
3. Bound roots		
DAY-AGO	1–10	number of days ago
AFTER-DAY	1–10	number of days from now
YUAN	1–10	quantity of yuan (RMB)
DEAF-SCHOOL	1–4	the ordinal number of deaf schools
DAY-OF-WEEK	1–7	the ordinal number of the day in a week

4.2.1 Root types in numeral incorporation

The base sign that allows numeral incorporation in Table 5 is either a free root or a bound root. A free root is further divisible into a root that has dual meaning and a root with a single meaning. A free root with dual meaning contains a '1' handshape. The base signs WEEK, DAY, TEN-THOUSAND, and GRADE in Figure 21 all involve a '1' handshape.

The four signs in Figure 21 have a dual meaning. First, they can denote the quantity one/the first order of the unit, i.e., ONE-WEEK, ONE-DAY, ONE-TEN-THOUSAND, and FIRST-GRADE, by incorporating the number handshape ONE.

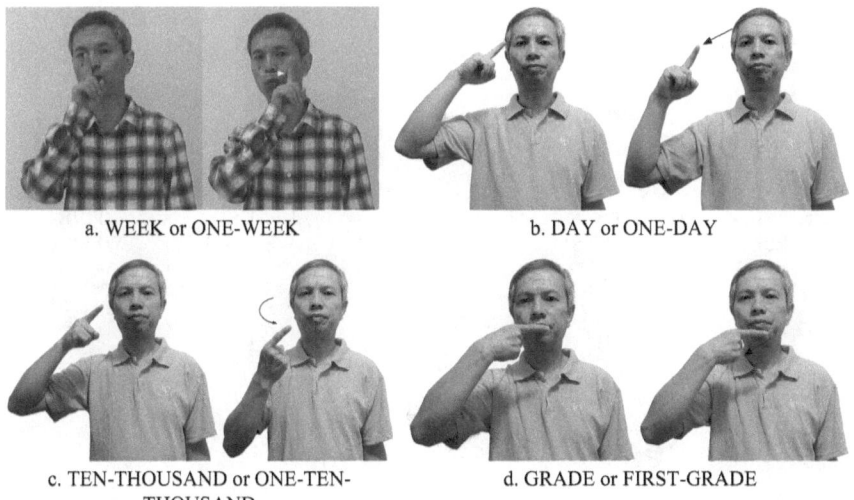

a. WEEK or ONE-WEEK   b. DAY or ONE-DAY

c. TEN-THOUSAND or ONE-TEN-THOUSAND   d. GRADE or FIRST-GRADE

Figure 21: Free roots with a dual meaning in SHSL numeral incorporation.

Besides numeral incorporation, they can be a bare form meaning WEEK, DAY, TEN-THOUSAND, and GRADE. They can combine with a separate number sign in a sequence to form a numeral phrase. For instance, the concept of sixteen weeks is expressed by a phrase consisting of SIXTEEN and WEEK, suggesting that the sign WEEK has no quantification as part of its internal meaning. By using other numeral handshapes that denote number two to five, etc., the quantity of the units is expressed. In WEEK, for instance, the expression of ONE-WEEK, TWO-WEEKS, and all the way to TEN-WEEKS is realized by inserting the number handshape for one to ten, as illustrated in Figure 22.

Such formation of signs with numeral incorporation is predictable so that only the base form is reckoned as part of the mental lexicon and the other signs are derivable from the base form in combination with the numeral incorporation rules.

Apart from free roots with a dual meaning, some SHSL roots that allow numeral incorporation are not necessarily specified with a '1' handshape. For instance, the base signs HALF-KILOGRAM and TEN-CENTS in Table 5 are articulated with thumb and index finger in closed aperture and a 'Y' handshape respectively, as illustrated in Figure 23a and 23c. Their incorporated forms with the number handshape ONE are illustrated in Figure 23b and 23d.

Figure 22: Numeral incorporation of numbers one to ten in the SHSL WEEK.

Figure 23: Free roots with a single meaning in SHSL.

Provided that the free roots for HALF-KILOGRAM and TEN-CENTS involve handshapes other than '1', these root forms are thus not homophonous to the incorporated forms with the meaning of one measurement of the base, i.e., ONE-HALF-KILOGRAM and ONE-TEN-CENTS. Whether a free root has a dual meaning is contingent on its underlying handshape specification.

The bound roots in Table 5 are only phonologically specified in movement, location, and orientation while the handshape features are unspecified. In these signs with a bound root {X}, the incorporation of number one exclusively refers to {one X}, i.e., a sign with quantification. Take the SHSL sign FIRST-DEAF-SCHOOL for example. The base form for numeral incorporation is a bound root by having the hand slightly move towards the contralateral side of the upper chest. The location, a little above the chest pocket, is motivated by the area for wearing a school badge (Fu and Mei 1986: 52). By incorporating the number one, two, three, and four, the phonological forms of the signs denoting the order in the naming of the four deaf schools in Shanghai are realized. The sign for FIRST-DEAF-SCHOOL is illustrated in Figure 24a. A similar process is attested in the group of signs that specifies the quantity of *yuan*, a basic unit of currencies in Chinese. The base sign is a bound root with a hand executing a movement released from the chin. The handshape of this bound root is unspecified and must be simultaneously combined with a number handshape, for instance, the '1' handshape that denotes one, to surface as a grammatical form in Figure 24b.

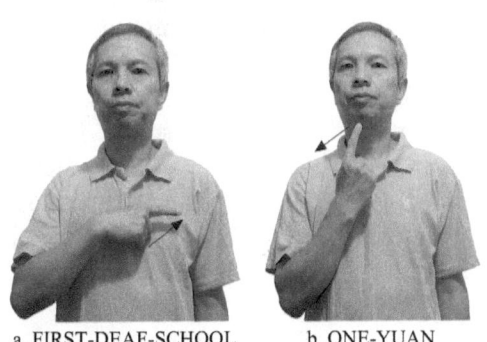

a. FIRST-DEAF-SCHOOL   b. ONE-YUAN

Figure 24: Bound roots with a single meaning in SHSL.

4.2.2 Restrictions in numeral incorporation

Despite the regularity and automaticity in numeral incorporation rules, a range of factors, including phonology, counting conventions in Mandarin, and iconicity, are at play in restricting numeral incorporation in SHSL. I analyze these factors with examples. In particular, I will show that one type of iconicity that blocks numeral incorporation is unique to SHSL, which sheds light on the relationships between Chinese orthography, iconicity, and phonology in SHSL.

First, the typical values for numeral incorporation in Table 5 are usually from one to ten. On par with other sign languages, SHSL does not allow incorporation of a number handshape that exceeds ten by the reason that numeral incorporation requires the number sign to not have a handshape change. The phonological restrictions that regulate numeral incorporation in SHSL is provided in (3):

(3) Phonological restrictions in numeral incorporation in SHSL:
Only a static handshape can be incorporated. In other words, a number handshape that involves a handshape change (i.e., a motion) is blocked from undergoing numeral incorporation.

In addition to phonological restrictions, some SHSL signs allow incorporation of value only up to 9, as instantiated in THOUSAND, HUNDRED, and TEN-CENTS. In these cases, incorporation of the value ten is blocked by an existing lexical sign with the same meaning. For instance, TEN-THOUSAND, although phonologically well-formed, is not attested in SHSL merely due to the fact that there is already a character sign for [ONE-[TEN-THOUSAND]]. The latter is preferred to the former by virtue of the counting conventions in Chinese wherein a five-digit number is formed by the modifying numeral in combination with ten-thousand(万), a basic unit in the Chinese counting system.

Lastly, some marked handshapes in the SHSL base signs block numeral incorporation due to iconicity. Here I discuss two such handshapes. The handshape in YUAN (Figure 25a) shows an association to the appearance of the physical referent. The other handshape in the character sign HUNDRED-MILLION (Figure 26a) exhibits an association with orthography, which is specific to SHSL and rarely attested in western sign languages. I propose the iconic restrictions on numeral incorporation in SHSL in (4).

(4) Iconic restrictions in numeral incorporation in SHSL:
A base sign with an iconic handshape blocks numeral incorporation. Numeral incorporation is only allowed when there is an alternative bound root with an unspecified handshape.

In Figure 25a, the handshape of YUAN assumes a configuration of the fingers that imitates the round outline of a coin, which establishes a motivated association between form and meaning. Such a blocking of numeral incorporation was also reported in Mathur and Rathmann (2010) on Japanese Sign Language (JSL), which employs a very similar handshape for *yen*, the basic unit in the Japanese currencies. This marked handshape arguably prevents signs from undergoing numeral incorporation. The strategy for expressing the quantification of YUAN in SHSL is as follows: The quantification with number one to ten, as illustrated by TEN-YUAN in Figure 25b, undergoes numeral incorporation by selecting an alternative bound root for YUAN. By virtue of the phonological restriction in (3), only a static handshape can undergo numeral incorporation. The quantification of a number over ten, as instantiated by {TWELVE YUAN} in Figure 25c, therefore appeals to a sequence of a number sign TWELVE followed by the free word YUAN.

a. YUAN   b. TEN-YUAN   c. {TWELVE YUAN}

Figure 25: SHSL sign YUAN and its quantification.

It is certain that sequencing the number signs such as TEN followed by YUAN in a phrase structure is grammatical as well in SHSL. Numeral incorporation is nonetheless preferred when the environment is satisfied by the reason that numeral incorporation is monosyllabic, which is strongly favored in sign languages (Coulter 1982, Brentari 1998, Sandler and Lillo-Martin 2006).

In Figure 26a, the handshape has to be preserved since HUNDRED-MILLION involves a configuration of the thumb and the fingers that represent the right radical, i.e., 乙, of the corresponding Chinese character 亿('hundred-million'). Numeral incorporation is disallowed given that the substitution of handshape would inevitably destroy the mapping from the Chinese orthography to the character sign. The possible alternative form that conveys the meaning of one hundred million is instead a phrase, i.e., a number sign denoting one followed by HUNDRED-MILLION, as shown in Figure 26b. HUNDRED-MILLION therefore favors a phrase-like structure to express all its quantifications.

Like fingerspelled words in ASL, character signs are foreign vocabulary and thus not native to a sign language lexicon. These signs occupy the peripheral component in the lexicon and they do not always obey phonological constraints (Brentari and Padden 2001). Being marginalized in the SHSL lexicon, the character sign HUNDRED-MILLION therefore does not fully conform to the phonological rules of numeral incorporation.

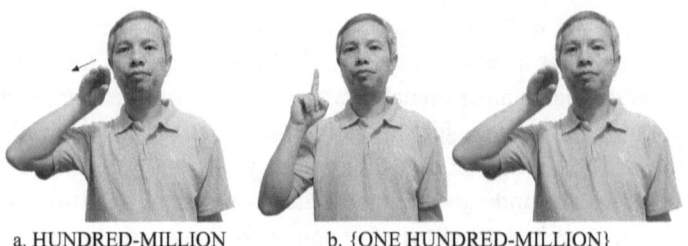

a. HUNDRED-MILLION   b. {ONE HUNDRED-MILLION}

Figure 26: The SHSL sign HUNDRED-MILLION and its quantification.

5 Conclusion

This study investigates phonological processes in the formation of SHSL complex words. I propose that compounding is a productive word formation device in SHSL. Regular patterns in phonological processes are identified in compounding and affixation in concatenative morphology, as well as in initialization and numeral incorporation in nonconcatenative morphology. In addition to regularity, idiosyncratic processes are found in the SHSL numeral system. Moreover, I show that modulations of some iconic sub-lexical units are disallowed in SHSL. In particular, the non-conformity of the character signs to the phonological regularity sheds light on the relationships between orthography, iconicity, and phonology in the sign structure. This kind of specific relationships manifested in character signs is unique to an East Asian sign language like SHSL and offers a dimension not seen in most western sign languages studied to date.

References

Aronoff, Mark, Irit Meir & Wendy Sandler. 2005. The paradox of sign language morphology. *Language* 81(2). 301–344.
Battison, Robin. 1974. Phonological deletion in American Sign Language. *Sign Language Studies* 5(1). 1–19.
Battison, Robin. 1978. *Lexical Borrowing in American Sign Language*. Silver Spring, MD: Linstok Press.
Bellugi, Ursula & Don Newkirk. 1981. Formal devices for creating new signs in American Sign Language. *Sign Language Studies* 30(1). 1–35.
Brennan, Mary. 1992. The visual world of BSL: An introduction. In David Brien (ed.), *Dictionary of British Sign Language/English*, 1. London: Faber and Faber.
Brentari, Diane. 1990a. Licensing in ASL handshape change. In Ceil Lucas (ed.), *Sign Language Research: Theoretical Issues*, 57–68. Washington, DC: Gallaudet University Press.

Brentari, Diane. 1990b. *Theoretical foundations of American Sign Language.* Chicago: University of Chicago dissertation.
Brentari, Diane. 1998. *A Prosodic Model of Sign Language Phonology.* Cambridge, MA: MIT Press.
Brentari, Diane. 2019. *Sign Language Phonology.* Cambridge, UK: Cambridge University Press.
Brentari, Diane & Carol Padden. 2001. Native and foreign vocabulary in American Sign Language: A lexicon with multiple origins. In Diane Brentari (ed.), *Foreign Vocabulary in Sign Languages: A Cross-Linguistic Investigation of Word Formation*, 87–119. Mahwah, NJ: Lawrence Erlbaum Associates.
Cheek, Davina. 2001. *The phonetics and phonology of handshape in American Sign Language.* Austin: University of Texas dissertation.
Chen, Yaqing & Qunhu Gong. 2020. Dialects or languages: A corpus-based quantitative approach to lexical variation in common signs in Chinese Sign Language (CSL). *Lingua*, 248(1). 102944.
Coulter, Geoffrey. 1982. On the nature of ASL as a monosyllabic language. Paper presented at the annual meeting of the Linguistic Society of America (LSA), San Diego, CA.
Crasborn, Onno & Han Sloetjes. 2008. Enhanced ELAN functionality for sign language corpora. In *Proceedings of the 3rd workshop on the Representation and Processing of Sign Languages: Construction and Exploitation of Sign Language Corpora*, 39–43.
Deuchar, Margaret. 1984. *British Sign Language.* Routledge & Kegan Paul.
Emmorey, Karen. 2002. *Language, Cognition, and the Brain: Insights from Sign Language Research.* Mahwah, NJ: Lawrence Erlbaum Associates.
Fernald, Theodore & Donna Napoli. 2000. Exploitation of morphological possibilities in signed languages: Comparison of American Sign Language with English. *Sign Language & Linguistics* 3(1). 3–58.
Fischer, Susan & Qunhu Gong. 2010. Variation in East Asian sign language structures. In Diane Brentari (ed.), *Sign Languages*, 499–518. Cambridge, UK: Cambridge University Press.
Fu, Yiting & Cikai Mei. 1986. *Longre Shouyu Gailun* [Introduction to the deaf sign language]. Shanghai: Xueling Press.
Geraci, Carlo. 2009. Epenthesis in Italian Sign Language. *Sign Language & Linguistics* 12(1). 3–51.
Gong, Qunhu. 2005. *Zhongguo Longren ji Yuyan Jiaoyu Wenti* [The language of Chinese deaf people and the issues in language education]. In Yulin Shen, An'an Wu & Chaoyu Zhu (eds.), *Shuangyu Longjiaoyu de Lilun yu Shijian* [Theory and practice in bilingual deaf education], 61–90. Beijing: Huaxia Press.
Greenberg, Joseph. 1963. *Universals of Language.* Cambridge, MA: MIT Press.
Grosvald, Michael & David Corina. 2012. Perception of long-distance coarticulation: An event-related potential and behavioral study. *Applied Psycholinguistics* 33(1). 55–82.
Gu, Dingqian, Ying Liu & Xirong He. 2019. Deaf education and the use of sign language in Mainland China. In Harry Knoors, Maria Brons & Marc Marschark (eds.), *Deaf Education Beyond the Western World: Context, Challenges and Prospects*, 285–306. New York: Oxford University Press.
Gu, Shengyun. 2018. *The feature system of handshapes and phonological processes in Shanghai Sign Language.* Shanghai: East China Normal University dissertation.
Hendriks, Berndina. 2008. *Jordanian Sign Language: Aspects of grammar from a cross-linguistic perspective.* University of Amsterdam dissertation. Utrecht: LOT.
Hochgesang, Julie, Onno Crasborn & Diane Lillo-Martin. 2021. *ASL Signbank.* New Haven, CT: Haskins Lab, Yale University. https://aslsignbank.haskins.yale.edu/ (accessed 20 November 2021).

Hurford, James. 2011. *The Linguistic Theory of Numerals*, Vol 16. Cambridge, UK: Cambridge University Press.

Katamba, Francis. 1993. *Morphology*. London: Macmillan.

Kegl, Judy & Ronnie Wilbur. 1976. When does structure stop and style begin? Syntax, morphology, and phonology vs. stylistic variation in American Sign Language. In Salikoko Mufwene, Carol Walker & Sanford Steever (eds.), *Papers from the 12th Regional Meeting, Chicago Linguistic Society*, 12, 376–396. Chicago: The University of Chicago Press.

Kiparsky, Paul. 1982. From cyclic phonology to lexical phonology. In Harry van der Hulst & Norval Smith (eds.), *The Structure of Phonological Representations* 1, 131–175. Cinnaminson, USA: Foris Publications.

Klima, Edward. & Ursula Bellugi. 1979. *The Signs of Language*. Cambridge, MA: Harvard University Press.

Lepic, Ryan. 2016. The great ASL compound hoax. In Aubrey Healey, Ricardo Napoleão de Souza, Pavlina Pešková & Moses Allen (eds.), *Proceedings of the High Desert Linguistics Society Conference* 11, 227–250. Albuquerque, NM: University of New Mexico.

Lepic, Ryan. 2019. A usage-based alternative to "lexicalization" in sign language linguistics. *Glossa: A Journal of General Linguistics* 4(1). 1–30.

Liddell, Scott. 1996. Numeral incorporating roots and non-incorporating prefixes in American Sign Language. *Sign Language Studies* 92(1). 201–226.

Liddell, Scott. 2003. *Grammar, Gesture, and Meaning in American Sign Language*. Cambridge: Cambridge University Press.

Liddell, Scott & Robert Johnson. 1986. American Sign Language compound formation processes, lexicalization, and phonological remnants. *Natural Language & Linguistic Theory* 4(4). 445–513.

Lin, Christina Mien-Chun, Barbara Gerner de García, & Deborah Chen-Pichler. 2009. Standardizing Chinese Sign Language for use in post-secondary education. *Current Issues in Language Planning* 10(3). 327–337.

Lin, Hao. 2021. Early development of Chinese Sign Language in Shanghai schools for the Deaf. *Frontiers in Psychology* 12.

Lytle, Richard, Kathryn Johnson & Junhui Yang. 2005. Deaf education in China: History, current issues, and emerging deaf voices. *American Annals of the Deaf* 5. 457–469.

Ma, Yunyi. 2020. *A Study of lexical variation, comprehension and language attitudes in deaf users of Chinese Sign Language (CSL) from Beijing and Shanghai*. London: UCL (University College London) dissertation.

Mak, Joe & Gladys Tang. 2011. Movement types, repetition, and feature organization in Hong Kong Sign Language. In Rachel Channon & Harry van der Hulst (eds.), *Formational units in Sign Languages*, 315–38. Berlin: De Gruyter Mouton.

Mathur, Gaurav & Christian Rathmann. 2010. Two types of nonconcatenative morphology in signed languages. In Mathur Gaurav & Donna Napoli (eds.), *Deaf Around the World: Impact of Language*, 54–82. New York: Oxford University Press.

Mauk, Claude. 2003. *Undershoot in two modalities: Evidence from fast speech and fast signing*. Austin: University of Texas dissertation.

Meier, Richard. 2002. Why different, why the same? Explaining effects and non-effects of modality upon linguistic structure in sign and speech. In Richard Meier, Kearsy Cormier & David Quinto-Pozos (eds.), *Modality and Structure in Signed and Spoken Languages*, 1–25. Cambridge, UK: Cambridge University Press.

Meir, Irit, Mark Aronoff, Wendy Sandler & Carol Padden. 2010. Sign languages and compounding. In Sergio Scalise (ed.), *Cross-Disciplinary Issues in Compounding*, 301–322. Amsterdam: John Benjamins Publishing Company.

Meir, Irit. 2012. Word classes and word formation. In Roland Pfau, Markus Steinbach & Bencie Woll (eds.), *Sign Language: An International Handbook*, 77–112. Berlin: De Gruyter Mouton.

Meir, Irit, Carol Padden, Mark Aronoff & Wendy Sandler. 2013. Competing iconicities in the structure of languages. *Cognitive Linguistics* 24(2). 309–343.

Mohanan, Karuvannur. 1986. *The Theory of Lexical Phonology*. Dordrecht: Reidel.

Napoli, Donna. 2019. Morphological Theory and Sign Languages. In Jenny Audring & Francesca Masini (eds.), *The Oxford Handbook of Morphological Theory*. DOI:10.1093/oxfordhb/9780199668984.013.37

Ormel, Ellen, Onno Crasborn & Els van der Kooij. 2013. Coarticulation of hand height in Sign Language of the Netherlands is affected by contact type. *Journal of Phonetics* 41 (3–4). 156–171.

Ormel, Ellen, Onno Crasborn, Gerrit Kootstra & Anne de Meijer. 2017. Coarticulation of handshape in Sign Language of the Netherlands: A corpus study. *Laboratory Phonology* 8(1). 1–21.

Östling, Robert, Carl Börstell & Servane Courtaux. 2018. Visual iconicity across sign languages: Large-scale automated video analysis of iconic articulators and locations. *Frontiers in Psychology* 9. 725.

Padden, Carol & David Perlmutter. 1987. American Sign Language and the architecture of phonological theory. *Natural Language & Linguistic Theory* 5(3). 335–375.

Perlmutter, David. 1993. Sonority and syllable structure in American Sign Language. In Geoffrey Coulter (ed.), *Current Issues in ASL Phonology: Phonetics and Phonology*, Vol 3, 227–261. New York: Academic Press.

Pfau, Roland. 2008. The grammar of headshake: A typological perspective on German Sign Language negation. *Linguistics in Amsterdam* 1(1). 37–74.

Quer, Josep, Carlo Cecchetto, Caterina Donati, Carlo Geraci, Meltem Kelepir, Roland Pfau & Markus Steinbach (eds.). 2017. *SignGram Blueprint: A Guide to Sign Language Grammar Writing*. Berlin: De Gruyter Mouton.

Russell, Kevin, Erin Wilkinson & Terry Janzen. 2011. ASL sign lowering as undershoot: A corpus study. *Laboratory Phonology* 2(2). 403–422.

Sandler, Wendy. 1987. Assimilation and feature hierarchy in American Sign Language. In Anna Bosch, Barbara Need, and Eric Schiller (eds.), *Papers from the 23rd Annual Regional Meeting of the Chicago Linguistic Society, Parasession on Autosegmental and Metrical Phonology*, 2, 266–278. Chicago: The University of Chicago Press.

Sandler, Wendy. 1989. *Phonological Representation of the Sign: Linearity and Nonlinearity* in American Sign Language. Providence, RI: Foris Publications.

Sandler, Wendy. 1993. A sonority cycle in American Sign Language. *Phonology* 10(2). 243–279.

Sandler, Wendy. 1996. Representing handshapes. In William Edmondson & Ronnie Wilbur (eds.), *International Review of Sign Linguistics*, 115–158. NJ: Lawrence Erlbaum Associates.

Sandler, Wendy & Diane Lillo-Martin. 2006. *Sign Language and Linguistic Universals*. Cambridge, UK: Cambridge University Press.

Santoro, Mirko. 2018. *Compounds in sign languages: The case of Italian and French Sign Language*. Paris: l'École des Hautes Études en Sciences Sociales dissertation.

Shanghai Municipal Statistics Bureau. 2020. *Total households, population, density of registered population and life expectancy (1978~2019)*. http://tjj.sh.gov.cn/tjnj/nj20.htm?d1=2020tjnjen/E0201.htm (accessed 20 November 2021)

Shanghai Disabled Persons' Federation. 2020. *2019 Nian Canjiren Jiben Shuju Qingkuang* [The basic data of disabled persons in 2019]. http://www.shdisabled.gov.cn/clwz/upload/file/2020/07/17/5b08eaa3ee93412fabe3cea74fc1aff0.pdf (accessed 20 November 2021)
Stokoe, William, Dorothy Casterline & Carl Croneberg. 1965. *A Dictionary of ASL on Linguistic Principles*. Washington, D.C.: Gallaudet University Press.
Sutton-Spence, Rachel & Bencie Woll. 1999. *The Linguistics of British Sign Language: An Introduction*. Cambridge, UK: Cambridge University Press.
Sze, Felix, Connie Lo, Lisa Lo & Kenny Chu. 2013. Historical development of Hong Kong sign language. *Sign Language Studies* 13 (2). 155–185.
Tang, Gladys. (ed.). 2007. *Hong Kong Sign Language*. Hong Kong: Chinese University Press.
Tkachman, Oksana & Irit Meir. 2018. Novel compounding and the emergence of structure in two young sign languages. *Glossa: A Journal of General Linguistics* 3(1). 1–40.
Van der Hulst, Harry. 1996. On the other hand. *Lingua* 98(1–3). 121–143.
Vogel, Irene. 2010. The phonology of compounds. In Sergio Scalise and Irene Vogel (eds.), *Cross-Disciplinary Issues in Compounding*, 145–164. Amsterdam: John Benjamins Publishing Company.
Wallin, Lars. 1983. Compounds in Swedish Sign Language in historical perspective. In James Kyle & Bencie Woll (eds.), *Language in Sign: An International Perspective on Sign Language*, 56–69. London: Croom Helm.
Wilbur, Ronnie. 1993. Syllables and segments: Hold the movement and move the holds. In Geoffrey Coulter (ed.), *Current Issues in ASL Phonology: Phonetics and Phonology*, Vol 3, 135–168. New York: Academic Press.
Woodward, James. 1973. Inter-rule implication in American Sign Language. *Sign Language Studies* 3(1). 47–56.
Woodward, James. 1974. Implicational variation in American Sign Language: negative incorporation. *Sign Language Studies* 5(1). 20–30.
Woodward, James. 1993. Intuitive judgments of Hong Kong signers about the relationship of sign language variations in Hong Kong and Shanghai. *CUHK Papers in Linguistics* 4. 88–96.
Woodward, James & Susan De Santis. 1977. Negative incorporation in French and American sign language. *Language in Society* 6(3). 379–388.
Yang, Junhui. 2006. *Deaf teachers in China: Their perceptions regarding their roles and the barriers they face*. Washington, D.C.: Gallaudet University dissertation.
Yang, Junhui. 2016. Numeral signs and compounding in Chinese Sign Language (CSL). In Ulrike Zeshan & Keiko Sagara (eds.), *Semantic Fields in Sign Languages: Color, Kinship and Quantification*, 253–268. Boston/Berlin: De Gruyter Mouton & Lancaster, UK: Ishara Press.
Yang, Junhui & Susan Fischer. 2002. Expressing negation in Chinese sign language. *Sign Language & Linguistics* 5(2). 167–202.
Yau, Shun-chiu. 1977. *The Chinese signs: Lexicon of the Standard Sign Language for the Deaf in China*. Hong Kong: Langages Croisés.
Yau, Shun-chiu. 1988. *Création gestuelle et débuts du langage* [Sign creation and language emergence]. Paris: Université de Paris VII dissertation.
Yi, Yumin. 2008. *Shanghai Shouyu de Yuyin Diaocha Baogao* [The survey of the phonology of Shanghai Sign Language]. Shanghai: Fudan University dissertation.
Zhang, Jisheng (ed.). 2019. *Shanghai Shoyu Yinxi* [Shanghai Sign Language phonology]. Shanghai: East China Normal University Press.

Ki-Hyun Nam and Kang-Suk Byun
Classifiers and gender in Korean Sign Language

Abstract: This chapter notices the agreement phenomena for classifier verb in Korean Sign Language (KSL). KSL expresses two types of gender, male and female: one with only the thumb out of the fist and the other with only the pinky out. In KSL, the gender handshape productively combines with not only kinship terms, name signs, agreement verbs but also with classifier verbs. In sign language the research on agreement has focused on the person features of agreement verbs. However, there has never been a case where gender agreement and classifier verbs were studied empirically. The contribution of this chapter is a close examination of the main characteristics of the gender agreement of classifier verbs. We discuss major characteristics of the classifier verbs and argument agreement phenomena in KSL, associating them with general agreement phenomena of sign language. We look at factors for selecting the gender handshape of classifier verbs. The hope is that this research on classifier verbs and gender agreement phenomena will contribute to the cross-linguistic studies of the agreement and gender marker in sign language in general.

Keywords: Korean Sign Language (KSL), Gender, Agreement, Classifier Verbs, Gender handshape

1 Introduction

In this chapter we discuss the gender agreement phenomena of classifier verbs in Korean Sign Language (KSL), for which there are two relevant issues. Firstly, the problem of classifier handshapes appearing in sign languages in which classifiers have been reported to exist. In sign language classifiers are made up of handshapes expressing referents such as human beings, animals, and things, and are seen as meaningful morphemes. KSL is very similar to other sign languages, in that it possesses entity classifiers, handling classifiers, and Size and Shape Specifiers (SASSes). The similarity is manifested both in the handshape signifying a human being with two legs (the index finger and the middle finger out of fist), and in the handshape meaning upright living beings (the index finger out of fist). These two handshapes have been confirmed to be in use in many countries worldwide. Additionally, KSL has two ways to depict gender (male and female), one with only the thumb out of the fist and the other with only the pinky out. These gender handshapes can refer to creatures including human beings and animals. Worldwide in sign languages it is hard to find handshapes that differentiate genders. Among Asian sign languages, the sign languages of Japan, Korea, and Taiwan are historically related. KSL, Japanese Sign Language (JSL), and Taiwan Sign Language (TSL) all use the gender handshape (McBurney 2002; Fischer and Gong 2010).

The second issue we will look at in this paper is the agreement phenomenon in sign language. Agreement verbs can either move between the referential loci or move toward the referential loci, depending on the person and number of the arguments. This is seen as agreement, as the agreement verb changes form according to the person and the number features. In many sign languages it is believed that the referential locus of the argument is involved in expressing the person feature, and in sign languages with gender handshapes, the handshapes involve the agreement phenomenon as well. Fischer and Osugi (2000) named gender handshapes "indexical classifiers" (ICs). Instead of the referential locus, these ICs represent the subject argument and the object argument (Smith 1989, in Fischer and Gong 2010: 511). American Sign Language (ASL) and many other sign languages have ICs for object agreement, yet the alternation between the locus and the ICs is not systematic, nor does it show gender (Fischer and Gong 2010: 511).

This chapter looks at the agreement phenomena for classifier verbs. The classifier verbs express, in the signing space, the motion and action of the referent, as well as the acts that handle referents. Thus, the classifier verbs come to include entity handshapes representing the referent itself (entity handshape), and handshapes that handle referents (handling handshape). Among these we will discuss in this chapter the classifier verbs including the entity handshapes. The classifier verbs and agreement verbs have in common the inclusion of gender handshapes and the use of signing space, but are different in whether the citation form is there or not. The aforementioned ICs mostly happen in frozen signs (Fischer and Gong 2010: 511). All the agreement verbs including ICs are listed in the sign language dictionary as frozen signs. However, because the classifier verb represents the movement, location, and handling of the referent, it is difficult to set the basic form, as the handshapes vary depending on the referent. This leads us to the non-listing of classifier verbs, which include the classifier handshapes, in the sign language dictionary. The agreement verbs can change the unmarked handshapes of the verb to marked handshapes, in order to represent the object of the verb as female. Likewise, the classifier verbs can change the handshape of the verb according to the gender. This chapter attempts to describe the phenomenon of productive combination of classifier verbs with gender handshapes, while at the same time discussing the agreement in classifier verbs conforming to gender features. This will show that KSL not only has characteristics in common with classifiers of other sign languages, but also some individual characteristics. In addition, this paper will discuss the implications of this for the discussion on gender markers in other sign languages.

This chapter is organized as follows. Section 2 introduces specific vocabulary in which the gender handshapes are particularly manifest, including kinship terms, name signs, and agreement verbs (in part). Section 3 explains the common characteristics of the classifier types and handshapes. In Section 4 we cover the general characteristics of agreement in sign language, as well as the grammatical characteristics of the gender agreement for agreement verbs in KSL. Section 5 presents the consequences of gender agreement for the subtypes of classifier verbs, while Section 6 debates the grammatical issues for gender agreement in KSL classifier verbs.

2 Gender markers in KSL

In most sign languages the genders (masc, fem, neu) do not exist, but the three historically related sign languages KSL, JSL, and TSL all have a binary gender system (McBurney 2002; Fischer and Gong 2010; Byun et al. 2015). In these sign languages the gender is based on natural gender and is applied only to animate entities. In this paper, we call the A handshape and the I handshape 'gender handshapes'. The gender handshapes occurring in KSL are portrayed in Figure 1 (Byun 2012: 10). The A handshape – with the thumb erect – refers to the male as well as neutral human being(s), whereas the I handshape – with the little finger erect – means the female.

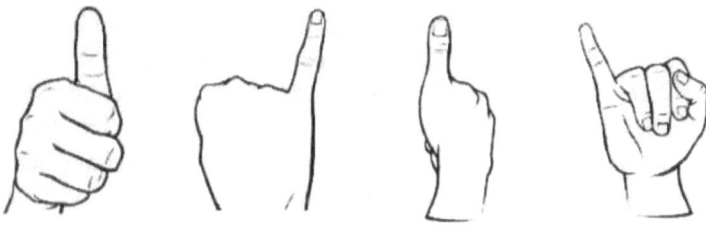

a. Viewpoint from the interlocutors   b. Viewpoint from the signers

Figure 1: Gender handshapes in KSL.

In KSL the A handshape and I handshape occur productively in kinship terms, name signs, agreement verbs (in part), and classifier verbs (in part).

2.1 Kinship terms

In the case of American Sign Language (ASL), the forehead and the chin are the positions representing gender (Liddell and Johnson 1989). For instance, the GRANDFATHER and FATHER are produced from the forehead, and [grandmother] and [mother] are produced from the chin. In KSL, [grandfather]/ [grandmother] are both produced from the wrinkled forehead, while the gestures for [daughter]/[son] begin from the belly, referring to the process of giving birth. By adding the male/female handshapes, it is possible to distinguish between [grandfather]/[grandmother] and [daughter]/[son]. Moreover, in [father]/[mother], the act of the index finger touching the face just beside the nose signifies blood kinship or physical connection (Kim 1998: 269), as in Figure 2.

a. [father]   b. [mother]

Figure 2: An example of kinship terms in KSL.

In the kinship terms of ASL and KSL, the non-positional functions of the signing space can be considered as the authority convention. In KSL, there is the belly location for [son]/[daughter], the higher cheek location for [father]/[mother], the even higher forehead location for [grandpa]/[grandma] and a forehead location for the male in ASL. All things considered, although not completely predictable, perceived or practically powerful referents are primarily associated with traces located in the upper part of the signing space, with authority status being depicted by a higher facial location. This phenomenon reflects the common metaphor of "power is up" (Lakoff and Johnson 1980; in Emmorey 2001).

2.2 Name signs

Generally, human beings receive names when they are born, and ordinarily use the names all their lives. The name can be said to refer to the person themselves. For deaf people, the custom is to keep the spoken language name given by the parents, but also to use the 'name sign' made in sign language (Lee, 2006). In KSL the way the name sign is made is generally descriptive or related to the owner's characteristics. For example, if the person is bearded, his name sign could reference 'beard'.

Let us now center our interest on the analysis by Lee (2006) of the gender-indicating handshapes in name signs. First, in the name signs of the male, there are twelve (a-i) handshapes with masculine form, and three (m-o) without. In handshapes present in the name signs for the male, 27 ▪ (36%), 15 ▪ (20%), and 10 ▪ (13.3%) have the highest frequencies. The male handshapes are outlined in red in Table 1.[1]

Table 1: The handshapes that appear in male name signs for KSL.

a.	b.	c.	d.	e.	f.
g.	h.	i.	j.	k.	l.
m.	n.	o.			

As indicated in Table 2, for female name signs, there are five handshapes (a-e) that have feminine forms, and two that have none(f-g). From all those handshapes appearing in name signs for the female, the ones most frequent are 37(48%, ▪), 28(36.36% ▪), and 5(6.49%, ▪).

Let us examine the examples of actual name signs in KSL. In Figure 3 we see the name sign for the author, Byun Kang-Suk: it is an iconic representation that references certain of Byun's congenital facial traits: the 'a' refers to his short eyebrows. The 'b', the name sign of his wife, is taken from the Chinese Sign Language (CSL). She is a Chinese deaf person from China. Her Chinese name is 倩('young') and thus takes the CSL name sign meaning 'young', whereby the hand brushes the chin with

---

[1] Tables 1 and 2 are taken from Lee (2006).

Table 2: The handshapes that appear in female name signs for KSL.

a.	b.	c.	d.	e.
f.	g.			

small left-right movements. In this handshape, the fist closes over the thumb and the ring finger to represent femininity. In other words, to make name signs include the gender in KSL, her name sign manifests the state in which the thumb and the ring finger are folded in the fist. Finally, 'c' shows the name signs for Byun's son, as given before his birth. Normally the name signs are created after the baby is born, to express something of his facial features, but under the circumstances, this did not work. Instead, the parents' name signs were combined to create a new name. The son's name was formed combining the 'a' handshape and the 'b' handshape, with the little finger folded in to indicate the gender of the son. The location also changed: the son's name sign is in the middle, between the father's eyebrows and the mother's chin. This is extremely rare, and a privilege for a child born to deaf parents.

a. Dad's name sign   b. Mom's name sign   c. Son's name sign

Figure 3: An example of name sign in KSL.

According to the research (Lee 2006) on name signs in KSL, name signs with male/female handshapes are more numerous than name signs without male/female handshapes. In comparison, male/female handshapes are omitted more often in JSL. Differences in the usage of handshapes are detected in name signs in KSL and JSL.

2.3 Agreement verbs

Verbs in sign language are divided into the following three types: plain verbs, agreement verbs, and spatial verbs according to morphological characteristics (Padden 1988). Most literature on KSL verbs was carried out based on these verb classifications. Before we get to Section 4 for details on gender agreement for agreement verbs in KSL, in this section we shall look into the grammatical characteristics of agreement verbs, including gender handshapes. Not all agreement verbs in KSL possess a person marker. As displayed in Figure 4, of all the proposed 95 agreement verbs, 40% carry the person marker, 25% have no person marker, and 35% optionally possess the person marker (Hong 2009). Whether obligatory or optional, this shows the very high percentage of 75% occupation of agreement verbs embracing the person marker. In KSL, the gender handshapes are a (clearly) dominant tool that indicates agreement. Also in KSL, there are a few verbs that allow the I handshape, which leads us to the A handshapes set as default, and rather the human being than the male classifier (Hong 2006, in Fischer and Gong 2010: 511).

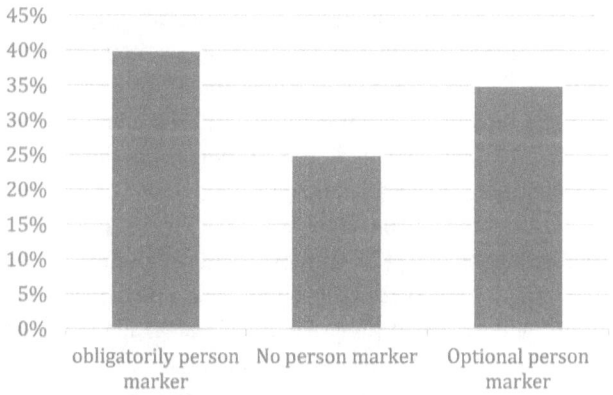

Figure 4: The inclusion and proportion of person markers in agreement verbs.

The citation form for "help" takes the A handshape (Figure 5). In this instance, it is more appropriate to 'help someone referred to' rather than to 'help a man'. Nonetheless, when the referenced subject is female, as in 'help a woman', the A handshape of the agreement verb can be used, but you could also modify the sign to the I handshape (Byun 2012: 56–57). The A handshape occurs more frequently because the A handshape can express not only the male but also a neutral-gendered human being. To emphasize the gender or to imply opposition with the male, the A handshape and the I handshape can be alternately and frequently exchanged. The I handshape signifies the female, and it is a marked gender. In frozen signs, the unmarked gender is male, but in part the frozen signs can be thawed, to allow the change of the object from male to female. This has been noted in the JSL (Fischer and Gong 2010: 511).

a. [help]   b. [help a woman]

Figure 5: The A and I handshapes in the agreement verbs of KSL.

For reference, although they are not agreement verbs, there are frozen signs with which the citation form has to be the I handshape. This is where we can use the I handshape to specify femininity. For instance, with the signs for [get pregnant] and [implantation], since physically only women can get pregnant, the citation form takes the I handshape (Figure 6a–b). This example proves that in KSL the gender marker included in the vocabulary is based on biological gender. By contrast, in JSL, the [get pregnant] sign excludes the female handshapes (Figure 6c). While KSL and JSL share the same gender handshapes, KSL employs them more often.

In the agreement verbs in KSL, the person classifiers pose as A and I handshapes with the non-dominant hand, and in almost all cases, the classifier manifests in the object argument (Hong 2006: 168). This is because in [help], the non-dominant hand takes a person classifier to represent the object argument and the dominant hand represents the act of applying to the referent, represented by the object. In ASL and many other languages, the ICs express the object argument, but in KSL and JSL the gender handshapes are developed, and in their agreement verbs, they not only express the object but also the subject argument. As in KSL "the husband said to his wife" is more precise than "he said", so when you refer to the location of the object in the syntactic space, the agreement verb can start in the location of the subject and move on to the object locus (Byun 2012: 31). This is illustrated in Figure 7.

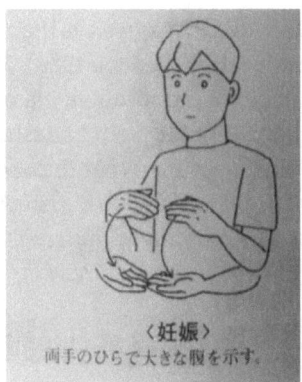

a. [get pregnant] in KSL   b. [implantation] in KSL   c. [get pregnant] in JSL[2]

Figure 6: 'get pregnant' in KSL and JSL.

'The husband said to his wife.'

Figure 7: Subject agreement in the KSL agreement verbs.

Up till now, a broad occurrence of gender handshape has been confirmed in kinship terms, name signs, and agreement verbs of KSL.[2]

3 Classifier verbs

Spatial verb signs express the location, the movement path, and movement manner of the referent. In ASL they include GO-TO, DRIVE-TO, MOVE, MOVE-AWAY, PUT,

---

2 Figure 6c is taken from Yonekawa (2011).

BRING/CARRY as well as the class of verbs described elsewhere as verbs of motion and location (Padden 1988). This class of verbs has various names such as verbs of motion and location, classifier constructions and depicting verbs (Schembri et al. 2018). The verb handshapes for this subset were called 'classifiers', as the handshapes represent the various categories of the referents. The gender handshapes are related to classifier handshapes insofar as they represent the human being. Accordingly, this chapter will use the term 'classifier verbs.'

3.1 The types of classifiers

Earnest discussion of classifiers in sign language goes back to Supalla (1982; 1986). In the 1970s, this form which we call nowadays 'classifier' was considered as pantomimes. However, Supalla (1982; 1986) compared verbs of motion and location of ASL with Navajo, proposing that the elements of these verbs are not gestures but morphemes with individual meanings. Supalla proposed five types among ASL-semantic classifiers: size and shape specifiers (SASSes), instrumental classifiers, bodypart classifiers, and body classifiers. This profoundly influenced subsequent studies. In this chapter, we will look at the type of reclassification involving handshape (Zwitserlood 2012: 161–162).

> Firstly, whole entity classifiers include classifiers that directly express referents by representing particular semantic and/or shape features. They include Supalla's semantic classifiers, static SASSes, body part classifiers, and tool classifiers.
>
> Secondly, handling classifiers (occasionally by human agents) include classifiers that express whether entities are being held or being moved. They cover Supalla's instrumental classifiers and body part classifiers.

According to Zwitserlood (2012: 161–162), the body classifier and tracing SASSes proposed by Supalla do not belong to the recent classification above. The body classifier is regarded as the means of referential shift that is not a classifier. The rest of the types and some differences have been pointed out for tracing SASSes. Because tracing movement is needed to present the shape of the referent, it cannot be combined with verbs of motion; it can, however, manifest specific shape information, and can be used in various syntactic contexts. The Body Classifier and Tracing SASSes have therefore recently been excluded from classifier types. In this chapter, we comply with types distinguishing whole entity classifiers and handling classifiers.

3.2 Classifier handshapes

Classifiers are defined as "morphemes with a non-specific meaning, which are expressed by particular configurations of the manual articulator (or hand) and which represent entities by denoting salient characteristics" (Zwitserlood 2012: 158). The handshapes that represent the entity itself or handle the entity in KSL show similarity when compared to the types of handshapes proposed in sign languages with classifiers.

3.2.1 Handshapes that present entities

Now we consider the handshapes that express the human being and the vehicle, among the handshapes that presents entities. Like other sign languages, KSL expresses entities according to animacy and shape. For handshapes signifying living beings (see Figure 8), not only are the A handshape and I handshape used, but also the 1 and 2 handshapes.[3] In KSL, 1 handshape is used to reference human beings, but is not productive. The inverted 2 handshape is used frequently to mean walking with two legs. The Y handshapes with the thumb and the little finger open can mean [family], [parent], [human rights], [society], and or [relatives]. However, it is difficult to find examples for this in classifier verbs.

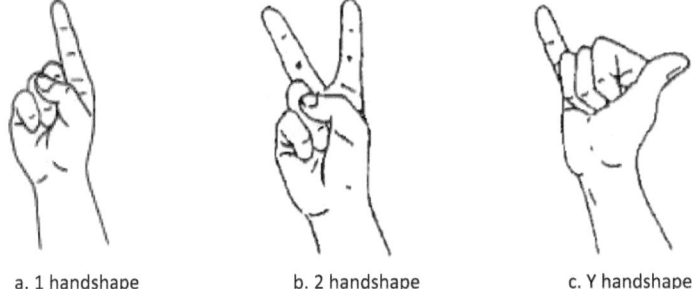

a. 1 handshape   b. 2 handshape   c. Y handshape

Figure 8: Whole entity classifiers meaning living beings in KSL.

---

3 To show the handshapes, we made use of HamNoSys 4 Handshapes, developed by Institute of German Sign Language and Communication of the Deaf. The 2 handshape, actually expressed by the tips of the index finger and the middle finger pointing under, represents a person walking by moving both legs.

Moving on to vehicles, in ASL a handshape with the thumb, index finger, and middle finger open is used for this meaning. But in KSL when you express the movements of a bus, car, etc. you do not use the same handshape. When you consider [bus] and [car], the hand below means the road and the hand above signifies the bus or car (Figure 9a, b). Both hands express the objects themselves. For the movement of the bus or car, each handshape for each sign is utilized, instead of the common handshapes. In other words, each handshape can be combined with classifier verbs.

a. [bus] b. [car] c. [motorcycle]

Figure 9: Signs for vehicle in KSL.

However, as you can see in Figure 9c the handshape of [motorcycle] cannot be combined with classifier verbs. Therefore, KSL signers utilize a handshape with the tips of the thumb and the index finger touching, imitating the roundness of the wheel of the motorbike. In Figure 10a, both hands express the land and the motorbike, in the same way as [bus] and [car]. In Figure 10b, both hands express

a. motorcycle runs b. lifts the front wheel of a motorcycle

Figure 10: The handshapes for motorcycle in KSL.

the front and back wheels to specify information such as which route the motorcycle is on, or whether the motorbike's front wheel is raised. The movement and motion of a motorbike is represented by the F handshape.

3.2.2 The handshape for handling objects

In KSL the handshapes for handling objects are varied according to their shapes, such as holding a slender object (Figure 11a), holding a flat object (Figure 11b–c), holding a thick object (Figure 11d), or holding a bulky object (Figure 11e).

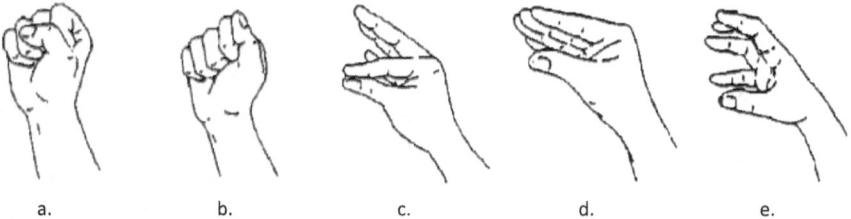

a.   b.   c.   d.   e.

Figure 11: Handshapes dealing with objects.

4 Agreement in sign language

Agreement in sign language means the correspondence between two elements, involving the features of person, number, and gender. In Korean language there is no agreement phenomenon with person, gender, and number. Instead, we can find agreement in honorifics, a grammatical category raising up the people whom the speaker deems as holding a higher position than themselves (Go and Gu 2009: 282). For example, in the sentence "Mother calls me", 'Mother' is the object of honor, to the effect that the honorific nominative postpositional particle '-kkeseo' is added to the subject of the sentence, making it 'Honorable Mother'. In the predicate also, the agreement with the subject is achieved by attaching the honorific pre-final ending '-(eu)si-'. The honorific feature of the subject is marked in the predicate, and thus the honorific is seen as an agreement phenomenon (Go and Gu 2009: 459). Nonetheless, in KSL, honorifics is not a feature for agreement.

Up till now in sign languages, the agreement phenomena have been studied for person and number features. Plain verbs do not change their forms to mark person and number. For instance, plain verbs such as [think] or [know] do not change forms to person and number of the argument. Plain verbs are produced close to the signer's body and do not utilize signing space. Thus, due to the phonological characteristics of the verbs themselves, they are limited when it comes to changing forms. Moreover, plain verbs cannot just include the handshape to indicate the referent. However, the agreement verbs employ the signing space and mark the agreement for the starting point, the end point, and the direction of the verb. For the agreement verb [give], the first location for the verb is the location for the subject and the final location is the location for the object. Moreover, the agreement verbs change their direction to the location of subject and object. In producing [help], the palm of the dominant hand faces the location of the object, and the back of the hand faces the subject. As such, the position and directional changes of the agreement verbs are analyzed as inflection by person. Agreement verbs realize agreement via the movement of the verbs and directional changes, and other non-manual features such as eye gaze and role shift (Schembri et al. 2018: 10). Finally, the spatial verbs have the usage of the signing space in common with the agreement verbs. However, the movement from the first location to the final location does not express the locations for the subject and the object, but articulates the locational relationship for before and after the transport of the referent.

Research on the gender agreement phenomena in KSL provides cases where the object argument and the agreement verb both have gender features, and other results where only one among the object argument and the agreement verb possesses agreement features, as below follow (Nam et al. 2019: 93–96).[4]

(1) a. IX_s $IX_{i.fem}$ [student] $_s$[help]$_{i.fem}$
'I helped the girl student.'
b. IX_s IX_i [father] $_s$[help]$_{i.fem}$
'I helped father.'

Regarding the acceptability of the cases where the object argument and the agreement verb both possess gender features, a high acceptability rate was shown

---

[4] Nam et al. (2019) asked seven male and female deaf persons who use KSL as their mother tongue to present sentences varying the instances when the features of agreement are shared between the argument and the verb, to judge their acceptability. The gloss of (1) is as follows (Nam et al. 2019: 76): 'IX' is indexing, 's' is the position of the signer, 'I' is the position of the argument, and 'i.fem' is the female agreement. In the verbs, the subject location features are shown before the verb and the object location features are exhibited after the verb ($_s$help$_i$). The content word borrows from the semantically nearest Korean word and is notated inside brackets (help).

where (see (1a)) the object is marked as female and was also shown when the verb [help] took the handshape showing the female (100%). This is an instance where exact match happens between the argument and the verb feature. In comparison, in (1b) the object [father] had in itself the meaning "male", thus when [help] took the handshape signifying female, the verb and the gender showed no agreement and this example ranked low in acceptability (14%). This result shows that when the object argument and the agreement verb have the same gender features, 100% acceptability is revealed, but that when the gender features are different, the acceptability rate is very low.

The following is the acceptability result in cases when only one of the argument and agreement verbs shows gender agreement features (Nam et al. 2019: 96–97).

(2) a. IX_s IX_i [student] $_s$[help]$_{i.fem}$
 'I helped the student.'
 b. IX_s $IX_{i.fem}$ [student] $_s$[help]$_i$
 'I helped the girl student.'
 c. IX_s IX_i [mother] $_s$[help]$_i$
 'I helped mother.'
 d. IX_s IX_i [mother] [gift] $_s$[give]$_i$
 'I gave a gift to my mother.'

(2a) is a sentence where there is a gender marker in the verbs, but no gender marker in the object. In (2b) there is gender marker in the object but none in the verbs. Both sentences displayed 100% acceptability. (2c) and (2d) both showed that the object [mother] was feminine in itself and had no gender marker in the verbs, and this resulted in comparably lower acceptability (71%, 43% each). Low acceptability in the argument was manifest in the argument [mother], and we asked some of the participants for their reaction if [mother] were replaced with [sister], and every one of them answered that it was more acceptable that way. Following this additional check-up, we can see that when the object argument has gender marker and the verb does not, the acceptability is rated at more than 86%. One explanation proposed for the high acceptability was that when the object argument had the I handshape and the verb argument made the A handshape, it meant that the A handshape did not conflict with the female feature of the argument, and also that the A handshape remained unmarked.

Corbett (2006) regarded agreement as feature sharing between the controller and the target. An exact match should be made among the corresponding features. However, from the point of view of feature sharing, in the case where no feature is marked in the controller argument, and the corresponding feature is marked in only the target verb, it is difficult to explain the high acceptability observed in KSL (Nam et al. 2019: 100). Therefore, it has been proposed that in KSL, the feature-checking method is more appropriate, because, in contract to feature sharing, it avoids any conflict of features (Nam et al. 2019: 101).

4.1 Gender agreement in KSL classifier verbs

Classifier verbs are divided into sub-categories. There are slight differences in the names and classifications according to the researcher. First of all, Liddell (2003) named classifier verbs as depicting verbs, because the classifier verbs include not only the act and the state generally expressed by verbs, but also the depiction. He divided them into three sub-categories. The first subtype represents the information telling us where the entity exists, for example, VEHICLE-BE-AT, or UPRIGHT-PERSON-AE-AT. The second subtype describes the surface. The examples for this type are: FLAT-NARROW-SURFACE-EXTEND-TO, BUMPY-BROAD-SURFACE-EXTEND-TO. The third subtype is divided into two categories: the verbs that represent the movement path and the verbs that describe the action. The examples of the former are VEHICLE-DRIVE-TO, BIPED-WALK-TO and the latter explains the handling of the entity. These verbs were named depicting verbs in Auslan, and included motion and location, handling, and SASSes (Johnston and Schembri 2007). Zwisterlood (2012) states that the classifier verbs exhibit the movement of the referents through space, the location or existence in space, any change of posture, or the handling of referents.

When the subtypes of classifier verbs are synthesized, the classifier verbs signify the location, movement, motion, the manner of movement for the referent, and the size and the shape of the referent. The verbs that represent the size and the shape cannot include the gender handshape and are therefore excluded from our discussion. We focus on the agreement phenomena of the classifier verbs according to the gender feature. We will describe the pattern and the constraints employed by the gender handshape in classifier verbs.

5 Data collection

We gave out Google questionnaires to the participants who agreed to participate in the survey from September 21 to 27, 2020.

5.1 Participants

Sociolinguistic backgrounds for participants are listed in [Table 3]. The participants are Deaf with KSL as their first language. In all they totalled seven individuals: two males and five females. Their ages ranged from 20 to 50. Their language acquisition period for KSL was between ages one to six. Six graduated from a school for the Deaf, and one from an ordinary school. The latter was from a Deaf family and naturally learned sign language when he/she was young. They came from various towns/cities: Seoul, Incheon, Jeonju, Daejeon, Daegu, and Chuncheon.

Table 3: The sociolinguistic background of the participants.

Participants	Gender	Age	Age when sign language was acquired	Graduation from school for the Deaf	Education	Region
A	Woman	26	3	Yes (Deaf family)	master's course	Seoul
B	Man	52	8	Yes	master's course	Incheon
C	Woman	47	5	Yes	Ph.D. program	Jeonju
D	Woman	31	3	Yes (Deaf family)	master's course	Daejeon
E	Woman	40	6	Yes	High school graduate	Daejeon
F	Woman	38	1	No (Deaf family)	College graduate	Daegu
G	Man	43	6	Yes	master's course	Chuncheon

5.2 Questionnaire

By alternating the handshapes for classifier verbs, we produced sentences where the gender for arguments and verbs agreed, as well as sentences where they did not (see Table 4). In sentences where the gender for argument and verbs did not agree, the 1 handshape with only the index finger out, meaning living beings, and the 2 handshape where only the index finger and the middle finger out of the fist, were included. In the sentence where you move on the kickboard (Appendix 801–804) the B handshape with the thumb and every finger were in an open state, and the F handshape with the end of the thumb and the index finger touching the palm and the rest of the fingers open, were intertwined.

Table 4: Sentences in which are included the sub-types of the classifier verbs.

Sub-types of the classifier verbs	handshapes
Twelve sentences were constructed to examine the gender agreement arguments of and verbs expressing a person's location. On the right is the handshapes included in the verb. (Same as below)	A, I, 2, BENT2, 1
Thirty-seven sentences were constructed to examine the gender agreement of arguments of the verbs expressing human and animal movements.	A, I, 2, BENT2, 1
Seven sentences were constructed to examine gender agreement of arguments of the verbs expressing the manner in which humans and animals move.	A, I, 2, B, BENT2, F

In 56 sentences, we confirmed the factor that influenced the choice of handshapes for the verbs, as well as the gender agreement for the argument and the verb. In KSL the [baby] has no gender but was included in the argument to better observe the factor for the choice of handshape. In addition, man and woman were replaced by the two authors of this paper [BYUN] and [NAM]. The Deaf author, whose first language was KSL, proposed sentences in KSL, and the participants were asked to look at the sentences and to choose whether they were natural or not. There were two question types. For the one type, they had to select whether the verb handshapes in the sentence were natural or not ; for the other type they simply had to select their favorite handshapes. The entire questions are presented in the appendix.

5.3 Results

5.3.1 Classifier verb and argument gender agreement

The following sentence presents the consequence for gender agreement in classifier verbs and the arguments.[5]

---

[5] The glossing for this chapter is as following.
1) The KSL words were notated with corresponding Korean language words: [help]
2) The gender agreement features were notated as subscript at the right side of the word: [father]$_A$

(3) a. [I] [father]_A [meet] [appointment] [I] [drive] [arrive] [find] [father] [be standing]_A
   b. *[I] [father]_A [meet] [appointment] [I] [drive] [arrive] [find] [father] [be standing]_I
   'I had an appointment to meet my father. I arrived at the place of appointment by car. I found him standing there.'

(3a), where the gender for argument [father] and the verb [be standing] agreed as male, was judged by all the participants to be natural. (3b), where the verb took the I handshape and had a different gender than the subject argument's, was judged by everyone as not natural (100%). All of the participants responded for (3b) that the sentence felt unnatural and was marked by*.

(4) a. [I] [mother]_I [meet] [appointment] [I] [drive] [arrive] [find] [mother] [be standing]_I
   b. [I] [mother]_I [meet] [appointment] [I] [drive] [arrive] [find] [mother] [be standing]_A
   'I had an appointment to meet my mother. I arrived at the place of appointment by car. I found his standing there.'

(4a), where the argument [mother] and the verb [be standing] coincided as female, all the participants judged as natural. However, in (4b) the gender of the verb was male, disagreeing with the gender of the subject, which only some of the participants judged as natural (43%). Since 43% of the participants judged it to be natural, it means that the verb is permitted to remain unmarked in gender when the argument is female. This was similar to the aforementioned study (Nam et al. 2019), where a marked-unmarked argument-verb relationship was permitted. It seems, however, that as the participants perceived that they were taking part in a questionnaire demanding a judgment over the usage of gendered handshapes, it led to (4b) seeming less natural than (4a), which was characterized by gender agreement.

---

3) Classifier verbs signifying the movement of the referent were notated with arrows: [Baby approach NAM]_{A→A}

5.3.2 Factors for selecting handshapes

To confirm whether the verb always contains the gender handshapes, we compared the verbs including the gender handshapes with the verbs where gender handshapes were not included.

(5) a.   [BYUN]$_A$ [mistake] [tree] [fall]$_A$
          'Byun fell from the tree by mistake.'
     b.   *[BYUN]$_A$ [tree] [jump]$_A$
          'Byun jumped off the tree.'
     c.   [BYUN]$_A$ [mistake] [tree] [fall]$_2$
          'Byun fell from the tree by mistake.'
     d.   [tree] [BYUN]$_A$ [BYUN climb the tree]$_2$ [NAM]$_I$ [NAM climb the tree]$_2$
          'Byun climbed the tree and Nam climbed the tree.'

The two sentences in (5a) and (5b) had different meanings: The subject [BYUN] either fell from the tree by mistake, or jumped off voluntarily. In both sentences the A handshape is embraced in the verb. For (5a), some members of the participants judged it as natural (57%). None of the participants deemed (5a) "unnatural". However, the reason for not responding that (5a) was natural, was that in the sentence, there is the expression [mistake] where the subject obviously did not mean to fall off, but that the environmental factor which caused the mistake was omitted. For instance: if you expressed [push] before the verb, the cause was certain ("someone pushed me so I fell from the tree"), and thus the verb [fall], which included the A handshape, would feel natural. (5b) was not accepted. That is because it was judged to be inappropriate to include the A handshape in the verb in case the fall from the tree was voluntary.

(5c), in contrast, where the verb contains the 2 handshape was determined to be natural by every participant. Likewise, in the verbs [fall], [jump] and [climb], the most natural handshape was the 2 handshape. Example (5), therefore, shows that the gender feature is not the only factor in choosing the handshape of verbs. We then looked at a couple of sentences to examine the factors determining the selection of the handshapes.

5.3.2.1 Referents displaying neutral gender

In [BYUN], [NAM], [mother], and [father], the vocabulary gender is certain; however, [baby] presents itself with no gender. We investigated what the preferred gender for [baby] was.

(6) a. [baby] [table] [baby fall from table]
'The baby fell down from the table.'
b. [NAM]$_I$ [with open arms to the baby] [baby] [baby approach NAM]$_{A \to I}$
'Nam opened her arms to the baby and the baby approached Nam.'
c. *[BYUN]$_A$ [with open arms to the baby] [baby] [baby approach BYUN]$_{I \to A}$
'Byun opened her arms to the baby and the baby approached Byun.'

Reflecting the response that for the [baby]'s gender the A handshape was preferred (71%) as well as the response that both the A handshape and the I handshape were acceptable (29%), it can be inferred that for the gender of [baby] the unmarked A handshape was preferred. (6a) was a sentence in which the subject argument, [baby], singularly formed the whole sentence. But in the case of (6b-c), besides the [baby], the arguments [NAM] and [BYUN] are also included. The judgment of the participants differed about the baby's gender. In (6b), where the [baby]'s gender was male, all of the participants judged it as natural (100%), whereas (6c), where the baby was female, received only (57%) votes for being "natural". According to the participants, this was because the baby was portrayed as merely a neutral human being, rather than as a specific male or female baby. Of course, in situations where gender identification was absolutely essential, inclusion of the gender handshapes was allowed. We searched (7) to discover the preference of handshapes for animals.

(7) a. [BYUN]$_A$ [be standing] [dog] [dog approach BYUN]$_{A \to A}$
b. [BYUN]$_A$ [be standing] [dog] [dog approach BYUN]$_{I \to A}$
'Byun was standing and the dog approached Byun.'

The subject of the sentences is male, [BYUN], and the response that the A handshapes were preferred for the dog was 57%. There was 43% preference for both A and I handshape. The latter response connoted the preference for male, and it could well be said that A handshape was favored for the handshape for the dog. In the case of the animals, same as with the baby, they are regarded as living beings rather than separate males and females.

5.3.2.2 Relationship among arguments
When the verb displays the relationship between two arguments, there is a call for clarity in showing the gender of the argument.

(8) a. [BYUN]$_A$ [In secret] [NAM]$_I$ [BYUN NAM follow]$_{A \rightarrow A}$
    b. [BYUN]$_A$ [In secret] [NAM]$_I$ [BYUN NAM follow]$_{I \rightarrow A}$
       'Byun follows NAM in secret.'

In (8), the verb [follow] signifies 'someone follows someone' and needs two arguments. In this sentence, the gender of the agent and the patient is certain, and the verb has a tendency to follow the gender of the argument. For (8a), which showed A handshapes in both arguments, most of the participants deemed it natural (71%). The A handshape is unmarked, and even as the gender of the verb is not distinguished, there is hardly any problem in grasping and communicating, and thus this finding is based on the judgment as natural. Everyone responded 'natural' for (8b) when it was expressed, according to the gender of the argument, with the I handshape and A handshape (100%). When elaborating the relationship between the two arguments, the usage of gender handshape can clearly articulate the arguments.

5.3.2.3 Impact of "frozen sign"
We were able to observe the influence of a frozen handshape in the determination of what felt natural to the respondents.

(9) a. *[BYUN]$_A$ [traffic accident] [hospital] [transfer]$_A$
    b. [BYUN]$_A$ [traffic accident] [hospital] [transfer]$_2$
       'Byun was in a traffic accident and was transferred to hospital.'

In (9), the subject [BYUN] is male, however, 43% of the participants responded that the A handshape, agreeing with the gender of the subject, was natural. Likewise, 100% responded that the 2 handshape was natural. The cause of the 2 handshape being judged as natural, was that, in KSL, the 2 handshape is used with [hospitalization]([hospital] + [lie down]), and this could be seen as being influenced by a frozen sign handshape.

5.3.2.4 Manner of movement
The verb is influenced by the content that the verb signifies. The manner of motion by referents influences the selection of handshapes.

(10) a. [BYUN]_A [kickboard] [mountain] [climb the mountain on the kickboard]
'Byun climbs the mountain on the kickboard.'
b. [rabbit] [jump] [go in circles]
'The rabbit jumped around in circles.'

For the verb in (10a) [ride the kickboard] the form most preferred was the F handshape, where the kickboard was seen as an entity (42%). Following that, the B handshape where the handle of the kickboard was held with one foot stamping was preferred, and after that, the 2 handshape expressing one foot stamping with two legs was preferred (both 29%). In (10b) with the verb [jump], the gender handshape was not preferred, and the participants preferred the 2 handshape, meaning the rabbit jumped (100%). The participants found noticeable difficulty with the form including the 1 handshape, with which an upright entity was expressed in the verb.

(11) a. ? [I] [father]_A [meet] [appointment] [I] [drive] [arrive] [find] [father] _A [be standing]₁
'I had an appointment to meet my father. I arrived at the place of appointment by car. I found him standing there.'
b. ? [I] [mother]_I [meet] [appointment] [I] [drive] [arrive] [find] [mother]_I [be standing]₁
'I had an appointment to meet my mother. I arrived at the place of appointment by car. I found her standing there.'
c. ? [BYUN]_A [NAM]_I [bench] [BYUN and NAM are sitting side by side]₁/₁
'Byun and Nam are sitting in a bench side by side.'
d. *[BYUN]_A [mistake] [tree] [fall]₁
'Byun fell off a tree by mistake.'
e. *[BYUN]_A [tree] [jump]₁
'Byun jumped from the tree.'
f. *[tree] [BYUN] _A [BYUN climbs the tree] [NAM] _I [NAM climbs the tree] ₁/₁
'Byun climbed the tree and Nam climbed the tree.'

For (11a-c), regardless of the gender of the arguments [mother] and [father], when the 1 handshape was included in the verbs [be standing] and [be sitting], 57% of participants responded that the 1 handshape was natural, while 43% declared not. There is no noticeable difference in the percentage of the response, but what is remarkable is that its three responding participants were all female and the same person. In contrast, in (11d-f) regardless of the argument's gender, the addition of the verbs [fall], [jump], [climb] with 1 handshape were seen as unnatural by every participant. In KSL, the 1 handshape does not occur often, but is used in frozen signs, such as in [come] and [meet]. For these frozen signs, the 1 handshape signifies the motion of the referents. Based on this phenomenon, when the use of the 1 handshape in (11d-f) was deemed unnatural, this was because the verbs [fall], [jump] and [climb] signify the manner of the referent's movement.

6 Discussion

In KSL, the gender handshape productively combines with not only kinship terms, name signs, and agreement verbs – but also with classifier verbs. However, there has never been a case where gender agreement was empirically researched with respect to classifier verbs and arguments. This chapter fills this research gap insofar as it observes the main characteristics of the gender agreement of classifier verbs. We will discuss below the major characteristics of the classifier verbs and argument agreement phenomena in KSL, associating them with agreement phenomena of sign language in general.

First of all, this is a gender agreement phenomenon occurring between classifier verbs and argument in KSL. In KSL, the gender markers are the A handshape and the I handshape, signifying respectively the female the male, as well as the human being. If the agreement is to be regarded as feature sharing between the controller and the target (Corbett 2006), the classifier verbs should show consistent agreement according to the gender of the argument. Not all the classifier verbs, however, possess gender agreement. Among the classifier verbs, the verbs indicating the location of the referent generally show agreement by gender feature, but this did not happen with the verbs of motion and movement of the referent. We take these characteristics as evidence that in sign language, not all the verb types – plain verbs, agreement verbs and spatial verbs (here, also classifier verbs) – participate in the principle of agreement. In KSL, the gender agreement of classifier verbs and arguments has led the features of gender handshapes to be confirmed as [+female] and [-female]. As a matter of course, the gender agreement of the agreement verb shows the same result. Gender agreement of classifier verbs and the arguments is forbidden when the argument is male and the classifier verbs are female, but it is almost allowed in cases where the argument is female and the classifier verbs are male. In other words, the A handshape can signify the female, the male, and the human being, but the I handshape signifies the female only. This means that the gender features in KSL are [+female] and [-female].

Secondly, there is the issue of there being several factors that decide the handshapes for the classifier verbs. There are three main factors that influence the choice of the handshape of classifier verb. Firstly, the gender handshape enables a very economical expression in that it clearly visually reveals the relationship between the arguments that the verb user wants to convey by expressing the gender of the argument. Next, the subtype of classifier verbs influences the handshape choice. In other words, the verbs, where the movement manner of the referent is indicated, impact the choice of handshapes. In expressing the movement manner of the referents, the phonemic constraints limit the gender handshape and the combination. These characteristics have been proposed in Auslan. The types of motion events effectively decide the classifier handshapes (Schembri et al. 2018: 4). Next, you can choose the handshape according to agent or experiencer of the event. The 2 handshape is a handshape meaning the two legs of the referent and connoting that the referent is the subject of the act. Thus, if the referent intentionally fell out of a tree, the person relating the event uses verbs including the 2 handshape, thereby referring to the two feet of the referent. When the referent unintentionally fell out of a tree, the verb containing the A handshape is used to refer to the referent him/herself. If one wants to add additional explanations to this, in KSL agreement verbs, the object argument uses the A handshape and the I handshape (Byun 2012). For instance, in [scold someone], [push someone], and [compliment someone], the object word can be applied with the non-dominant hand making the A handshape. Just as the front of the A handshape means 'face', the back means 'back', and the underside means 'buttocks', the dominant hand faces a specific location. Re-examining the classifier verb [fall] already dealt with in this chapter, the 2 handshape is used for the intentional fall, but for an event in which someone pushes you and you fall out of the tree, the falling person was represented with the A handshape. As seen here, the choice between the 2 handshape and the A handshape complies with the fact that *how* the agent or patient is involved with the event decides what the handshape expresses. Lastly, the classifier verbs are influenced by frozen signs. Seeing that the classifiers have been through lexicalization and became frozen signs, this is a very natural phenomenon.

Research on agreement in sign language has largely focused on the person features of agreement verbs. With this study we hope to broaden the discussion by bringing the elements of the classifier verbs and gender agreement into the cross-linguistic studies of agreement and gender markers in sign language.

7 Appendix

number	type	Sentence
1	101	location	[I] [father]_A [meet] [appointment] [I] [drive] [arrive] [find] [father] [be standing]_A
2	102	location	[I] [father]_A [meet] [appointment] [I] [drive] [arrive] [find] [father] [be standing]_A
3	103	location	[I] [father]_A [meet] [appointment] [I] [drive] [arrive] [find] [father] [be standing]_A
4	104	location	[I] [father]_A [meet] [appointment] [I] [drive] [arrive] [find] [father] [be standing]_A
5	105	location	[I] [mother] [meet] [appointment] [I] [drive] [arrive] [find] [be standing]
6	106	location	[I] [mother] [meet] [appointment] [I] [drive] [arrive] [find] [be standing]
7	107	location	[I] [mother] [meet] [appointment] [I] [drive] [arrive] [find] [be standing]
8	108	location	[I] [mother] [meet] [appointment] [I] [drive] [arrive] [find] [be standing]
9	201	location	[BYUN]_A [NAM]_I [bench] [BYUN and NAM are sitting side by side]_{A/I}
10	202	location	[BYUN]_A [NAM]_I [bench] [BYUN and NAM are sitting side by side]_{I/I}
11	203	location	[BYUN]_A [NAM]_I [bench] [BYUN and NAM are sitting side by side]_{BENT2/BENT2}
12	204	location	[BYUN]_A [NAM]_I [bench] [BYUN and NAM are sitting side by side]_{1/1}
13	301	movement	[BYUN]_A [mistake] [tree] [fall]_2
14	302	movement	[BYUN]_A [mistake] [tree] [fall]_A
15	303	movement	[BYUN]_A [mistake] [tree] [fall]_1
16	304	movement	[BYUN]_A [mistake] [tree] [fall]_I
17	305	movement	[BYUN]_A [tree] [jump]_A
18	306	movement	[BYUN]_A [tree] [jump]_2
19	307	movement	[BYUN]_A [tree] [jump]_I
20	308	movement	[BYUN]_A [tree] [jump]_1
21	309	movement	[tree] [BYUN]_A [BYUN climb the tree] [NAM]_I [NAM climb the tree]_{2/2}
22	310	movement	[tree] [BYUN]_A [BYUN climb the tree] [NAM]_I [NAM climb the tree]_{I/I}
23	311	movement	[tree] [BYUN]_A [BYUN climb the tree] [NAM]_I [NAM climb the tree]_{A/A}
24	312	movement	[tree] [BYUN]_A [BYUN climb the tree] [NAM]_I [NAM climb the tree]_{1/1}
25	401	movement	[NAM]_I [with open arms to the baby] [baby] [baby approach NAM]_{I/I}
26	402	movement	[NAM]_I [with open arms to the baby] [baby] [baby approach NAM]_{I/A}
27	403	movement	[NAM]_I [with open arms to the baby] [baby] [baby approach NAM]_{A/A}

(continued)

number		type	Sentence
28	404	movement	[NAM]₁ [with open arms to the baby] [baby] [baby approach NAM]_{A/I}
29	405	movement	[BYUN]_A [with open arms to the baby] [baby] [baby approach BYUN]_{A/I}
30	406	movement	[BYUN]_A [with open arms to the baby] [baby] [baby approach BYUN]_{A/A}
31	407	movement	[BYUN]_A [with open arms to the baby] [baby] [baby approach BYUN]_{I/I}
32	408	movement	[BYUN]_A [with open arms to the baby] [baby] [baby approach BYUN]_{I/A}
33	501	movement	[BYUN]_A [in secret] [NAM]₁ [BYUN NAM follow]_{A/A}
34	502	movement	[BYUN]_A [in secret] [NAM]₁ [BYUN NAM follow]_{I/A}
35	503	movement	[BYUN]_A [in secret] [NAM]₁ [BYUN NAM follow]_{A/I}
36	504	movement	[BYUN]_A [in secret] [NAM]₁ [BYUN NAM follow]_{I/I}
37	601	movement	[BYUN]_A [NAM]₁ [motorcycle] [motorcycle]_{A/I}
38	602	movement	[BYUN]_A [NAM]₁ [motorcycle] [ride side by side]_{I/I}
39	603	movement	[BYUN]_A [NAM]₁ [motorcycle] [ride side by side]_{BENT2/BENT2}
40	701	movement	[get on a bus]
41	702	movement	[police] [grandmother]₁ [bus] [get on a bus]₁
42	703	movement	[BYUN]_A [traffic accident] [hospital] [transfer]_A
43	704	movement	[BYUN]_A [traffic accident] [hospital] [transfer]₁
44	705	movement	[BYUN]_A [traffic accident] [hospital] [transfer]₁
45	706	movement	[BYUN]_A [traffic accident] [hospital] [transfer]₂
46	901	movement	[baby] [table] [baby fall from table]_A
47	902	movement	[baby] [table] [baby fall from table]₁
48	903	movement	[BYUN]_A [be standing] [dog] [dog approach BYUN]_{A/A}
49	904	movement	[BYUN]_A [be standing] [dog] [dog approach BYUN]_{A/I}
50	801	manner	[BYUN]_A [kickboard] [mountain] [climb the mountain on the kickboard]_B
51	802	manner	[BYUN]_A [kickboard] [mountain] [climb the mountain on the kickboard]_A
52	803	manner	[BYUN]_A [kickboard] [mountain] [climb the mountain on the kickboard]_F
53	804	manner	[BYUN]_A [kickboard] [mountain] [climb the mountain on the kickboard]₂
54	905	manner	[rabbit] [jump] [go round]_A
55	906	manner	[rabbit] [jump] [go round]₁
56	907	manner	[rabbit] [jump] [go round]₂

References

Byun, Kang-suk. 2012. *The grammatical functions of the A-handshape and the I-handshape in Korean Sign Language: Regarding gender realization and verb classification.* Chungnam National University MA thesis.
Byun, Kang-suk, Inge Zwitserlood, and Connie de Vos. 2015. Classifiers and gender in sign language: The case of Korean Sign Language. Paper presented at the conference on "Gender and classifiers: areal and genealogical perspectives" at the Max Planck Institute for Psycholinguistics, Nijmegen, 26–27 January.
Corbett, Greville. 2006. *Agreement.* Cambridge, UK: Cambridge University Press.
Emmorey, Karen. 2001. *Language, cognition, and the brain: Insights from sign language research.* New York: Psychology Press. https://doi.org/10.4324/9781410603982
Fischer, Susan and Qunhu Gong. 2010. Variation in East Asian sign language structures. Brentari, Diane (ed.), *Sign languages.* Cambridge: Cambridge University Press.
Fischer, Susan and Yutaka, Osugi. 2000. Thumbs up vs. giving the finger: Indexical classifiers in NS and ASL. Paper presented at the International Conference on Theoretical Issues in Sign Language Research, Amsterdam, July 23–27.
Go, Young-geun and Gu, Bongwan. 2009. *Korean grammar theory.* Seoul: Jimpoon.
Hong, Sung Eun. 2006. Agreement verbs in Korean Sign Language. Paper presented at the International Conference on Theoretical Issues in Sign Language Research, Florianopolis, Brazil, December 6–9.
Hong, Sung Eun. 2009. An empirical investigation of agreement verbs in Korean Sign Language. *Sign Language and Linguistics* 12(2). 228–234.
Johnston, Trevor and Adam Schembri. 2007. *Australian Sign Language: An introduction to sign language linguistics.* Cambridge, UK: Cambridge University Press.
Kim, Chil-gwan. 1998. *The study of the etymology of Korean Sign Language.* Incheon, South Korea: Incheon Seongdong School for the Deaf.
Lakoff, George and Mark Johnson. 1980. *Metaphors we live by.* Chicago: University of Chicago Press.
Lee, Hanna. 2006. *A study pertaining to name signs for deaf people.* Korea Nazarene University MA thesis.
Liddell, Scott K. 2003. *Grammar, gesture, and meaning in American Sign Language.* Cambridge, UK: Cambridge University Press.
Liddell, Scott K. and Robert E. Johnson. 1989. American Sign Language: The phonological base. *Sign Language Studies* 64(1). 195–277. https://doi.org/10.1353/sls.1989.0027
McBurney, Susan Lloyd. 2002. Pronominal reference in signed and spoken language: Are grammatical categories modality-dependent? In Richard Meier, Kearsy Cormier and David Quinto-Pozos (eds.), *Modality and structure in signed and spoken languages,* 329–369. Cambridge: Cambridge University Press.
Nam, Ki Hyun, Cho, Jun-Mo, and Kim, Yeon Woo. 2019. Agreement phenomena in Korean Sign Language. *Korean Semantics* 64. 75–107.
Padden, Carol. 1988. *Interaction of morphology and syntax in American Sign Language.* New York: Garland.
Smith, Wayne H. 1990. Evidence for auxiliaries in Taiwan Sign Language. In Susan D. Fischer and Patricia Siple (eds.), *Theoretical Issues in Sign Language Research* (1), 211–228. Chicago: University of Chicago Press.

Schembri, Adam, Kearsy, Cormier and Jordan Fenlon. 2018. Indicating verbs as typologically unique constructions: Reconsidering verb 'agreement' in sign languages. *Glossa: A journal of general linguistics* 3(1). 89. DOI: http://doi.org/10.5334/gjgl.468

Supalla, Ted. 1982. *Structure and acquisition of verbs of motion and location in American Sign Language*. San Diego: University of California dissertation.

Supalla, Ted. 1986. The classifier system in American Sign Language. In Craig, Colette. (ed.), *Noun classes and categorization: Typological studies in language*, 181–214. Amsterdam: John Benjamins.

Yonekawa, Akihiko. 2011. *The New Japanese Sign Language Dictionary*. Edited in Kyoto by the Japanese Sign Research Centre. Tokyo: Japanese Deaf Federation.

Zwitserlood, Inge. 2012. Classifiers. In Roland Pfau, Markus Steinbach, and Bencie Woll (eds.), *Sign Language: An International Handbook*, 158–186. Berlin: Mouton de Gruyter.

Jia He and Gladys Tang
Causative alternation in Tianjin Sign Language

Abstract: This paper examines the phenomenon of causative alternation in Tianjin Sign Language (TJSL), a variety sign language used by deaf people in Tianjin, China, and addresses the long-standing debate about the relationship between classifier handshape and the verb argument structure of classifier predicates using TJSL data. Initially, we adopt the classifier typology of Benedicto and Brentari (2004) and identify three types of causative alternation in TJSL. First, lexical causatives such as BREAK, which alternate between causative and unaccusative predicates without any change of the verb's morphological form and in the absence of classifier morphemes. Second, causative-unaccusative alternation in classifier predicates requiring classifier handshape change, namely a handling classifier for transitive predicates and a whole entity classifier for unaccusative predicates. Third, causative-unaccusative alternation in classifier predicates involving no change of classifier handshape and verb root. We argue that neither is the handling classifier a causative marker nor is the whole entity classifier an unaccusative marker in TJSL. Additionally, Benedicto and Brentari's (2004) proposal that classifier type determines the argument structure of predicates fails to apply to TJSL straightforwardly. The paper also attempts to align the current observations in TJSL with Haspelmath's (1993) typology of causative alternation in the world's languages, namely, TJSL displays properties of subtypes of non-directed alternation – labile and equipollent alternation. Such a typological alignment enables us to appreciate the nature of the verb root and the classifier morpheme of classifier predicates in TJSL.

Keywords: classifier predicates, causative alternation, argument structure

1 Introduction

There has been pervasive research on causative alternation in spoken languages, in particular the correlation between causativity and unaccusativity, and how

Acknowledgements: This research was supported by Hong Kong GRF Grant #450513 to Gladys Tang. We are also grateful to the audiences at FEAST 2017 for their comments. We wish to thank the deaf signers in Tianjin, China who participated in this research.

https://doi.org/10.1515/9781501510243-005

this correlation reveals the interaction of morphology, syntax and argument structure alternation. Causative alternation is often assumed to be lexical, which characterizes verb pairs that stand in both an intransitive use and a transitive use. The intransitive use typically denotes a change of state undergone by an entity, whereas the transitive use typically denotes that such a change of state is caused by some different entity (Levin and Rappaport Hovav 1995, Schäfer 2009). Therefore, verbs that undergo causative alternation generally incorporate the meaning of a change of state. Examples (1) and (2) illustrate causative-inchoative alternation with typical pairs of alternating verbs in English.

(1) a. John broke the vase.
 b. The vase broke.

(2) a. Mary opened the door.
 b. The door opened.

As shown in examples (1a) and (2a), the causative-transitive verbs *break* and *open* require an agent to act on a theme to bring about a change of state, whereas examples (1b) and (2b) are the intransitive-inchoative counterparts denoting a change of state of the theme argument. An underlying assumption of the alternation is that the object of the transitive verb and the subject of its intransitive-inchoative counterpart must bear the same thematic role (i.e. *theme*), and the causative-transitive verb involves an external argument that bears the thematic role of *agent* or *causer*.

Haspelmath (1993) examines such a relationship from a typological perspective and puts forward a causative, inchoative and non-directed alternation distinction based on 21 languages and the morphological characteristics of 31 verb pairs identified. In alternation of the causative type, the inchoative form is the basic and the causative form is derived. In alternation of the inchoative type, the causative form is the basic and the inchoative form is derived. In non-directed alternation type, neither the causative nor the inchoative verb is derived from the other. It can be further divided into three subtypes – equipollent, labile and suppletive, and each subtype comes with different morphological characteristics (see Section 1.1 below).

Research on causative alternation in signed languages so far has seldom attempted to compare spoken languages and signed languages from the perspective of Haspelmath's typology. Such a comparison is timely. It has been argued that signed languages are agglutinating in nature where different morphemes for lexical and grammatical functions combine to form words/signs (Dyer 1976;

Schwager 2004; Schuit 2007; Schuit, Baker and Pfau 2011). Additionally, classifier predicates from which most discussions on causative alternation originate are said to be morphologically complex. Seen in this light, whether there is morphological marking for causative alternation in signed languages constitutes a legitimate research question. For instance, Kegl (1985, 1990) argues that in ASL the handling classifier is a causative marker and the SASS an inchoative marker. Rather than taking up Kegl's causative/inchoative morphological marking proposal, Benedicto and Brentari (2004: 744) treat the classifier morphemes in ASL as agreement markers. They also argue that "changes in argument structure alternation are triggered by specific morphological items (the classifier morphemes) projecting as heads in the syntax". The morphosyntactic properties triggering the projections will accommodate either the internal argument only, the external argument only, or both the external and internal arguments hence potentially reflecting argument structure alternation. Their proposal has led to series of debates about whether classifier type in signed languages determines the argument structure of predicates.

This paper contributes to the continuing debate with evidence from TJSL, an underreported signed language in China. We will focus on verifying whether the descriptions of causative alternation in signed languages put forth by Benedicto and Brentari (2004) also exist in TJSL. Our analysis involves the commonly discussed handling classifiers and whole entity classifiers. We also examine bodypart classifiers, arguing for their participation in causative alternation. We assume that if evidence suggests that a certain classifier type can enter both a causative and an inchoative predicate, it will at least suggest that the pattern of causative alternation in TJSL differs from that reported in ASL. Last, analysing TJSL data from the perspective of Haspelmath's (1993) typology of causative alternation has the advantage of enriching our understanding of the relationship between the movement-as-verb-root and classifier morpheme in causative alternation in signed languages in a better light. Our findings show that TJSL does not have causative morphology for alternation. While the commonly cited causative-inchoative alternation with a corresponding change of classifier morpheme from the handling classifier to the whole entity/SASS also obtains in TJSL, we also found evidence for causative alternation that does not involve classifier change in our data. The findings thus suggest that crosslinguistic variation may be at work, especially in the correlation between classifier type and (in)transitivity of the predicates in signed languages (Benedicto and Brentari 2004). Due to space limitations, we will leave aside discussions concerning the syntactic representations of the different types of causative alternation to a separate report (He and Tang, In preparation).

The paper is organized as follows. First, we introduce Haspelmath's (1993) typology of causative alternation in spoken languages, followed by a summary of previous studies on causative alternation in signed languages and the debates relevant to the current study. After this introduction on the literature, we will present our study, including the backgrounds of the Deaf signers, data collection procedures, transcription methods and criteria for identifying causative alternation. The section on data discussion is organized according to classifier types to verify if a relationship exists between classifier types and argument structure alternation. The last part of the paper discusses the nature of verb root and how it accounts for the lack of a direct association between classifier morpheme change and causative alternation. Given the findings, we call for a crosslinguistic re-examination of Benedicto and Brentari's (2004) prediction on the correlation between classifier morpheme and argument structure.

1.1 Causative alternation in spoken languages

As mentioned in the introduction, Haspelmath (1993) makes a distinction among causative, inchoative and non-directed alternation. However, he also points out that crosslinguistically languages do show substantial variation in the direction of alternation based on morphological marking. Within the causative and inchoative alternation types, either the causative-transitive alternate is the basic and the causative verb is derived (causative type); or the causative verb is basic and the inchoative verb is derived (inchoative type). In example (3), one finds morphological marking on the causative-transitive variant only.

Causative: Morphological marking on the causative-transitive variant

(3) Georgian
        a. duy-s   'cook (intr)'
        b. *a*-duy-*ebs* 'cook (tr)'
        (Haspelmath 1993: 91)

The causative variant (3b) is marked by affix *a-+-eb*, whereas the inchoative variant (3a) is left unmarked. However, this causativization view is challenged by the existence of a reversed pattern in some languages in which the inchoative variant is overtly marked by specific morphology while the causative variant is unmarked.

Inchoative: Morphological marking on the inchoative-intransitive variant

(4) Russian
    a. katat'-*sja*   'roll (intr)'
    b. katat'   'roll (tr)'
               Haspelmath (1993: 91)

(5) Polish
    a. złamać-*się*   'break (intr)'
    b. złamać   'raise (tr)'
               (Piñon 2001: 347)

In examples (4) and (5), the morphological marking is on the inchoative variant. The inchoative verbs are marked by an affix (i.e. *-sja* in Russian and *-się* in Polish), whereas the causative verbs are unmarked.

In addition to morphological marking, some languages exhibit non-directed alternation, namely, neither the causative verb nor the inchoative verb contains morphological marking to indicate the direction of alternation. Such alternations can be further subdivided into *equipollent*, *labile* and *suppletive* alternations.

Non-directed causative alternation

(6) Japanese (equipollent)
    a. atum-*aru*   'gather (intr)'
    b. atum-*eru*   'gather (tr)'
               (Haspelmath 1993: 91–92)

(7) English (labile)
    a. break   (intr)
    b. break   (tr)
               (Haspelmath 1993: 91–92)

(8) English (suppletive)
    a. die   'die' (intr)
    b. kill   'cause to die' (tr)

(9) Russian (suppletive)
    a. goret'   'burn (intr)'
    b. žeč   'burn (tr)'
    (Haspelmath 1993: 91–92)

(10) German (suppletive)
    a. sterben   'die' (intr)
    b. töten   'kill' (tr)
    Schäfer (2009: 36)

According to Haspelmath (1993: 91), "in non-directed alternations, neither the inchoative nor the causative verb is derived from the other. In equipollent alternations, both are derived from the same stem which expresses the basic situation, by means of different affixes, different auxiliary verbs, or different stem modifications". In the Japanese example in (6), the causative/inchaotive verbs are derived from the same verb stem -*atum*. An independent affix -*aru* is attached to the stem to derive the causative verb, while -*eru* to derive the inchoative verb.

Example (7) illustrates *labile* alternation in English in which the same verb form *break* is used as either a causative verb or an inchoative verb. Examples (8), (9) and (10) exemplify *suppletive* alternation, in which different verbs are adopted for the causative and the inchoative verbs.

Crosslinguistically, languages also vary in terms of whether they display different combinations of types of causative alternation. Examples (7) and (8) above show that there are languages such as English which has more than one subtype of non-directed alternation – labile and suppletive alternation. There are also languages like German which involve two or three major types of alternation types, including causative, inchoative and non-directed alternation.

German
(11)   a. Hans verändert die Temperatur.
        Hans changes the temperature
    b. Die Temperatur veränderte *sich*
        The temperature changed REFL

(12)   a. Hans schmilzt die Schokolade
        Hans melts the chocolate
    b. Die Schokolade schmilzt
        The chocolate melts

Schäfer (2009: 29)

Examples (11a) and (11b) manifest inchoative alternation in which a reflexive pronoun 'sich' in (11b) occurs to mark the inchoative variant. This pronoun is absent in the causative-transitive predicate, as shown in (11a). Non-directed labile alternation is shown in examples (12a) and (12b), where the causative (12a) and inchoative (12b) share the same verb and a reflexive pronoun is not required with the inchoative (12b).

From the review above, we observe that spoken languages do vary in the morphological realization of causative alternation as well as types of causative alternation that may occur in a language. In the following section, we will review the literature on causative alternation in signed languages.

1.2 Causative alternation in signed languages

Not many studies have focused on causative alternation in signed languages. (Kegl 1985, 1990 on ASL; Lau 2002 on HKSL). Kegl (1985, 1990) claims that causative alternation occurs in the classifier predicates in ASL, analogous to that observed in spoken languages.

ASL

Transitive/causative classifier predicate

(13) a. topic   head nod
 STICK$_{10}$, M-A-R-I-S-A$_0$ SBP$_0$#$_{10}$CL: HAND [S/S]+BREAK
 'Marisa broke the stick.'

(Kegl 1990: 157)

Intransitive/inchoative classifier predicate

(13) b. topic   avert
 STICK$_{10}$ SBP$_{0\#10}$ CL:G/G +BREAK [inchoative]
 stick-topic RP-negated-Ito-break

(Kegl 1990: 158)

According to Kegl, the handling classifier of a two-handed[1] CL:*HAND[S/S]* sign as shown in (13a) serves as a causative marker in a transitive predicate. The role

---

[1] Most of the previous research of classifier predicates focus on one-handed classifier predicates only. Yet two-handed classifier predicates are also found to represent different types of events,

prominence clitic (SBP$_0$#$_{10}$²) in this example is used to encode an agent (i.e. Marisa) from whose perspective the action of the verb BREAK is construed. *CL: HAND [S/S]+BREAK* is articulated at the locus of the sign STICK$_{10}$ previously established in space. In (13b), the two-handed SASS sign represented by *CL:G/G* (i.e. long thin object) refers to STICK$_{10}$ only. Additionally, the nonmanuals of the signer, a head twist and aversion of the eyes, signal non-involvement of an agent. Therefore, the predicate is unaccusative-intransitive. Kegl (1985) further claims that the handling classifier is associated with both the external and the internal argument of a causative-transitive predicate while the SASS is only associated with the internal argument in an unaccusative inchoative. According to her, other verbs that show similar properties of causative alternation are SPILL, OPEN, SLIDE, MOVE, and CLOSE.

Similarly, Lau (2002) observes causative alternation in classifier predicates of HKSL (see examples 14a and 14b). Just as in ASL, the causative-transitive predicates involve a handling classifier and unaccusatie-intransitive predicates an SASS (a subtype of whole entity classifier). However, she rejects Kegl's (1985) proposal that the handling classifier is a causative marker. Instead, she argues that the classifiers serve a reference tracking function since they are co-referential with either the agent or theme NP hence behaving like a proform. She further claims that the causative-transitive variant requires a volitional agent to be an external argument.

(14) a. MALE-CHILD BALL CL:BOUNCE_A 3D_ROUND_OBJECT [HANDLE]
'A boy bounced a ball.'
b. BALL CL:A_3D_ROUND-OBJECT_BOUNCE [SASS]
'A ball bounced.'

(Lau 2002: 60–61)

The handling classifier in (14a) refers to two arguments at the same time – the external argument MALE-CHILD and the internal argument BALL. In contrast, the unaccusative variant in (14b) involves an SASS that outlines the size and shape of the internal argument BALL. In sum, while the grammatical status of the classifier morpheme remains arguable, both ASL and HKSL offer evidence reflecting a typical pattern of causative alternation in the classifier predicates.

---

among which sometimes two-handed classifier as a whole refers to one event participant, and sometimes each of the two hands represents a separate event participant of the predicate.

2 The subscript 10 indicates that the sign BREAK is located at position$_{10}$ (agreeing with STICK$_{10}$).

Benedicto and Brentari[3] (2004) explicitly argue for a correlation between the classifier morpheme and the valency of the predicate in ASL, namely, morphosyntactic properties of classifier morphemes determine the valency of the predicate.

(15) a. 'MOVE_FROM_VERTICAL_TO_HORIZONTAL_POSITION'
          [ø] BOOK C+MOVE
          pron.3sg book obj_grab$_{hdlg}$ +move_vert. > hor.
          's/he took the (standing) book and load it down on its side'
      b. 'BOOK B+MOVE.'
          book 2D_flat_obj$_{w/e}$ + move_vert. > hor.
          'The (standing) book fell down on its side'
                              (Benedicto and Brentari 2004: 752)

In (15a) and (15b), while the meaning of the predicate remains the same, i.e. 'move from vertical to horizontal position', example (15a) exemplifies a transitive classifier predicate which involves a handling classifier (C-handshape) referring to both an external argument *s/he* and an internal argument BOOK (meaning 'someone flips the book). Example (15b) exemplifies an unaccusative classifier predicate which involves an SASS (B-handshape) referring only to the internal argument BOOK (i.e. the book flips). According to Benedicto and Brentari (2004), since example (15a) and (15b) share one movement, they present themselves as transitive-unaccusative alternation in ASL. Instead of treating the handling classifier as a causative marker, these researchers propose that it is an agreement marker which bears the relevant morphosyntactic features for a syntactic projection to accommodate both the external and internal argument of a causative predicate. Alternatively, properties of a whole entity classifier will lead to a syntactic projection to accommodate only the internal argument. Benedicto et al. (2007: 1208) further confirm the correlation in Argentina Sign Language (LSA) and Catalan Sign Language (LSC). According to them, 'LSA and LSC should display transitive-unaccusative alternation of the same sort we find in languages such as English (e.g., 'they opened the door' versus 'the door opened'). This prediction is borne out in examples (16a) and (16b):

---

[3] Although Benedicto and Brentari (2004) do not focus on causative alternation per se, since causative alternation belongs to one typical type of transitivity alternation, we believe their proposal on the correlation between classifier type and argument structure also covers causative alternation.

(16) a. LAURA LIBRO...C+PONER_DE_COSTADO [LSA]
Laura book book_hndl$_{hndl}$+turn_on_its_side
'Laura put the book on its side.'
b. LIBRO....B+CAER_DE_COSTADO
book book$_{w/e}$+turn_on_its_side
'The book fell down on its side.'

(Benedicto et al. 2007: 1208)

To conclude this section, we have summarized research on causative alternation in spoken languages, where the focus is primarily on the change (or no change) of the morphological structure of the verb form in the causative and unaccusative alternates. On the other hand, research in signed languages focuses on the change of classifier morphemes in the alternates, the latter of which assumes that classifier morphemes are affixes merged to a verb root expressed by movement (i.e. movement-as-root). The claim that it is the classifier morpheme that determines the argument structure of predicates as put forward in Benedicto and Brentari (2004) has subsequently attracted much debate. While not all discussions center upon causative alternation, but explore if other classifier types (e.g. bodypart classifiers and instrumental classifiers) exert similar morphosyntactic constraints on argument structure or (in)transitivity and if such a constraint holds crosslinguistically. In the ensuing section, we will provide a brief summary of other researchers' views on this claim, and by way of which we identify insights to guide our current analysis. We will focus on the correlation between classifier type and argument structure/(in)transitivity.

1.2.1 Interim discussion

Although Zwitserlood (2003, 2008) does not examine causative-unaccusative alternation in the Sign Language of the Netherlands (NGT), she also highlights the relatively more systematic occurrence of the handling classifier in transitive predicates and the whole entity classifier in intransitive predicates. Contrary to Benedicto and Brentari (2004), Zwitserlood (2003) proposes that 'the choice between an entity classifier and a handling classifier is determined by the argument structure of the verb' (Zwitserlood 2003: 141). She also highlights that sometimes it is difficult to differentiate between a handling classifier and a whole entity classifier. She cites the C-handshape in NGT as an example, which is either a handling classifier in transitive predicates (i.e. 'someone is holding a cup') or in other contexts an entity classifier (i.e. a 'cup exists here'). According to Zwitserlood (2003: 128), it is the movement root that gives clues to its morphological status.

Enlightened by Benedicto and Brentari's (2004) proposal, de Lint (2010, 2018) developed two experimental studies to further verify the correlation between classifier type and argument structure in ASL and NGT. For both experiments, she observes consistent occurrences of the handling classifier in transitive predicates and a whole entity classifier in intransitive predicates, thus justifying the transitive-intransitive alternation. However, the informants' performance on unergative-unaccusative and transitive-transitive alternation shows various degrees of variation. Interestingly, she also predicts that whole entity instrumental classifiers can appear in transitive predicates involving SAW-type manner verbs where the agent is semantically/implicitly realized. Clearly, these findings challenge Benedicto and Brentari's (2004) claim, especially classifier predicates involving a whole entity instrumental classifier must be intransitive because it involves a non-agentive internal argument only.

Kimmelman et al. (2019) examines whether Benedicto and Brentari's (2004) proposal can be extended to Russian Sign Language (RSL). They argue that whole entity classifiers also occur in contexts other than unaccusative-intransitive predicates. Also, whole entity-semantic classifier for vehicles, such as planes, cars and buses, can occur in clauses where the subjects are not vehicles but agents such as driver, pilot and passenger. Instead of adopting a lexicalization approach, they propose that the whole entity classifier is an agreement marker only and does not determine argument structure. They also examine the transitivity properties of bodypart classifiers. They observe that bodypart classifiers behave similarly to whole entity classifiers in terms of its occurrence in transitive predicates. Their analysis assumes that the whole entity and bodypart classifiers (excluding the moving legs classifiers) are agreement markers, hence they are merged at the specifier of the relevant agreement nodes. Moreover, they postulate that handling classifiers and moving-legs classifiers (i.e. 2B_handshape) are arguments hence bearing eventive properties, as such, they occupy the specifier position of the verbal projections, not agreement nodes. Clearly, this proposal assumes that classifiers serve different linguistic functions and occupy different positions in the syntactic structure, contrary to the previous analysis that classifiers belong to one morphology subgroup. Based on the variable results, these researchers conclude that classifiers in RSL do not straightforwardly determine the argument structure of classifier predicates.

In the spoken language literature, the criterion for identifying causative alternation rests upon the existence of certain verb pairs from which either the causative-transitive or the inchoative-intransitive variants are derived, plus all other mechanisms reflecting change of valency and argument structure. In the current analysis, we will adopt the same set of criteria as observed in spoken languages and resolve to analyzing the occurrence of classifier morphemes in classifier predicates of TJSL. Assuming the movement as root hypothesis, we pay attention to the properties of movement in identifying and analyzing the alternating verbs.

2 Causative alternation in TJSL: The current study

2.1 Some background information

Before providing the backgrounds, it is necessary to clarify why we adopt TJSL in the analysis. This language is used by deaf people in Tianjin, a northern city next to Beijing, China's capital city. According to our research experience, Tianjin Sign Language (TJSL), Beijing Sign Language (BJSL) and Hong Kong Sign Language (HKSL) are not necessarily mutually intelligible. While lexical variation abounds, it is currently unclear to what extent their syntax overlaps, as few studies have been conducted to verify the dialectal status of these signing varieties. Additionally, since none of these varieties has been claimed to be an official sign language in China, we decide to adhere to the name Tianjin Sign Language (TJSL) to refer to the signing variety used by deaf people in that region.

According to an informal source,[4] there are about 140,000 deaf people in Tianjin. The sign language variety used by Deaf people in Tianjin can be dated back to almost 150 years ago, although formal historical documentation about TJSL is lacking. Similar to BJSL, TJSL has not been considered as a natural language officially in the past and has never enjoyed a social status equal to Putonghua, the spoken language in the deaf community. This is partly due to a lack of linguistic research on the signing varieties in mainland China previously. He (2011) marks the first attempt to investigate the grammar of TJSL, focusing on some of the basic morphosyntactic properties of classifier predicates that involve an instrument argument.

2.2 Methodology

The current study aims to address the following research questions:
a) Does causative alternation exist in TJSL? If yes, does it pattern like HKSL and ASL? In other words, does it show a change of classifier morpheme between the handling classifier in a causative-transitive predicate and the whole entity classifier in an inchoative predicate?

---

[4] The total number of the deaf population in Tianjin was not officially announced. This figure and the historical information of TJSL is obtained through personal communication with a deaf person who is interested in sign language research and deaf culture. This figure might not be very accurate.

b) Are there other patterns of causative alternation in TJSL?
c) How to characterize these patterns of causative alternation in TJSL within the typological framework set up by Haspelmath (1993)?

Crucially, we will attempt to verify whether the theoretical argument put forward by Benedicto and Brentari (2004) that classifier morpheme determines the argument structure of a classifier predicate also applies to TJSL. If evidence suggests that the handling classifier only occurs in causative-transitive predicates and the whole entity classifier only occurs in unaccusative-intransitive predicates, Benedicto and Brentari's prediction is borne out in TJSL. If there is evidence pointing to the otherwise, their proposal would need to be modified to address crosslinguistic variation, in the sense that different signed languages may adopt different mechanisms for causative-unaccusative alternation. Our data suggest this second possibility.

The TJSL data came from a larger project in which we examined patterns of causative alternation and resultative constructions in HKSL, BJSL and TJSL. In this paper, we will focus on causative alternation in TJSL only. Two deaf signers in TJSL were informants. One was an adult native deaf signer who grew up in a deaf family since birth. The other one was born in a hearing family but acquired TJSL when he entered a deaf school in Tianjin at the age of 7. These two signers were invited to respond to 72 vignettes designed to induce production of causatives, inchoatives and resultatives. They were also invited to attend interviews with the researchers to confirm data or their intuitions about grammaticality, based on their productions on the vignettes. Both the elicited production and interview data were transcribed using ELAN, and we extracted tokens of causative alternation for our analysis. We focus on the morphological make-up of the verb root and change of classifier types in the predicates. Note that some of the contrastive data presented below were elicited during the interview sessions with the deaf signers.

The design of the 72 vignettes was based on the following considerations: (1) classifier types: handling classifiers, whole entity classifiers, bodypart classifiers, (2) different types of dynamic predicates involving a change of state and a change of location, (3) animacy of event participants, and (4) the predicted argument structure and the semantic roles involved, namely the external argument (agent/inanimate causer), theme (animate being/inanimate being) and instrument (see Table 1).

In identifying classifier types, some researchers generally divide classifiers into two types: entity classifier and handling classifier (Zwitserlood 2003); other researchers provide a more detailed classification based on the semantic properties that the classifier handshape entails (Supalla 1982). The typology of classifier handshapes adopted in this study was adapted from Benedicto and Brentari

Table 1: Experiment design for data elicitation.

Argument Structure	Subject	Object	Classifier Types
1-place predicate	animate	--	CL_{WE_SASS} & CL_{WE_SEM}
	inanimate	--	CL_{WE_SASS} & CL_{WE_SEM}
	inanimate	--	CL_{BP}
2-place predicate (agent/causer+theme)	agent/causer	inanimate theme	action verb
			CL_{HL}
			CL_{WE_SASS} & CL_{WE_SEM}
			CL_{BP}
		animate theme	action verb
			CL_{HL}
			CL_{WE_SASS} & CL_{WE_SEM}
	inanimate causer	inanimate theme	CL_{HL}
			CL_{WE_SASS} & CL_{WE_SEM}
			Natural force
		animate theme	CL_{HL}
			CL_{WE_SASS} & CL_{WE_SEM}
			Natural force
3-place predicate (agent+instrument+theme)	agent	inanimate theme	CL_{HL}
			CL_{WE_SASS} & CL_{WE_SEM}
			CL_{BP}

(2004) which was based on the semantically driven inventory proposed in Engberg-Pederson (1993).

Classifier handshape morphemes

a) Whole entity classifier ($CL_{w/e}$) makes use of the shape of the hand to refer to a whole entity.
   Subtypes of whole entity classifier:
   i. SASS (CL_{WE_SASS}) refers to whole objects defined mainly by their shape (e.g. a 'closed 4 handshape' refers to objects such as a knives that are flat in surface). B&B (2004) use the term *descriptive classifier* for SASS
   ii. Semantic classifier (CL_{WE_SEM}) refers to abstract classes of objects such as human beings, animals, vehicles ... .etc (e.g. an 'upright 6 handshape' refers to human beings in TJSL).
b) Handling classifier (CL_{HL}) refers to the way that objects or instruments are held or manipulated.

c) Extension-and-surface classifier (CL_{EXT}) refers to the physical properties of the objects but not the whole objects themselves
d) Bodypart classifier (CL_{BP}) refers to a part of the body such as head, leg, ear, etc . . . (e.g. an 'S-handshape' refers to the head of human beings)

Benedicto and Brentari's (2004) proposal on the correlation between classifier type and valency of the predicates entails that the above classification on classifier morphemes should be in complementary distribution, because any overlap of one particular classifier handshape with more than one classifier type may cause confusion with the argument structure it is associated with. Yet, puzzles remain concerning whether the inventory of classifier handshapes can systematically reflect distinctive patterns of valency of the corresponding classifier predicate. In this study, we will show that there is no direct one-to-one correspondence between the valency of the predicate and the classifier type, as readers will see some classifier types in TJSL can occur in predicates with different valency and predicates of a particular valency can accommodate more than one classifier type.

In the following two sections, we will first show that the widely reported pattern of causative alternation that entails a change of classifier type also exists in TJSL. However, we will also include some data that violate this constraint of classifier type in causative alternation.

2.3 Causative alternation with classifier handshape change

This section will show that causative alternation accompanied with classifier handshape change can also be found in TJSL. However, such data do not necessarily suggest that classifier type determines argument structure because there also exist causative alternations without classifier handshape change.

TJSL

(17) a. MAN IRON-ROD CL_{HL}: bend the iron rod
'The man bends an iron rod (by holding it with his hands).'
b. IRON ROD CL_{WE_SASS}: bends
'The iron rod bends.'
c. WALL CL_{WE_SASS}_be located$_a$, MAN PICTURE CL_{HL}: hang the picture on the wall$_a$
'The man hangs the picture on the wall.'

d. WALL CL$_{WE\_SASS}$_be located$_a$, PICTURE CL$_{WE\_SASS}$: picture hangs on the wall$_a$
'The picture hangs on the wall.'

HKSL

(18) a. BOOK-SQUARE MALE-CHILD BOOK CL: STAND_BOOK_ON_BOOK-SQUARE
'A boy stood the books on a book-shelf.'
(Lau 2002: 65)

b. BOOK-SQUARE BOOK CL: BOOK_STAND_ON_BOOK-SQUARE
'The books stand on a book-shelf.'
(Lau 2002: 65)

Examples (17a) and (17b) represent a typical case of causative alternation where the verb root (i.e. 'bend') remains the same phonologically (i.e. pronation of the wrist of both hands) but there is a classifier handshape change, from a handling classifier (i.e. S-handshape) in the causative predicate to a whole entity classifier (i.e. 1-handshape) in the inchoative predicate. Examples (17c) and (17d) represent similar examples, where the causative variant 'someone hangs a picture' is realized by a handling classifier and the inchoative variant 'a picture is hanging on the wall' adopts a whole entity classifier. Similar cases of causative alternation accompanying with classifier change has also been reported in HKSL (Lau 2002), as illustrated in examples (18a) and (18b) where the verb root (i.e. 'stand') remains the same whereas classifier handshape changes from a handling classifier (i.e. square-C-handshape) in the causative predicate to a whole entity classifier (i.e. B-handshape) in the inchoative predicate. Therefore, this phenomenon aligns with what has been reported in previous studies.

In what follows, we will show that classifier type as discussed in the literature, i.e. the handling classifier and the whole entity classifier, does not necessarily determine argument structure hence alternation. To verify it, we first tackle whether the handling classifier consistently marks causativity. We will show that although the handling classifier occurs in causative predicates, it is not necessarily a causative marker because it can also occur in non-causative-transitive predicates. Secondly, we examine whether the whole entity classifier occurs only in unaccusative predicates but not in transitive or causative predicates. Again, the data show that it occurs in both types of predicates. Given these findings, we argue that the handling classifier is not a causative marker, neither is the whole entity classifier an unaccusative marker.

2.3.1 Handling classifier is not a causative marker

When analyzing causative alternation represented by the handling classifier predicate and SASS predicate in ASL, Kegl (1985: 120) argues that 'the causative marker in ASL is a handling classifier, a gerund of sorts which refers to the handling of some object'. This claim was reiterated in Kegl (1990: 157), 'The causative/inchoative alternation exists in ASL, but the transitive verb is explicitly marked with causative morphology, which involves the presence of a handling classifier in the position of the verb generally associated with the theme (the element that undergoes the change of state).' That argument structure alternation manifests itself via different classifier types is confirmed in Benedicto and Brentari (2004), who further claim that the external argument in a handling classifier predicate is restricted to agents and classifier type determines the valency of the predicate.

Although the data so far reveal that causative alternation is associated with a change between handling and whole entity classifiers, there may be possibilities where the predicate in which a handling classifier occurs is just transitive but not necessarily causative. The answer to this question helps to disconfirm the proposal that the handling classifier is causative in nature.

The examples in (19a) and (19b) both adopt a typical handling classifier meaning 'holding' an object; however, the predicate it occurs in is just transitive. The predicate itself is not causative since no change of state or change of location of the internal argument is entailed.

(19)   a.   CUP MAN CL_{HL}: hold a cup
               'The man is holding a cup.'
       b.   YOGURT-JAR MOM CL_{HL}: shake jar
               'Mom shakes the yogurt jar by holding it.'

The examples in (19a) and (19b) encode an event of holding an object by an agent, as expressed by a handling classifier, such as 'holding a cup' in (19a) and 'holding a jar' in (19b). As such, the internal argument does not undergo a change of state, a criterial property of causatives. Based on these findings, the predicates in (19a) and (19b) which find a handling classifier are transitive but not causative.

Although the handling classifier is not a causative marker, can it demonstrate causative alternation without classifier handshape change, meaning that both the causative and the inchoative predicates involve a handling classifier? Such data do not seem to exist, as the handling classifier never occurs in intransitive predicates. We predict that it is due to the lexical meaning of 'manner of holding' which is already incorporated into the classifier handshape with a specific configuration denoting how the agent holds the object (i.e. the manner of holding it).

Such a requirement means that the argument structure with a handling classifier is transitive and agentive if a human hand is configured into the classifier handshape. He (2011, 2020) proves that predicates with a handling classifier can either involve an agent argument or an inanimate handler,[5] implying that the handling classifier may be defined broadly allowing both animate and inanimate handlers.

2.4 Causative alternation without classifier change

2.4.1 Lexical causative and the handling classifier

Causative alternation based on lexical rather than classifier verbs is highly restrictive. Only one verb BREAK was identified during personal interviews. This verb seems to be lexicalized from a handling classifier predicate. During one of the interviews, the signers were given a context 'X borrowed a car from Y. While X was driving, a bus hit the car at its back and a part of the car came off. When Y saw the broken car, she asked X who broke it'. The following sentences were extracted from the narrative above.

(20)   _____top
 a. IX-a   CAR BAD // WHO BREAK?
     'As for this car, it is broken. Who broke (it)?'
 b. IX-3 DRIVE BUS//IX-1 CAR CL_{WE_SASS} + CL_{WE_SASS}: bus hits car at the back// IX-CL_{WE}: car BREAK.
     'Someone drove a bus. I drive a car. The bus hit my car at the back, the car broke'
 c. STICK   MAN CL_{HL} + CL_{HL}: break the stick
     'The man broke a stick into two with his hands.'

The causative verb BREAK occurs in both a causative predicate (20a) and an inchoative predicate (20b). Although this verb has its origin as a handling classifier predicate, lexicalization results in the loss of meaning in the manner of handling an object encoded by the handling handshape configuration. As a consequence,

---

5 Whether or not the handling classifier is associated with an agent argument depends on how the handling classifier is defined. If it only refers to a human being manipulating something with the hand, then the handling classifier can only be associated with an agent argument. If the handling classifier is defined broadly as anything that handles something, it can refer to an inanimate handler such as a machine or other instruments such as a plier, a clamp or a clip which 'acts on' a theme by holding.

the handshape component of the lexical causative no longer varies according to the size and shape of the object. When BREAK is used as a causative verb in (20a), it expresses an abstract notion of causation whereby the manner of causation is unspecified, similar to causative alternation in spoken languages. In English, when the alternating verb 'break' is used as a causative verb, the manner of direct causation is also unspecified, as shown in (21a) and (21b):

(21) a. John broke the car.
      b. The car broke.

Note that it is common for certain lexical verbs with a classifier origin to re-emerge as a classifier predicate. For instance, when the lexical verb BREAK re-emerges as a handling classifier predicate, the manner of direct manipulation will be specified through the handshape configuration of the handling classifier. Therefore, we predict that causative predicates in which the causing event does not encode manner of direct manipulation will not involve a handling classifier. In (20b), the breaking of the car is not caused by an agent directly manipulating the car by the hand, but by its crashing with another vehicle. Under these circumstances, use of a handling classifier will crash semantically. However, when the change of state of the theme is caused by the manner of direct manipulation of an agent, the handling classifier will surface. As shown in (20c), the change of state of the theme STICK from one whole stick into two parts is caused by the agent MAN holding and breaking it in a certain manner. In other words, only when the meaning of manner of direct manipulation is bleached can the lexical verb BREAK be used in a causative-transitive predicate. Similar cases have also been reported in Danish Sign Language (Engberg-Pedersen 2010: 49–50).

2.4.2 Whole entity classifier in causative alternation

Whole entity classifiers are consistently observed in unaccusative-intransitive predicates (Kegl 1985, 1990; Zwitserlood 2003, 2008; Lau 2002; Benedicto and Brentari 2004; Benedicto et al. 2007; de Lint 2010; Kimmelman et al. 2019). In this section, we will discuss a subtype of whole entity classifiers, namely SASS classifiers (WE_SASS henceforth), and argue that they behave differently from that has been reported in the literature in terms of argument structure.

WE_SASS classifiers represent the most typical of whole entity classifiers. In TJSL, they may occur in both causative-transitive and inchoative predicates, as shown in examples (22a), (22b), (22c) and (23).

(22) a. BOOK MAN (ON PURPOSE) CL$_{WE\_SASS}$: open book
'A man opens the book (on purpose).'
(causative-transitive)

b. BOOK CL$_{WE\_SASS}$: book opens
'The book opens.'
(inchoative)

c. BOOK THICK MAN CL$_{HL}$: open book
'A man opens the book.'

(23) BOOK THIN CL$_{WE\_SASS}$: be located$_a$
WIND WIND-BLOW$_a$ CL$_{WE\_SASS}$: book opens$_a$
'The wind blows at the book and it opens.
(inchoative)

(22a) and (22b) show causative alternation based on the same verb root 'open' and the classifier type 'WE_SASS'. It is the presence of the external argument MAN but not the classifier that yields a causative-transitive reading to the predicate. To test for agentivity, an agent-oriented adverb ON-PURPOSE is inserted in (22a) and it is still compatible with the external argument MAN. Note that the WE_SASS classifier in this transitive predicate, which denotes the theme argument's size and shape only, bears no lexical meaning about how the agent 'handles' the book while causing it to open. If this meaning is incorporated into the predicate, a handling classifier will merge with the predicate instead, as shown in (22c). In other words, whether or not a handling classifier is required in the causative-transitive variant of the alternation depends on whether the manner of direct manipulation (e.g. holding/bending an object) is specified or not, rather than whether it is triggered by the requirement for encoding causativity of the predicate.

In (23), WIND, a natural force serving as an external argument for the causative predicate occupies the subject position and the internal argument BOOK is represented by a WE_SASS classifier established at locus.$_a$. This sentence is followed by a resultative classifier predicate indicating a change of state of the internal argument (i.e. the book 'opens'). While researching on HKSL, Tang and Yang (2007) and Lau (2011) analyze it as a resultative, a sub-type of serial verb constructions. According to Lau, the central argument supporting a resultative analysis rests upon the existence of a shared internal argument between the primary and the secondary predicate in the construction. Applying this analysis to (23), the complex predicate is constituted by a causative predicate 'blow at' and an inchoative predicate 'book opens' (i.e. result). Syntactically, the shared internal argument is the direct object of the causative predicate (i.e. 'wind blows at *the book*') but subject of the result predicate which is inchoative in nature (i.e. *the book* opens').

One piece of evidence justifying the shared argument analysis comes from locus assignment. In (23), locus-a is consistently selected for signing the locative predicate CL_{WE_SASS}: *be located$_a$*, the transitive predicate WIND-BLOW-a and the resultative predicate CL_{WE_SASS}: *book opens$_a$*.

There are different types of serial verb constructions, and resultatives represent a sub-type whose syntactic structure is different from causative alternation. Resultatives are monoclausal constructions structurally analyzed as a complex predicate consisting of a series of verbal projections to accommodate the cause and result predicates. On the other hand, causative alternation is analyzed using pairs of sentences whose verb forms display specific morphemes to mark the alternation. For instance, the lexical causative BREAK in example (20) shows no change of verb form in the alternation, analogous to example (1) in English. Obviously, the resultative construction in example (23) is a serial verb construction, hence the causative and the inchoative predicates do not share the same verb root. The verb of the causative is 'blow at', and that of the inchoative is 'open'.

In fact, it is not difficult to find a causative predicate that involves a handling classifier and a resultant predicate with an WE_SASS classifier, as shown in (24):

(24) BOOK CL_{WE_SASS}:be located$_a$ with cover facing upward+$CL_{WE\_SASS:}$ table MAN CL_{HL}: turn the book over$_a$ CL_{WE_SASS}: book with cover facing downward$_a$+-$CL_{WE\_SASS:}$ table
'The man turns a book over by holding it.'

In example (24), the primary predicate of the resultative construction is *MAN CL_{HL}: turn the book over*, the secondary inchoative predicate is CL_{WE_SASS}: *book with the cover facing downwards*. Taken as a whole, the handling classifier and the whole entity-SASS are generally observed in both causative alternation and resultative constructions. Necessarily, the syntactic representations of the constructions involved in causative alternation and resultative as a subtype of serial verb constructions are different (see Lau 2002 & 2012 for a detailed syntactic analysis).

To recall, the causative predicate in (22a) does not involve a handling classifier, but a WE_SASS classifier. One question may arise as to whether this WE_SASS classifier predicate in the causative variant is an output of lexicalization, just as INJECT (i.e. a shot with a needle)...etc. In the context of a transitive classifier predicate in TJSL, one can easily find a handling classifier occurring in those contexts. However, examples (25a) – (25d) below show a variety of ways in which the WE_SASS classifier can be used in a causative context, implying that these WE_SASS classifier predicates are not necessarily lexicalized verbs.

(25) a. TABLE$_a$ SMALL KNIFE CL$_{WE\_SASS}$: be located$_a$ MAN CL$_{WE\_SASS}$: turn over$_a$ (H-handshape)
'The man turns the small knife on the table over.'
b. TABLE$_a$ BOOK CL$_{WE\_SASS}$: be located$_a$ MAN CL$_{WE\_SASS}$: turn over$_a$ (B-handshape)
'The man turns the book on the table over.'
c. WINDOW$_a$ CL$_{WE\_SASS}$: located$_a$ with one panel on top of the other
MAN CL$_{WE\_SASS}$: open$_a$ (2B-handshape$_{vertical}$)
'The man opens the window by moving one panel upwards'
d. TABLE$_a$ LAPTOP CL$_{WE\_SASS}$: be located vertically on a surface
MAN CL$_{WE\_SASS}$: open$_a$ (2B-handshape$_{vertical}$)/*(2B-handshape$_{horizontal}$)
'The man opens the laptop vertically.'

Both (25a) and (25b) show that the WE_SASS classifier appears in a causative-transitive predicate. All share the same verb root 'turn over' but different handshapes are adopted to reflect the semantic properties of the internal argument (i.e. H-handshape for a thin and long object vs B-handshape for a flat object). In (25c) and (25d), the causative verbs require a different orientation for the handshape morpheme to encode 'open the window horizontally' or 'open the laptop vertically'. The morphological property of the manner of causation (i.e. open X horizontally/vertically) as a meaning component to be merged with the verb root 'open' signals their status of a classifier predicate rather than a lexical verb. Native signers' intuitions also confirm that changing the orientation of the classifier handshape in signing (see example (25d)) leads to unacceptability, although they had no difficulty comprehending the predicates 'open the laptop'.

Next, we examine if the causative-transitive predicates involving WE_SASS classifiers are passives. Here, we report on the use of imperatives as diagnostics because imperatives only allow active sentences with an agent argument as subject (Jary and Kissine 2014). In imperatives, the null element has three important properties: (1) it is located in the subject position; (2) it refers to the addressee; (3) it is interpreted as involving an agent argument.

(26) a. IX-2! COMPUTER CL$_{WE\_SASS}$: open
'You! Open the computer!'
b. IX-2! CALENDAR CL$_{WE\_SASS}$: open
'You! Open the calendar!'
c. IX-2! BOOK CL$_{WE\_SASS}$: open
'You! Open the book!'

Examples (26a), (26b) and (26c) show that the whole entity-SASS (i.e. CL$_{\text{WE\_SASS}}$) occurring in the causative predicates is compatible with imperatives. Therefore, it excludes the possibility that these sentences are passives.

In this section, we have shown that whole entity-SASS can participate in causative alternation without changing the handshape into a handling one in the causative-transitive variant. In the following section, we will examine the argument realization and syntactic properties of bodypart classifiers by showing that bodypart classifiers, proposed to occur only in unergative predicates in ASL, do participate in causative alternation in TJSL.

2.4.3 Bodypart classifier in causative alternation

This section investigates whether the bodypart classifier participates in causative alternation, an area not tackled by Benedicto and Brentari (2004).[6] To recall, they propose that the bodypart classifier in ASL only occurs in unergative predicates, revealing its status as referring to the external argument of the predicates.

(27) a. ROSIE S+BOW
Rosie head$_{\text{limb=BPCL}}$ +bow
'Rosie bowed.'
b. ROSIE WILLING S+BOW
Rosie willingly head=BPCL+bow
'Rosie bowed willingly.' (in a theater play, for instance)
(Benedicto and Brentari 2004: 763)

Based on (27b), in which the bodypart classifier is compatible with an agent-oriented adverb WILLING, they argue that the argument associated with the bodypart classifier is agentive and the predicate is unergative.

Grose et al. (2007) challenge these assumptions of Benedicto and Brentari (2004). Instead, they argue that the bodypart classifier patterns with the handling classifier as encompassing both external and internal arguments, since both have handpart for external arguments and selected fingers for internal arguments in their morphophonological representations. The distinction between them is that the internal argument as referred to by the predicate's bodypart classifier is ana-

---

[6] Benedicto and Brentari (2004) using S+BOW for unergative (S=bodypart classifier) and 1+BOW for unaccusative (1=whole entity classifier) in ASL as evidence to argue for unergative-unaccusative alternation.

lyzed as 'part' of the external argument. Also, predicates with a bodypart classifier can be correlated with telic and atelic events. Invoking the Event Visibility Hypothesis (Wilbur 2003, 2008), they claim that the possibility of internal arguments which can be quantified or delimited will give rise to a telic event reading.

(28) a. S+SHAKING (atelic)
'She shook her head'.
b. S+BOW (telic)
'She bowed her head.

(Grose et al. 2007; 1259)

c. ACTOR S+BOW NOTHING
#'None of the actors bowed.
'The actors didn't bow at all.

(Grose et al. 2007;1280)

d. BUTTER MELT NOTHING
'None of the butter melted.'

(Grose et al. 2007; 1279)

e. INDEX S+BOW_TO_EACH.
'S/he bows to each of them.'

(Grose et al. 2007; 1281)

Two pieces of evidence are put forward by Grose et al. to counteract Benedicto and Brentari's proposal. First, (28a) shows that the bodypart classifier (i.e. head) as represented by S-handshape occurs in an atelic predicate. The event as encoded in (28b) is telic because the bodypart classifier shows a wrist-orientation change to a halt denoting an endpoint of the event of BOW. Second, they claim that the NOTHING & distributive tests are not reliable syntactic tests for the presence of internal arguments. Briefly state, NOTHING in (28c) does not scope over the external argument, or the reading 'None of the actors bowed' would be acceptable. In (28d), NOTHING scopes over the internal argument BUTTER, thus 'none of the butter melted' is acceptable. Last, (28e) yields a reading that 'the woman' directs a bowing movement at 'each of them' (i.e. internal argument) at different loci (see Grose et al. 2007 for a detailed discussion). Based on these observations, they conclude that the predicate involving a bodypart classifier is not unergative, and the type of alternation may be transitive or unaccusative. However, since the bodypart classifier does not encode a change of internal state, it does not participate in causative alternation (Grose et al. 2007: 1270). Here, we will expand this discussion of Grose et al. (2004) by investigating the bodypart classifier in TJSL.

The findings in TJSL suggest that bodypart classifier predicates are not necessarily unergatives. Firstly, examples in (29) and (30) show that bodypart classifiers may occur in unaccusative-intransitive predicates (as shown in Type 1) as well as causative predicates (as shown in Type 2) respectively. Bodypart classifiers in TJSL do participate in causative alternation, in which the bodypart classifier is associated with the internal argument in both the causative variant and the unaccusative variant.

Type 1. *Bodypart classifiers in unaccusative-intransitive predicates*

(29) a. RABBIT FALL ASLEEP //
 CL_{BP_EAR}: drops sideway
 'The rabbit falls asleep; (one of its) ears drops sideway.'
 b. MAN SLEEPY //
 IX-eye CL_{BP_EYE}: close
 'The man is sleepy; his eyes close.'

The context of (29a) indicates the situation that the rabbit falls asleep, thus it does not have volitional control over its ears. By the same token, the context provided in the first clause of (29b) also implies that the sleepy man does not have volitional control over his eyes. These two examples suggest that an agentive reading is unavailable. We argue that the bodypart classifier in these examples occurs in an inchoative-intransitive predicate, despite the presence of an animate being in the context (i.e. RABBIT in (29a) and MAN in (29b). In other words, the bodypart classifiers represent an internal, theme argument that undergoes a change of state. In (29a), 'the ear drops sideway' and in (29b), the eyes close.

Type 2. *Bodypart classifiers in causative-transitive predicates*

(30) a. CAT HAPPY   IX-3 CL_{BP_TAIL}: raises
 'When a cat is happy, it raises its tail high.'
 b. MAN WANT SLEEP //
 IX-3 CL_{BP_EYE}: close
 'The man wants to go to sleep, so he closes his eyes'

The causatives in (30a) and (30b) involve an internal argument represented by a bodypart classifier that undergoes a change of state through the internal control of an external argument whose referent is the possessor of the bodypart, CAT in (30a) and MAN in (30b). As shown, the internal control of the external argument is expressed through a bodypart classifier realized phonologically by extending the selecting finger of a 1-handshape (i.e. 'raises its tail') in (30a) and flexing of selected fingers (i.e. closes the eyes) of C-handshape in (30b). That the bodypart classifier occurs in a causative-transitive predicate in (30a) and (30b) demonstrates that not only the handling classifier but also the bodypart classifier that may occur in a transitive or a causative predicate, under the condition that the causative reflects the semantics of 'internal bodily control of the agent'. In examples (30a) and (30b), the eventuality is under direct control of the external argument, CAT and MAN, who perform the activity leading to a change of state of the internal argument. If the change of state of the bodypart is caused by some accident or not under the direct internal bodily control of the causer or agent, e.g. the cat's tail is raised by another person in (30a), the existing structure with the bodypart classifier would be incompatible with such an interpretation.

Taken together, the data show that when a bodypart classifier represents an internal argument of a causative predicate, the change of state of the bodypart must be caused directly by the agent or causer exerting direct bodily control over the bodypart.

As said, if the change of state of the bodypart is caused by some accident or not under the direct bodily control of the causer, a similar structure like the one in the examples in (30) would fail to yield such an interpretation.

(31) a. ...(signer describing a car accident)... MAN IX-man LEG-BONE CL_{BP_LEG}: breaks
'The man's leg-bone broke.'
*b. LEG-BONE MAN CL_{BP_LEG}: break.
*'The man breaks his own leg (by exerting his will to break his own leg).'

In (31a), the bodypart classifier occurring in an inchoative-intransitive predicate denotes a change of state of a man's leg-bone. (31b) is unacceptable for the denotation that 'the man exerts direct bodily control over the leg causing it to break'. This is not the intended meaning for (31b) because one cannot break one's leg by exerting his will over it, unlike the 'opening eyes' events. The sentence could mean 'The man breaks his own leg', which is not the intended interpretation against the context of interaction.

The idea of direct bodily control leads us to propose that the bodypart classifier in a causative predicate has a [+volition] feature, following Grose et al.'s (2007) proposal that bodypart classifier embodies both external and internal arguments in the predicate. Our data in TJSL to some extent corroborate with their assumption that the bodypart classifier predicate can involve both an external argument and an internal argument.⁷ The internal argument, which is a part of the body, is subject to 'direct bodily control' by the external argument. In other words, an inherent possessor – possessee relationship is entailed between the agent and a part of the body that the classifier refers to, and only the bodypart that belongs to the agent can it be subject to direct control by the agent. This criterion of direct bodily control in the case of bodypart classifier can be further confirmed by the imperative test, as imperatives generally require an active voice realized by an external argument 'you'. In (32), the presence of an external argument IX-2 and an internal argument MOUTH with a causative verb 'open' clearly implies that the predicate is causative-transitive.

(32) IX-2! MOUTH CL$_{BP\_MOUTH}$: open one's mouth! CANDY?
'You! Open your mouth! Any candy (in it)?'

(32) further disconfirms Benedicto and Brentari's (2004) proposal that bodypart classifiers only appear in predicates that are necessarily unergative. Here, the bodypart classifier morphologically represents the theme argument which is a part of the body, and the agent argument IX-2 is just a pronoun and is not morphologically realized through any classifier handshape. As we have argued previously, it is not necessarily the case that all arguments in a classifier predicate must be morphologically represented through a classifier handshape; it is possible to find other morphological components for argument realization, such as signer's body,⁸ imperative constructions offer a litmus test for this condition.

Do predicates with a bodypart classifier participate in causative alternation? Our data confirms such a claim. Comparing (33a) and (33b), the same bodypart classifier handshape and movement (i.e. selected fingers change from open to close near the eyes) are used. What distinguishes the argument structure of the predicates is the grammatical subject, IX-man serving as the external argument of the causative predicate in (33a) and IX-eye serving as the internal argument of the unaccusative predicate in (33b).

---

7 The agentivity and (in)transitivity of bodypart classifiers also has something to do with the morphological status of the signer's body and signing perspective. Due to the limitation of space, we won't spell this out. Interested readers are recommended to refer to Perniss (2007) and the Ph.D thesis of He (2020).
8 We predict that the signer's body can also be a morphological marker in classifier predicate. Interested readers are suggested to refer to He (2020) for a detailed discussion on signer's body and signing perspective, and their relation to argument realization.

(33) a. MAN SLEEP WANT SLEEP //
　　　　IX-3 MAN (ON-PURPOSE) CL$_{BP\_EYE}$: close
　　　　'The man wants to go to sleep, so he closes his eyes (on purpose)'
　　b. MAN SLEEPY //
　　　　IX-eye　CL$_{BP\_EYE}$: close
　　　　'The man is sleepy; his eyes close'

Another example to further confirm the existence of causative alternation is shown in (34a) and (34b)

(34) a. RABBIT IX-3 PLAY//INDEX RABBIT^EAR ON_PURPOSE CL$_{BP\_EAR}$: drops.
　　　　'The rabbit drops its ears.
　　b. …LOOK! RABBIT^EAR CL$_{BP\_EAR}$: drop, IX-3 APPEARANCE CUTE!
　　　　'Look! The ears of the rabbit are dropping (in front of its head), the rabbit's appearance is cute!'

In (34a) and (34b), the bodypart classifier morphologically represents the internal argument RABBIT^EAR which undergoes a change of state from an erected to a flexed position on the rabbit's head. The presence of an animate entity RABBIT in (34a) invokes a reading of direct causation, initiated by the external argument exerting direct bodily control over the internal argument, causing it to change its state. On the contrary, the occurrence of the grammatical subject RABBIT^EAR in (34b), especially when signed from an observer's perspective via the use of a vocative 'LOOK!', entails an eventuality of an unaccusative-intransitive predicate denoting a change of state of the internal argument of 'ears drop'. The same bodypart classifier occurs in a causative-transitive as well as an inchoative-intransitive predicate while the verb root remains the same, revealing a typical case of causative alternation in TJSL, contrary to Benedicto and Brentari's prediction that bodypart classifiers occur in unergatives denoting an external argument only.

With handling classifiers, the agent acts upon the theme argument by manipulating his hand 'hand as handler' in a certain manner. On the other hand, causation by direct bodily control of the agent on an internal argument may involve adoption of a bodypart classifier. As shown in the above examples, the change of state of the rabbit's ears from standing to lying on its head is not caused by the rabbit using its hand (i.e. hand as handler) to manipulate its position, but some direct internally bodily control, thus a directly caused eventuality. Under these circumstances, the bodypart classifier pattern after CL$_{WE\_SASS}$ in the sense that both may represent an internal argument undergoing a change of state. However, they differ in terms of the types of causation: direct internally bodily control for the bodypart classifier but direct manipulation for the CL$_{WE\_SASS}$.

To conclude this section, it seems that causative alternation involving a bodypart classifier represents a case of labile alternation because of the absence of any morphological marking on the one hand, and on the other hand, absence of manner of manipulation in the eventuality as expressed by the handling classifier in specific handshape configuration or orientation.

3 Discussion

This paper discusses the phenomenon of causative alternation in TJSL. We have explored the claim put forward in Benedicto and Brentari (2004), namely, that classifier type determines the argument structure of a predicate. In particular, we examine the handling classifier and the whole entity classifier in TJSL systematically to verify if the claim holds crosslinguistically. The data discussed above reveal that the patterns of causative-unaccusative alternation in TJSL are similar to HKSL but some differ from ASL. Additionally, we have examined the bodypart classifier and shown that it participates in causative alternation, contrary to the claim that it only represents an external argument in unergatives. As a whole, the data show that causative alternation is not driven by properties of the classifier morpheme in TJSL. What seems to be the case is that classifier morphemes behave quite independently grammatically of the requirements for causativity, in(transitivity) and argument structure of predicates. Although the handling classifier only occurs in transitive predicates, it is not necessarily a causative marker because the handling classifier can also occur in non-causative-transitive predicates (see Section 2.3.1, example 19). The WE_SASS classifier as a subtype of whole entity classifiers occurs not only in unaccusative-intransitive but also in transitive predicates, hence not an unaccusative marker. In other words, both the handling classifier and the whole entity classifier do not systematically alternate between the causative and inchoative pair of constructions and each assumes its own argumental and grammatical functions as required by the predicate. Incorporating the bodypart classifier into our analysis, we observe that it occurs in either inchoative-intransitive predicates or causative-transitive predicates, providing further evidence to argue against the correlation between classifier type and argument structure.

Despite these findings concerning the correlation between classifier type and argument structure, we did observe some patterns of causative alternation in TJSL. To interpret the current findings within the framework of Haspelmath's (1993) typology of causative alternation, we have the following observations. Firstly, we have not observed data that suggest causative or inchoative alternation in TJSL. Secondly, we observe data suggesting that TJSL manifests itself more systematically with two subtypes of non-directed alternation – labile alternation and equipollent alternation. While the data are highly restrictive, instances of labile alternation are observed with lexical causatives realized by a lexical verb like BREAK, whose lexicalization pathway seems to originate from handling classifier predicates. With this verb, at least the handshape and movement are phonologically frozen, and, unlike the classifier morphemes, the handshape bears no anaphoric relation with the argument of the predicate.

The second piece of data suggesting labile alternation came from some causative alternation of classifier predicates in which we observe no change of the morphophonological form of the verb root as well as the classifier morpheme that merges with it. The occurrence of a WE_SASS classifier (see Section 2.4.2; example 22a and 22b) or a bodypart classifier (see Section 2.4.3; example 29 and 30) in both the causative and unaccusative predicates is consistent. This third type of causative alternation in classifier predicates in TJSL has not been reported in other signed languages in the literature and more research is necessary to confirm this preliminary observation. As for equipollent alternation, our evidence came from the language's systematic adoption of handling classifiers in causative-transitive predicates and WE_SASS classifiers in inchoative-intransitive predicates, hence instances of causative alternation (see Section 2.4.2 example 22b and 22c) Note that the phenomenon of change of classifier type is also observed in the causative alternation of HKSL, while researchers working on NGT and RSL adopt this distinction in exploring other types of alternation (e.g. transitive-intransitive alternation). In other words, this type of causative alternation involves a change of classifier type while the verb root remains phonologically the same. To summarize our observation, we provide a taxonomy of causative alternation in TJSL in Figure 1 below.

A corollary issue is what counts as the verb root of a classifier predicate and where argument structure is encoded in this type of constructions. Benedicto and Brentari (2004) adopt the movement-as-root proposal, but they put forward a syntactic approach to account for the correlation between classifier type and argument structure, arguing that eventualities can be built into syntax and the classifier morpheme triggers different syntactic projections to accommodate the different types of argument structure in classifier predicates. For instance, they assume that the verb root of a classifier predicate, such as MOVE or BE, only encodes information about the number of argument(s) within a predicate, but the assignment of external or internal arguments as well as their associated theta roles rests with the classifier morpheme. In their model, classifier morphemes are functional heads at which the corresponding argument is interpreted as external or internal.

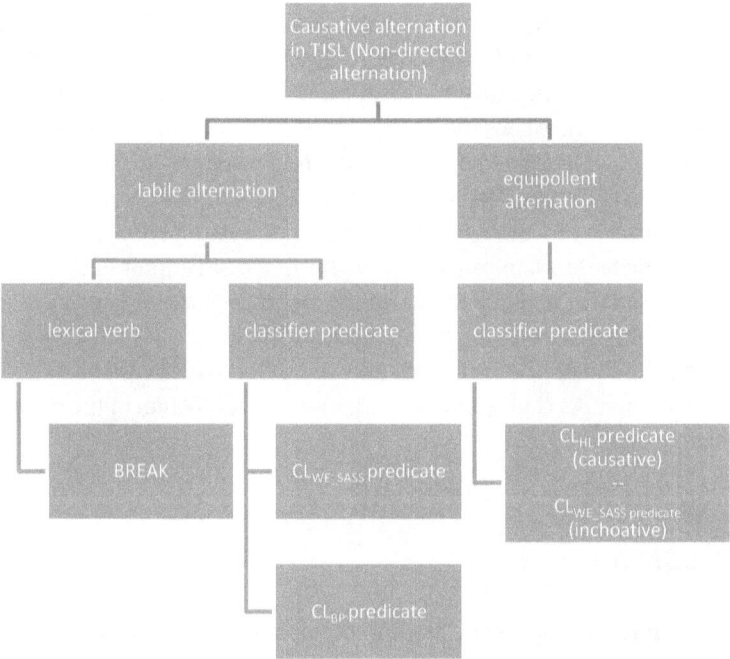

Figure 1: Taxonomy of causative alternation in TJSL.

One must point out that in order to appreciate the debate about the function of classifier morpheme in determining argument structure, it also requires a corresponding understanding of whether the verbal root expressed by the movement component of the sign plays a role in determining the argument structure of a predicate. Apparently, Benedicto and Brentari rejects this assumption. Tang (2003) and Tang and Yang (2007) adopt the 'movement-as-root' hypothesis, arguing that classifier morphemes provide information about the arguments of a predicate via co-reference between the classifier and the NP antecedent. It is the movement component that encodes information about the qualitative domain of predication such as event, state and location, as well as number of arguments to participate in these eventualities, hence argument structure information resides with the verb root. Zwitserlood (2003, 2008) and Kimmelman et al. (2019) are also in favor of it, arguing that the verb root encodes argument structure. For instance, adopting the analysis of First Phase Syntax (Ramchand 2008) where syntactic structure is motivated by eventualities, Kimmelman et al. (2019) argue that the MOVE root projects *proc* head to account for motion predicates, which encodes a dynamic event denoting the movement of an UNDERGOER argument. Syntactically, this argument is merged to the specifier of *procP* while the whole entity classifier or the bodypart classifier that refer to the UNDERGOER argument are heads of agreement projections to fulfil the referent identification function. Another evidence to support this alternative proposal came from labile and equipollent alternation in TJSL, where we observe that no matter whether the classifier morpheme changes or not to encode the external or internal argument, the verb root remains the same in causative alternation. In other words, the verb root encodes conceptual information, including eventualities and event participants with associated semantic features, to constrain the selection of an appropriate classifier morpheme to satisfy the requirements of the argument structure encoded in the verb root. Certainly, more research is necessary to verify this assumption and an understanding of the nature of the verb root and the classifier morpheme will enlighten how researchers conceptualize the grammatical function of the classifier morpheme.

4 Conclusion

This paper examines the nature of classifier morpheme from the perspective of argument structure in causative alternation, with TJSL data suggesting that causative-unaccusative alternation in classifier predicates does not necessarily trigger a change in classifier type. In other words, classifier morpheme does not necessarily determine the status (as external or internal) of the argument that lands. Whereas the handling classifier consistently occurs in transitive predicates, other classifier types – whole entity and bodypart classifiers–occur either in causative-transitive, transitive or unaccusative or intransitive predicates. Such evidence leads us to conclude that the classifier morpheme does not necessarily determine the argumental status of the predicate, be it external or internal. Based on these observations, we revisit the 'movement-as-root-hypothesis', and argue that it is the verb root that provides information about argument structure and constrains the selection of classifier morpheme as either external or internal argument. Couching the data analysis within the framework of Haspelmath 1993 typology, the verb root + classifier morpheme morphophonological template enables us to identify some predicates to be manifestations of labile and equipollent alternation, which are subtypes of non-directed causative alternation. As sign linguistics research on Asian signed languages is not as extensive as non-Asian signed languages, the current observations in TJSL, while corroborating the findings in HKSL, need to be further verified with data from other Asian signed languages for confirmation of areal properties and crosslinguistic variation.

Appendix: Annotations

In this paper, we follow the annotation conventions as adopted in the sign linguistics literature as follows:
1. Lexical signs are capitalized. For instance: BOOK
2. Pointing signs are glossed as IX. When an IX sign is followed by '-1/2/3', these signs refer to pronouns with person specifications. When it is followed by '-a/b/..', these alphabets refer to loci in space that the index signs are pointing at. This applies to localization of nouns in space, e.g. GROUND$_s$, showing a locus in space the sign GROUND is located. When IX points at an object, the object will be named directly, e.g. IX-mouse (pointing at a mouse)
3. Annotations for classifier predicates
    - General format: the type or sub-types of classifier predicate will appear first, to be followed by a colon ':' and a meaning translation of the predicate, e.g. CL$_{SASS}$: book moves.
    - Signs for two handed classifier predicates will be annotated by a '+' sign to show the combination of classifier handshapes. The annotation on the left of the '+' is for glossing the classifier on the dominant hand (i.e. H1) and the one on the right of the '+' is for the classifier on the non-dominant hand (i.e. H2). For instance, CL$_{WE\_VEH}$ + CL$_{WE\_VEH}$: bus hits car at the back
    - Types of classifiers will be presented in the following formats:
        - Whole entity_SASS – CL$_{WE\_SASS}$
        - Whole entity_semantic classifiers– CL$_{WE\_HUM}$ refers to semantic classifier that classifies human being, CL$_{WE\_VEH}$ refers to semantic classifier that classifies vehicle.
        - Handling classifier – CL$_{HL}$
        - Bodypart classifier – CL$_{BP}$
4. Lines on the glosses will be used to mark the following:
    $\underline{\qquad}$nms: with difficulty
    - Adverbial nonmanuals, e.g. BOY CL$_{BP}$: standing on one leg.
    $\underline{\qquad}$top
    - Syntactic nonmanuals, e.g. BOY   MAN LIKE.

References

Benedicto, Elena, Sandra Cvejanov & Josep Quer. 2007. Valency in classifier predicates: A syntactic analysis. *Lingua* 117(7). 1202–1215.

de Lint, Vanja. 2010. *Argument Structure in Classifier Constructions in ASL: an experimental approach*. Utrecht: Utrecht University MA dissertation.

de Lint, Vanja. 2018. NGT classifier constructions. *Sign Language and Linguistics* 21(1). 3–39.

de Lint, Vanja. 2020. From meaning to form and back in American Sign Language verbal classifier morphemes. *Word Structure* 13(1). 69–101.

Dyer, Eugene R. 1976. Sign language agglutination: a brief look at ASL and Turkish. *Sign Language Studies* 11(1). 133–148.

Engberg-Pedersen, Elisabeth. 1993. *Space in Danish Sign Language*. Hamburg: Signum Verlag.

Engberg-Pedersen, Elisabeth. 2010. Expressions of causation in Danish Sign Language. *Sign Language and Linguistics* 13(1). 40–67.

Grose, Donovan, Ronnie B. Wilbur & Katharina Schalber. 2007. Events and telicity in classifier predicates: A reanalysis of body part classifier predicates in ASL. *Lingua* 117(7). 1258–1284.

Hale, Ken & Samuel Jay Keyser. 1993. On argument structure and the lexical expression of syntactic relations. In Hale Ken & Samuel Jay Keyser (eds.), *The View from Building 20*, 53–109. Cambridge, Mass.: The MIT Press.

Haspelmath, Martin. 1993. More on the typology of inchoative/causative verb alternations. In Bernard Comrie & Maria Polinsky (eds.), *Causatives and transitivity* (23), 87–121. Amsterdam & Philadelphia: John Benjamins Publishing Company.

Harley, Heidi. 1995. *Subjects, events, and licensing* (Doctoral dissertation), Massachusetts Institute of Technology.

Harley, Heidi. 2008. On the causative construction. In Shigeru Miyagawa (ed.), *The Oxford Handbook of Japanese Linguistics*, 1–48. Oxford: Oxford University Press.

He, Jia. 2011. *Instrument Classifier Predicates in Tianjin Sign Language*. Hong Kong: The Chinese University of Hong Kong MA thesis.

He, Jia. 2020. *Classifier Realization in Hong Kong Sign Language, Beijing Sign Language and Tianjin Sign Language*. Hong Kong: The Chinese University of Hong Kong dissertation.

Hovav, Malka Rappaport & Beth Levin. 2012. Lexicon uniformity and the causative alternation. In Martin Everaert, Marijana Marelj &Tal Siloni (eds.), *The Theta System: Argument Structure at the Interface*, 150–176. Oxford: Oxford University Press.

Jary, Mark & Mikhail Kissine. 2014. *Imperatives*. Cambridge: Cambridge University Press.

Kegl, Judy. 1985. Causative marking and the construal of agency in ASL. In Karen L. Peterson, Paul D. Kroeber & William H. Eilfort (eds.), *Papers from the Parasession on Causatives and agentivity at the twenty-first regional meeting* 120–137. Chicago: Chicago Linguistic Society.

Kegl, Judy. 1990. Predicate argument structure and verb class organization in the ASL lexicon. In Ceil Lucas (ed.), *Sign Language Research: Theoretical Issues*, 149–175. Washington, D.C.: Gallaudet University Press.

Kimmelman, Vadim, Roland Pfau & Enoch O. Aboh. 2019. Argument structure of classifier predicates in Russian Sign Language. *Natural Language and Linguistic Theory* 38. 539–579.

Lau, Sin Yee Prudence. 2002. *Causative Alternation in Hong Kong Sign Language*. Hong Kong: The Chinese University of Hong Kong MA thesis.
Lau, Sin Yee Prudence. 2012. *Serial Verb Constructions in Hong Kong Sign Language*. Hong Kong: The Chinese University of Hong Kong dissertation.
Levin, Beth & Malka Rappaport Hovav. 1995. *Unaccusativity: At the Syntax-Lexical Semantics Interface*. Cambridge, Mass.: MIT Press.
Perniss, Pamela M. 2007. Achieving spatial coherence in German Sign Language narratives: The use of classifiers and perspective. *Lingua* 117(7). 1315–1338.
Piñón, Christopher. 2001. A finer look at the causative-inchoative alternation. *Semantics and Linguistic Theory* 11. 346–364.
Ramchand, Gillian. 2008. *Verb meaning and the lexicon: A first-phase syntax*. Cambridge: Cambridge University Press.
Schäfer, Florian. 2009. The causative alternation. *Language and Linguistics Compass* 3(2). 641–681.
Schuit, Joke. 2007. *The typological classification of sign language morphology*. Amsterdam: Universiteit van Amsterdam MA thesis.
Schuit, Joke, Anne Baker & Roland Pfau. 2011. Inuit Sign Language: a contribution to sign language typology. *Linguistics in Amsterdam* 4(1). 1–31.
Schwager, Waldemar. 2004. *Polymorphemische Gebärden in der Russischen Gebärdensprache (Polymorphemic Signs in Russian Sign Language)*. Amsterdam: Universiteit van Amsterdam MA thesis.
Supalla, Ted Roland. 1982. *Structure and Acquisition of Verbs of Motion and Location in American Sign Language*. San Diego: University of California, San Diego dissertation.
Tang, Gladys & Gu Yang. 2007. Events of motion and causation in Hong Kong Sign Language. *Lingua* 117(7). 1216–1257.
Wilbur, Ronnie. 2003. Representations of telicity in ASL. *Proceedings from the Annual Meeting of the Chicago Linguistics Society* 39(1). 354–368. Chicago: Chicago Linguistics Society.
Wilbur, Ronnie. 2008. Complex predicates involving events, time and aspect: Is this why sign languages look so similar. In Susan D. Fischer and Patricia Siple (eds.), *Theoretical issues in sign language research*, 217–250. Chicago: University of Chicago Press.
Zwitserlood, Inge. 2003. *Classifying Hand Configurations in Nederlandse Gebarentaal (Sign Language of the Netherlands)*. Utrecht: LOT.
Zwitserlood, Inge. 2008. Morphology below the level of the sign: frozen forms and classifier predicates. In Josep Quer (ed.), *Signs of the time: Selected papers from TISLR* 8, 251–272. Seedorf: Signum Press.

Kazumi Matsuoka, Uiko Yano and Kazumi Maegawa
Epistemic modal verbs and negation in Japanese Sign Language

Abstract: Epistemic modality conveys the speaker's commitment of how likely the content of the proposition will be true. Sign languages show variation in how they express epistemicity: manually, non-manually, or a combination of both. Japanese Sign Language (JSL) uses manual modal verbs to indicate epistemic modality. In the current study, using Cinque's (1999) model of cartographic syntax as a basis, we reclassified nine modal verbs which were previously identified as exclusively epistemic into three categories (possibility, epistemic, evidential). This reclassification is done based on the syntactic (word-order) restrictions and speaker judgements about the quality of commitment entailed by each modal category. Two different JSL expressions of negation, which take different scopes, also provided a clue for identifying the different categories of modal verbs. The modal verbs discussed in this paper are used also as lexical signs, which indicates that they might have acquired modal usage as JSL developed into an established language of the deaf community over 140 years. The issue of ordering between the evidential and the epistemic modal verbs are addressed in the discussion.

Keywords: cartography, epistemic modality, evidential, negation, possibility, Japanese Sign Language

1 Introduction

Modality refers to grammatical expressions of the speaker's judgements or attitude toward the content of the proposition, or "situations which need not be real"

Acknowledgements: A part of the current study was presented at the 153th Bi-annual meeting of Linguistic Society of Japan, the 35th Meeting of the English Linguistic Society of Japan, Formal and Experimental Advances in Sign language Theory (FEAST Reykjavik 2017), Ling 50 at the University of Connecticut, and Evolinguistics Meets Signed Language Symposium in 2018. We appreciate the discussion and comments of the audience. Hiroshi Baba and Shogo Nishiwaki helped us with additional information of non-manual expressions included in the current study. Comments from Margaret Ruth Crabtree, Yuta Sakamoto, Asako Uchibori, and two anonymous reviewers to an earlier version significantly contributed to the discussion. John Helwig provided editorial help. The handshape fonts are created by Centre for Sign Linguistics and Deaf Studies (CSLDS), the Chinese University of Hong Kong (CUHK). This study was funded by JSPS KAKENHI Grant 26284061 and 19H01259 (PI: Kazumi Matsuoka). All errors are our own.

https://doi.org/10.1515/9781501510243-006

(Portner 2009: 1). It is also defined as the "conceptual domain of necessity and possibility" (Shaffer 2004: 176). Specifically, epistemic modality indicates the speaker's judgements or commitment of how likely the content of the proposition will be true (Bybee et al. 1994; Palmer 2001, etc.). For example, the linguistic expression, *John might eat sushi* implies that the speaker has less confidence about John's food preference, as opposed to saying *John absolutely eats sushi*.

Sign languages employ a variety of manual or non-manual options to express epistemic modality. Ferreira Brito (1990) studied modal expressions in Brazilian Cities Sign Language (BCSL) and concludes that the use of epistemic modal expressions relies on contextual information and hence are not linguistically established (or "concrete"). In a more recent study, Herrmann (2013) claims that epistemic modal meanings are predominantly expressed non-manually in German Sign Language (DGS). Her cross-linguistic research revealed a similar pattern in Sign Language of the Netherlands (NGT), and Irish Sign Language (ISL). At the same time, in other sign languages, manual expressions of modality have also been identified, and their historical or iconic properties have been discussed extensively. For example, lexical signs of French Sign Language (LSF) are considered to have undergone various degrees of grammaticization and came to be used as modal expressions in American Sign Language (ASL) (Shaffer 2002, 2004; Shaffer and Janzen 2016). Other sign languages have lexical signs which have acquired modal usage: Herrero-Blanco and Salazar-García (2010) reported that modality in Spanish Sign Language (LSE) is expressed by lexical items such as verbs, nouns, adjectives, and adverbs.

Among sign languages with manual signs of epistemic modality, it has been pointed out that syntactic positions of the modal correspond to different semantic interpretation. Shaffer (2002, 2004) noted that in ASL, the pre-verbal position is typically associated with agent-oriented discourse functions of modality (i.e., ability or permission), while epistemic modals appear in the clause-final position. Similarly, the same ASL sign (e.g., SHOULD) may receive deontic or epistemic interpretation according to its syntactic position (Wilcox and Shaffer 2006; Shaffer 2004).

In fact, syntactic positions have been considered as a manifestation of hierarchical relationships between functional heads. According to the cartography approach in Cinque (1999), unique functional heads are assigned to different types of functional projection such as aspect (Asp), modality (Mod), mood, or speech act. Cinque assumes that the order of those functional heads is universally determined. The universal hierarchy of clausal functional projections has been proposed based on the ordering patterns of adverbs in spoken languages. In Cinque's (1999: 106) hierarchy, shown in (1) below, the epistemic modal head ($Mod_{epistemic}$) is placed between $Mood_{evidential}$ and the tense (T):

(1) [*frankly* Mood$_{speech\ act}$ [*fortunately* Mood$_{evaluative}$ [*allegedly* Mood$_{evidential}$ [*probably* Mod$_{epistemic}$ [*once* T(past) [*then* T(future) [*perhaps* Mood$_{irrealis}$ [*necessarily* Mod$_{necessity}$ [*possibly* Mod$_{possibility}$ [*usually* Asp$_{habitual}$ [*again* Asp$_{repetitive(I)}$ [*often* Asp$_{frequentative(I)}$ [*intentionally* Mod$_{volitional}$ [*quickly* Asp$_{celerative(I)}$ [*already* T(Anterior) [*no longer* Asp$_{terminative}$ [*still* Asp$_{continuative}$ [*always* Asp$_{perfect(?)}$ [*just* Asp$_{retrospective}$ [*soon* Asp$_{proximative}$ [*briefly* Asp$_{durative}$ [*characteristically*(?) Asp$_{generic/progressive}$ [*almost* Asp$_{prospective}$ [*completely* Asp$_{SgCompletive(I)}$ [*tutto* Asp$_{PlCompletive}$ [*well* Voice [*fast/early* Asp$_{celerative(II)}$ [*again* Asp$_{repetitive(II)}$ [*often* Asp$_{frequentative(II)}$ [*completely* Asp$_{SgCompletive(II)}$

One of the early attempts to apply the cartographic approach to sign language was Bross and Hole (2017), and soon other researchers began to adopt this approach (Karabüklü et al. 2018; Crabtree et al. 2018; Salazar-García 2018; Crabtree 2020). Bross and Hole (2017) demonstrated that scope relations of different expressions of modality in German Sign Language (DGS) can be effectively described by cartography. Bross (2020) more fully investigated functional heads in the higher and lower CP regions, using the data of multiple spoken and signed languages in addition to DGS. He proposed the bodily-mapping hypothesis, which states that the range of semantic scope of modal expressions systematically corresponds to the location on the body of the articulators employed. For example, an articulator such as the eyebrows scopes over a lower articular such as the hands (Bross 2020: 275).

Japanese Sign Language (JSL henceforth) is one of the sign languages which uses manual modal verbs to express epistemic modality. The current study is an attempt to provide descriptions of expressions of modality in JSL, based on the framework of the cartography of syntactic structure in Cinque (1999).[1] As described in the following sections, we considered word-order interactions of JSL modal verbs and two types of negation, inspired by the method adopted in previous studies of modality in spoken Japanese.

As we leave the introductory section, a brief introduction to JSL is in order. JSL refers to the language acquired and used by the deaf Japanese who were exposed to the language since birth. An earlier version of JSL has developed into the language of the deaf community by 1878, which was used as a language of instruction at the first school for the deaf and blind (Yonekawa 1984; Ito 1998;

---

[1] Crabtree (2020) independently applied Cinque's hierarchy to re-categorize modal expressions based on the JSL modal analyses provided in Matsuoka (2016, 2017).

Kimura 2011). JSL is fundamentally different from spoken Japanese in phonology, syntax, semantics, and discourse (Yonekawa 1984; Ichida 2010; Oka and Akahori 2011; Matsuoka 2015, etc.). The number of native signers of JSL is far smaller than non-native signers (the deaf born to hearing parents). Though there are no official statistics for native JSL signers, the number of users of JSL is estimated to be 35,000–57,000, which is approximately 10% of the deaf and hard-of-hearing population in Japan (Ichida et al. 2001; Kanda, Kimura, and Hara 2008). The status of JSL is overshadowed by the political supremacy of manually coded Japanese (sign-supported Japanese, typically referred to as *nihongo taio shuwa* [sign language corresponding Japanese]). Nevertheless, native and near-native signers have formed organizations to study and promote JSL, at least in urban areas.[2]

JSL declaratives follow the basic SOV word order (Yonekawa 1984; Ichida 2010; etc.), which may undergo alterations caused by information-structure, such as the topic-comment sequence. Modal verbs[3] follow the main verb. In the following example, the proposition TANAKA GO is followed by the modal verb REAL 'surely'.

(2) TANAKA GO REAL
 'I'm sure that Tanaka goes/went.'

Even though the modal verb typically appears in the sentence-final position in the surface structure, we will demonstrate that there are multiple positions available for modal verbs in the right periphery of a JSL sentence.

The organization of the paper is as follows. In Section 2, results of the previous research of word-order phenomena of modal verbs in spoken Japanese and JSL are briefly summarized. Two types of negation will be introduced in Section 3. They play an important role to establish the order of constraints among modal verbs in JSL. After that, linguistic descriptions of three categories of modal verbs in JSL are presented in Section 4. The final section is the conclusion with issues raised for future research.

---

[2] A detailed overview of the history of JSL, written in English, can be found in Nakamura (2006). Readers should note, however, that the two NHK TV shows described in chapter 11 (*Everyone's Sign* and *Sign News*) have been reformed in later years and now feature authentic JSL.

[3] The term 'modal verb' is used to refer to the signed expressions of modality. However, as Quer et al. (2017: 119) mentions, their verbal status is 'may yet have to be determined'.

2 Previous studies of modality in Japanese and JSL

2.1 Spoken Japanese

In the tradition of Japanese linguistics, epistemic modality was often associated with subjectivity (the speaker's judgment or attitude toward the proposition). Though researchers agree that subjectivity does not directly translate to modality (Takubo 2009), it has been widely recognized that subjectivity plays an important role in the syntactic behavior of epistemic modals (Masuoka 1991; Nitta 1991; Inoue 2007). Based on the degrees of subjectivity, epistemic modals have been classified into Quasi and True modals. According to Halliday, modality refers to "the speaker's assessment of probability and predictability" (Halliday 1970: 349), while modulation (quasi-modalities) is "a characterization of the relation of the participant to the process – his ability to carry it out" (Halliday 1970: 349). In other words, modulation is a quasi-modality which is not necessarily connected to the subjectivity.[4] Because quasi-modals in Japanese do not state the speaker's own judgement or attitude toward proposition, it may be denied by the negation morpheme and/or modified by the tense morpheme, as shown in examples (3–4). Halliday's distinction between True and Quasi modals has been widely assumed in studies of modality in Japanese linguistics.

Researchers, in recent years, have adopted the syntactic approach to study modals in Japanese (Inoue 2007; Ueda, 2007; Saito 2015). By using syntactic tests with different ordering of modals, negation, and the tense morpheme, they confirmed that True and Quasi modals were distinct syntactic categories. First, the Quasi modal *yoo* ('seem'), in (3a), may be followed by the negation morpheme *-nai* ('not'), which is not possible for the true modal *daroo* ('would be the case'), as shown in (3b).

(3) a. Hanako-wa   kuru   yoo-dewa-**nai**   (Quasi modal)
       Hanako-TOP   come   yoo-NEG[5]
       'It does not seem that Hanako comes.'

---

4 Chapin (1973: 8) also argues for treating expressions such as *has to* as a Quasi modal. For the sentence *John has to go*, the Quasi modal describes "a particular sort of relation between John and the act of going, a modality of the proposition".
5 TOP: topic, NEG: negation, PAST: past-tense morpheme, ACC: accusative, NML: nominalizer, COP: copula.

b. *Hanako-wa   kuru   daroo-**nai**   (True modal)
   Hanako-TOP   come   daroo-NEG
   'It would not be the case that Hanako comes.'
   (cf. Hanako-wa ko-nai daroo 'It would be the case that Hanako does not come.')

Moreover, the following examples show that Quasi modals (4a), but not True modals (4b), may be followed by the tense morpheme.

(4) a. Hanako-wa   kuru   yoo   dat-**ta**   (Quasi modal)
       Hanako-TOP   come   seem   copula-PAST
       'Hanako seemed to come.'
    b. *Hanako-wa   kuru   daroo- ta   (True modal)
       Hanako-TOP   come   would-PAST
       'Hanako would have come.'
       (cf. Hanako-wa ki-ta daroo.)

Based on those observations, Inoue (2007) argues that the Quasi modal is a type of predicate (verb), which takes IP (TP) as its complement. According to her analysis, a True modal is placed structurally higher than a Quasi modal, which results in the linear ordering of Quasi-True in a sentence, but not vice versa. To sum up, Quasi and True modal expressions are ordered as below.

(5) Quasi modals<negation<tense<True modals

As the framework of cartography is widely adopted in the analysis of different languages, observations made in the traditional Japanese linguistics were re-interpreted further. Based on the syntactic restrictions observed with various grammatical elements, including modal particles and adverbial clauses, Endo (2007, 2012a, 2012b, 2014) proposed the hierarchical ordering of functional heads in Japanese as in the following (Endo 2012a: 366):

(6) Voice<Aspect<Polarity (Negation)<Tense<Speaker's Mood<Interpersonal Mood

The syntactic analysis based on the ordering patterns is applicable to the study of JSL. We will now turn to the analysis of modal verbs in JSL.

2.2 JSL modality project: Interaction of modal expressions and negation

Our JSL modality project was initiated in 2013, based on the observation made in spoken Japanese. Our research questions are as follows:
(i) Which signs express negation and epistemic modality in JSL?
(ii) What are the syntactic and semantic properties of JSL modal verbs?

Throughout the project, the grammatical judgement data were collected from two native signers (including the co-authors Yano and Maegawa) who were born and raised in deaf families. One of the original deaf co-researchers was replaced by a person with similar background. Both current deaf co-authors are bimodal bilinguals (of JSL and written Japanese) with graduate degrees, whose first (the most dominant) language is JSL. They have experience in participating in or conducting linguistic research projects and are considered as representative JSL signers in the community of JSL signers in Japan.

Ten modal verbs were identified in early works of the author's group (Akahori et al. 2013; Matsuoka et al. 2016).[6] Those modal verbs were numbered by the order of the strength of the speaker's belief about the validity of the proposition. All of the signs were considered to be expressions of epistemic modality since they can modify a JSL proposition without an agent with volition such as AME-FURU '(It) rains'. In addition, the speaker's attitude can be modulated with different degrees of epistemic non-manuals (eye gaze and head tilts). With a diverted eye gaze and a head tilt, for example, the speaker's commitment regarding the factual validity of the proposition is weakened (to be discussed more in Section 5).

There is an ordering pattern among different types of modal verbs in JSL. The reversed order of the modal verbs DECIDE and REAL leads to the ungrammaticality of the sentence, as shown in (7):

(7) a. MAN COME DECIDE REAL
      'It is for sure that the man is definitely coming.'
    b. *MAN COME REAL DECIDE

Based on the grammaticality judgements about possible orderings of multiple modal verbs, Matsuoka, Yano and Maegawa 2016 classified the ten modal verbs

---

[6] The list of ten modal verbs is never meant to be exhaustive. There are other signs such as THINK, which indicates much less commitment of the speaker than the Japanese equivalent. Another relevant expression is SORT-OF (/mitai/ in Japanese gloss), which have at least two different regional variations (Matsuoka, Yano and Maegawa 2016).

into three groups. In Table 1, below, the Japanese gloss of the JSL sign is given in italics with forward slashes (e.g., /kimari/), while the English gloss is given in the standard style for sign language glossing, all capital letters (e.g., DECIDE).

Table 1: Three categories of JSL modal verbs (cf. Matsuoka, Yano and Maegawa 2016: 9).

	Modal verbs	Ordering restrictions
Type 1	DECIDE /kimari/, SHOULD /beki/, PLAN /yotei/, IMAGINE /sozo/	May be followed by Types 2 and/or 3
Type 2	MEAN /imi/, SEEM /yoo/, NO-ERROR /chigainai/,	May be followed only by Type 3
Type 3	REAL /honto/, DIFFER /chigau/, NO-IDEA /fumei/	May not be followed by any modal verbs

The three categories of modal verbs follow the ordering pattern in (8).

(8) VP>Type 1>Type 2>Type 3

The next step would be identifying the functional head corresponding to each type. Though JSL does not have an overt tense marker, the perfective mouth gesture "pa" (Kimura 2011) provides us with a clue. As seen in the following example, the mouth gesture may co-occur only with the modal of Type 1, which indicates that it appears in a syntactic position within the range of (i.e., syntactically lower than) the Aspect head.

(9)   *____pa   ____pa   *____pa
        MAN COME   DECIDE   MEAN
        'It's that the man certainly has shown up.'
        (Matsuoka, Yano and Maegawa 2016: 10)

In the following section, we will demonstrate that the ordering patterns between modal verbs and negation will provide us with further evidence for placing Type 1 modals lower than the other two types. After providing descriptions of two types of negation, we will demonstrate how those negation signs interact with modal verbs in terms of word order.[7] As will be shown below, negation plays an important role to determine the ordering of different types of modal expressions.

---

[7] We excluded NO-ERROR /chigai-nai/ from the current research since it is a compound consisting of two words. The semantic and syntactic status of this signed expression is left for future research.

3 Negation in JSL and the word-order constraints

JSL has various signs to express negative meaning, which have not been fully investigated in linguistic studies.[8] We also need to note that these "negation signs" are sometimes glossed differently by individual researchers. The glosses chosen in our project and used in Matsuoka, Yano and Maegawa (2016) are as follows: NOT /nai/, NO-WAY /iyaiya/, and DIFFER /chigau/. As Ichida (2005: 90) noted, the basic negator is NOT, which negates existence, while NO-WAY is associated with a negative habit or personal preference or value. Ichida (2005) and Matsuoka (2015) independently argue that DIFFER is an expression of metalinguistic negation (to be discussed later).

In this section, two expressions of negation, NOT and DIFFER, will be described. The third expression mentioned above, NO-WAY /iyaiya/, does not indicate any systematic ordering patterns with NOT, DIFFER, or modal verbs, and thus requires a different approach to investigate its syntactic properties.

3.1 Two types of negation in JSL

The standard sign of negation in JSL is NOT /nai/ (Figure 1). All fingers are extended and spread apart (similar to the handshape 🖐). Both hands are repeatedly waved with quick twisting at the wrists.[9]

---

[8] Morgan (2006: 112) presented descriptions of ten "negative signs", identified in his own video corpus as well as in other previous studies of JSL. However, he did not clearly distinguish negation markers such as NOT or DIFFER from lexical signs with negative meaning (e.g., NOT-YET, NOT-ABLE).

[9] It is not totally clear from previous research if the non-manual expression of negation (side-to-side headshake) is required in JSL negation. Based on the claim in Morgan (2006) that the headshake is "not mandatory" (Morgan 2006: 111), Zeshan (2006) classifies JSL (which she refers to by the Japanese name *Nihon Shuwa*) as one of the sign languages with the "manual dominant system" of negation and "clause cannot be negated non-manually only, a manual negator is required" (Zeshan (2006: 43, Table 2). On the contrary, Akahori et al. (2000), based on the data from their corpus of natural conversation of four deaf participants, claim that the non-manual expression (side-to-side headshake) does not have to occur with the manual sign of negation. The grammatical judgements informally collected on our own, using minimally different sentences such as the ones in (i), below, indicate that JSL is not either manual or non-manual dominant: a sentence can be negated with manual-only, non-manual only, or both.

(i) a. MAN COME NOT 'The man does/did not come.'
    ___neg
 b. MAN COME 'The man does/did not come.'
    ___neg
 c. MAN COME NOT 'The man does/did not come.'

Further study of non-manual expression of negation is beyond the scope of the current study.

Figure 1: NOT /*nai*/.

When used without a predicate, it negates the existence of the person or the item.

(10)   TANAKA NOT
        'Tanaka is not here.'

As indicated by the translation in the following example, NOT can also negate the semantic content of the VP.

(11)   TANAKA COME NOT
        'Tanaka is not coming.' or 'Tanaka does/did not come.'

The second sign of negation is DIFFER /*chigau*/ (Figure 2). The dominant hand, with the index finger and the thumb extended, while other fingers are closed against the palm (handshape), is quickly flipped, or repeatedly wiggled at the wrist. This sign is frequently accompanied by the mouth gesture "ii", particularly when it is signed with quick, repeated movements.

Figure 2: DIFFER /*chigau*/.

The same sign may be interpreted as the adjective DIFFERENT[10] (e.g. JAPAN AMERICA DIFFERENT 'Japan and America are different'.)

DIFFER can also follow the noun, as shown in (12a) below:

(12) a. BOOK DIFFER
 'It is not the book.'
 b. BOOK NOT
 'The book does not exist (the book is not here.)'

As indicated in the English translation, DIFFER negates the proposition equivalent to "(It) is a book". In fact, DIFFER is the expression of metalinguistic negation (Ichida 2005, Matsuoka 2015). In the following example of a conversation between two persons, the speaker A used DIFFER to indicate the utterance of the other speaker (B) is incorrect. Note that NOT is not a possible choice here.

(13) A: IX$_3$ STUDENT 'S/he is a student.'
 B: DIFFER '(That is) wrong.' *NOT

In addition, Matsuoka (2015: 72) reports that DIFFER may be used to give a correction of non-linguistic body movements (e.g., when a tennis coach is teaching how to swing the racket). Such an example also suggests that DIFFER is an expression of meta-linguistic negation.

Both NOT and DIFFER may be used in a sentence, though they are not construed as negative concord reported in previous studies such as Makharoblidze and Pfau (2018). As indicated in the translation, DIFFER negates the proposition containing NOT.[11]

(14) a. MAN COME NOT DIFFER
 'It's not that he is not coming.'
 b. *MAN COME DIFFER NOT
 (No coherent meaning)

Now, we will look at the ordering restrictions between the two types of negation, introduced in this section, and JSL modal verbs.

---

10 There is a two-handed version of DIFFER, though the one-handed sign is used more frequently, either as a main verb or a sign of negation.
11 Note that the sentence contains the negation marker DIFFER, not the modal verb DIFFER-PE (accompanied with the mouth gesture "pe"). DIFFER-PE will be introduced in Section 4.

3.2 Interaction of negation and modal verbs

The interaction of the two types of negation and modal verbs shows systematic ordering patterns. As shown in the following examples, DECIDE must be followed by NOT, while REAL must precede it.

(15) a. MAN COME DECIDE NOT
'It's not certain that he is coming.'
b. *MAN COME REAL NOT
'It's not that he is surely coming.'

(16) a. *MAN COME NOT DECIDE
'He is absolutely not coming.'
b. MAN COME NOT REAL
'He is surely not coming.'

In contrast, DECIDE must precede DIFFER.

(17) a. TANAKA COME DECIDE DIFFER
'It's not that Tanaka certainly comes.'
b. *TANAKA COME DIFFER DECIDE
(No coherent meaning)

DIFFER may follow any modal verb. This can be expected from the fact that it is a meta-linguistic negation.

(18) a. TANAKA COME TRUE DIFFER
'It's not that Tanaka absolutely comes.'
b. *TANAKA COME DIFFER TRUE
'Absolutely, Tanaka does not come.'

The grammatical judgements of sentences with all possible combinations of modal verbs and negation can be summarized in the following hierarchy (Matsuoka, Yano, and Maegawa 2017):

(19) VP<Type 1<NOT<Type 2<Type 3<DIFFER

It was confirmed that Type 1 modal verbs take a syntactically lower position than the other two types. However, there are many unresolved issues with the pattern summarized in (19): which functional category is Type 1? Why do Types 2 and

3 need to be separated, which is not predicted under the two-way ("Quasi" or "True") distinction of modals in Japanese? We now need to consider the semantic properties of the three categories to determine which functional categories they belong to. We will argue that the three types of JSL epistemic modals correspond to different categories that follow Cinque's (1999) hierarchy.

4 Expressions of epistemic modality in JSL

Based on the syntactic constraints on word-order patterns, nine manual expressions of epistemic modality in JSL are now re-interpreted as in the following:[12]

    Type 1. Possibility (Mod$_{possibility}$): DECIDE, SHOULD, IMAGINE, PLAN
    Type 2. Evidential (Mod$_{evidential}$): MEAN, SEEM
    Type 3. Epistemic (Mod$_{epistemic}$): REAL, NO-IDEA, DIFFER-PE

The modality of possibility (Mod$_{possibility}$) appears in the lowest position among three groups of modals. Type 3 modals, which takes the highest syntactic position, are assumed to be epistemic modals (Mod$_{epistemic}$). We will argue that the usage of Type 2 modals is sensitive to the availability of evidence, and hence they can be classified into evidential modals (Mod$_{evidential}$). The re-labeled hierarchy, which contains NOT and DIFFER, would be as follows:

(20)   VP<Modal of possibility (Mod$_{possibility}$)<NOT<evidential (Mod$_{evidential}$)<epistemic modality (Mod$_{epistemic}$)<DIFFER

As will be shown, many of the modals to be discussed are also used as lexical signs (verbs, nouns, adjectives).[13] The modal and non-modal uses of the same sign can, however, be distinguished with different non-manual expressions in many cases. Considering the historical development of sign languages reported in previous studies such as Shaffer (2002, 2004), we assume that JSL modal verbs have emerged through grammaticalization of lexical signs. See Section 5 for more discussion.

---

12 It is not realistic to accurately translate the intricate nuance of the modality into a different language, and hence the English translations in the following examples should be taken as approximations.
13 In her discussion of JSL data, Engberg-Pederson (2020: 34) independently argued that SENSE (labeled as MEAN in the current study) and DIFFERENT (labeled DIFFER in the current study) were developed from lexical sources.

In Sections 4.1 and 4.2, we will first provide linguistic descriptions of possibility and epistemic modals. In Section 4.3, we will discuss evidential modals, which are sensitive to the availability of evidence.

4.1 Modal verbs of possibility (Mod_possibility)

In this section, four modal verbs of possibility are introduced: DECIDE /kimari/, SHOULD /beki/, IMAGINE /sozo/, and PLAN /yotei/.

4.1.1 DECIDE /kimari/ 'certainly'

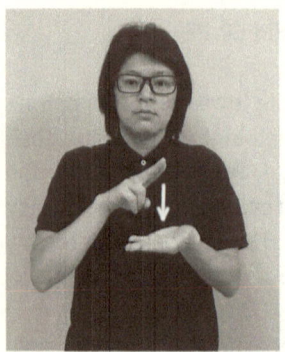

Figure 3: DECIDE /kimari/ 'certainly'.

DECIDE /kimari/ 'certainly' (Figure 3) indicates that the speaker is fairly sure about the factual status of the proposition. The dominant hand with the index and middle fingers extended together (handshape ✌) sharply hits the palm of the non-dominant hand.

(21)   MAN COME DECIDE
       'The man is certainly coming.'

The same sign may be used as a verb DECIDE or as a noun DECISION.

(22)   MAN COME DECIDE
       'The man decided to come.'

(23) SELECT DECISION
'The decision was made about selecting a person/thing.'

There are different non-manual features that co-occur with DECIDE, depending on whether the sign is used as a modal verb or lexical item (noun or verb). When DECIDE is used as a modal verb, Japanese-based mouthing[14] "kimari ('to decide, decision')" typically co-occurs, and there is no break allowed between the verb and the modal. On the other hand, the different mouth gesture "mm" is optionally used when the same sign is used as a noun or a verb. Moreover, there may be a prosodic break before DECIDE. The non-manuals associated with the different use of the sign are summarized in Table 2.

Table 2: Non-manuals for the different uses of DECIDE.

	Modal ('certainly')	Verb/Noun ('to decide, decision')
Prosodic features	No break allowed between the main verb and the modal	A prosodic break is possible before DECIDE
Typical mouth actions	Japanese mouthing *kimari* ('to decide, decision')	Mouth gesture 'mm'

4.1.2 SHOULD /*beki*/ 'should/ is supposed to'

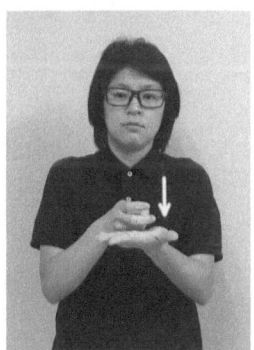

Figure 4: SHOULD /*beki*/ 'should'.

---

14 It is not unusual that mouthing indicates abstract grammatical features (in this case, indicating the sign expresses epistemic modality). Matsuoka (2021) discussed examples of mouthing-based mouth gestures, which were originally taken from the ambient spoken language, but later acquired grammatical properties unique to the sign language.

The usage of SHOULD /*beki*/ (Figure 4) indicates that the speaker feels that s/he can reasonably expect the content of the proposition to be realized. The dominant hand with the index and middle finger bent (handshape) is lightly tapped on the palm of the non-dominant hand.

(24)   MAN COME SHOULD
       'The man is should/supposed to come.'

SHOULD can be used to express deontic modality.

(25)   MAN COME SHOULD
       'The man is obliged to come.'

The same sign may be used as a noun (often glossed as LAW 'law'). When the sign is used as a noun, it is typically signed with two repeated small movements, which are widely reported as a characteristic of nouns in sign languages (Supalla and Newport 1978).

(26)   LAW EXIST
       'There is a law.'

4.1.3 IMAGINE /*sozo*/ 'could be/maybe'

Figure 5: IMAGINE /*sozo*/ 'could be'.

The use of IMAGINE /*sozo*/ (Figure 5) indicates that the speaker has clear evidence or a reason to believe that the content of the proposition is likely to occur (the meaning similar to *imaginable* in English). The dominant hand, loosely opened with all fingers bent (similar to the handshape), bounces upward from the temple of the signer.

(27) MAN COME IMAGINE
   'The man may come.'

Similar to other signs for weaker commitment (SEEM and NO-IDEA, to be introduced later), it is signed with light, repeated movements.

When the same sign is used as a verb ('to imagine'), however, it is signed with one movement, which is widely observed as a typical pattern of verbs in sign languages (Supalla and Newport 1978).

(28) FUTURE IMAGINE
   'I imagine the future.'

4.1.4 PLAN /yotei/ 'expectedly'

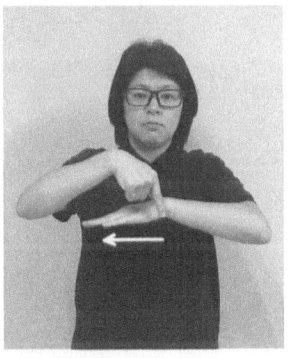

Figure 6: PLAN /yotei/ 'expectedly'.

PLAN /yotei/ (Figure 6) expresses a moderate expectation of the speaker about the content of the proposition being realized. The dominant hand with the index finger extended (handshape) touch the ulnar side of the non-dominant hand and is moved horizontally (from the base to the tip).

(29) MAN COME PLAN
   'The man is expected to come.'

The same sign may be used as the noun ('a plan').

(30) PLAN EXIST
 'I have a plan.'

Compared to other modal verbs in the same category, PLAN seems to show a weaker ordering effect with DECIDE. The reason for the weaker effect is left for further research.

(31) a. MAN COME DECIDE PLAN
 'It is supposed to be the case that the man is absolutely coming.'
 b. ??MAN COME PLAN DECIDE
 'The man is supposed to come, absolutely.'

In the following section, modal verbs of epistemic state ($Mod_{epistemic}$) will be introduced. Grammaticality judgement data of native signers collected in the current study suggest strongly that they appear in a structurally higher position than $Mod_{possibility}$.

4.2 Modal verbs of epistemic state ($Mod_{epistemic}$)

In this section, three modal verbs of epistemic state are introduced: REAL /*honto*/, NO-IDEA /*fumei*/, and DIFFER-PE /*chigau-pe*/.

4.2.1 REAL /*honto*/ 'really, surely'

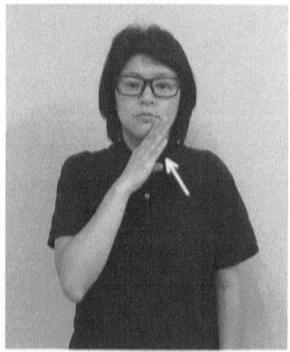

Figure 7: REAL /*honto*/ 'really, surely'.

REAL /honto/ (Figure 7) indicates that the speaker is fairly certain about the factual status of the proposition. The dominant hand with all fingers and the thumb extended straight (handshape 👋) lightly taps the chin in one movement.

(32) MAN COME REAL
      'The man is surely coming.'

The same sign may be used as the adjective ('true').

(33) IX$_2$ $_2$EXPLAIN$_1$ REAL[15]
      'What you said was true.'

4.2.2 NO-IDEA /fumei/ 'maybe'

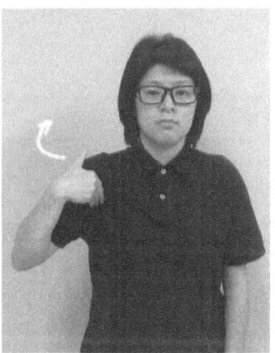

Figure 8: NO-IDEA /fumei/ 'maybe'.

All fingers are bent at the base and the thumb is extended up (handshape 🤟). The fingertips brush the ipsilateral side of the shoulder, in two light and quick upward movements. This is one of the two signs which are typically translated as 'maybe'. According to the follow-up interview in Matsuoka, Yano and Maegawa (2016), NO-IDEA /fumei/ (Figure 8) indicates that the speaker's degree of confidence is 50% (i.e., no commitment to the content of the proposition).

---

15 Numbers in subscript refers to first (1), second (2), third (3)-person, respectively. For example, IX$_2$ refers to the pointing toward the hearer. $_2$EXPLAIN$_1$ is a gloss of agreeing verbs (Padden 2018 [1983]), which is an equivalent to an expression in English such as 'you tell (something) to me.'

(34) MAN COME NO-IDEA
'The man might come.'

NO-IDEA is phonologically identical to the JSL sign DON'T-KNOW.

(35) ANSWER DON'T-KNOW
'(I) don't know the answer.'

Signers use mouthing to distinguish the usage (NO-IDEA 'maybe' vs. DON'T-KNOW 'don't now'). The Japanese mouthing *kamo* ('maybe') typically accompanies NO-IDEA, which is signed with one brushing movement (though one informant noted that even when the sign is used as a modal expression, the movements may be repetitive.) On the other hand, the mouth gesture "he" or "ho" is typically used for DON'T-KNOW, though one informant reported that the Japanese mouthing *wakaranai* ('I don't know') may be used instead. The information is summarized in the following table:

Table 3: Distinguishing NO-IDEA/DON'T-KNOW as a modal or a verb.

	Modal ('maybe')	Verb ('do not know')
Mouth action	The Japanese mouthing *kamo* ('maybe')	Mouth gesture 'he', 'ho', or Japanese mouthing *wakaranai* ('I don't know')
Phonological features	One movement	At least two small, repeated movements

4.2.3 DIFFER-PE /*chigau-pe*/ 'isn't it?'

DIFFER-PE /*chigau-pe*/[16] is also used to confirm the speaker's guess, with non-manual expressions similar to the ones for asking a polar question (eyebrow raise, wide-open eyes). The handshape and movement are virtually identical to the negation DIFFER, introduced in Section 3.1. When it is used as a modal verb, the dominant hand (handshape 👆) is flipped in one movement, and the mouth gesture "pe" typically appears (note that the negator DIFFER is accompanied by a different mouth gesture of "ii", as mentioned in the section 3.1.).

(36) MAN COME DIFFER-PE
'I guess the man comes.'

---

16 We chose to mention the mouth gesture "pe" in the gloss, since it is the only (and the most notable) difference from a similar sign of negation DIFFER.

As seen in the following example, the sentence which contains DIFFER-PE cannot be negated by DIFFER. Hence, the mouth gesture "pe" is possibly a non-manual affix of modality, attached to the negation marker DIFFER.

(37) *MAN COME DIFFER-PE DIFFER
'(lit.) It's not the case that I thought the man is coming.'
(cf. MAN COME DIFFER DIFFER-PE 'Isn't it that the man does not come?')

It is not uncommon that the meta-negation has multiple grammatical functions, particularly when it is marked with a prosodic cue. In the following example of spoken Japanese, the negative sentence (38a) can be converted to the confirming question with the rising intonation at the end of the sentence.

(38) a. Tanaka-ga   kuru-n-ja-nai
       Tanaka-NOM   come-NML-COP-NEG
       'It's not the case that Tanaka comes.'
     b. Tanaka-ga   kuru-nja-nai? (with the rising intonation)
       Tanaka-NOM   come-NML-COP-NEG
       'Isn't it the case that Tanaka comes?'

The addition of the mouth gesture "pe" to DIFFER in JSL could be an instance of prosodic alteration comparable to the intonation in Japanese. We will leave this issue open for future research.

Modal verbs of evidentiality in JSL appear in a lower position than modality of possibility as shown in (39):

(39) Modal of possibility ($Mod_{possibility}$)>NOT> evidential modality ($Mod_{evidential}$)> epistemic modality ($Mod_{epistemic}$)>DIFFER

Finally, we will give descriptions of expressions of evidential ($Mod_{evidential}$). Crucially, we assume that there is a class of modal verbs of evidential, which takes a position lower than Mood in Cinque's hierarchy.

4.3 Modal verbs of evidentiality ($Mod_{evidential}$)

Evidential refers to the system with which the speaker indicates the evidence when they make judgements about the content of the proposition. It is "a linguistic category whose primary meaning is source of information" (Aikhenvald 2004: 3). Direct or indirect evidence frequently affects the epistemic state of the speaker. For example, the modal verb in English *must* indicates that the speaker has evidence to be sure about the factual status of the proposition. For example, when the speaker states *John must be in his office*, s/he has evidence to make judgement, such as noting that the lights of John's office are on (Palmer 2001). Languages show a wide variety of methods to express evidentiality. Hence, some researchers do not consider the grammatical category of evidential as 'modality' (Murray 2017). In the history of Japanese linguistics, evidentiality is mentioned in discussions of a variety of grammatical categories (Nihongo Kijutsu Bunpo Kenkyukai 2003; Takubo 2009), which indicates that it does not always constitute a single functional head.

Results of our previous research (Matsuoka, Yano, and Maegawa 2016) revealed that MEAN /*imi*/ and SEEM /*yoo*/ can be separated from other modal verbs, because the signer may use them when a hearsay is the only available evidence ("reported evidence" in Palmer's (2001) terminology).

(40) a. OLDER-SISTER CAKE EAT MEAN
'It's that the older sister eats/ate the cake.'
b. OLDER-SISTER CAKE EAT SEEM
'It seems that the older sister eats/ate the cake.'

Moreover, those two modal verbs belong to Type 2, which takes a syntactic position lower than Mod$_{epistemic}$ (i.e., Type 3). Based on their semantic and syntactic properties, we will classify MEAN and SEEM as a separate category of modal verbs, which is sensitive to the availability of hearsay as evidence.

4.3.1 MEAN /*imi*/ 'meant to'

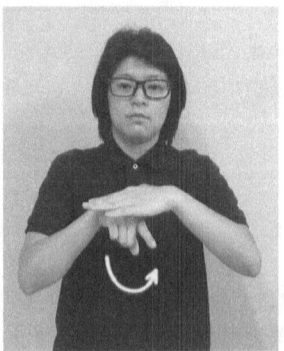

Figure 9: MEAN /*imi*/ **'meant to'**.

MEAN /imi/ (Figure 9) indicates that the speaker is certain about the content of the proposition, which s/he is explaining to the hearer. The dominant hand with the index finger extended (handshape 🖐) passes through the space under the palm of the non-dominant hand. It may be translated to 'it is that . . .' or 'it is meant to. . .'.

(41)   MAN COME MEAN
       'It's that the man comes.'

It can be used as the verb ('to mean') or as the noun ('meaning'). There are no notable non-manuals associate with the lexical use of the sign.

(42)   MEANING UNDERSTAND
       'I understand (its) meaning.'

The same sign can be used as WHY when it is combined with the non-manuals for wh-questions (i.e., eyebrow raise or furrow with a quick horizontal headshake).

(43)   ___wh
       MAN   COME   MEAN?
       'Why did/does the man come?'

4.3.2 SEEM /yoo/ 'seem'

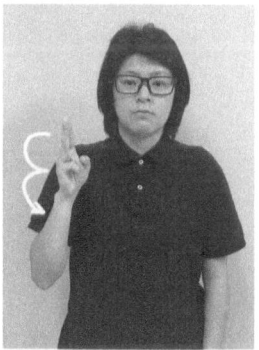

Figure 10: SEEM /yoo/ 'seem'.

SEEM /yoo/ (Figure 10) indicates that the speaker is uncertain about the factual status of the proposition. The dominant hand with the index and middle fingers extended (handshape 🖐) undergoes a bouncing downward movement. According to the interview with twenty native JSL speakers in Matsuoka, Yano and Maegawa (2016), the possibility that the content of the proposition would be true was about 50%. This sign cannot be used in any other lexical categories.

(44) MAN COME SEEM
'The man seems to come.'

MEAN and SEEM must follow the negation marker NOT, as shown in the following examples.

(45) a. *MAN COME MEAN NOT
'(lit.) It's not that the man comes/came.'
b. MAN COME NOT MEAN
'It's that the man does/did not come.'

(46) a. *MAN COME SEEM NOT
'(lit.) It does not seem the man comes/came.'
b. MAN COME NOT SEEM
'It seems that the man does/did not come.'

In addition, they may not follow epistemic modals (Type 3), which means that they take a structurally lower position. The ordering we observed here (evidential being structurally lower than epistemic) does not match the ordering of epistemic and evidential proposed by Cinque (1999).

(47) a. MAN COME MEAN REAL
'Surely, it's that the man comes/came.'
b. * MAN COME REAL MEAN
'(lit.) It's that the man surely comes/came.'

(48) a. MAN COME SEEM NO-IDEA
'It seems that the man might come.'
b. *MAN COME NO-IDEA SEEM
(No coherent meaning)

We will maintain the hypothesis that the ordering of the functional heads is universal among spoken and signed languages. There are some possible interpretations of the ordering patterns observed in JSL. As discussed at the beginning of this section, evidentiality is recognized as a separate grammatical category from modality (it is a mood in the Cinque's hierarchy[17]). However, some researchers have suggested a possibility regarding syntactic positions of evidential. In his review paper, Squartini (2016: 61) stated that there are two conflicting views regarding whether the entire set of evidential functions belongs to modality or not. Hence, it could be the case that multiple functional heads, above or below $Mod_{epistemic}$, are available for expressing evidentiality. For now, we assume that there is an additional set of modal verbs which are sensitive to evidentiality, which appear in a syntactically lower position than functional head of epistemic modality. Further research is necessary to confirm the nature of the category of $Mod_{evidential}$.

5 Summary and conclusion

In this study, we investigated the syntactic positions of JSL epistemic modal verbs by considering their ordering restrictions. Based on their syntactic properties, they are now classified into the three categories: possibility ($Mod_{possibility}$), epistemic ($Mod_{epistemic}$), and evidential ($Mood_{evidential}$).

(49) **Possibility ($Mod_{possibility}$)**: DECIDE/kimari/, SHOULD/beki/, IMAGINE/sozo/, PLAN /yotei/
 Epistemic ($Mod_{epistemic}$): REAL /honto/, NO-IDEA /fumei/, DIFFER-PE /chigau-pe/
 Evidential ($Mood_{evidential}$): MEAN /imi/, SEEM /yoo/

The ordering pattern of those three types of modals and two types of negation (NOT, DIFFER) is summarized in (50):

(50) VP> Modal of possibility ($Mod_{possibility}$)>NOT> evidential ($Mod_{evidential}$)> epistemic modality ($Mod_{epistemic}$)>DIFFER

Our observations mostly match the hierarchy proposed by Cinque (1999), except the ordering between evidential and epistemic modals. The unexpected hierarchical order between $Mod_{epistemic}$ and $Mod_{evidential}$ could be a reflection of multifaceted nature of evidentiality.

Another issue to be pursued in future research is more in-depth analysis of the items currently classified into "modality of possibility ($Mod_{possibility}$)". It is

---

[17] Crabtree (2019, 2020) did not include the evidential in her analysis of modal verbs with an intention to maintain Cinque's ordering hierarchy (p.c.).

obvious that they are located syntactically lower than NEG, but it is possible that some of them belong to different categories such as modality of necessity or irrealis mood. Their syntactic interaction with the perfective aspectual marker in JSL (FINISH) and the perfective mouth gesture "pa" needs to be considered to determine their position in the Cinque's (1999) hierarchy.

The current study also revealed that some JSL signs may be used as modal verbs or lexical items. Herrero-Blanco and Salazar-García (2010) stated that modality is expressed by lexical items of verbs, nouns, adjectives, and adverbs in Spanish Sign Language (LSE). We have made a similar observation in JSL. In many cases, modal and lexical use of the JSL sign can be clearly distinguished by non-manuals including mouth actions, or movements. Such a usage of non-manuals indicates that lexical items in JSL have been in the process of undergoing phonological grammaticalization[18] to form their own grammatical category of modals.

Our findings, combined with the results of previous work in different sign languages, suggest that sign languages employ different paths to develop their own systems to express modality; some of them have non-manual expressions only, while others use a combination of manual and non-manual expressions. In her (2013) analysis of DGS, NGT, and ISL, Herrmann concluded that there were no manual equivalents to express epistemic modality in those languages. In her data sets, uncertainty was expressed by non-manuals such as slow head nods, pursed lips, and body lean, which may be accompanied by eyebrow furrow and slight squinting. In ISL, for example, body and head position shifting from one side to the other indicates the speaker's feeling of indecisiveness (Herrmann 2013: 156). She conjectures that the lack of manual signs of epistemic modality could be a universal feature of sign languages in the world.

JSL does not seem to support Herrmann's hypothesis: it has manual expressions of both deontic and epistemic modality.[19] However, non-manuals certainly play an important role in expressing modality in sign languages. While ASL has manual signs such as MAYBE, non-manuals are required for epistemic interpretation (Wilcox and Wilcox 1995: 146). Herrmann (2013: 133) states that facial expressions are used to gradually modify different degrees of uncertainty, which is similar to the observation of Shaffer (2004: 191) that non-manuals in ASL are used to change "the strength of the epistemic commitment". A similar use of non-manuals was observed in our studies of JSL. It is possible that the use of non-manuals developed from co-speech gestures, such as tilting one's head to show a weaker commit-

---

[18] Japanese mouthing consistently appears when signs are used to express epistemic modality, which implies that the modal usage could have developed later, possibly through contact with spoken Japanese.
[19] Descriptions of deontic modal verbs can be found in Matsuoka, Yano and Maegawa (2016).

ment of the speaker. Cross-linguistic comparisons suggest that sign languages have developed different ways to express epistemic modality: lexical items developed modal usage by adding designated phonological features and/or non-manuals (ASL, JSL), or non-manual expressions are used solely (DGS, NGT, ISL).

Another issue left for future research is whether JSL confirms the (potentially) universal pattern of the bodily-mapping hypothesis (Bross 2020). We did not specifically investigate the locations of non-manuals associated with items with different semantic scope in the current study. However, we did observe that the modal verbs discussed in this paper can be augmented with head-tilt and eye gaze that indicates the degree of confidence of the signer, regarding how likely the event described by the proposition is to be true (for more information, see Matsuoka et al. 2016). In their analysis of mouth gestures that co-occur with gradable adjectives, Matsuoka and Gajewski (2013: 40) presented examples in which attitudinal polarity (i.e., the signer's personal judgement about "good" or "bad") is expressed by eyebrows and eyes, while lexical polarity (i.e., polarity included in the lexical meaning of an adjectives such as *big/small*) is associated with a certain mouth gesture in an emphatic context. Those examples suggest that the height of the body part may reflect the semantic scope of linguistic expressions in different sign languages.[20]

Investigating modality is a challenging but rewarding endeavor: it illuminates possibilities regarding when cognitive state and the linguistic system interact. In spoken languages, one's epistemic state may be expressed paralinguistically with increased voice features, facial expressions, and gestures such as head tilt. Those paralinguistic aspects are also observable in sign languages, but many other non-manual components are utilized in signed communication. Modality is one of the topics which motivate cross-linguistic, as well as cross-modal, studies, which leads to a better understanding of the nature of our mind.

References

Aikhenvald, Alexandra. 2004. *Evidentiality*. Oxford: Oxford University Press.
Akahori, Hitomi, Uiko Yano, Kazumi Matsuoka & Norie Oka. 2013. Expressing modality: a descriptive study of Japanese Sign Language. Paper presented at the 147th Meeting of the Linguistic Society of Japan. Kobe City University of Foreign Studies, 23–24 November.

---

[20] In fact, in their analysis of the modal in JSL, Crabtree et al. (2018) argue that epistemic modals scope over lower produced modals. In addition, Crabtree (2019) reports that eye squint distinguishes 'possibility' and 'necessity' JSL in her analysis of 15 sentences produced by a JSL signer.

Akahori, Misato, Kazuko Noritomi, Hitomi Akahori, Minako Tsuyama & Yumiko Fukuda. 2000. *Nihon shuwa no hitei no hyogen ni kansuru kenkyu* [A study of negative expressions of Japanese Sign Language]. Paper presented at the 26th Annual Meeting of Sign Language Studies in Japan, Tokyo University of Foreign Studies, 24–25 June.

Bross, Fabian. 2020. *The clausal syntax of German Sign Language*. BoD–Books on Demand. https://refubium.fu-berlin.de/bitstream/handle/fub188/26812/978-3-96110-218-1.pdf?sequence=1&isAllowed=y

Bross, Fabian & Daniel Hole. 2017. Scope-taking strategies and the order of clausal categories in German Sign Language. *Glossa: A Journal of General Linguistics* 2(1). 76, 1–30.

Bybee, Joan, Revere Perkins & William Pagliuca. 1994. *The evolution of grammar: tense, aspect, and modality in the languages of the world*. Chicago: The University of Chicago Press.

Chapin, Paul G. 1973. Quasi-modals. *Journal of Linguistics* 9(1). 1–9.

Cinque, Guglielmo. 1999. *Adverbs and functional heads. A cross-linguistic perspective*. Oxford: Oxford University Press.

Crabtree, Margaret Ruth. 2019. Non-manual marking of the epistemic modality in Japanese Sign Language. Poster presented at the Office of Interdisciplinary Graduate Programs' Spring Reception, Purdue University, 1 May.

Crabtree, Margaret Ruth. 2020. *Universal Grammar (UG) and Japanese Sign Language (JSL)*. Purdue University major paper.

Crabtree, Margaret Ruth, Serpil Karabüklü & Ronnie B. Wilbur. 2018. Looking for Sign Language Universal in JSL Modals. Paper presented at the 7th Meeting of the Signed and Spoken Language Linguistics Conference, National Museum of Ethnology (minpaku), 29–30 September.

Engberg-Pedersen, Elisabeth. 2020. Markers of epistemic modality and their origins: Evidence from two unrelated sign languages. *Studies in Language* (Online first). https://doi.org/10.1075/sl.19065.eng.

Endo, Yoshio. 2007. *Locality and information structure: A cartographic approach to Japanese*. Amsterdam/Philadelphia: John Benjamins.

Endo, Yoshio. 2012a. The syntax-discourse interface in adverbial clauses. In Lobke Aelbrecht, Liliane Haegeman & Rachel Nye (eds.), *Main clause phenomena: New Horizons*, 365–384. Amsterdam/ Philadelphia: John Benjamins.

Endo, Yoshio. 2012b. Illocutionary force and discourse particle in the syntax of Japanese. In Werner Abraham & Elisabeth Leiss (eds.), *Modality and theory of mind elements across languages*, 405–424. Berlin/Boston: Mouton de Gruyter.

Endo, Yoshio. 2014. *Nihongo caatogurafi josetsu* [Introduction to the cartography of Japanese syntactic structures]. Tokyo: Hituzi Shobo.

Ferreira Brito, Lucinda. 1990. Epistemic, alethic, and deontic modalities in a Brazilian Sign Language. In Susan D. Fisher & Patricia Siple (eds.), *Theoretical Issues in Sign Language Research. Vol 1: Linguistics*, 229–259. Chicago & London: The University of Chicago Press.

Halliday, Michael A.K. 1970. Functional diversity in language as seen from a consideration of modality and mood in English. *Foundations of language* 6. 322–361.

Herrero-Blanco, Ángel & Ventura Salazar-García. 2010. The expression of modality in Spanish Sign Language. *Web Papers in Functional Discourse Grammar* (WP-FDG) 83. 19–42.

Herrmann, Annika. 2013. *Modal and focus particles in sign languages: a cross-linguistic study*. Boston/Berlin: Walter de Gruyter.

Ichida, Yasuhiro. 2005. Nihon shuwa no gengogaku (dai 11-kai): Bunpouka – nihon shuwa no bunpou (7): Jodousi, hiteigo, koubun-reberu no bunpouka [Sign Language Linguistics (part 11): Grammaticalization – JSL Grammar (7) Auxiliary verbs, negative words, and construction-level grammaticalization]. *Gengo* [Language] 34(11). 88–96.

Ichida, Yasuhiro. 2010. Introduction to Japanese Sign Language: iconicity in language. *Studies in Language Sciences* 9. 3–32.

Ichida, Yasuhiro, Yuka Namba, Momoko Fushihara, Mieko Miyake & Miki Yoshii. 2001. *Nihon shuwa bogo washa jinko tokei no kokoromi* [A preliminary statistics of the population of the native signers of Japanese Sign Language]. Paper presented in the 27th Annual Meeting of the Japanese Association for Sign Language Studies, Kanazawa University, 23–24 June.

Inoue, Kazuko. 2007. *Nihongo no modaru no tokucho saiko* [Reconsidering modals in Japanese]. In Hasegawa, Nobuko (ed.), *nihongo no shubun gensho: togo kozo to modariti* [Matrix phenomena in Japanese: syntactic structure and modality], 227–260. Tokyo: Hituzi Shobo.

Ito, Masao. 1998. *Rekishi no naka no roasha* [The deaf and mute in the history]. Tokyo: Kindai Shuppan.

Kanda, Kazuyuki, Tsutomu Kimura & Daisuke Hara. 2008. *Nihon no rosha jinko no suikei* [An estimate of the size of deaf population in Japan]. Paper presented at the 34th Annual Meeting of the Japanese Association for Sign Language Studies. Kobe Academic Park Association for the Promotion of Inter-University Research and Exchange UNITY Academic Community Hall, Kobe, 14–15 September.

Karabüklü, Serpil, Fabian Bross, Ronnie B. Wilbur & Daniel Hole. 2018. Modal signs and scope relations in TID. *FEAST. Formal and Experimental Advances in Sign Language Theory* 2. 82–92.

Kimura, Harumi. 2011. *Nihon shuwa to nihongo taio shuwa: aida ni aru fukai tani* [Japanese sign language and signed Japanese: a deep gap between them]. Tokyo: Seikatsu Shoin.

Makharoblidze, Tamar & Roland Pfau. 2018. A negation-tense interaction of Georgian Sign Language. *Sign Language and Linguistics* 21(1). 136–151.

Masuoka, Takashi. 1991. *Modariti no bunpo* [The grammar of modality]. Tokyo: Kurosio Publishers.

Matsuoka, Kazumi. 2015. *Nihon shuwa de manabu shuwa gengogaku no kiso* [Foundations of sign language linguistics with a special reference to Japanese Sign Language]. Tokyo: Kurosio Publishers.

Matsuoka, Kazumi. 2021. Grammatical patterns of 'mouthing-based mouth gestures' in Japanese Sign Language. A keynote talk at the ninth meeting of the Formal and Experimental Advances in Sign Language Theory (FEAST), at the Chinese University of Hong Kong (online).

Matsuoka, Kazumi & Jon Gajewski. 2013. The polarity-sensitive intensifier mouth gestures in Japanese Sign Language. *Journal of Japanese Linguistics* 29(1). 30–49.

Matsuoka, Kazumi, Uiko Yano, Hitomi Akahori & Norie Oka. 2016. Notes on Modals and Negation in Japanese Sign Language. *Studies in Language Sciences: Journal of the Japanese Society for Language Sciences* 15. 1–20.

Matsuoka, Kazumi, Uiko Yano & Kazumi Maegawa. 2016. *Nihon shuwa no modariti hyogen ni mirareru shokosei* [Evidentiality in modality expressions in Japanese Sign Language]. Paper presented at the 153th Bi-annual meeting of Linguistic Society of Japan. Fukuoka University, 3–4 December.

Matsuoka, Kazumi, Uiko Yano & Kazumi Maegawa. 2017. Modal-negation interactions in Japanese Sign Language. Poster presented at the sixth meeting of the Formal and

Experimental Advances in Sign language Theory (FEAST Reykjavik 2017), University of Iceland, 21–22 June.

Morgan, Michel W. 2006. Interrogatives and negatives in Japanese Sign Language. In Ulrike Zeshan (ed.), *Interrogative and negative constructions in sign languages*, 91–127. Nijmegen: Ishara Press.

Murray, Sarah. 2017. *The semantics of evidentials*. Oxford: Oxford University Press.

Nakamura, Karen. 2006. *Deaf in Japan: Signing and the Politics of Identity*. Ithaca: Cornell University Press.

Nihongo Kijutu Bunpo Kenkyukai [A research group of descriptive grammar of Japanese]. 2003. *Gendai nihongo bunpo 4: dai 8-bu modariti* [Grammar of modern Japanese 4: 8 Modality]. Tokyo: Kurosio Publishers.

Nitta, Yoshio. 1991. *Nihongo no modariti to ninsho* [Modality and person agreement in Japanese]. Tokyo: Hituzi Syobo.

Oka, Norie & Hitomi Akahori. 2011. *Nihon shuwa no shikumi* [Structure of Japanese Sign Language]. Tokyo: Taishukan.

Padden, Carol. 2018 [1983]. *Interaction of Morphology and Syntax in American Sign Language*. Ph.D. dissertation, UCSD. New York: Routledge.

Palmer, Frank R. 2001. *Mood and Modality*. Cambridge: Cambridge University Press.

Portner, Paul. 2009. *Modality*. New York: Oxford University Press.

Quer, Josep, Carlo Cecchetto, Caterina Donati, Carlo Geraci, Meltem Kelepir, Roland Pfau & Markus Steinbach (eds.). 2017. *SignGram Blueprint. A Guide to Sign Language Grammar Writing*. Berlin & Boston: Mouton de Gruyter.

Saito, Mamoru. 2015. Cartography and selection: case studies in Japanese. In Ur Shlonsky (ed.), *Beyond Functional Sequence*, 255–274. Oxford: Oxford University Press.

Salazar-García, Ventura. 2018. Modality in Spanish Sign Language (LSE) revisited: a functional account. *Open Linguistics* 4(1). 391–417.

Shaffer, Barbara. 2002. CAN'T: the negation of modal notions in ASL. *Sign Language Studies* 3(1). 340–353.

Shaffer, Barbara. 2004. Information ordering and speaker subjectivity: modality in ASL. *Cognitive Linguistics* 15(2). 175–195.

Squartini, Mario. 2016. Interactions between modality and other semantic categories. In Jan Nuyts & Johan van der Auwera (eds.), *Oxford Handbook of Modality and Mood*, 50–67. Oxford: Oxford University Press.

Supalla, Ted & Elissa Newport. 1978. How many seats in a chair? The derivation of nouns and verbs in American Sign Language. In Patricia Siple (ed.), *Understanding language through sign language research*, 91–132. New York: Academic Press.

Takubo, Yukinori. 2009. Conditional modality: two types of modal auxiliaries in Japanese. In Barbara Pizziconi & Mika Kizu (eds.), *Japanese modality: exploring its scope and interpretation*, 150–182. New York: Palgrave Macmillan.

Ueda, Yukiko. 2007. Nihongo no modariti no togo kozo to ninsho seigen [Syntactic structure and Restriction of person agreement of Japanese modality]. In Nobuko Hasegawa (ed.), *nihongo no shubun gensho: togo kozo to modariti* [Matrix phenomena in Japanese: syntactic structure and modality], 261–294. Tokyo: Hitsuji Shobo.

Wilcox, Sherman & Barbara Shaffer. 2006. Modality in American Sign Language. In William Frawley (ed.), *The expression of modality*, 207–237. Berlin: Mouton de Gruyter.

Wilcox, Sherman & Phyllis Wilcox. 1995. The gestural expression of modality in ASL. In Joan Bybee & Suzanne Fleischman (eds.), *Modality in grammar and discourse*, 135–162. Amsterdam: Benjamin Publishing.

Yonekawa, Akihiko. 1984. *Shuwa gengo no kijutsuteki kenkyu* [A descriptive study of sign languages]. Tokyo: Meiji Shoin.

Zeshan, Ulrike. 2006. Negative and interrogative constructions in sign languages: A case study in sign language typology. In Ulrike Zeshan (ed.), *Interrogative and negative constructions in sign languages*, 28–68. Nijmegen: Ishara Press.

Part 2: **Non-manuals and space**

Sung-Eun Hong, Seong Ok Won, Hyunhwa Lee, Kang-Suk Byun and Eun-Young Lee

The Korean Sign Language (KSL) corpus and its first application on a study about mouth actions

Abstract: KSL Corpus Project is an ongoing project and aims to create a corpus for the documentation and research of the Korean Sign Language (KSL). For this purpose, language material has been collected from 148 deaf informants at five locations since 2015, and the plan is to collect more data in the coming years. The data is collected with the help of elicitation materials that have been used in other western sign language data collections. We describe how the cultural aspect influenced the efficiency of the elicitation materials, and present how the corpus data has been annotated so far. As a first sample of corpus-based research, we will introduce a study on mouth actions in KSL. Mouth actions have not been described yet and represent a new research area in Korea. The mouth actions are grouped by their different function and their frequency distribution is compared to other sign languages.

Keywords: Korean Sign Language Corpus, elicitation material, lexical database, glosses, mouth action

1 Introduction

Korean Sign Language (KSL) is the Sign Language of the Deaf people in South Korea. Due to the Korean Sign Language Act, which was enacted in 2016, KSL has now gained legal recognition and status as an official language in South Korea. The first purpose of the Korean Sign Language Act is to declare that KSL is a language in its own right with an equal status to that of the spoken Korean language. Its second purpose is to enhance the quality of life and protect the linguistic rights of deaf communities and KSL users through a variety of KSL-related projects (Hong et al. 2019). In view of the Korean Sign Language Act, the National Institute of Korean Language (NIKL) has provided funding to build a KSL Corpus. The KSL Corpus Project began in 2015 and has been extended every year since then.

The corpus was built gradually, taking multiple steps. At the time of writing (Dec 2020), the KSL Corpus Project had collected data from 148 deaf informants in five areas of South Korea. The plan is to collect more data in the coming years.

https://doi.org/10.1515/9781501510243-007

The collected sign language data amounts to about 180 hours. Part of it has been tagged and annotated using ELAN (2021), a professional tool for the creation of complex annotations on video and audio resources developed by the Max Planck Institute of Psycholinguistics in the Netherlands.

The first part of the chapter describes the building of the Korean Sign Language Corpus with a focus on the elicitation materials used in the data collection. We will describe how we have adapted the elicitation material developed in Western countries to an East Asian cultural environment and we will present insights we gained from the process of adaptation.

The second part of this chapter will present findings based on the KSL Corpus. We decided to study the non-manual elements in KSL, because there is very little research about them in Korea. Sign Language in Korean is expressed as *suhwa* or *sueo*, which means 'hand language'. This might be a reason why the primary focus of sign language research in Korea is on the manual articulator in KSL. In this study, however, we have looked at what is probably the most prominent element of the non-manual articulator: the mouth. Our mouth action study is based on the KSL Corpus data collected in Seoul, which was the first location – and also the first annotated data – of the entire data collection.

2 Building of the KSL corpus

The term *linguistic corpus*, in this study, refers to a large-scale collection of language data in a machine-readable and machine-searchable form assembled for the purpose of studying the language. A corpus contains transcriptions and annotations in a standardized format, and the language data is associated with metadata, which gives information about the informants and the circumstances in which the data was collected (Johnston 2008, 2010). Different from a spoken language corpus, it is essential for a sign language corpus to be multimodal, because sign languages are visual-gestural languages that are typically used face-to-face. In other words, a sign language corpus must include language data in the form of videos (Johnston 2008; Schembri et al. 2013). In the past, it was almost impossible to create and manage such a large number of videos. Nowadays, thanks to the advanced technology in the field of digital video data representing and computer storage capacity, an increasing number of linguists can document sign language in the form of a corpus to conduct corpus-based research. There are numerous sign language corpus projects such as the Auslan Corpus Project (Johnston 2008), NGT Corpus Project (Crasborn and Zwitserlood 2008), DGS-Corpus Project (Prillwitz 2008; Nishio et al. 2010), BSL Corpus Project (Schembri et al. 2013), among others.

2.1 Informants and locations of the data collection

For the purpose of data collection, 148 deaf native and near-native signers were invited in pairs. Many informants have been recruited with the help of the local branches of the Korea Association of the Deaf. In the selection process, we realized how important it was to recruit the informants with the help of the Deaf Association. Not only does the Korea Association of the Deaf have an important and central role within the Deaf community and was therefore able to reach the deaf people, but also the informants then had a certain trust in the research project, knowing it was supported by the Deaf Association. In addition to the Deaf Association, a project homepage on Facebook was also used to recruit deaf people. The use of social media also served to inform deaf people about the ongoing project.

All informants were at least 19 years old. The language they use most and are most comfortable with is KSL. They have graduated from a deaf school (except for those informants born to deaf parents), and have either lived or worked in their location for at least 10 years. Another criterion was that they meet deaf people at least three times a week. Informants have been prioritized in the process of selection, depending on whether they had deaf parents, siblings or partners, as well as if they had learned KSL before they entered school.

Further information about the informants was collected with a questionnaire which was sent to them before the data collection. The informants were divided in age groups (Table 1). Among the age groups, the largest number of the informants were in their forties (47 of 148), followed by the informants in the fifties and thirties (35 and 34 of 148). The age group of the seventies has the lowest in number (4 of 148).

Table 1: Age group of the informants.

Age groups	Number of informants	Percentage
19–29	12	8%
30–39	34	23%
40–49	47	31%
50–59	35	24%
60–69	16	11%
70–79	4	3%

There are more female informants than male informants who participated in the data collection. Eighty-three (56.1%) of the informants were female and 65 (43.9%) were male informants. About two-thirds of the informants (67%) indicated that they were born deaf or became deaf before the age of three. Fifteen (10%) of the informants have a deaf father and 17 (11%) have a deaf mother. Twelve (8%) of the informants state that both of their parents are deaf.

When the informants were asked how they communicate with their mother, the answer given most often was body language/gestures (23%) and writing (18%). One-eighth (12.8%) of the informants indicated that they use spoken Korean with their mother. The communication used most often for communicating with their father is written Korean (31%), followed by body language/gestures (20.9%). Nine percent of the informants state that they use mainly spoken Korean to communicate with their father.

The questionnaire contains questions about personal information, family, language acquisition and use, education and profession, and activities in the deaf community. All of the data collected matches the IMDI metadata standards for sign language corpora proposed in Crasborn and Hanke (2003). There is a second questionnaire concerning the relationship of the two informants to each other and to the moderator. It notes (a) whether the informants knew each other and if so, how well and (b) whether the moderator knew the informants, and if so, how well. The second questionnaire[1] is important because their usage and register might change according to whether the conversation partner is well known to the informant or the moderator.

At the time of writing, data has been collected in five areas of South Korea, covering five of eight provinces in Korea. The first location where the data collection took place in 2015 is Seoul, the capital city of South Korea. Sixty informants from Seoul and the surrounding province, Gyeongi-do, participated in the data collection. In the following years, the data collection took place in the provinces Jeollabuk-do (8 informants), Jeollanam-do (46 informants), Gangwon-do (8 informants) and Gyeongsangnam-do (26 informants). The provinces Jeollabuk-do, Chungcheongbuk-do, Chungcheongnam-do and, if possible, the Island Jeju will be added to data collection locations in the coming years. The biggest drawback of this step-by-step data collection is that the data is that the time of collections are years apart. However, this is not an uncommon situation, as seen in how the Korean National Corpus, also known as the Sejong Corpus[2] was also built (NIKL 2007).

---

[1] The two questionnaires are Korean translations of the questionnaires originally used in the DGS Corpus Project.
[2] The Sejong Corpus is part of the 21st Century Sejong Project which aimed to build various kinds of language resources. The Project started in 1998 as a long-term, 10-year project and contains a collection of corpora of modern Korean (written and spoken), North Korean, Korean used abroad, old Korean, and oral folklore literature (Kang and Kim 2004).

2.2 Elicitation materials

There are many ways to collect language data from deaf signers. The KSL Corpus has used following types of elicitation materials (see Hong et al. 2009 for each type's advantages and disadvantages):
- pictures (cartoons, single drawings, picture stories, photographs)
- movies, animation
- topics for an open conversation or discussion
- combination of pictures and words
- words in written language, written texts
- signed videos

The most ideal method is certainly to develop our own materials that correspond to the local environment and culture. Due to limited resources, however, we have decided to adapt the elicitation materials from the DGS Corpus (Nishio et al. 2010) for our purpose. After two phases of testing, we shortened or adjusted some tasks in order to carry them out smoothly and efficiently in the new cultural environment, while in other cases, we removed certain tasks or replaced them with other tasks. As a result, the elicitation material of the KSL Corpus consists of 13 tasks. Each task is introduced and explained using a sign language instruction. In order to ensure that all informants receive the same input, the instructions were presented in a video. Each data collection is about three hours long with a break for twenty minutes. In the following, each task of the data collection is explained.

Task A: Sign name
In the first task, the informants are asked to show their sign names and to explain where these names come from. The task is convenient to start the session, since the informants can introduce themselves to each other. It is also a good warming up task, because usually a deaf person has explained his/her sign name numerous times, and such a familiar task made it easy for informants to do to start the data collection. The goal of the task is to collect name signs with the explanation of their origin, which play an important role in Deaf culture.

Task B: Jokes (funny stories)
Prior to the data collection, each informant is asked to prepare a joke to present to his/her partner informant on the day of filming. The idea of having one task for a prepared signing at the beginning of the session is adapted from the DGS Corpus and Auslan Archive and Corpus Projects. This task is meant to make the

informants feel confident by signing something they are familiar with. The goal of this task is also to collect Deaf jokes, which is a part of the Deaf culture.

Task C: Movie retelling

One of the informants is shown the cartoon movie clip 'Canary Row' featuring Tweety and Sylvester (Warner Brothers 1950) and asked to retell the story to the other informant. The video clip doesn't contain any spoken words and is thus suitable to use for deaf informants. This stimulus has been used in eliciting retellings in various languages and our KSL corpus can be used as a source material for cross-linguistic research. The movie is presented twice. First, the approximately six-minute video clip is shown as a whole. In the second showing, the story is divided into seven movie clips. After each section, the informant retells the respective part of the story.

Task D: Retelling of a signed story

The other informant, who was the addressee in Task C above, watches a funny story in KSL. The original story titled "how people select a tie in various countries" explains how people should choose a tie when they make a purchase. The criterion in each country points out a national characteristic of the culture. The story contains countries such as French, United States, China, and ends with the story how people in Korea select a tie. The original KSL story was broadcast in iDBN, an Internet Broadcast Network for Deaf people in Korea (cf. Figure 1). The original video is about 4.5 minutes long but was shortened to 2.3 minutes, including only the countries China, Japan and Korea. This task is the only task in which the video stimulus is in sign language.

Figure 1: How people select a tie.

Task E: Discussion
The two informants are provided with four controversial statements from which they are asked to choose one each to discuss. The aim of this task is to get the informants engaged in a discussion in which they concentrate on the content and don't think about their language use. The four discussion topics included three Deaf related issues and one general issue. All four issues were explained in KSL.

Task F: Warning and prohibition signs
In this task, the informants look at warning and prohibition signs collected from different places around the world. The informants are asked to discuss what the warning and prohibition signs could mean. Informants are not familiar with most of the signs, and they have to guess what they mean. There is no explicit answer to this task. The goal of the task is to make the informants use negated sentences. The negation occurs when the informants describe the warning signs (e.g. this sign means not to) and prohibition signs (e.g. it is forbidden to), as well as when one informant disagrees to the other informant's suggestion (e.g. 'I don't think that is what this sign means'). This task, which contains 11 warning and prohibition signs, has been adopted from the DGS Corpus Project without editing. As in the DGS Corpus Project, this task proceeded smoothly. This was the last task before the break.

Task G: Description of incidents
The informants are shown visual cues of shocking incidents, tragic accidents or moving events from the past (cf. Figure 2) and are asked to describe them to their conversation partner and to explain what they did, when they heard about the incident. The selected incidents are: the assassination of the First Lady of the Republic of Korea (1974), the Sampoong Department Store collapse (1995), a significant soccer game of World Cup 2002, the suicide of the Former President Roh Moo-Hyun (2009), the Namdaemun fire (2013) and the sinking of the ferry MV Sewol (2014). These historical incidents, which are from various decades in order to suit all ages, are named first in KSL. Immediately after that, well-known photographs of the events are presented in order to evoke memories. The goal of the task is to encourage the informants to engage in lively monologues or dialogues. The task also aims at documenting the way Deaf people, who have limited access to information, come to know the news. Often deaf people come to know news much later than hearing people, or they have to guess the details since they don't have the same amount of information available as hearing people do.

Figure 2: Description of incidents (overview slide).

Task H: Subject areas

The informants are shown various photographs and pictures from different subject areas in order to make them initiate a conversation about the shown topics. The aim of this task is to cover basic vocabulary of subjects which cannot be covered in the rest of the tasks. We prepared 12 subjects areas: weather and climate, economics, emotions and feelings, food, communication, town and country, events and celebration, vacation and leisure, fashion, religion, traffic and four seasons. Each informant chooses one subject, so the pair talks freely about two different topics. Each subject is presented with titles in Hangul and 4–8 photographs or drawings to stimulate the informant's association. If the informants are not able to keep up the conversation about the subject, the moderator helps the informants by asking related questions, which are supposed to focus on different aspects of the event and motivate the informants to pay attention to a new sub-topic related to the subject.

Task I: Elicitation of isolated signs

This is the only task in the data collection that aims at eliciting isolated signs in order to document regional sign variation. The chosen terms (e.g. aunt, bean sprouts, flavor enhancer, seven basic colors) are expected to have many different variations even in the same regional area. We don't suppose that the signs are still undergoing the process of conventionalization; we rather suspect that it is the nature of sign language that many different signs for the same meaning exist in the deaf community. Nevertheless, this task will provide valuable information about regional sign variation in Korea when the data collection continues in other areas of Korea. Each term is shown in Hangul and/or pictures and the informants are asked to show the KSL sign they use.

Task J: Deaf events
In this task, the informants are shown three different posters of Deaf events (cf. Figure 3). The three events are: World Deaf Day Event, Cultural Festival of Sign Language, and the 100th anniversary of the Seoul Deaf School. The first two events are celebrated every year in the Deaf community. The posters help to call the Deaf event to the mind of the informants. Together with Task A (Sign names) and Task M (Experience of Deaf individuals), this task is specifically related to the Deaf community, and provides good material to collect Deaf culture related sign language data.

Figure 3: Posters of Deaf events used in Task J.

Task K: Picture retellings
One informant is shown the Korean fairy tale 'Heungbu' and 'Nolbu' described in 10 pictures. Those fairy tales are well-known in Korea. First, the pictures are shown from the beginning to the end. In the second time, the pictures are shown in groups. After each group of pictures is shown, the monitor switches to black and the informant is asked to retell the respective part of the fairy tale to the other informant.

Task L: New vs. old signs
Informants are invited to show signs that have changed over time. The older generation might use a sign that is not used among the younger generations anymore. Young deaf people might use new signs that are unknown to the older deaf people. The goal of the task is to find out age-related sociolinguistic variance.

Task M: Experience in deaf school
The informants are asked to share their experiences from Deaf schools. Both informants take turns signing. Deaf schools are a location where deaf students can be together and use sign language. This task therefore aims at documenting typical experiences from Deaf lives in narratives. This task is used as the last task of the data collection because it is useful to elicit lively and spontaneous signing of informants, who might be exhausted from the data collection.

2.2.1 Cultural aspects that have influenced the efficiency of the elicitation materials

Although the elicitation materials were tested before the data collection, we noticed some points that may be relevant to cultural differences. In this section, we describe the tasks we feel have been affected by the Korean culture.

Task B: Jokes (funny stories)
It is a task which went differently from what we expected. Many informants didn't understand the term 'joke'. The KSL sign for 'joke' was ambiguous and many informants interpreted the signs as a wordplay. It is not only that some informants didn't understand that we meant a short story which ends with a punchline and makes people laugh.[3] The underlying problem is that there is not a culture (neither hearing nor deaf) in Korea where people share jokes in private settings. Most people understand a joke and even like to hear one, but they would not try to remember it because there is no opportunity to share it.

Task C: Movie retelling
It contains the 'Canary Row' featuring Tweety and Sylvester movie clip (Warner Brothers 1950) which was presented to the informants. Older informants in our data collection had problems understanding and remembering the content of the movie clip. We suppose that there are two reasons for this: first, the characters in the cartoon move very fast, because 'Canary Row' featuring Tweety and Sylvester is a story about a cat chasing a yellow bird. Second, this American cartoon is unfamiliar to the older generation, who were only exposed to Japanese and Korean cartoons in their young age. They therefore seemed to feel overburdened when they were asked to watch the American cartoon and retell it. This was

---

[3] The best evidence that such jokes exist in Korea is task D, where a deaf person is telling a joke.

different among the younger informants, who had been exposed to American cartoons in their childhood.

Task E: Discussion
It is an example that shows very strongly how much different cultural background affects the data collection. People in the Western culture are used to discussing topics from a very early age and are even taught discussion skills in school. In Korea, a country with a strong Confucianism influence, students are taught to respect the opinion of older people. Koreans do discuss issues openly, for example in the political and journalistic sector, but they are more reticent when it comes to expressing their opinions in front of older people, unknown people, and authorities. The discussion task in the data collection didn't consider this cultural aspect. If a young informant had an elder and unknown informant as a conversation partner, the Korean social manners prevented them from expressing their opinions freely, or disagreeing openly with the opinions of the older informant. Certainly, the chances to elicit an engaged discussion between the two informants is higher if the informants are similar in age, but our experience shows that same-aged pairs of informants can also have problems discussing controversial topics. Discussion seems not to be a suitable conversation form for collecting signed language data in Korea, because discussions in general take place in much more private circumstances than they do in the Western culture.

Task G: Description of incidents
The original instruction was to choose one of the incidents and to describe what they did and/or felt when they heard about the incident. Results of our first pilot test of this task showed that the deaf informants tended to describe the incidents, rather than to report what they did when they received the news. We therefore modified the instruction and left it to the informant if they wanted to describe the incident or to report what they did when they heard about it. As in the pilot test, the majority of the informants decided to describe the incidents, instead of recounting their own reaction when they heard about the news. We suppose that in the West, individuality is more emphasized and the informants are used to telling about their personal experience and opinion, while in Asian cultures the focus will be on the community, not on the individual. The Korean informants therefore seem to be more comfortable with the objectively reporting the incidents.

In task I: Elicitation of isolated signs
Some informants didn't use the sign they would ordinarily use, but rather a sign they considered as the standardized sign. In such cases, the role of the moderator was to

assure that we were interested in the sign the informants would use. The standardization of signs, as well as the standardization of Korean, has been an important issue in the Korean language policy. We suppose that this is due to the Korean cultural mindset in which standing out of the crowd makes one feel uncomfortable.

The difficulties described above did not undermine the data collection itself; the collected material still served its purpose. However, our experience shows that the testing phase needs to be much more extensive. For example, it is important that informants of different ages are made to participate in the testing phase, because the problem in Task C (movie retelling) was not observed among young informants. In the testing phase, we also did not take into account whether the informants knew each other. This made an impact on Task E (discussion).

2.2.2 Role of the moderator

The moderator's role is to make the informants feel comfortable enough, so they are to be able to sign as naturally as possible during the whole session. The informants can notify the moderator if they don't understand the instruction video of the task or if they need to watch any stimuli again. The moderator is also responsible for balancing the amount of language data each informant is uttering: if an informant's proportion of language data is much greater than that of the other informant, the moderator has to regulate the conversation by encouraging an informant to sign or by politely interrupting the signer. The challenge of the moderator is to support the informants, but also not to interfere too much, since the point is that the participants can talk to each other comfortably.

Figure 4: The moderator with two informants.

Before the data collection starts, the informants are given a consent form which allows us to use all sign language data for research purposes. The content of the consent form was translated in KSL and sent to the informants, on a CD along with the metadata questionnaire, a few days before the data collection. Because the informants had received all information ahead of time, the moderator only needed to clarify and answer additional questions about the consent form and the questionnaire. After that formality, the informants and the moderator take their seat to start the data collection (cf. Figure 4).

2.3 Studio setup

The data collection took place in a studio which was at least $32m^2$: 5.3 m wide and 6 m long. It was important that the studio is reachable by public transportation. All windows in the studio had blinds to darken the space. No hearing person was allowed to be present during the recording in the studio, which was a rule used in the DGS and BSL Corpus Projects. It is because that deaf people get influenced by spoken language (that means more code-switching between Korean and KSL) when hearing signers are present (Lucas and Valli 1992). The hearing technicians, assistants and researchers avoided being seen by the informants by staying in a separate room, where they were able to watch the recording through a monitor if necessary.

The setting of the data collection involves two informants interacting with each other and a moderator who leads the session. During a recording session, the two informants are sitting facing each other at a distance of approximately three meters. Each session was filmed with three cameras. Each informant was filmed separately with one camera, and the third camera filmed the overall scene including the moderator. The cameras for the two informants were located above each informant's head: the camera above the head of informant A filmed informant B and vice versa (cf. Hanke et al. 2010).

The moderator sat between (but off to the side) the two informants, so that all three participants of the data collection formed a triangle and could face each other easily. Each informant sat in front of his/her own monitor, since there were tasks where both informants were shown different materials. The moderator controlled the elicitation materials with two desktop computers. Each computer displayed the elicitation material and the informant's monitors mirrored the screen of the moderator's desktop computer.

A blue background screen was installed behind the two informants as well as the moderator. Five lights were used in order to control the lightening in the studio. The moderator and the informants were seated in armless chairs, in order to prevent them from resting their elbows while signing. This is because it was reported in the BSL Corpus Project group (Schembri et al. 2013) that the signers tend not to hit target locations that are higher on the body when they are resting their elbows. This would mean that resting elbows on the chair would interfere with sign language production. All informants were asked to wear plain-colored shirts, since patterned clothes make it harder for the transcriber to recognize the handshape.

3 Basic annotation and the building of a lexical database

Each session of the naturalistic, controlled, and elicited sign language sample has a length of about three hours. The video material has been cut into the length of each task, converted, compressed into MPEG format and synchronized in order to process the data with the software ELAN.[4] In ELAN is possible to add an unlimited number of annotations to a video stream. Each annotation is entered on a tier and assigned to a time interval (cf. Figure 5).

Figure 5: Annotation in ELAN.

---

4 The research group of the KSL Corpus Project has translated the interface of ELAN into Korean (Hangul). The Korean version of ELAN is available since version 4.9.3

The edited sign language data has a length of about 180 hours. The language data is collected from 148 informants and about one-third of the data is translated in Korean. Almost 23 hours of the sign language data has been annotated in ELAN. Most of the annotated data is collected in Seoul; 144 of 962 tasks are at least annotated for dominant and non-dominant hands.

The main goal of the first process of annotation is the lemmatization – the classification or identification of related word forms under a single label or lemma. Johnston (2008) sees lemmatization of a corpus as a requirement for it to become machine-readable. The KSL Corpus Project has followed Johnston (2008) by using ID glosses. An ID gloss is a "word that is used to label a sign all of the time within the corpus, regardless of what a particular sign may mean in a particular context or whether it has been systematically modified in that context" (Johnston 2008: 84).

In this sense, the basic annotation of the KSL data consists of tagging and matching signs (tokens) with its sign type using ID glosses. The annotation does not contain any phonological transcriptions such as HamNoSys. This process of lemmatization would be usually much easier when a reference dictionary or a lexical database existed, but since neither was available in South Korea,[5] it was necessary to annotate the data to establish a lexical database from scratch. The first version of such lexical database was a list of sign types created in the form of a Google Sheet, in which each sign type was linked to a video presenting the sign. Later, the Google Sheet was changed into a lexical database in the ISKSLR (Integrative System for Korean Sign Language Resources), an online platform developed for the KSL Corpus Project not only for the list of sign types, but also for the elicitation material and the KSL corpus video data with all its metadata and annotation files (see Hong et al. 2018 for further information). The lexical database in the ISKSLR keeps track of all sign types from the annotation of the KSL Corpus (KSL Online Dictionary 2022). There are no signs added from other sources (such as a sign language lexicon) and all entries of the sign type database have occurrences (tokens) from the KSL Corpus, which can also be searched in the token list of the ISKSLR. At the time of writing, the lexical database consists of 2,870 entries. A sign type entry contains the ID gloss of the sign type, a video showing the citation form of the sign type, an image of the sign type, the meaning (or Korean equivalents) of the sign type, and the name of the annotator who entered the sign type. There is no phonological information about the sign type, but a handshape of the sign can be seen in form of a drawing. It is possible to look up, for example, the history of an entry: the viewer

---

5 There are numerous KSL dictionaries in South Korea, but none of them follow lemmatization practices and are therefore not suitable for corpus purposes (see Schembri et al. 2010 and Fenlon at al. 2015 for further discussion).

can find out whether the name of the sign type has changed, or if a sign type used to be separated from or has been united with another type. This historical information, as well as the image and meaning of the sign type, have been added to the database in a later stage, so this information is not yet available for all entries.

The annotations are created by hearing and deaf annotators. The annotators are fluent in KSL, but have no previous linguistic knowledge and must therefore be trained. The annotators work at home, as the project cannot provide any workplace. They come together for training and (online) meetings if necessary.

All annotation rules of the KSL Corpus are summarized in the Annotation Conventions, which are included in the annual report of the KSL Corpus Project (see NIKL 2020 for the latest version). The KSL Annotation Conventions contain general information such as file names, name of the tiers, segmentation principles, as well as conventions on ID-glosses concerning lexicalized signs, variants, productive signs, number signs, name signs, fingerspelling, compounds and index signs. There are also annotations concerning non-manual signals and meaning and image-producing techniques (Koenig et al. 2008) described in the Annotation Conventions. In the following section, we will present results of our analysis of mouth actions in KSL, based on the data collected for our corpus project.

4 Mouth actions

As has been demonstrated for all sign languages today, sign languages are not only articulated by the signer's hand, but also by non-manual articulators, which are typically the upper part of the body, the head, the face including the mouth, cheeks, eyes and eyebrows (Pfau et al. 2012; Herrmann and Steinbach 2011). These non-manuals are usually expressed simultaneously with the manual articulators. Sign language linguists consider the role of the mouth important and have distinguished the action of the mouth into two types: mouthings and mouth gestures. Mouthings are derived from a spoken language, whereas mouth gestures are not (Boyes Braem and Sutton-Spence 2001). Although researchers in Korea (e.g. Yoon 2003) have observed mouth gestures in KSL, there has not yet been many discussion about the function of mouth gestures in KSL. Furthermore, many deaf people in Korea deny the existence of mouthing in KSL, because mouthing is generally seen as 'borrowing' from spoken Korean and not as a genuine part of KSL. Hence, our case study concerning mouth actions based on our corpus data will be a contribution to a fuller description of KSL. Our naturalistic data clearly show that mouthing is a part of the modern KSL.

In the following, we will outline the function of mouth gestures in previous studies. Then we will describe the type of annotation that we used for the corpus

data, and introduce mouth action and its occurrences in KSL. Our research deals with the following questions:
- How is the distribution between mouthing and mouth gestures and signs without mouth actions in the KSL Corpus?
- What kind of mouth gestures are found in the KSL Corpus?
- What kind of function do mouth gestures have in the KSL Corpus?
- How different is the distribution of mouth gestures in the KSL Corpus compared to those in other signed language corpora?

4.1 Mouth gestures in other sign languages

4.1.1 Types and functions of mouth gestures

Sutton-Spence and Day (2001) divided the functions of mouth gestures in British Sign Language into two functions: gestural and lexical. The gestural function is a non-verbal gesture produced by the signer, such as a smile that shows the signer's emotion while he/she is signing. Mouth gestures with a lexical function are seen as a substantial part of signs. An example is the mouth gesture which occurs together with the sign KISS showing the mouth movement in the act of kissing.

Vogt-Svendsen (2001) compared mouthings and mouth gestures in the Norwegian Sign Language and classified their functions into 1) non-morphemic functions, 2) morphemic bound morphemes, 3) morphemic free morphemes, 4) redundant function and 5) illustrator function. Vogt-Svendsen's classification can be understood as a morphological analysis of mouth actions with a lexical function. When the function of a mouth action is non-morphemic, it can be described as a phonological function. When the function of a mouth action is a morphemic bound morpheme, it usually is construed as adverbs or adjectives. The third type refers to mouth gestures that can occur by themselves without a manual articulator. Mouth actions with a redundant function appear simultaneously with the hands, but don't have their own meaning. They have a redundant function and mostly apply to mouthing. Vogt-Svendsen's last type of function seems to hold only for mouth gestures. It refers to cases in which the mouth gesture depicts the mouth of a character, described by the signer. Among KSL mouth actions ,we have observed that there are several mouth gestures which seem to belong to more than one type. One example is the KSL sign EAT. in which the mouth gesture depicts the mouth eating something. The mouth gesture in EAT also belongs to type 4, however, because it occurs simultaneously with the manual articulator and has a redundant function.

Crasborn et al. (2008) analyzes the function of the mouth actions further through a classification based on a comparative study of mouth actions in British

Sign Language (BSL), the Sign Language of the Netherlands (NGT), and Swedish Sign Language (SSL). They categorized mouth gestures into four types:

1) Adverbial mouth gestures (A-type)
This category contains mouth gestures that contribute adverbial information additional to the meaning of the manual sign. Since these kind of mouth gestures are productively combined with the manual articulator, they are usually seen as bound morphemes. An example is the closed and lightly protruding lips (relaxed 'mm') during the articulation of a verb phrase, in which the mouth gesture indicates that the action is executed 'comfortably' or 'at ease' (Sutton-Spence and Woll 1999 as cited in Crasborn et al. 2008).

2) Semantically empty mouth gestures (E-type)
Mouth gestures in this category appear with manual signs, but don't carry any additional or independent meaning, and are therefore called 'semantically empty'. Although these mouth gestures don't have their own meaning, they can be seen as obligatory because signs without the accompanied mouth action are not considered well-formed. Woll (2001) has analyzed these kind of mouth gestures as 'echo phonology': the movement of mouth parallels the movement of the hands. An example is the BSL sign DISAPPEAR in which the closing movement and abrupt stop of the hands are echoed by the mouth (inter-dental fricative followed by a bilabial stop).

3) Enacting mouth gestures (4-type)
Mouth gestures of this category perform the action of the mouth itself such as biting, chewing, and shouting. These mouth gestures either occur with signs which have the same meaning as the mouth action, or represent an action by themselves so that the manual articulators are free to express other related information. An example is the BSL sign RUN accompanied by a 'shouting' mouth action, which would indicate the meaning 'run while shouting'. Enacting mouth gestures are mouth gestures in which the mouth represents the mouth ('mouth for mouth', 4-type).

4) Mouth activity in the context of whole-face activity (W-type)
The mouth gestures are not independent and must be seen with other facial actions as a whole. The mouth is part of the facial expression such as in the KSL sign DISGUST, in which the face including the mouth is expressing 'disgust'. W-type of mouth action is a group which is not covered by the Vogt-Svendsen (2001).

The classification above makes it possible for us to analyze mouth gestures found in the KSL Corpus by assigning them into corresponding categories. We will analyze mouth actions in KSL by using the types proposed by Crasborn et al. (2008).

4.1.2 Distribution of mouth action

Crasborn et al. (2008) have analyzed data from the ECHO (European Cultural Heritage Online) corpus (Crasborn et al. 2007). The data were collected from one male and one female Deaf native signer of BSL, NGT and SSL, respectively. A total of six signers were asked to sign their own versions of five Aesop's fables. The sign language data of 51 minutes were coded for manual and non-manual features in ELAN. A special focus was on the analysis of the temporal relationship between manual articulation and mouth actions. Mouth actions were categorized and counted. The results are shown in Table 2.

Table 2: Distribution of mouth action types in three sign languages (Crasborn et al. 2008: 51).

	M-Type	A-Type	E-Type	4-Type	W-Type	Total
BSL	560 (51%)	231 (21%)	20 (2%)	63 (6%)	225 (20%)	1099
NGT	299 (39%)	230 (30)	58 (8%)	45 (6%)	125 (17%)	757
SSL	831 (57%)	205 (14%)	99 (7%)	87 (6%)	233 (16%)	1455

The above data reveals that mouthings are the largest category across all three languages. The following are the percentage of mouthings derived from a spoken language: 51% of mouth action in BSL, 39% in NGT and 57% in SSL. Adverbial mouth actions (A-type) account for 21% of mouth actions in BSL, 30% in NGT, and 14% in SSL. A-type mouth actions represent the largest category among the mouth gestures classifications. Semantically empty mouth gestures (E-Type) and enacting mouth gestures (4-type) together account for 8% to 14% of all mouth actions and the whole face actions (W-type) represent 16% to 20% in all three sign languages.

Although the NGT signers seem to use fewer mouthings than the signers in BSL and SSL, it is significant to observe that the distribution pattern of the different mouth action types is similar in all three sign languages. Crasborn et al. (2008) offer three explanations of this phenomenon. 1) The sample data might be too small and a larger corpus might show a different result, 2) The sign language data from all three countries belong to the register 'storytelling'. Signing from other registers (e.g. personal narratives, lectures, or dialogues) could possibly show different results, and 3) Similarities in the data are due to similar sociolinguistic factors in the three Deaf communities. Signers from all three countries, for example, have experienced similar educational systems and therefore the influence on spoken language might be similar (for a discussion on the influence of the oral education on occurrence of mouthings in NGT, see Bank 2015). Hence, it is beneficial to add KSL data from our corpus for better understanding of mouthing in sign languages.

4.2 Data collection and research method

In order to explore mouth gestures and their function in KSL, we analyzed data from the KSL Corpus, which have been translated and annotated the manual components.[6] The data chosen for the analysis include narrations and dialogues,[7] taken from three tasks: retelling of a signed story (task D), warning and prohibition signs (task F), and a description of incidents (task G). Table 3 shows the length of the annotated data.

Table 3: KSL Corpus material annotated for mouth action.

Task	Retelling of a signed story (Task D)	Warning and prohibition signs (Task F)	Description of incidents (Task G)	Total
Number of annotation files	4	5	2	11
Duration (hh:mm)	16:30	57:10	39:13	112:53

Nine of the 16 informants are male and seven are female. The age of the informants is not matched and they all live in Seoul and attended a deaf school. The informants have deaf family members or partners and all of them consider KSL as their first language.

After experimenting with different ways to distinguish and annotate mouth gestures in the data (cf. Nonhebel et al. 2004; Hanke 2014), we coded mouth gestures by using roman alphabets. The rationale behind the decision was simply convenience. Roman alphabets are available on a computer keyboard and can be used without installing any additional fonts or software. This would be also true for the Korean alphabet Hangul, but these letters have the disadvantage that the annotators get influenced by the (Korean) spoken language, because Hangul is a very phonemic alphabet. For example, the mouth gesture code system from

---

[6] Mouth actions without manual activity are not taken into account.
[7] In contrast to Crasborn et al. (2008) our data includes not only narrations, but also dialogues. Although sign language linguists expect different mouth actions in different registers (cf. Sutton-Spence and Day 2001), our data hasn't revealed any relevant difference.

Sutton-Spence and Day (2001), which is very hard to learn, we decided to use the roman alphabets in our own system, based on iconicity of the form of the letter. The form of the letters depicts the form of the mouth: the open mouth in a rounded form represents 'O', for example, while stretched lips with the furrow on the right and left side of the mouth is represented by the letter 'H'. The codes for the mouth gestures in KSL with their description are shown in Table 4. These codes can also be combined to describe more complex mouth gestures.

Table 4: Mouth gesture codes in KSL.

No	Description	Code	
1	The mouth is open as little as possible	O1	
2	The mouth is open	O2	
3	The mouth is open wide	O3	
4	Protruding lips	B	
5	Lips are stretched, mouth is slightly open, teeth are visible	H1	
6	Lips are stretched, mouth is open, teeth are visible	H2	
7	Mouth is closed	−1	
8	Mouth is closed and lips are pressed together	−2	
9	Corner of the mouth curved down slightly	^1	
10	Corner of the mouth curved down strongly	^2	
11	Left corner of the mouth is raised	<	

Table 4 (continued)

No	Description	Code	
12	Right corner of the mouth is raised	>	
13	Air in the left cheek	(–	
14	Air in the right cheek	–)	
15	Air in both cheeks	(·)	
16	Air in both cheeks is sucked out	)–(	
17	Tongue pushes from the inside of the cheek	o>	
18	Only lower teeth are visible	M	
19	Only upper teeth are visible	W	
20	Continuous or repetitive movement	~	–
21	Upper and lower teeth are moved in alternate directions	Z	
22	Both cheeks blow out air	(=)	
23	The tongue is bitten in the inside of the mouth	C	
24	The stretched out tongue is pulled into the mouth	UJ	

4.3 Results

4.3.1 Distribution of mouthing, mouth gestures and signs without mouth actions

An analysis of the annotated data (112 min.) shows that there are 10,879 manual signs in total; 3,246 signs (29.8%) of these are articulated with mouthing and 1,351 signs (12.4%) appear with mouth gestures. The remaining 6,282 signs (57.7%) are articulated with no mouth action. In other words, more than half of the signs in the data don't have any mouth actions. About one third of the signs are accompanied with mouthing, and only 12.4% of the signs show a mouth gesture. The result might be surprising for many Korean deaf people who accept mouth gestures as a substantial part of KSL, but see mouthing solely as an influence of the spoken language and more or less as a supportive method to help hearing people understand the signed utterances of deaf people. It was expected that signs are articulated with mouthing when there are hearing people around. This is not the case with the data of the KSL Corpus. The two informants and the moderator were all deaf and no hearing person was allowed to enter the studio during the data collection. Nevertheless the annotated corpus data show clearly that informants articulate signs with mouthing and that the portion of signs with mouthing is greater than the portion of signs with mouth gestures.

4.3.2 Comparing the distribution of mouth action in KSL to other sign languages

We have compared our results with data of NGT and Auslan. In order to consider both of the signs accompanied by mouth action, and the number of signs not accompanied, we chose the data in Bank et al. (2016) for NGT, and Johnston and Roekel (2014) for Auslan.

Bank et al. (2016) have investigated the frequency of mouthings in order to study the meaning of spoken language elements in NGT. When they compare the mouth action frequency to manual signs, they reported that 36 signers used 8,386 signs and produced 6,125 mouth actions, containing 5,106 mouthings and 870 mouth gestures. In the remaining 149 cases, it was unclear what the type of mouth action was used (Bank et al. 2016: 10).

Johnston and Roekel (2014) have examined the distribution and characteristics of mouth actions in Auslan to describe the degree of language-specific conventionalization of these forms. In their preliminary findings, they do not reveal the exact number of their analyzed signs, but reported that 51% of the signs occurred with mouthings, 19.2 % occurred with mouth gestures, and 29.8% signs were articulated without mouth action (Johnston and Roekel 2014: 85).

A summary of the mouth actions in three sign language would be as follows.

Table 5: Distribution of signs with mouth action and without.

	Total of signs	Signs with mouthing	Signs with mouth gesture	Signs with unclear mouth action	Signs with no mouth action
KSL	10,879	3,246 (29.8%)	1,351 (12.4%)		6,282 (57.7%)
NGT	8,386	5,106 (60.9%)	870 (10.3%)	149 (1.8%)	2,112 (25.2%)
Auslan	–	(51.0%)	(19.2%)		(29.8%)

The table above shows that the percentage of signs with mouth gestures is quite similar in all three sign languages (12.4% for KSL, 10.3% for NGT and 19.2% for Auslan). Most signs in NGT (60.9%) and Auslan (51.0%) are articulated with mouthings, while most KSL signs are articulated without any mouth actions. The reason for the comparably lower number of mouthings in KSL might be because of the different educational background of deaf students in South Korea. We suppose that the oral method made deaf students mimic the mouth shapes, which in turn led to mouthing, and that this occurred to a much greater degree in the Netherlands and Australia than in South Korea.

The comparably lower number of mouthings might also be a characteristic of East Asian sign languages, but this would need further research with other sign languages such as Japanese Sign Language, Hong Kong Sign Language, and Taiwan Sign Language. However, the above observation might explain why mouthing in KSL seem to be less perceived by researchers and deaf people than in European sign languages.

4.3.3 Frequent mouth gesture types and their function in KSL

The mouth gesture with the highest number of occurrences (151) is O1, in which the mouth is open as little as possible. The second most used mouth gesture is O3 (137 tokens) in which the mouth is open widely. The third mouth gesture is –O3, in which the mouth is first closed and then opened widely (128 tokens), and then mouth gesture H1 (119 tokens), in which the lips are stretched, the mouth slightly open and the teeth visible. The mouth gesture -1, in which the mouth is closed, has 77 tokens. The following table shows the various mouth gestures with more than 50 occurrences in our data.

Table 6: Most used mouth gestures with their number of occurrences.

Code	Description	Number of occurrences
O1	The mouth is open as little as possible	151
O3	The mouth is open widely	137
–O3	The mouth is closed and then opened widely	128
H1	Lips are stretched, mouth is slightly open, teeth are visible	119
–1	Lips are closed	77
O2	The mouth is open	68
B	Protruding lips	57
(·)	Air in both cheeks	52

An examination of the mouth gesture functions by using the mouth gesture types of Crasborn et al. (2008) shows that most gestures are of the E-type (67%), which means that those mouth gestures don't carry any additional or independent meaning. The A-type adverbial mouth actions occur at 18.9%, the whole-face mouth gesture (W-type) at 11.0%, and the enacting mouth gesture (4-type) have the lowest number of occurrences, at 3.1%.

In the following, a KSL example for each mouth gesture type will be presented (figure 6–9 are taken from the KSL Online Dictionary).

1. E-type
Mouth gesture code: -O3 (the mouth is closed and then opened widely)

Figure 6: ABLE-TO.

2. A-type
Mouth gesture code: -O3~ (the mouth is closed and then opened widely repeatedly)

Figure 7: SUBWAY.

The mouth gesture is expressing the repetitive movements of the subway and adds an adverbial meaning to the lexical sign (cf. Figure 7).

3. W-type
Mouth gesture code: H103 (lips are stretched, teeth are visible, mouth then opened widely)

Figure 8: WASTE.

The W-type mouth gesture is part of the whole face which depicts a negative expression (cf. Figure 8).

4. 4-type
Mouth gesture code: <H (lips are stretched, teeth are visible and the left corner of the mouth is raised)

Figure 9: EAT-BURGER.

The mouth performs the action of chewing a burger (cf. Figure 9).

4.3.4 Mouth gesture types and their functions compared to other sign languages

The comparison of the mouth gesture types in KSL with BSL, NGT and SSL (Crasborn et al. 2008) shows that the most frequently used mouth gesture in KSL is E-type (67%). In BSL (43%) and NGT (50.2%) it is A-type, and in SSL it is W-type (37.3%). The second most used mouth gesture type in KSL and SSL is A-type, whereas it is W-type for BSL and NGT.

The table above reveals that regarding the distribution of the mouth gesture types, BSL and NGT seem to be similar, while KSL looks quite different due to the number of mouth gestures of E-type being much more frequent than in the other three sign languages. The reason is that the KSL sign ABLE (Figure 6) with its prominent mouth gesture -O3, categorized as an E-type mouth gesture, occurs very frequently in the annotated data.

4.4 Summary

On the basis of the KSL Corpus data, we found evidence that mouth actions exist in KSL just as they do in many other sign languages. In order to describe roles of

Table 7: Distribution of mouth gestures types in four sign languages.

SL	A	E	4	W	Total
KSL	**255** (18.9%)	**904** (67%)	42 (3.1%)	150 (11%)	1351
BSL	**231** (43%)	20 (3.7%)	63 (11.6%)	225 (41.7%)	539
NGT	**230** (50.2%)	58 (12.7%)	45 (9.8%)	125 (27.3)	458
SSL	205 (32.9%)	99 (15.9%)	87 (13.9%)	**233** (37.3%)	624

mouth gestures and mouthings in KSL, we annotated 112 minutes from 16 informants of the KSL Corpus data collected in Seoul.

Among 10,879 signs we found, 1,351 (12.4%) signs were accompanied with mouth gestures and 3,246 signs (29.8%) were articulated with mouthing. Compared to NGT (60.9%) and Auslan (51%), the portion of signs with mouthing is lower in KSL. We suppose that the reason is the oral method in deaf education, which had an impact on the use of mouthing in other sign languages, was less widespread in Korea. Alternatively, we observed that there are hardly any signs in KSL which are distinguished by mouthing; mouthing doesn't have a disambiguating function for homonym signs as it does, for example, in the NGT signs BROER (brother) and ZUS (sister) (Crasborn et al 2008).[8] Further research within KSL is needed to explore this explanation.

The frequency of KSL signs with mouth gestures is very similar to that of mouth gestures in previous studies of mouth action in Auslan and NGT. We have described the most frequent mouth gestures in KSL by showing the number of occurrences. The mouth gesture occurring most often – with 151 tokens – is O1, in which the mouth is open as little as possible. The second most often occurring mouth gesture – with 137 tokens – is O3, in which the mouth is open wide. Mouth gesture -O3 (the mouth is first closed and opens widely) occurs 128 times, H1 (stretched lips with slightly visible teeth) occurs 119 times, and -1 (closed mouth, lips are stretched) occurs 77 times.

By analyzing the function of mouth gestures, we have adopted the classification of mouth action types in Crasborn et al. (2008). Our data shows that most mouth gestures belong to the E-type mouth action. Sixty-seven percent of all

---

[8] It can be observed for KSL that this disambiguating function is often realized by the handshape that corresponds to the Korean finger alphabets (initialized signs).

mouth gestures are semantically empty, which means that they don't carry any additional or independent meaning – such as the mouth gesture in the KSL sign ABLE-TO. The second most used type of mouth gesture (18.9%) belongs to A-type, which means that the mouth gesture contributes adverbial information to the meaning, such as the KSL sign SUBWAY, in which the repetitive movement of the subway is expressed by the mouth gesture -O3. The portion of mouth gesture of W-type is 11.0%. W-type mouth gestures are not as isolated, but embedded within the entire facial expression. A KSL example is the sign WASTE, which is accompanied by a negative face expression. Mouth gestures belonging to the 4-type occur the least in our data (3.1%). Those mouth gestures reflect the action of the mouth itself, such as biting, chewing, and shouting. A KSL example would be the sign EAT-BURGER. The distribution of the mouth gesture types in KSL, compared with data in BSL, NGT, and SSL, shows a higher number of E-type mouth gestures in KSL than in the other three European sign languages.

The results of this mouth action study are based only on data collected in Seoul. Further data and research is needed to find out if our results are a phenomenon characterizing all East Asian sign languages, or a feature of KSL alone.

5 Conclusion

In this chapter, we have provided descriptions of the KSL Corpus Project, starting with the data collection procedures, the background of the informants, and the studio setup. The tasks in the data collection were presented in detail, highlighting the issue of modifying the elicitation material developed in the Western culture for the use in an Asian culture. We have also described our first phase of annotation in ELAN using ID glosses. The KSL Corpus is currently collecting data in other areas of South Korea. The ongoing annotation work of the KSL Corpus will enlarge the proportion of data which can be applied for further research of KSL. As a first sample of corpus-based research, we have introduced a study on mouth actions in KSL.[9] Further research is needed in order to determine if the observations that differ from the those of the European sign languages have to be considered as language-specific.

---

9 For further KSL corpus-based research see Song et al. 2020 and Lee et al. 2020.

References

Bank, Richard. 2015. *The ubiquity of mouthings in NGT. A corpus study*. Utrecht: LOT.
Bank, Richard, Onno Crasborn & Roeland van Hou. 2016. The prominence of spoken language elements in a sign language. *Linguistics* 54(6). 1–25.
Boyes Braem, Penny & Rachel Sutton-Spence (eds.). 2001. *The Hands are the Head of the Mouth: The Mouth as Articulator in Sign Languages*. Hamburg: Signum.
Crasborn, Onno & Thomas Hanke. 2003. Additions to the IMDI metadata set for sign language corpora. Paper presented at the ECHO workshop, Nijmegen University, The Netherlands, 8–9 May.
Crasborn, Onno, Els van der Kooij, Dafydd Waters, Bencie Woll & Johanna Mesch. 2008. Frequency distribution and spreading behavior of different types of mouth actions in three sign languages. *Sign Language & Linguistics* 11(1). 45–67.
Crasborn, Onno, Johanna Mesch, Dafydd Waters, Annika Nonhebel, Els van der Kooij, Bencie Woll & Brita Bergman. 2007. Sharing sign language data online: experiences from the ECHO project. *International Journal of Corpus Linguistics* 12(4). 537–564.
Crasborn, Onno & Inge Zwitserlood. 2008. The Corpus NGT: an online corpus for professionals and laymen. 6th International Conference on Language Resources and Evaluation. Workshop Proceedings. 3rd Workshop on the Representation and Processing of Sign Languages: Construction and Exploitation of Sign Language Corpora, 44–49. Paris: ELRA.
ELAN (Version 6.2) [Computer software]. 2021. Nijmegen: Max Planck Institute for Psycholinguistics, The Language Archive. Retrieved from https://archive.mpi.nl/tla/elan
Hanke, Thomas. 2014. Annotation of mouth activities with iLex. 9th International Conference on Language Resources and Evaluation. Workshop Proceedings. 6th Workshop on the Representation and Processing of Sign Languages: Beyond the manual channel, 67–70. Paris: ELRA.
Hanke, Thomas, Lutz König, Sven Wagner & Silke Matthes. 2010. DGS Corpus & Dicta-Sign: The Hamburg Studio Setup. 7th International Conference on Language Resources and Evaluation. Workshop Proceedings. 4th Workshop on Representation and Processing of Sign Languages: Corpora and Sign Language Technologies, 106–109. Paris: ELRA.
Herrmann, Annika & Markus Steinbach (eds.). 2013. *Nonmanuals in Sign Language*. Amsterdam & Philadelphia: John Benjamins Publishing Company.
Hong, Sung-Eun, Thomas Hanke, Susanne König, Reiner Konrad, Gabriele Langer, Christian Rathmann. 2009. Elicitation materials and their use in sign language linguistics. Poster presented at Sign Language Corpora: Linguistic Issues Workshop 2009, London, 24–25 July.
Hong, Sung-Eun, Hyunhwa Lee, Mi-Hye Lee, Seung-Il Byun. 2019. The Korean Sign Language Act. In Maartje De Meulder, Joseph J. Murray & Rachel McKee (eds.), *Recognizing Sign Languages: An International Overview of National Campaigns for Sign Language Legislation and their Outcomes*, 36–51. Multilingual Matters.
Hong, Sung-Eun, Seongok Won, Il Heo & Hyunhwa Lee. 2018. Development of an "Integrative System for Korean Sign Language Resources". 11th International Conference on Language Resources and Evaluation. Workshop Proceedings. 8th Workshop on the Representation and Processing of Sign Languages: Involving the Language Community, 75–78. Paris: ELRA.

Johnston, Trevor. 2008. Corpus linguistics and signed languages: no lemmata, no corpus. 6th International Conference on Language Resources and Evaluation. Workshop Proceedings. 3rd Workshop on the Representation and Processing of Sign Languages: Construction and Exploitation of Sign Language Corpora, 82–87. Paris: ELRA

Johnston, Trevor. 2010. From archive to corpus: Transcription and annotation in the creation of signed language corpora. *International Journal of Corpus Linguistics* 15. 106–131.

Johnston, Trevor & Jane van Roekel. 2014. Mouth-based non-manual coding schema used in the Auslan corpus: explanation, application and preliminary results. 9th International Conference on Language Resources and Evaluation. Workshop Proceedings. 6th Workshop on the Representation and Processing of Sign Languages: Beyond the manual channel, 81–88. Paris: ELRA.

Kang, Beom-mo & Hunggyu Kim. 2004. Sejong Korean Corpora in the Making. 6th International Conference on Language Resources and Evaluation, 1747–1750. Paris, ELRA.

Konrad, Reiner, Susanne König & Gabriele Langer. 2008. What's in a Sign? Theoretical Lessons From Practical Sign Language Lexicography. In Josep Quer (ed.), *Signs of the time. Selected papers from TISLR 2004*, 379–404. Hamburg: Signum.

KSL Online Dictionary (2022) KSL Online Dictionary, https://sldict.korean.go.kr/ (accessed 02.07.22).

Lee, Hyun-hwa, Mi-yeon Song, Sung-eun Hong, Eun-young Lee, Chang-wook Kang, Seong-ok Won. 2020. Hangugsueoui Sunchajeog Gyeolhab Gujo Teugseong Tamsaeg - Hangugsueo Malmungchi Seoul Jiyeog Jalyoleul Jungsim-eulo [A Study on the Characteristics of Sequential Combination Structure of Korean Signs - Focused on the Seoul Data of the Korean Sign Language Corpus -]. *Hangugcheong-gag-eon-eojang-aegyoyug-yeongu [The Korean Society of Education for Hearing-Language Impairments]* 11(2). 177–199.

Lucas, Ceil, Clayton Valli. 1992. *Language contact in the American Deaf Community*. San Diego, CA: Academic Press.

Mayer, Mercer. 1969. *Frog, Where Are You?* New York: Dial Books for Young Readers.

National Institute of Korean Language. 2007. 21segi Sejong Gyehoeg Gug-eo Teugsujalyo Guchug [21st Century Sejong Plan. Building special resources of Korean]. Annual Research Report.

National Institute of Korean Language. 2020. 2020 Hangukssuo Malmungchi Guchuk mit Yongu [Building and Research of the Korean Sign Language Corpus]. Annual Research Report.

Nishio, Rie, Sung-Eun Hong, Susanne König, Reiner Konrad, Gabriele Langer, Thomas Hanke & Christian Rathmann. 2010. Elicitation methods in the DGS (German Sign Language) Corpus Project. 7th International Conference on Language Resources and Evaluation. Workshop Proceedings. 4th Workshop on Representation and Processing of Sign Languages: Corpora and Sign Language Technologies, 178–185. Paris: ELRA.

Nonhebel, Annika, Onno Crasborn & Els van der Kooij. 2004. Sign language transcription conventions for the ECHO Project: BSL and NGT mouth annotation University of Nijmegen.

Pfau, Roland, Markus Steinbach & Bencie Woll (eds.). 2012. *Sign Language. An International Handbook.* (Handbooks of Linguistics and Communication Science HSK 37). Berlin: De Gruyter Mouton.

Prillwitz, Siegmund, Thomas Hanke, Susanne König, Reiner Konrad, Gabriele Langer & Arvid Schwarz. 2008. DGS Corpus Project – Development of a Corpus Based Electronic Dictionary German Sign Language / German. 6th International Conference on Language Resources and Evaluation. Workshop Proceedings. 3rd Workshop on the Representation and Processing of Sign Languages: Construction and Exploitation of Sign Language Corpora, 159–164. Paris: ELRA

Schembri, Adam, Jordan Fenlon, Ramas Rentelis, Sally Reynolds & Kearsy Cormier. 2013. Building the British Sign Language Corpus. *Language Documentation and Conservation* 7. 136–154.

Song, Mi-yeon, Sung-eun Hong, Chang-wook Kang, Seong-ok Won, Kang-suk Byun, Hyun-hwa Lee. 2020. Hangugsueoui Saengsanjeog Sueo Eohwieseo Natanan Dosangseong - Imiji Hyeongseong Gibeob-eul Jungsim-eulo [A Study on the Iconicity of productive signs in the Korean Sign Language (KSL) Corpus - by describing the different image-producing techniques]. *Hangugcheong-gag-eon-eojang-aegyoyug-yeongu [The Korean Society of Education for Hearing-Language Impairments]* 11(1). 109–139.

Sutton Spence, Rachel & Linda Day. 2001. Mouthings and Mouth Gesture in British Sign Language (BSL). In Penny Boyes Braem & Rachel Sutton-Spence (eds.), *The Hands are the Head of the Mouth: The Mouth as Articulator in Sign Languages*, 69–85. Hamburg: Signum.

Vogt-Svendsen, Marit. 2001. A comparison of mouth gestures and mouthings in Norwegian Sign Language(NSL). In Penny Boyes Braem & Rachel Sutton-Spence (eds.), *The Hands are the Head of the Mouth: The Mouth as Articulator in Sign Languages*, 41–50. Hamburg: Signum.

Warner Brothers. 1950. Canary Row. Broadcast on Oct. 7th, 1950.

Woll, Bencie. 2001. The sign that dares to speak its name: echo phonology in British Sign Language (BSL). In Penny Boyes Braem & Rachel Sutton-Spence (eds.), *The Hands are the Head of the Mouth: The Mouth as Articulator in Sign Languages*, 87–98. Hamburg: Signum.

Yoon, Byong-Chen. 2003. *Hangugsuhwaui Bisujisinho-e daehan Eon-eohagjeog Teugseong Yeongu* [A Study on the Linguistic Characteristics of Non-manual Signals in Korean Sign Language]. Daegu: Daegu University dissertation.

Felix Sze and Helen Lee
Negative polar questions in Hong Kong Sign Language

Abstract: This paper investigates how Hong Kong Sign Language (HKSL) expresses different types of negative polar questions (NPQs). NPQs can be ambiguous between an outer and inner reading. For the outer reading, the NEG is outside the proposition and the speaker tries to confirm that what he believes is true. For the inner reading, the NEG is inside the proposition, and the speaker wants to confirm an unexpected inference. NPQs can be used as an urge/request for an action, too. Our findings suggest that HKSL signers mainly adopt non-manuals to differentiate these three types of NPQs. Unlike other sign languages which directly combine the non-manuals of polar questions and negation when forming NPQs, HKSL has not incorporated the backward movements of the head/body associated with negation into the non-manuals of NPQs, probably because such backward movements contradict the forward head tilt of polar questions, which are more dominant. In addition, the varying degree of consistency of the non-manual markings within and across signers might suggest that the non-manual markers of the three types of NPQs are at different stages of grammaticalization.

Keywords: Hong Kong Sign Language, negative polar questions, non-manual markings, grammaticalization.

1 Introduction

This paper aims at investigating how Hong Kong Sign Language (HKSL) expresses negative polar questions (NPQs).[1] Three main research issues are addressed. First, how are different sub-types of NPQs expressed syntactically? Second, how do non-manuals interact with different sub-types of NPQs? Third, how may indi-

---

[1] Part of the data and analysis of this research was supported by the General Research Fund of the Research Grant Council, Hong Kong SAR Government (Project title: Basic Word Order in Asian Sign Languages: A Cross-Linguistic Perspective, Ref.: 450113).

Acknowledgements: We would like to express our heartfelt thanks to all the deaf native signers participating in this project – Aaron Wong, Pippen Wong, Connie Lo, Brenda Yu and Kenny Chu. Without their sign language data and judgment, we would not have been able to conduct the analysis and prepare this paper.

https://doi.org/10.1515/9781501510243-008

vidual variations associated with some of these NPQ non-manuals illuminate the process of grammaticalization by which facial/head gestures are gradually incorporated into the grammar of sign languages?

In natural languages, polar questions fall into two major classes – positive polar questions and negative polar questions (NPQ). In most spoken languages, NPQs are formed by combining the negative and interrogative markings directly (Miestamo 2009). NPQs can be ambiguous between an outer reading and an inner reading (Ladd 1981; Büring and Gunlogson 2000; Romero and Han 2004). For an outer reading, the NEG is outside the proposition under question and the speaker wants to confirm what he believes is true (e.g., *Isn't there a cafeteria nearby* uttered in a context where the speaker believes there is a cafeteria nearby and is trying to confirm this). In contrast, for an inner reading, the NEG is inside the proposition under question, and the speaker wants to confirm an unexpected inference (e.g., *Isn't there a cafeteria nearby* uttered by a speaker who thought there was a cafeteria but realizes that this might be incorrect). Beside these two types, NPQ can also be used as an urge/request for action when an expected action or event has not taken place (e.g., *Won't you go to work?*).

Not much is known about the differentiation of NPQs in sign languages. Previous studies mentioned that NPQs involve the syntactic structure of a negative statement plus a straightforward combination of the non-manual markers of polar questions (i.e., brow raise, head tilt forward) and negation (i.e., headshakes) (Bergman 1984; Bahan 1996; McKee 2006), without a further differentiation of NPQs. Interestingly, in HKSL, there is a potential conflict between the two sets of non-manuals: negation usually involves the head and body leaning backward, and polar questions typically require a forward head tilt. How would HKSL signers resolve these conflicting head movement directions? Our data suggest that HKSL signers mainly adopt non-manuals to distinguish different types of NPQs, but with a considerable amount of variation across signers. NPQs that serve as an urge for actions have the most consistent non-manuals across signers: a combination of brow raise (AU 1+2) and furrow (AU 4), lips pressing together tightly with two corners turned down, and a forward head tilt or thrust.[2] We propose to explain the suppression of backward head movements of negation in favour of the forward head movement of polar questions by the notion of non-manual dominance. Since non-manual markers for polar questions are mostly obligatory, they are more "dominant" than the optional non-manual

---

[2] Following the suggestion of a reviewer, we adopt the Facial Action Coding System (FACS) (Ekman, Friesen and Hager 2002) to describe different brow positions. (AU=Action Unit; AU 1=inner portion of the brows is raised; AU 2=outer portion of the brows is raised; AU 4=brows lowered and drawn together)

markers for negation, and are therefore retained in NPQs. As for the inner and outer NPQs, a variety of strategies are adopted by signers: a combination of brow raise (AU 1+2) and furrow (AU 4), head movements, varying degree of muscle tensions, etc. Despite some variability across signers, a high degree of consistency of non-manuals are found within individual signers. In addition, deaf viewers can still distinguish the inner and outer reading even when other deaf signers adopt non-manual features that differ from their own. We would like to argue that the internal consistency of non-manual signals within a signer, and the variability across signers, might actually suggest that these facial gestures and body movements are undergoing different stages of grammaticalization as they are gradually incorporated as non-manual markers for negative polar questions in HKSL, which is a relatively young sign language. We hypothesize that, at the initial stage of such grammaticalization process, individual deaf signers may have more than one set of non-manual marking for a particular grammatical function. At a later stage, signers begin to have more consistent non-manual markings, and individual variabilities across signers begin to level off. At the final stage, all signers use consistent non-manuals for a particular grammatical function. This hypothetical model may help explain why some non-manual makers are consistent while some are highly variable across different structures and functions in sign languages.

This paper is organized in the following way. Section 2 is the literature review. Section 3 is the methodology. Section 4 is the findings, and Section 5 is the discussion and conclusion.

2 Literature review

2.1 Negative polar questions in spoken languages

In natural languages, polar questions come in two major classes – positive polar questions and negative polar questions – as shown in examples (1) and (2) below respectively:

(1) Is she left-handed?

(2) Isn't she left-handed?   (Büring and Gunlogson 2000: 1)

In most of the 322 languages included in Miestamo's typological survey, negative polar questions are formed by combining the negative and interrogative marking (Miestamo 2009) directly. Example (3a) and (3b) show a declarative sentence and a polar question in German respectively, and their main difference lies in the syntactic position of the main verb: it follows the subject in the former, but precedes the subject in the latter. In a negative statement, the negator is placed post-verbally (Example 3c). The negative polar question (as in 3d) involves a straightforward combination of the syntactic characteristics of a polar question and negation.

(3) German (Miestamo 2009)
    a. *du   singst*
       2SG sing.2SG
       'You sing.'
    b. *singst   du?*
       sing.2SG 2SG
       'Do you sing?'
    c. *du   singst   nicht*
       2SG sing.2SG NEG
       'You don't sing.'
    d. *singst   du   nicht?*
       sing.2SG 2SG NEG
       'Don't you sing?'

In a few languages, however, negative polar questions are coded by a unique marker not derivable from negative declaratives or polar interrogatives (Miestamo 2009). In Estonian (Erelt 2003), for instance, positive polar interrogatives are marked by the particle *kas* (4b) and negative declaratives by a negative auxiliary *ei* (4c). Negative polar interrogatives are marked by a special particle *ega* (4d).

(4) Estonian (a, b and d quoted from Erelt 2003: 108; c quoted from Miestamo 2009)
    a. *sa   tule-d   täna   meile*
       2SG come-2SG today 2PL.ALL
       'You will come to visit us today.'
    b. *kas sa   tule-d   täna   meile?*
       Q   2SG come-2SG today 2PL.ALL
       'Will you come to visit us today.'
    c. *sa   ei   tule   täna   meile*
       2SG NEG come today 2PL.ALL
       'You won't come to visit us today.'
    d. *ega   sa   (ei)   tule   täna   meile?*
       NEG.Q 2SG NEG come-2SG today 2PL.ALL
       'Won't you come to visit us today?'

Regarding the interpretations of negative polar questions, one hotly discussed area in the spoken language literature is the ambiguity between an inner reading and an outer reading (Ladd 1981; Büring and Gunlogson 2000; Romero and Han 2004). Ladd (1981) provided the first observation that negative polar questions in English are ambiguous between *outer negation reading* (i.e., outer negative polar questions (ONPQ)) and *inner negation reading* (i.e., inner negative polar questions (INPQ)) due to a difference in the scope of negation (NEG). For ONPQ, the NEG is outside the proposition under question, and the speaker wants to confirm what he believes is true. In contrast, for INPQ, the NEG is inside the proposition under question, and the speaker wants to confirm an unexpected inference.

In the two examples (Example 5a and 5b) provided by Ladd (Ladd 1981: 164) below, the same negative polar question 'Isn't there a vegetarian restaurant around here?' is used but they render different interpretations. (5a) is an ONPQ whereas (5b) is an INPQ.

(5a) ONPQ
(Situation: Kathleen and Jeff have just come from Chicago on the Greyhound bus to visit Bob in Ithaca)
Bob: You guys must be starving. You want to get something to eat?
Kathleen: Yeah, isn't there a vegetarian restaurant around here – Moosewood, or something like that?
Bob: Gee, you've heard about Moosewood all the way out in Chicago, huh? OK, let's go there.

In this example, Kathleen believes that there is a vegetarian restaurant and uses the negative polar question to 'ask for confirmation of something she believes to be true' (Ladd 1981: 164). This is an instance of ONPQ because 'what is being questioned is the speaker's belief P'.

(5b) INPQ
(Situation: Bob is visiting Kathleen and Jeff in Chicago while attending the CLS (Chicago Linguistics Society meeting))
Bob: I'd like to take you guys out to dinner while I'm here – we'd have time to go around here before the evening session tonight, don't you think?
Kathleen: I guess, but there's not really any place to go to in Hyde Park.
Bob: Oh, really, isn't there a vegetarian restaurant around here?
Kathleen: No, about all we can get is hamburgers and souvlaki.

In Example (5b), the speaker previously assumed the truth of the proposition P 'there is a vegetarian restaurant around here' as in (5a). However, after listening to Kathleen's comment (i.e., 'but there's not really any place to go in Hyde Park'), the speaker has inferred that this proposition is actually false. The speaker then uses the negative question to check this new inference. Hence, what is being questioned is the inference -P.

Building on Ladd's initial insight, Büring and Gunlogson (2000) argued that the ambiguity associated with negative polar questions could be differentiated with *not some* and *no* in English:

(6a) Isn't there some vegetarian restaurant around here? (ONPQ)

(6b) Is there no vegetarian restaurant around here? (INPQ)

According to Büring and Gunlogson, (6a) only allows an ONPQ reading, whereas (6b) must be interpreted as INPQ.[3]

Büring and Gunlogson further elaborated on how inner and outer negative polar questions interact with different types of contextual evidence: while INPQs are only felicitous in negatively-biased contexts (as in 5b), ONPQ are in fact possible in both neutral context (as a suggestion as in 5a) and negatively-biased contexts (as in 5b). Example (7) illustrates how ONPQ and INPQ can be licensed in the same negatively-biased context (Büring and Gunlogson 2000: 9):

---

[3] As pointed out by Büring and Gunlogson (2000), ONPQ and INPQ in English can be differentiated by the use of 'some' in the ONPQ context and 'no' in the INPQ context. Upon the suggestion from an anonymous reviewer, we seriously looked into the possibility of using NO and SOME as a diagnostic test to distinguish the two types of negative polar questions in HKSL. However, we arrived at the conclusion that the two signs may not reliably differentiate the two contexts. In terms of semantics, SOME in HKSL is slightly different from 'some' in English. In both the English ONPQ and INPQ examples (Example 6a and 6b), the speaker has in mind a specific restaurant, and uses the negative polar question to confirm his original belief that this restaurant exists or to confirm his new inference that there is no such restaurant. Basing on our earlier study (Sze and Tang 2018), SOME/SOMEONE is typically used in an impersonal context where the identity of the referent is not known to the speaker. Hence, SOME in HKSL is compatible with neither the ONPQ nor the INPQ context, and as such it cannot be used as a diagnostic test. In addition, 'some' and 'no' in English are restricted to contexts where the existence of a referent is asserted or negated. They do not appear to fit other negative polar question contexts that involve other kinds of negation, e.g., negation of a state or an action. In the current study, the contexts were carefully designed to elicit the ONPQ and INPQ. In fact, individual signers do show consistent non-manuals to distinguish the two types. Hence, we still decide to posit that there exists empirical evidence for the separation of ONPQ and INPQ.

(7) (Situation: A(ddressee) and S(peaker) want to go out for dinner.)
A: Since you guys are vegetarians, we can't go out in this town, where it's all meat and potatoes (compelling contextual evidence against *p* – the proposition that there is a vegetarian restaurant nearby)
  a. S: Isn't there a vegetarian restaurant around here? / Isn't there some vegetarian restaurant around here? (ONPQ)
  b. S: Isn't there a vegetarian restaurant around here? / Is there no vegetarian restaurant around here? (INPQ)

Büring and Gunlogson suggested that to use an ONPQ in a negatively biased situation (as in 7a), the speaker must not just expect the proposition *p* on some general grounds. The speaker must have some particular (and possibly private) evidence for the proposition under question. In other words, ONPQs have a stronger implication than INPQs, as the speaker's belief is based on his own evidence while it is based on general opinions for INPQs.

In brief, the inner and outer readings of negative polar questions are disambiguated mainly by contextual cues and the speaker's intent in English. Some spoken languages, however, do employ overt grammatical means to differentiate these two readings. As the three sub-types of negative polar questions (i.e., ONPQ in a neutral context, ONPQ in a negatively-biased context, and INPQ in a negatively-biased context) differ in the speaker's epistemic stance towards a certain proposition, they can be aptly differentiated by sentence-final particles *me1* and *aa4* in Cantonese.[4] There are over 30 sentence-final particles in Cantonese (Wakefield 2010). *Me1* is typically used in interrogations to express doubt and/or surprise when something runs counter to the speaker's original belief, and it serves the function of seeking confirmation from the addressee (Chan 2001; Kwok 1984; Matthews and Yip 1994). A speaker may adjust the voice and pitch quality of *me1* to show a varying degree of doubt and/or surprise (Wakefield 2010). The meaning of *aa4* is similar to *me1* when used in questions, but the speaker usually does not hold a strong presupposition, and only intends to confirm the truth of a proposition (Chao 1969; Matthews and Yip 1994). Unsurprisingly, *me1* can be used in both ONPQs and INPQs (8 a-c), while *aa4* is suitable for marking INPQs (8c):

---

4 Cantonese is the Chinese variety that is widely spoken in Hong Kong, and deaf signers in Hong Kong have varying degree of exposure to Cantonese through speech training or daily interactions with hearing people. As far as we know, there are no published studies on negative polar questions in Cantonese. The examples here are based on our intuitions as native speakers of this language.

(8a) **ONPQ in a neutral context (as a suggestion) (*me1* only)**
(Situation: the addressee is writing an article about Americans living in Hong Kong, and asks the speaker to recommend someone for an interview)

Aah3 Sam ng4hai6 mei5gwok3jan4 me1, nei5 ho2ji3 man6haa5 keoi5
Sam   not-be   American   SFP, you   can   ask him

'Isn't Sam an American? You can ask him.' (spoken in an ordinary, relaxed tone)

(8b) **ONPQ in a negatively-biased context (*me1* only)**
(Situation: Speaker A read the profile of Sam's Facebook page a while ago, and Sam stated himself to be an American. Speaker A and B are talking about how Sam spends his summer vacation. Speaker B says Sam has gone to France to meet his relatives there, and both his parents are French. Speaker A doubts if Speaker B is correct, and this is what Speaker A says.)

Aah Sam ng4hai6 mei5gwok3jan4 me1, keoi5 FACEBOOK hai6 gam2 se2 wo3
Sam   not-be   American   SFP, he   FACEBOOK be   like write SFP

'Isn't Sam an American? That's what he wrote on FaceBook.' (spoken with emphasis)

(8c) **INPQ in a negatively-biased context (*me1* or *aa4*)**
(Situation: Sam looks like an American and speaks English fluently with an American accent. Speaker A thought Sam came from the United States. Speaker A and Speaker B are talking about summer vacation, and Speaker B says Sam has gone to France to meet his relatives there and Sam is French. Realizing that his previous assumption about Sam's country of origin is wrong, Speaker A utters the following sentence.)

Aah Sam ng4hai6 mei5gwok3jan4 aa4/me1, ngo5 ji5wai4 keoi5 hai6 tim1
Sam   not-be   American   SFP,   I   think   he   be   SFP

'Isn't Sam an American? I thought he was.' (spoken in an ordinary, relaxed tone)

Apart from the above three types of negative polar questions, there is at least one more type of negative polar question in Cantonese involving the negator *m4* as in (9):

(9) (Situation: There will be an examination tomorrow. Seeing that his friend is still watching TV rather than reviewing, the speaker asks the following question:)

nei5 m4   heoi3 wan1syu1
you   not go   study
'Won't you go to study?'

The negative polar question in Example (9) is distinguished from its negative statement counterpart by a rising intonation pattern towards the end of the question. Unlike INPQs or ONPQs, this type of negative polar questions is not meant to check the truth or falsity of the proposition in question. Rather, they are used when the speaker assumes that some action should have been done according to his/her expectation but that has not yet happened. The negative polar question is used as an urge for action or as a request for an explanation.

In sum, Cantonese employs sentence-final particles and intonation as overt grammatical means to differentiate the several types of NPQs.

Table 1 below shows the four types of NPQs discussed so far in this paper:

Table 1: Four types of negative polar questions.

Types of negative polar questions	Interpretations
1. ONPQ in neutral context	The speaker believes in the proposition *p* and uses it as an suggestion.
2. ONPQ in negatively-biased context	The speaker strongly believes in the proposition *p* even though contextual evidence or the previous utterance of the addressee suggests otherwise. The speaker wants to confirm what he believes is correct.
3. INPQ in negatively-biased context	The speaker originally believed in the proposition *p*. But the contextual evidence or the previous utterance of the addressee implies that *p* is in fact false. The speaker wants to check if his inference of – *p* is correct.
4. Negative polar questions in the context of the non-occurrence of an expected event or action	The speaker expects that some event or action should have taken place but it has not. The speaker urges for the action or requests an explanation for the delay.

2.2 Negative polar questions in sign languages

Previous literature suggests that in negative polar questions, non-manual markers of polar questions and negation are combined directly in several historically unrelated sign languages. Example (10) below shows a negative polar question in Swedish Sign Language:

(10)

       <u>   neg+q </u>
       DEAF/YOU
       'Are you not deaf?' (Swedish Sign Language, Bergman 1984: 54)

('neg' and 'q' represent the non-manual markers for negation and polar questions respectively: head tilt forward, brow raise and headshakes)

Direct combination of non-manual markers in negative polar questions is observed in ASL (Bahan 1996) as well.[5] In New Zealand Sign Language, the non-manual marking of a negative polar question combines a negative headshake (i.e., neg) with brow signals in two distinct ways (McKee 2006). When the signer strongly expects a negative confirmation of the proposition (i.e., agreement) from the addressee, the eyes are squinted or brows furrowed, and the head may be moved forward or down. When the signer less strongly expects the addressee's agreement with the negative proposition, the brows are raised just like a normal polar question, and the head may be moved forward or down. Since McKee said these questions seek confirmation of a negative proposition, they are likely to be INPQ instead of ONPQ. In Turkish Sign Language (Gökgöz 2010), negative polar questions are marked with a backward head tilt associated with the postverbal negator, and an optional brow raise that scopes over the entire question.

Theoretically speaking, such combination of non-manual markers may be viewed as a further step of grammaticalization of non-manuals within a sign language. Would the same combinatory process occur in HKSL as well? In HKSL, signers make use of brow raise (AU 1+2) and forward head tilt for polar questions (Tang 2006) in most cases (Example 11), but occasionally brow furrow (AU 4) plus head thrust may be used to express doubt or surprise (Example 12):

---

[5] In a recent study on answering negative questions in ASL, Gonzalez et al. (2018) mentioned in passing that the negative headshakes associated with negators such as NOTHING, NOT, NEVER and NONE would not be realized in a negative polar question. This brief note contradicts what Bahan suggested in his 1996 study.

(11)

<pre>
                         forward head tilt
                         brow raise (AU 1+2)
―――――――――――――――――――――――――――――――――――
IX [=you]   KNOW   MATTER   KNOW   IX [=you]
</pre>

'Do you know this matter?'

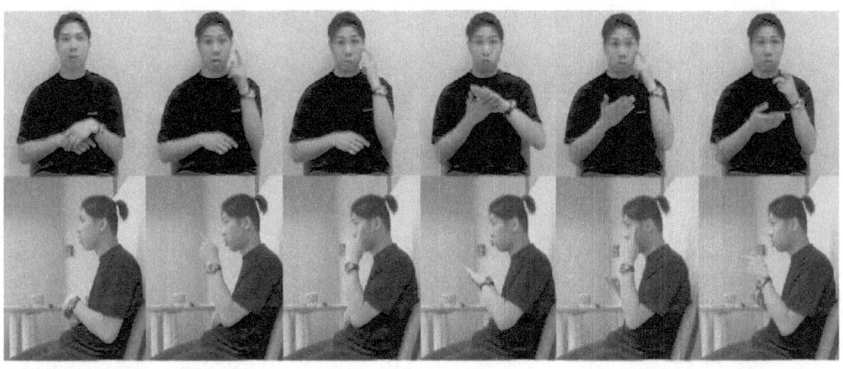

(before question)   IX[=you]   KNOW   MATTER   KNOW   IX[=you]

(12)

<pre>
              forward head thrust
              brow furrow (AU4)
―――――――――――――――――――――――――――――――
DRUG-TAKING   SMELL   HAVE?
</pre>

'Does drug-taking have any smell?'

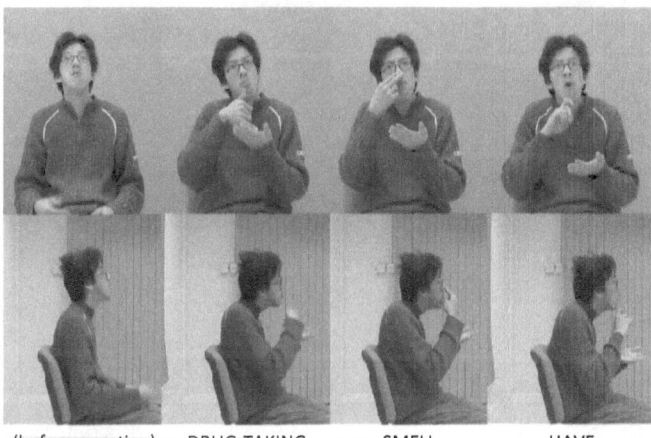

(before question)   DRUG-TAKING   SMELL   HAVE

As for negation involving the negator NOT, backward head movements are frequently used (Lee 2006) (Example 13):

(13)

<u>backward head movement</u>
IX[=I] FLY-TO U.S.A. START STUDY START COMPUTER DESIGN NOT
'I did not start studying computer design right away when I flew to the States.'

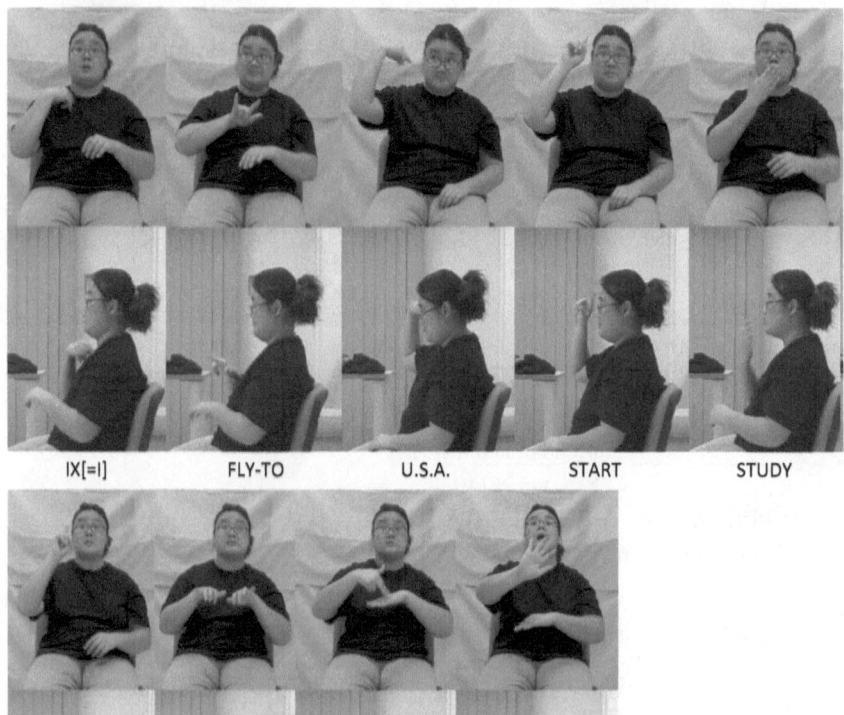

Obviously, the two types of head movements associated with polar questions and negations are contradictory to each other. How would HKSL resolve this potential movement conflict? Furthermore, whether and how sign languages express different types of negative polar questions has not been investigated before. In what follows, we will explore these issues with data from HKSL, with a hope that our findings may further shed light on the nature of grammaticalization of non-manuals in sign languages.[6]

3 Methodology

As far as we know, no studies have been done on how different types of negative polar questions are differentiated in sign languages. In this study, we would like to find out if negative polar questions in HKSL can be used in these four contexts, and, if they exist, whether and how they can be distinguished from one another. Attention was particularly given to how the non-manual markers of polar questions and negation interact in a specific context. Negative polar questions are far less common than polar questions and negations, as they only arise in highly specific pragmatic contexts. We checked one hour of transcribed HKSL conversation data by four signers (two signers for half-an-hour), and only one instance was observed. Hence, elicitation tasks with different contextual features were designed to elicit INPQs and ONPQs from several native signers. These tasks are described below (Section 3.1, 3.2 and 3.3).

3.1 Elicitation task for Type 1: ONPQs in neutral contexts as suggestions

In the hour-long conversation data analyzed in this study, no negative polar questions used as suggestions were observed. Direct consultation with four native

---

[6] In fact, the first author of this paper has published an article on the grammaticalization of non-manuals in polar questions in negation in HKSL (Sze 2022). The paper compares the co-speech gestures of Cantonese speakers when they produce polar questions as well as negation, and the non-manuals of polar questions and negation in HKSL. Cantonese speakers occasionally raise their eyebrows when asking yes-no questions. In contrast, HKSL signers consistently raise their eyebrows in polar questions. Given that eyebrow raise is a universal facial gesture associated with questioning, and eyebrow raise also serves a variety of other functions in both Cantonese and HKSL, the paper argues that eyebrow raise evolved from a universal facial expression and later became a grammatical marker of polar questions within HKSL itself, without involving any cross-linguistic borrowing from Cantonese. On the other hand, Cantonese speakers frequently shake their heads when producing negative sentences, yet HKSL has not incorporated this as a grammatical marker of negation. Instead, HKSL signers developed backward head tilt/backward lean of body and head as a non-manual marker for negation.

signers suggests that HKSL does not use negative polar questions as suggestions in a neutral context. To confirm their judgment, five hypothetical situations were set up. In all these situations, it is possible to use ONPQs in English and Cantonese as a suggestion. One of the situations is shown below. The rest of them are listed in Appendix I.

Situation 1:
The deaf awareness public education project needs extra helping hands in editing the videos, but all the deaf colleagues at the research centre are very busy with their existing workloads. You are discussing who else to look to for help.

    A: We need someone to help us. Who do you suggest?
    B: Isn't Aaron free on Tuesdays and Wednesdays?

The five situations were explained to them in HKSL and they had an open discussion among themselves to find out if negative polar questions were felicitous.

3.2 Elicitation task for Type 2 and 3: ONPQs and INPQs in negatively-biased contexts

To find out if outer and inner negative polar questions can be distinguished in HKSL, another elicitation task with six negatively-biased situations was designed, each with an ONPQ and INPQ context. The situations were described in HKSL to each of the four native signers participating in this experiment. They were required to sign out a negative polar question with the negator NOT without any restrictions on the choice of words preceding the sentence-final negators in their responses. One of the situations is shown below. The rest of them can be found in Appendix II.

Situation 1, context (a): Outer negation – Type 2:
    You received an email from someone called Jacky Lam. Jacky Lam said s/he is hearing and saw you in several activities of Deaf Power. Jacky said s/he wanted to learn sign language from you. You thought Jacky should be a boy as this is a boy's name. You checked Jacky's Facebook account and saw a boy's face as the profile picture. You talked about this with Kenny. Kenny said Jacky Lam was the girl who wore a long pink dress in the last Deaf Power gathering. You asked, 'Isn't Jacky a boy?'.

    Expected negative polar question: IX[=that] MALE NOT?

Situation 1, context (b): Inner negation – Type 3:
>You received an email from someone called Jacky Lam. Jacky Lam said s/he is hearing and saw you in several activities of Deaf Power. Jacky said s/he wanted to learn sign language from you. You thought Jacky should be a boy as this was a boy's name.[7] You asked Kenny about this. Kenny said Jacky Lam was the girl who wore a long pink dress in the last Deaf Power gathering. You asked, 'Isn't Jacky a boy?'.
>
>Expected negative polar question: IX[=that] MALE NOT?

Following Büring & Gunlogson (2000), in the ONPQ context (i.e., context (a)), the speaker has much stronger evidence for his belief because he actually checked the Facebook of Jacky, and found a boy's face in the profile picture. This is different from the INPQ context (i.e., context (b)) where the speaker thought Jacky was a boy on a general ground.

3.3 Elicitation task for Type 4: Negative polar questions in the non-occurrence of an expected action/event

The last category of negative polar questions involves the non-occurrence of an expected action/event. Five elicitation situations were designed. Each of them was explained individually in HKSL to the five deaf native signers who participated in this task. They were then asked to produce a response with NOT, with no restrictions on the words that appear before the sentence-final negator.[8] One of the situations is listed below, and the rest of them can be found in Appendix III.

Situation 1:
>Your father usually leaves home for work at 8 am on weekdays. Today is Monday and it is now ten o'clock, but he is still reading the newspaper at home. What do you think your mother will say to him? (Expected answer: YOU GO-TO WORK NOT? 'Won't you go to work?')

The five stimuli were presented in signing to each of the five native signers of HKSL participating in this experiment. Four out of these five informants also participated in the elicitation experiment of Type 1, 2 and 3.

---
7 Although 'Jacky' can be used for females, it is used mainly for males in Hong Kong.
8 The five stimuli were designed by Lee for her MA thesis on the same topic (Lee 2011).

3.4 Participants

Four native deaf signers of HKSL participated in the elicitation tasks for Type 1, 2 and 3. One more native deaf signer participated in the task for Type 4. Their personal information is presented in Table 2:

Table 2: Background information of the deaf native signers participating in this study.

Signer	Age	Background	Participating in elicitation tasks
Signer 1 (F)	Mid-twenties	Native signer with deaf parents and a deaf sibling	Type 1, 2, 3 and 4
Signer 2 (M)	Early-thirties	Native signer with deaf parents and a deaf sibling	Type 1, 2, 3 and 4
Signer 3 (M)	Mid-twenties	Native signer with deaf parents and a deaf sibling	Type 1, 2, 3 and 4
Signer 4 (F)	Early-thirties	Native signer with deaf parents	Type 1, 2, 3 and 4
Signer 5 (F)	Late-twenties	Native signer with deaf parents	Type 4 only

*All five signers graduated from the same deaf school in Hong Kong.

4 Findings

4.1 Type 1: ONPQs in neutral contexts as suggestions

For the five situations intended for Type 1 ONPQs (See Appendix I), an open discussion session in HKSL was held with the four native signers. All of them pointed out that in such situations negative polar questions could not be used in HKSL. Instead, they preferred to give a suggestion directly, e.g., AARON FREE EVERY-TUESDAY EVERY-WEDNESDAY, ASK-HIM HELP-US CAN (Aaron is free every Tuesday and Wednesday. We can ask him to help us). As this kind of ONPQ was not found in the hour-long conversation data either, we would like to conclude that there is no evidence that HKSL allows ONPQs as suggestions in a neutral context.

4.2 Type 2 and 3: ONPQs and INPQs in negatively-biased contexts

In this elicitation task, six negatively-biased situations were created (See Appendix II), each with two distinct contexts, one for ONPQ and one for INPQ. The four participating signers commented that negative polar questions were felicitous in these situations. All of them made use of a sentence-final negator and a specific brow position to mark the negative polar questions. In addition, they used non-manual signals to differentiate the outer and inner readings, but individual variation was observed. Here the Facial Action Coding System (FACS) (Ekman et al. 2002) is used to describe the brow positions observed in the signers' responses.

Example (14a) and (14b) show the ONPQ (Type 2) and INPQ (Type 3) of Signer (1) in the negatively-biased contexts respectively. Example (14c) shows a close-up comparison of the signer's neutral facial expression without signing in the same experiment, and the facial expressions associated with her ONPQ and INPQ sentences. Example (14d) shows the brow furrowing (i.e., brows are lowered and drawn together) and raising of the same signer in other conversation data to facilitate comparisons of different brow positions.

(14a) ONPQ in negatively-biased context of Signer (1)

	forward head thrust
	forward head tilt
	AU 1 +2 +4
IX[=that]	MALE NOT

'Isn't that person a male?'

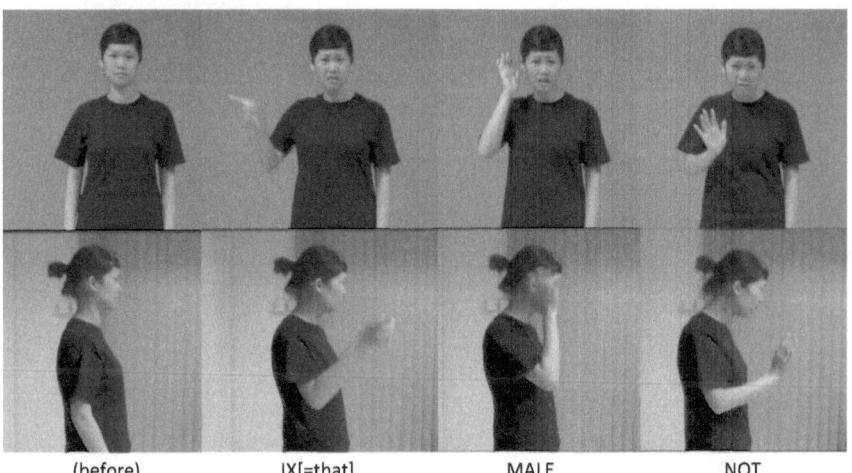

(before)   IX[=that]   MALE   NOT

(14b) INPQ in negatively-biased context (Type 3) of Signer (1)

	backward head mov	
		forward head tilt
		AU 1 +2 +4
IX[=that]	MALE	NOT

'Isn't that person a male?'

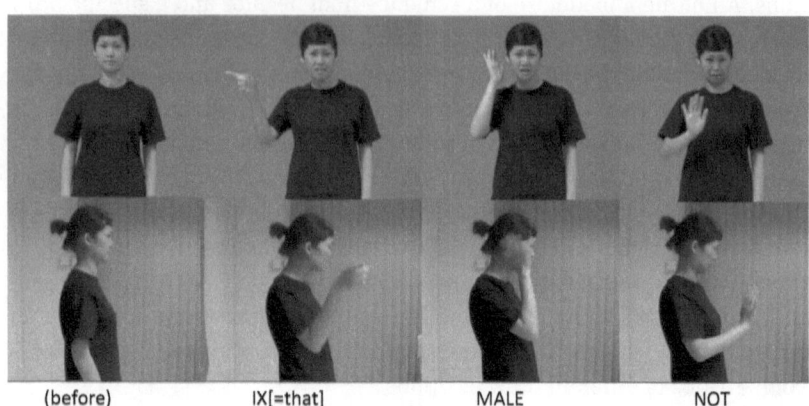

| (before) | IX[=that] | MALE | NOT |

(14c) A comparison of Signer (1)'s facial expressions of a neutral state, ONPQ and INPQ in the negatively-biased contexts.

| Neutral expression | ONPQ | INPQ |

(14d) Brow raising and furrowing of Signer (1) in other signing data for reference.

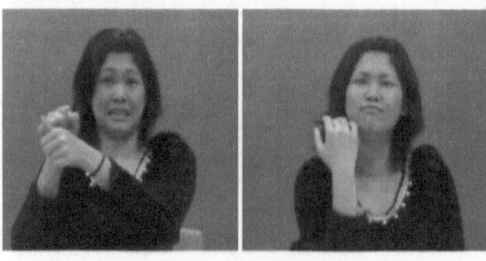

| Brows raise (AU 1+2) | Brows lowered & drawn together (AU 4) |

As shown in the examples above, for both types of negative polar questions, the brows of Signer (1) were pulled together and upward (i.e., AU 1+2+4)(AU=Action Unit; AU 1=inner portion of the brows is raised; AU 2=outer portion of the brows is raised; AU 4=brows lowered and drawn together). Hence, the brow position assumed by Signer (1) is in essence a combination of brow raising and furrowing. As mentioned in our previous discussion, brow raising is an obligatory marker in the majority of polar questions in HKSL, while furrowing signals that the signer is suspicious of the situation under question. Negative polar questions are a subtype of polar questions, and it is natural for brow raising to be used. On the other hand, negative polar questions are mostly found in situations where an inference runs counter to the speaker's expectation, therefore offering a felicitous context for brow furrowing as well. We hypothesize that this non-manual combination of raising and furrowing of Signer (1) stems from the grammaticalization of the two eyebrow movements within the HKSL grammar, and is used specifically to code negative polar questions. Signer (1) also adopted head movements and mouthings to differentiate the inner and outer readings: INPQ is functionally akin to negation, and is signaled with a backward head movement (which is common in negation), accompanied with a forward head tilt (which is frequent in polar questions). She also mouthed the Cantonese negator *m4hai6* 'not'. On the other hand, one purpose of ONPQs is to confirm the speaker's own belief despite unfavorable evidence with no intention to negate the proposition under question. Hence, for ONPQ, no negation-related backward head movement is observed. In contrast, forward head tilt (common in polar questions) and head thrust (used when the signer is surprised/suspicious) are used simultaneously. In addition, she mouthed the Cantonese negator *m4hai6* 'not' followed by the sentence-final particle *me1*. In brief, Signer (1) distinguished ONPQ and INPQ by non-manual features, and this distinction was consistently found in the five remaining pairs of stimuli.

However, the three other signers did not employ the same non-manual strategy to differentiate ONPQs and INPQs. Their expressions of ONPQs and INPQs are shown in Examples (15), (16) and (17) respectively.

(15a) ONPQ in negatively-biased context of Signer (2)

       <u>forward head thrust</u>
         <u>forward head tilt</u>
           <u>AU 1 +2 +4</u>
IX[=that]   MALE   NOT
'Isn't that person a male?'

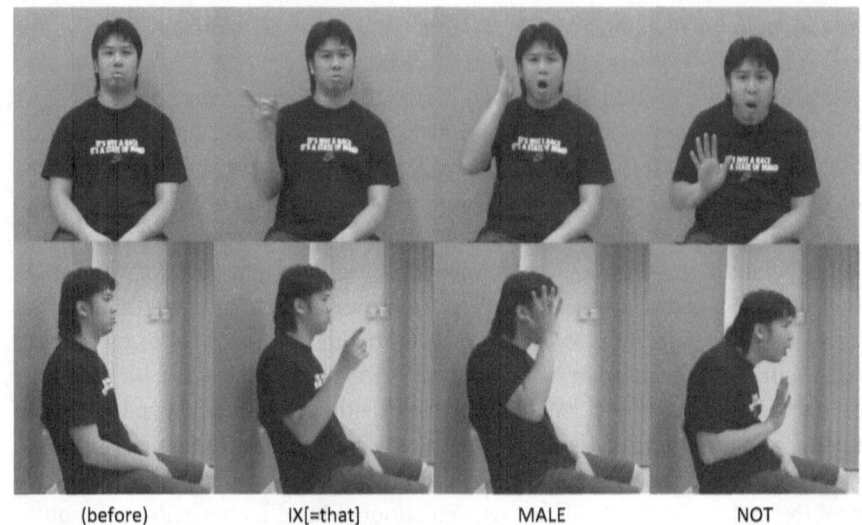

(before)   IX[=that]   MALE   NOT

(15b)   INPQ in negatively-biased context of Signer (2)

```
                    forward head thrust
             _____forward head tilt
        _____AU 1 +2 +4
IX[=that]  MALE   NOT
```
'Isn't that person a male?'

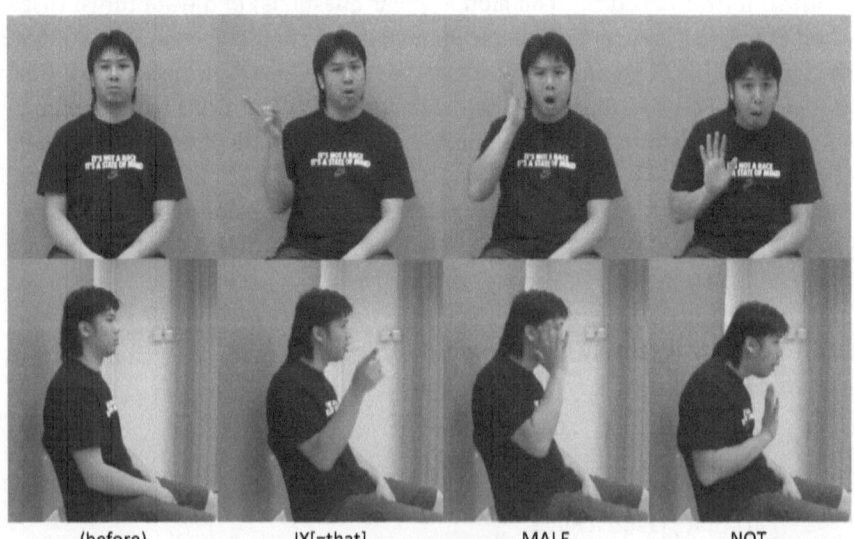

(before)   IX[=that]   MALE   NOT

Example (15c): A comparison of Signer (2)'s facial expressions of a neutral state, ONPQ and INPQ in the negatively-biased contexts.

Neutral expression　　　　　　ONPQ　　　　　　　　　INPQ

(15d) Brow raising and furrowing of Signer (1) in other signing data for reference.

Brows raise (AU 1+2)　　Brows lowered & drawn
　　　　　　　　　　　　together (AU 4)

As shown in Example 15 (a) to (c), Signer (2) adopted basically the same set of non-manual features for the two types of negative polar questions: forward head tilt, forward head thrust, the brows are pulled together and upward (AU 1 + 2 + 4), and the mouthing of the Cantnese negator m4hai5 'not'. However, the ONPQs showed a larger amplitude of brow furrowing (i.e., brows pulled together), and a lesser amplitude of browing raising. Given the distribution of brow raise and furrow in polar questions in HKSL, we would like to argue that for Signer (2), ONPQ indicates a stronger degree of suspicion towards the negative inference, hence a larger degree of frowning and a smaller degree of raise.

(16a) ONPQ in negatively-biased context of Signer (3)

```
                        forward head thrust
                                   AU 1 +2 +4
gesture[=attention]  TODAY  HOLIDAY  NOT
```
'Isn't today a holiday?'

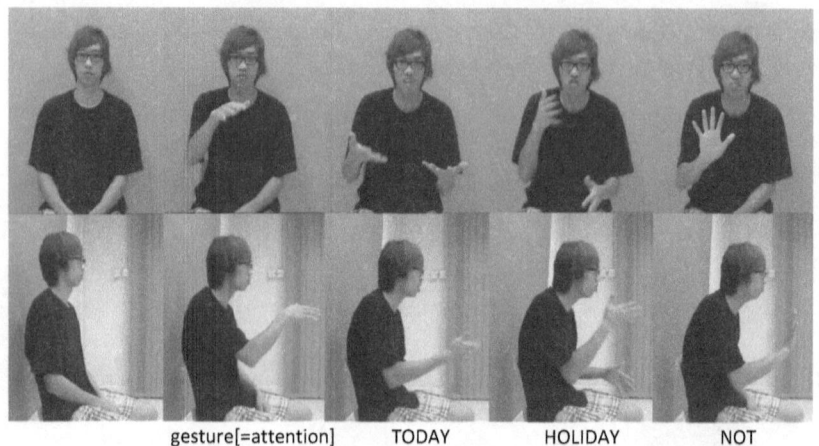

gesture[=attention]   TODAY   HOLIDAY   NOT

(16b) INPQ in negatively-biased context of Signer (3)

```
                              forward head thrust
_____
                                       AU 1 +2 +4
gesture[=attention]   TODAY   HOLIDAY   NOT
```

gesture[=attention]   TODAY   HOLIDAY   NOT

(16c) A comparison of Signer (3)'s facial expressions of a neutral state, ONPQ and INPQ in the negatively-biased contexts.

Neutral expression   ONPQ   INPQ

Example (16d): Brow raising and furrowing of Signer (3) in other signing data for reference.

Brows raise (AU 1+2)   Brows lowered & drawn together (AU 4)

Similar to Signer (1) and (2), Signer (3) produced a forward head thrust in both types of negative polar questions, and his brows were pulled together and upward (AU 1+2+4). However, his lips were pressed together instead of mouthing the Cantonese negator during the articulation of NOT. What differentiated the two types of questions was that ONPQs involved a tighter pressing of the lips, faster signing with a larger movement amplitude, and a tenser overall facial expression. We regard the tensing of movement and facial expression as an indicator of the signer's stronger belief in the proposition in the contexts of ONPQs.

(17a)　ONPQ in negatively-biased context of Signer (4)

				forward head thrust
				AU 4
INCORRECT,	TODAY	AFTERNOON	HOLIDAY	NOT

'Isn't today a holiday?'

(Before)　INCORRECT,　TODAY　AFTERNOON　HOLIDAY　NOT

(17b): INPQ in negatively-biased context of Signer (4)

			forward head thrust
			AU 1 + 2
TODAY	AFTERNOON	HOLIDAY	NOT

'Isn't today a holiday?'

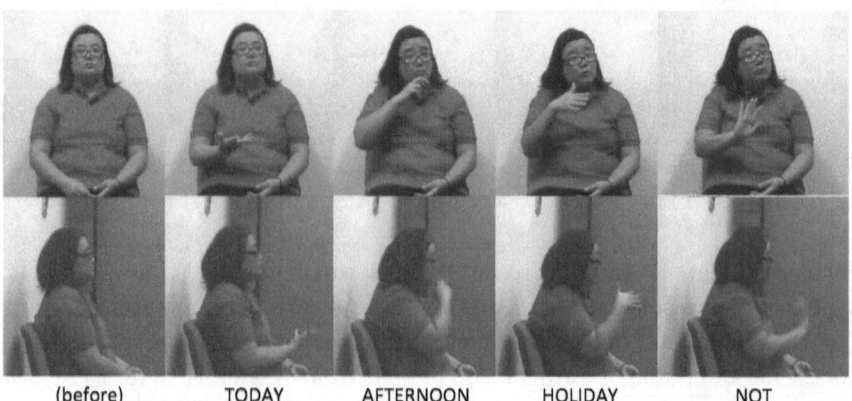

(before)   TODAY   AFTERNOON   HOLIDAY   NOT

(17c) A comparison of Signer (3)'s facial expressions of a neutral state, ONPQ and INPQ in the negatively-biased contexts.

Neutral expression   ONPQ   INPQ

(17d) Brow raising and furrowing of Signer (4) in other signing data for reference.

Brows raise (AU 1+2)   Brows lowered & drawn
                         together (AU 4)

Signer (4) mainly differentiated the two types of negative polar questions by brow positions. All six ONPQs in this task were marked with brow furrowing (AU 4), while the INPQs were accompanied with brow raising (AU 1+2). This difference suggests that while the signer was merely surprised in the contexts for INPQs, she was puzzled in the ONPQ contexts as the negative evidence actually ran counter to her own knowledge. Like Signers (1) and (2), she mouthed the Cantonese negator plus the sentence-final particle *m4hai5me1* when signing the negator.

Regarding the brow movements, Signer (4) appears to be different from the other three signers. However, Signer (4) did sometimes combine brow raise and furrow together. As mentioned before, we observed one negative polar question in our one-hour conversation data. It was actually produced by Signer (4). From the context, she was using an INPQ, and both brow raise and furrow were used simultaneously.

(18)

			AU 1 + 2
			AU 4
Brenda	TOGETHER-WITH-YOU	STUDY	NOT

'Didn't Brenda study together with you?'

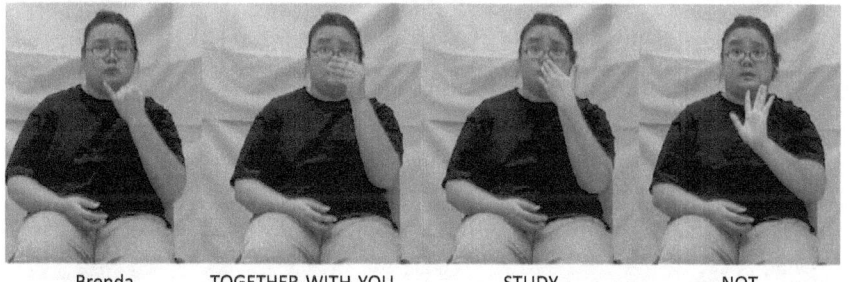

| Brenda | TOGETHER-WITH-YOU | STUDY | NOT |

How could we explain the inconsistency of Signer (4)'s non-manuals? One possibility is that she has not yet developed a stable differentiation of the outer and inner readings. That HKSL signers have not yet had consistent non-manual markers for INPQs and ONPQs is possibly related to the degree of grammaticalization of the non-manual signals. We will have a more detailed discussion on this issue in Section (5).

4.3 Type 4: Negative polar questions in the non-occurrence of an expected action/event

For this task, five situations were designed. The responses of the five participating signers showed a consistent use of non-manuals involving a forward head tilt and thrust, brow raise and furrow (AU 1+2+4), and the corners of one's mouth turned down.

(19)

	Mouth corners down
	Forward head tilt
	Forward head thrust
	AU 1 + 2 + 4
IX[=you] GO-TO WORK	NOT?

'Won't you go to work?'

(before)   IX[=you]   GO-TO   WORK   NOT

Example (19) shows Signer (1) using the following non-manual markers: brows pulled together and upward, lips pressing together tightly with two corners turned down, forward head tilt and forward head thrust. In fact, the remaining four signers all adopted a similar set of non-manual markers. Example (20) shows that Signer (4) used similar non-manual markers, except that the outer portion of the brows was not raised. Example (21) illustrates the snapshots of the facial expressions of all five deaf signers. As the elicitation experiments were conducted individually, our findings provided strong evidence that the non-manual markers for this particular type of negative polar questions are consistent among the five participating native signers.

(20)

		AU 4		AU 1 + 4 Forward head thrust Mouth corners down	
IX[=you]	GO-TO	WORK	NOT	IX[=you]?	

'Won't you go to work?'

(before)   IX[=you]   GO-TO   WORK   NOT   IX[=you]

(21)

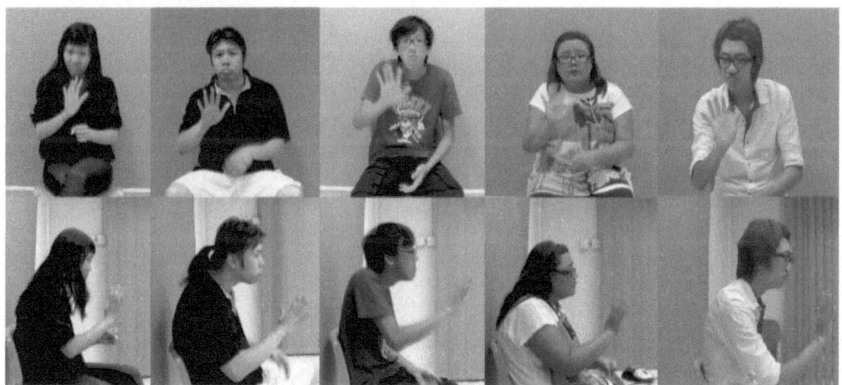

5 Discussion and conclusion

In this paper, we set up several elicitation tasks to find out how different types of negative polar questions are distinguished non-manually in HKSL and came up with the following observations. First, unlike English and Cantonese, HKSL does not use negative polar questions in a neutral context as a suggestion. This suggests that there exist cross-linguistic differences in the contexts for negative polar questions. Second, HKSL signers mostly use brow raise (i.e., AU 1+2), furrow (i.e., AU 4) or a combination of the two (i.e., AU 1+2+4) for INPQs and ONPQs in negatively-biased contexts (Type 2 and 3), but there are individual differences as to how the two readings are differentiated non-manually.[9] Third, HKSL signers can use a negative polar question as an urge or query if an expected action/event has not taken place, and they use consistent non-manual markers for this specific type of questions, which include simultaneous brow raise and furrow (i.e., AU 1+2+4), forward head thrust, and downward turning of the two corners of one's mouth.

As the non-manual markers for Type 2 and 3 NPQs were inconsistent across signers, an additional judgment task was created to see if the signers could still understand each other and accept these differences.[10] The judgement task was presented in a powerpoint format. Each slide showed the two contexts of the same situation in written Chinese and the sentences of one signer (Example 22). The main difference between the two contexts was highlighted in yellow. Each of the four signers was asked to match the contexts with the 12 signed sentences of each of the other three signers.

---

[9] That the two types of negative polar questions are mainly distinguished by non-manual features in Hong Kong Sign Language is not surprising at all. As argued by Dachkovsky and Sandler (2009), facial expressions on the upper face can be used as intonational markers for signers' attitudes or disbelief. For both the outer and inner readings, the inference based on the situation runs counter to the signer's original belief. For the outer reading, the function of the outer negative polar questions is to assert one's original belief, while the inner reading seeks to confirm the new inference which contradicts one's original belief. As mentioned in the literature review, Cantonese mainly employs sentence-final particles to distinguish different types of negative polar questions, and sentence-final particles in Cantonese are closely related to speakers' attitudes and beliefs as well.

[10] This judgment task was created upon the suggestion of one of the reviewers.

(22) A snapshot of the judgment task for Type 2 and 3 NPQs.

1a	你收到一位名叫 Jacky Lam 的人的電郵。他說他是健聽人，曾在數次聾會活動中見過你。Jacky 說想跟你學手語。Jacky 一般是個男孩子的名字，所以你以為 Jacky 是個男的，你跟 Mary 提起這個人，Mary 說上次在聾會活動中穿上粉紅色長裙的就是 Jacky，於是你問 Mary。
1b	你收到一位名叫 Jacky Lam 的人的電郵。他說他是健聽人，曾在數次聾會活動中見過你。Jacky 說想跟你學手語。Jacky 一般是個男孩子的名字，所以你以為 Jacky 是個男的，而且你曾看過 Jacky Lam 的面書，見到首頁的個人照是個短髮男孩。你跟 Mary 提起這個人，Mary 說上次在聾會活動中穿上粉紅色長裙的就是 Jacky，於是你問 Mary。

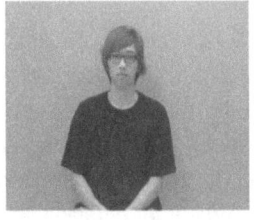 

Table 3 below shows the percentage of correct matching of the contexts with the signing of each signer. For Type 2 and 3 NPQs, each signer produced 12 sentences. Hence, each signer was asked to judge 36 signed sentences produced by the other three signers.

Table 3: Percentage of the four signers correctly matching the signed sentences of the other three signers for Type 2 and 3 NPQs.

	Signed sentences of Signer (1)	Signed sentences of Signer (2)	Signed sentences of Signer (3)	Signed sentences of Signer (4)
Correct matching by Signer (1)		100%	100%	66.7%
Correct matching by Signer (2)	66.7%		100%	100%
Correct matching by Signer (3)	83.3%	100%		100%
Correct matching by Signer (4)	100%	100%	100%	

In the majority of cases, the four signers correctly matched the signed sentences for Type 2 and 3 NPQs produced by the other signers. Among the four signers, Signer (1) received the lowest percentage of correct matching. For Signer (1), the major non-manual difference between Type 2 (ONPQ) and Type 3 (INPQ) lies in the head movements and mouthing. For Type 2 (ONPQ), she used forward head thrust and head tilt, and mouthed *m4hai6me1* in Cantonese. For Type 3 (INPQ), she used forward head tilt and backward head movement, and mouthed *m4hai6*. Since only the front views of the signed sentences were provided in the judgment task (note: this is what deaf people normally see in a signed conversation), the difference of head movements might be missed by the other signers. In addition, the mouthed words in the two NPQs also look very similar, and may be missed by other deaf viewers.

Their judgments confirm that even though the signers showed considerable individual differences in the non-manual expressions for the two types of NPQs, overall speaking, they were still able to distinguish the other three signers' signing for the two contexts. This suggests that this variation does not significantly impact the interpretation of the two types of NPQs. Hence, the grammatical markings for the two contexts are still relatively stable from the perceptual perspective.

Our most noticeable finding in the several elicitation tasks was that HKSL does not always directly combine the non-manual markers of polar questions with those of negations in negative polar questions. In our data, the most commonly found non-manuals involve a combination of brow raise and furrow (i.e., AU 1+2+4), plus forward head tilt and/or forward head thrust, which are all markers for polar questions. Backward head movements, a frequent non-manual marker for negation, are only found in the INPQs of Signer (1). We would like to argue that this phenomenon may be accounted for using the concept of non-manual dominance. According to the typological study conducted by Zeshan (2004, 2006), non-manual markings are very often the only means by which polar questions can be distinguished from statements, and are obligatory for polar questions in all of the sign languages covered in her study. We may consider this type of non-manual markers 'dominant' in the sense that their presence is obligatory. On the other hand, Zeshan proposed that sign languages fall into two types with regard to the combination of manual negator (e.g., NOT) and negative non-manuals (e.g., headshakes). For sign languages that are manual-dominant, the manual negator must be present in negation, while non-manual markers are optional. HKSL belongs to this type (See Lee (2006) for the optionality of non-manual markers for negation and the impossibility to negate a sentence with non-manual markers alone in HKSL). In contrast, nonmanual-dominant sign languages allow the use of just the non-manual marker to negate a sentence without a manual negator. American Sign Language, Swedish Sign Language and New Zealand Sign Language belong to this type according to Zeshan. We would like to argue that in these three sign languages, as the non-manual markers for polar questions and negations are equally dominant and there are no potential conflicts between them, they are both kept in the event of negative polar questions. In HKSL, however, only the non-manual markings for polar questions are dominant, and as such, the forward head tilts or thrusts associated with polar questions override the backward head movement for negation, which is optional in nature. As a result, we observed a suppression of negative non-manual marking in negative polar questions in HKSL for most signers.

With regard to the non-manual markers of negative polar questions in HKSL, we observed consistent non-manual markings across all signers only in Type 4 but not in Type 2 (ONPQ) and 3 (INPQ). However, for Type 2 and 3, most of the deaf informants used similar brow and head movements. In addition, three out of four signers had their own consistent non-manual markings for negative polar questions. Only Signer (4) seemed to be a bit unsettled in her use of non-manuals. Based on these empirical evidence, we would like to hypothesize that the (in)consistencies within and across signers might have reflected different stages in the grammaticalization of non-manual markers for negative polar questions in HKSL.[11] We hypothesize that there exist at least three stages:

a. Stage 1: individual deaf signers may have more than one way of non-manual markings for a particular grammatical function (i.e., Signer (4) in her production of INPQs and ONPQs).
b. Stage 2: Signers begin to have more consistent non-manual markings, and individual variabilities across signers are gradually levelled off (i.e., Signer (1), (2) and (3) in their productions of INPQs and ONPQs in negatively-biased contexts).
c. Stage 3: All signers use consistent non-manual markers for a particular grammatical function (i.e., Type 4 negative polar questions).

---

11 One anonymous reviewer pointed out to us that the variation of facial expressions across the deaf informants is in some ways similar to prosody variation in spoken languages. However, we suggest that this variation can be analyzed from the perspective of grammaticalization because of two reasons. First, it has been pointed out that some non-manual signals, which originally were para-linguistic in nature, have undergone the process of grammaticalization to become grammatical markers in sign languages. Two examples that have been discussed in depth are brow raise in polar questions and headshakes in negation (Janzen 1999, 2012; Janzen and Shaffer 2002; Pfau and Steinbach 2011; Pfau 2015). As our current focus is about negative polar questions, which involve the exact combination of polar questions and negations, it is likely that some form of grammaticalization of non-manuals is involved as well. The second reason to justify the grammaticalization perspective is that at least one type of negative polar question shows consistent non-manual markers across signers, while for the remaining types the deaf individuals show high internal consistency in the use of facial expressions. It is well known that grammaticalization is a process of conventionalization in which variability in forms is levelled off gradually. Hence, our observations of the non-manuals associated with different types of negative polar questions provide prima facie evidence for grammaticalization, though more research is needed to further verify this hypothesis.

If our hypothesis is correct, the non-manual markings of negative polar questions are likely to be in the process of being grammaticalized in the language. HKSL is a fairly young sign language, when compared with some of the western sign languages, and it is not surprising for it to have grammatical features that are not fully stabilized yet. The current form of HKSL originated from several deaf schools established in 1940s and 50s. Some of these schools were signing schools which used Nanjing/Shanghai Sign Language as their medium of instruction, while the others adopted a strict oralist education approach but the students there still developed their own signing varieties naturally among themselves. These signing varieties gradually blended with each other in the deaf community over the years, giving rise to today's HKSL (Sze et al. 2013). The deaf native signers who participated in this study are the offspring of the graduates of these deaf schools in the early days. These native signing participants can be considered the second generation of HKSL users, and they are in fact the first generation of native signers who acquired HKSL from birth. We believe that some of the grammatical features of HKSL are still going through the process of stabilization as they grew up. Regarding the grammaticalization of the non-manuals, it could be the case that some aspects go faster while some slower, and individual differences remain to a significant extent. However, more vigorous research with more signers and data is certainly needed to verify our hypothesis, and the findings will be of significant value for us to fully understand the grammaticalization of non-manual grammatical markers in sign languages.

Appendix I: Hypothetical situations for negative polar questions as suggestions in a neutral context

Hypothetical situation 1:
The deaf awareness public education project needs extra helping hands in editing the videos, but all the deaf colleagues at the research centre are very busy with their existing workload. You are discussing who else to look to for help.
    A: We need someone to help us. Who do you suggest?
    B: Isn't Aaron free on Tuesdays and Wednesdays?

Hypothetical situation 2:
A and B are hungry.

    A: I am very hungry right now. Let's find a restaurant to have lunch.
    B: Isn't there a nice Italian restaurant in the Science Park?

Hypothetical situation 3:
A and B are discussing the work schedule for this Friday.

   A: Do we have any specific work plan for this Friday.
   B: Isn't Prof. Padden giving a talk this Friday?

Hypothetical situation 4:
A and B are discussing where to bring Prof. Carol Padden for sight-seeing this Sunday.

   A: Where do you think we can bring Carol Padden for sight-seeing this Sunday?
   B: Isn't there a traditional festival on Cheung Chau Island this Sunday?

Hypothetical situation 5:
A and B are discussing where to bring the children for the coming Easter Holiday.

   A: The children are having their Easter holiday next week. Where can we take them out?
   B: Doesn't the Ocean Park have some new amusement rides?

Appendix II: Stimuli for Type 2 and 3 negative polar questions in negatively biased contexts

	Situations	Expected negative polar question
1a	**ONPQ context** You received an email from someone called Jacky Lam. Jacky Lam said s/he is hearing and saw you in several activities of Deaf Power. Jacky said s/he wants to learn sign language from you. You thought Jacky should be a boy as this is a boy's name. You checked Jacky's FaceBook account and saw a boy's face as the profile picture. You talked about this with Kenny. Kenny said Jacky Lam was the girl who wore a long pink dress in the last Deaf Power gathering. You asked, 'Isn't Jacky a boy?'.	IX[=that] MALE NOT? 'Isn't that person a male?'

(continued)

(continued)

	Situations	Expected negative polar question
1b	**INPQ context** You received an email from someone called Jacky Lam. Jacky Lam said s/he is hearing and saw you in several activities of Deaf Power. Jacky said s/he wants to learn sign language from you. You thought Jacky should be a boy as this is a boy's name. You asked Kenny about this. Kenny said Jacky Lam was the girl who wore a long pink dress in the last Deaf Power gathering. You asked, 'Isn't Jacky a boy?'.	IX[=that] MALE NOT? 'Isn't that person a male?'
2a	**ONPQ context** Today is Christmas Eve. You remember that staff members can have a half-day off last Christmas Eve. Also you received a mass mail from the university administration last week about this half-day-off arrangement. In the afternoon, however, staff are still working and you are puzzled. You asked Agnes, 'Don't we have a half-day off today?'	TODAY AFTERNOON OFF NOT 'Don't we have a half-day off today?'
2b	**INPQ context** Today is Christmas Eve. You remember that staff members can have a half-day off last Christmas Eve. In the afternoon staff are still working and you are puzzled. You asked Agnes, 'Don't we have a half-day off today?'	TODAY AFTERNOON OFF NOT 'Don't we have a half-day off today?'
3a	**ONPQ context** Sam looks like an American and can speak excellent English. You read his Facebook account and saw that he put down 'American' in his personal information. One day you check the Centre website and found out that his nationality is Japanese. You go to check with Agnes and ask 'Isn't he an American?'	SAM AMERICAN NOT? 'Isn't Sam an American?'
3b	**INPQ context** Sam looks like an American and can speak excellent English. One day you check the Centre website and found out that his nationality is Japanese. You go to check with Agnes and ask 'Isn't he an American?'	SAM AMERICAN NOT? 'Isn't Sam an American?'
4a	**ONPQ context** You know a lot of Sri Lankan people are Muslims and they don't eat pork. In the orientation week of the APSL Program, each of the students introduced themselves and you remembered Brayan said he is a Muslim. One day you go out to have lunch with the deaf students and see that Kenny orders a pork dish for Brayan. You are puzzled. You ask Kenny, 'Isn't Brayan a Muslim?'	BRAYAN MUSLIM NOT? 'Isn't Brayan a Muslim?'

(continued)

	Situations	Expected negative polar question
4b	**INPQ context** You know a lot of Sri Lankan people are Muslims and they don't eat pork. One day you go out to have lunch with the Sri Lankan deaf students and see that Brayan orders a pork dish. You are puzzled. You ask Kenny, 'Isn't Brayan a Muslim?'	BRAYAN MUSLIM NOT? 'Isn't Brayan a Muslim?'
5a	**ONPQ context** Your elder brother is now taking an evening course every Friday. He usually stays at home for other evenings. Yesterday was Tuesday. You were watching TV but your brother asked you not to do so because he needed to prepare for the quiz the coming Friday. Today is Wednesday. Now is evening time but your brother is not at home. You ask your mom where your brother is. She says he has gone to school. You ask your mother, 'Doesn't elder brother go to class every Friday evenings?'	ELDER-BROTHER STUDY EVERY-FRIDAY NOT? 'Doesn't elder brother go to class every Friday evenings?'
5b	**INPQ context** You know your brother is taking an evening course. As he is usually not at home on Monday evenings, you have the impression that the evening course is held every Monday evening. Today is Wednesday. Now is evening time but your brother is not at home. You ask your mom where your brother is. She says he has gone to school. You ask your mother, 'Doesn't elder brother go to class every Monday evening?'	ELDER-BROTHER STUDY EVERY-MONDAY NOT? 'Doesn't elder brother go to class every Monday evenings'
6a	**ONPQ context** Woody flies back to Vietnam to teach every two weeks. Last week he wasn't in Hong Kong. Before he left you saw him telling Jafi that he had prepared a gift for his wife in Vietnam and he was sure that she would be very happy. Today Woody is supposed to be back but he is not here. You asked Agnes about this. She said his return flight from Fiji was delayed because of the hurricane. You are puzzled. You asked Agnes, 'Didn't Woody fly to Vietnam last week?'	WOODY LAST-WEEK FLY VIETNAM NOT? 'Didn't Woody fly to Vietnam last week?'
6b	**INPQ context** Woody flies back to Vietnam to teach every two weeks. Last week he wasn't in Hong Kong. You thought he went to Vietnam as usual. This morning Woody is back. He has just put his hotel receipt on Agnes' desk for reimbursement. You walk past Agnes' desk and see that the hotel receipt is printed in Chinese. You ask Agnes, 'Didn't Woody fly to Vietnam last week?'	WOODY LAST-WEEK FLY VIETNAM NOT? 'Didn't Woody fly to Vietnam last week?'

Appendix III: Type 4: Negative polar questions in the non-occurrence of an expected action or event

Situation (1)
Your father usually leaves home for work at 8 am during weekdays. Today is Monday and it is now ten o'clock, but he is still reading the newspaper at home. What do you think your mother will say to him? (Expected answer: YOU GO-TO WORK NOT? 'Won't you go to work?')

Situation (2)
The daughter usually goes to bed at 10 pm at night. Right now it is already 12 am, the light of the daughter's room is still on. The mother opens the door, and sees that her daughter is still not gone to bed. What do you think the mother will say to the daughter? (Expected answer: YOU GO-TO SLEEP NOT? 'Won't you go to sleep?')

Situation (3)
The office hours of the research centre are from 9 am to 6 pm. It is now ten at night. You have just finished your work and are ready to leave. You notice that a colleague is still working. What would you say to him? (Expected answer: YOU GO-TO HOME NOT? 'Won't you go home?')

Situation (4)
The daughter usually leaves home for school at 8 am in the morning. Today is Monday and is not a school holiday. It is now 8 am but she is still watching TV. What do you think the mother will say to her daughter? (Expected answer: YOU GO-TO SCHOOL NOT? 'Won't you go to school?')

Situation (5)
June is the examination month for all students. It is a Sunday afternoon in June. Your roommate in the dormitory said he was going to a movie with his friends and would come back late. What would you say to him? (Expected answer: YOU STUDY NOT?)

References

Bahan, Ben. 1996. *Non-manual realization of agreement in American Sign Language*. Boston: Boston University Ph.D dissertation.
Bergman, Brita. 1984. Non-manual components of signed language: some sentence types in Swedish Sign Language. In Filip Loncke, Penny Boyes Braem & Yvan Lebrun (eds.),

Recent Research on European Sign Languages, 49–59. The Netherlands: Swets & Zeitlinger B.V.

Büring, Daniel & Christine Gunlogson. 2000. *Aren't positive and negative polar questions the same?* Manuscript. University of California Santa Cruz.

Chan, Marjorie K.M. 2001. Gender-related use of sentence-final particles in Cantonese. In Marlis Hellinger & Hadumod Bussmann (eds.), *Gender across language*, 57–72. Amsterdam: John Benjamins.

Chao, Yuen Ren. 1969. *Cantonese primer*. New York: Greenwood Press.

Dachkovsky, Svetlana & Wendy Sandler. 2009. Visual intonation in the prosody of a sign language. *Language and Speech* 52(2/3). 287–314.

Ekman, Paul, Wallace Friesen & Joseph Hager. 2002. *Facial Action Coding System: The Manual on CD Rom*. Salt Lake City, UT: A Human Face.

Erelt, Mati. 2003. Syntax. In Mati Erelt (ed.), *Estonian language*, 93–129. Tallinn: Estonian Academy Publishers.

Janzen, Terry. 1999. The Grammaticization of Topics in American Sign Language. *Studies in Language* 23(2). 271–306.

Janzen, Terry. 2012. Lexicalization and grammaticalization. In Roland Pfau, Markus Steinbach & Bencie Woll (eds.), *Sign Language: An International Handbook*, 816–840. Berlin: Mouton de Gruyter.

Janzen, Terry & Barbara Shaffer. 2002. Gesture as the substrate in the process of ASL grammaticization. In Richard Meier, Kearsy Cormier & David Quinto-Pozos (eds.), *Modality and Structure in Signed and Spoken Languages*, 199–223. Cambridge: Cambridge University Press.

Gökgöz, Kadir. 2010. What negative polar questions can teach us about the C domain for Turkish Sign Language (Turk Isaret Dili–TID). Poster presented at TISLR 2010, Purdue University, U.S.A., 30 September – 2 October.

Gonzalez, Aurore, Kathryn Davidson & Kate Henninger. 2018. Answering negative questions in American Sign Language. Paper presented at NELS 49, Cornell University, 5–7 October.

Kwok, Helen. 1984. *Sentence particles in Cantonese*. Hong Kong: Centre of Asian Studies, University of Hong Kong.

Ladd, Robert. 1981. A first look at the semantics and pragmatics of negative questions and tag questions. *Papers from the Seventeenth Regional Meeting of the Chicago Linguistic Society*. 164–171. Chicago: Chicago Linguistic Society.

Lee, Helen. 2011. *Negative polar questions in Hong Kong Sign Language*. Hong Kong: The Chinese University of Hong Kong MA thesis.

Lee, Jafi. 2006. *Negation in Hong Kong Sign Language*. Hong Kong: The Chinese University of Hong Kong MPhil thesis.

Matthews, Stephen & Virginia Yip. 1994. *Cantonese: A Comprehensive Grammar*. London: Routledge.

McKee, Rachel. 2006. Aspects of interrogatives and negation in New Zealand Sign Language. *Sign Language Typology: Interrogatives and Negation*, ed. by Ulrike Zeshan, 69–90. Nijmegen: Ishara Press.

Miestamo, Matti. 2009. Negative interrogatives. Paper presented at the 8th Biennial Conference of the Association for Linguistic Typology, July 23–26. Berkeley: University of California.

Pfau, Roland & Markus Steinbach. 2011. Grammaticalization in sign languages. In Heiko Narrog & Bernd Heine (eds.), *The Oxford handbook of grammaticalization*, 683–695. Oxford: Oxford University Press.

Pfau, Roland. 2015. The grammaticalization of headshakes: From head movement to negative head. In Andrew D.M. Smith, Graeme Trousdale & Richard Waltereit (eds.), *New Directions in Grammaticalization Research,* 9–50. Amsterdam, Philadelphia: John Benjamins.

Romero, Maribel & Han Chung-Hye. 2004. On Negative Yes/No Questions. *Linguistics and Philosophy* 27(5). 609–658.

Sze, Felix. 2022. From gestures to grammatical non-manuals in sign language: a case study of polar questions and negation in Hong Kong Sign Language. *Lingua* 267. 103–188.

Sze, Felix & Gladys Tang. 2018. R-Impersonal constructions in Hong Kong Sign Language. *Sign Language & Linguistics* 21(2). 284–306.

Sze, Felix, Connie Lo, Lisa Lo, & Kenny Chu. 2013. Historical development of Hong Kong Sign Language. *Sign Language Studies* 13(2). 155–185.

Tang, Gladys. 2006. On interrogatives and negation in Hong Kong Sign Language. In Ulrike Zeshan (ed.) *Sign Language Typology: Interrogatives and Negation,* 198–224. Nijmegen: Ishara Press.

Wakefield, John. 2010. *The English equivalents of Cantonese sentence-final particles: a contrastive analysis.* Hong Kong: The Hong Kong Polytechnic University dissertation.

Zeshan, Ulrike. 2006. Negative and interrogative constructions in sign languages: A case study in sign language typology. In Ulrike Zeshan (ed.) *Interrogative and negative constructions in sign languages,* 28–68. Nijmegen: Ishara Press.

Zeshan, Ulrike. 2004. Interrogative constructions in sign languages: Cross-linguistic perspectives. *Language* 80(1). 7–39.

Natsuko Shimotani
Analyzing head nod expressions by L2 learners of Japanese Sign Language: A comparison with native Japanese Sign Language signers

Abstract: This study analyzed the use of prosodic head nods in narratives by Deaf native signers of Japanese Sign Language (JSL) and hearing L2 learners of JSL. Head nodding in JSL is frequently observed at the end of an Intonational Phrase (IP), and either overlaps with the final movement of the manual sign to indicate a clause boundary (named "concurrent head nods") or appears after the final movement of the manual sign to indicate certain syntactic information (named "successive head nods"). Since head nods in spoken Japanese do not have these linguistic functions, the research examined how the head nodding was being used by the hearing JSL signers. The quantitative analysis found that there were no significant differences of head nodding frequencies between the two groups; however, the qualitative research revealed differences between the interactions of the head nodding and the manual sign. Successive head nods by the hearing signers that co-occurred with a manual sign were rarely observed in the Deaf signers, which indicated that the hearing signers of JSL were not as sensitive to the relationships between the manual signs and head nods as the Deaf signers of JSL, creating non-native accent.

Keywords: Japanese Sign Language, prosody, head nods, second language acquisition

1 Introduction

Prosodic structure has been an area of research interest in sign language linguistic studies and has been discussed in the literature (Nespor and Sandler 1999; Brentari and Crossley 2002; Herrmann 2010; Tang et al. 2010; Brentari et al. 2012,

---

Acknowledgments: This work was supported by JSPS Grant-in-Aid for Scientific Research (C) Grant Number JP19K00779.
 I would like to thank the Deaf and hearing people who participated in the study. I am also very much indebted to Kazumi Maegawa, Kazumi Matsuoka, and anonymous reviewers for their helpful comments, John Helwig for editorial help, and Enago (www.enago.jp) for the English language review on this paper. Any remaining inaccuracies are my own responsibility.

https://doi.org/10.1515/9781501510243-009

etc.). The prosodic hierarchy, proposed in Nespor and Vogel (1986: 16) in spoken language phonology was adopted in these studies of the phonology of sign languages, such as American Sign Language (ASL) (Brentari and Crossley 2002, Brentari et al. 2012), Israeli Sign Language (Nespor and Sandler 1999), German Sign Language (DGS) (Herrmann 2010), and Hong Kong Sign Language (HKSL) (Tang et al. 2010), shown in (1).

(1) Prosodic hierarchy
Utterance (U) > Intonational Phrase (IP) > Phonological Phrase (PP) > Prosodic Word (PW)

In a DGS study, Herrmann (2010) stated that prosody comprised three main aspects: rhythm, prominence, and intonation, all of which are commonly realized across sign languages through both manual and nonmanual features. Table 1 illustrates the manual and nonmanual prosodic features found for these three aspects.

Table 1: Prosodic features of DGS (Herrmann, 2010).[1]

	Manual features	**Nonmanual features**
Rhythm	Holds, pauses, lowering of the hands, lengthening, gestures	Eye blinks, head nods, breathing
Prominence	Tense signing, lengthening, enlarging signs	Head movements, eyebrow movements, eye aperture
Intonation	N/A	Facial expressions, eyebrow movements, eye aperture, eye gaze, head and body movements, mouth gestures

It has been found that adult learners of sign language often find it difficult to learn some of the prosodic features of language which are used by native signers. Boyes Braem (1999) compared the side-to-side torso movements of deaf people who had learned Swiss German Sign Language (DSGS) as children and those who had learned it as adults. Boyes Braem observed that the deaf people who had learned DSGS as adults (late signers) were more influenced by the prosodic components of spoken German than the native signers. The early learners' torso movements tended to coincide with the sentence boundaries or with discourse units, whereas the torso movements with the stressed words in the late learners' sentences appeared at several different positions.

---

[1] For details, see Herrmann (2010: 10–11).

Therefore, it was surmised that adult learners of Japanese Sign Language (JSL) could exhibit similar behaviors. In fact, when Deaf[2] JSL native signers are asked about the sign language production of hearing JSL learners, they often claim that the hearing JSL learners have unnatural expressions and unclear meanings because of either insufficient or excess rhythms, nonmanuals, and/or flow. Even after having acquired sufficient vocabulary and grammatical knowledge, hearing JSL learners seem unable to express themselves in the same way as Deaf JSL native signers. This suggests that there may be characteristic, non-native accent differences from the JSL production of Deaf native signers. It was hypothesized that when Deaf signers feel that the sign language sentences of hearing JSL learners are unnatural, there may be some kind of prosodic error occurring. Therefore, this study analyzed the expressions of both JSL learners and JSL native signers and particularly assessed the head nodding in hearing adult learners of JSL as a second language. Maynard (2011) claimed that head nods were widespread in natural interactions in spoken Japanese; therefore, the head nodding by the hearing JSL learners that Deaf people judged to be expression errors might have been influenced by the head nodding in spoken Japanese.

Head nodding in JSL is not normally demonstrated to students in an educational setting. While some textbooks provide some grammatical explanations for head nodding,[3] as far as the author was aware, no JSL teaching methods include prosody analyses. For a brief history and the current status of JSL education, please refer to the Appendix. The next section explains the details of head nodding in JSL and its acquisition, followed by the research questions.

2 Functions of head nodding

2.1 Head nodding in sign language

Previous studies in sign languages have claimed that head nodding contains syntactic functions such as conditionals, topics, relative clauses, and Wh-clauses (Herrmann 2010; Brentari and Crossley 2002). This is also applicable to JSL, as

---

[2] The word "Deaf" with initial capitalization is used to refer to individuals who use sign language as a primary means of communication and members of the Deaf community. The use of "deaf" without capitalization refers to an inability to hear.
[3] For example, in *Hajimete no Shuwa* [Sign language for beginners] by Kimura and Ichida (2014), in addition to the conversational practice, there are grammatical explanations where the function of head nodding is stated as "playing the role of connecting other components" with examples including the parallel relationship of nouns.

shown in Ichida (2014), which concluded that JSL head nods indicated topicalized noun, conditional clause, Wh-clause, relative clause, and subordinate clause functions and various linguistic functions, such as syntactic markers, semantic markers, and discourse markers. Ichida (2010) also noted that the timing of head nodding (simultaneous and delayed) further differentiated the sentence type and the signer's intentions, as shown in Table 2.

Table 2: Head-nod timing and sentence types.[4]

Head movement	Timing	Sentence type
Nod	Simultaneous	Judgment, Yes/No question
	Delayed	Request for agreement
	Repetitive	Request for agreement/confirmation

In addition to these syntactic elements, head nods have been identified as a prosodic component of other sign languages (Wilbur 2000; Sandler 2010; Brentari et al. 2012; Puupponen et al. 2015). Wilbur (2000) and Puupponen et al. (2015) respectively studied head nods in ASL and Finnish Sign Language (FinSL) and divided them into the three categories shown in (2):

(2) Functions of head nods in ASL and FinSL
  a. Single head nod: boundary marker occurring after clause-final signs;
  b. Slow or deliberate single head nod: focus marker that co-occurs with lexical signs indicating emphasis, assertions, or existence; and
  c. Repetitive head nods: semantic markers indicating assertion, hedging, or counterfactuals.

Therefore, head nods have a prosodic component and also function as semantic markers, with the function and timing of head nods differing depending on the speed and repetition. Furthermore, Puupponen et al. (2015) believed that FinSL head nodding had a "copying manual movements" function, that is, when the head synchronizes with the path movement of the manual sign, it is expressed as a head nod.

Head nods frequently mark an IP boundary. Tang et al. (2010) reported the high frequency of head nodding in JSL. Of the prosodic levels, the IP boundary

---

[4] Ichida (2010) claimed that there are a total of five head movement types in JSL: 1) Set (head downward), 2) Shake, 3) Nod, 4) Chin up, and 5) Move. For details, see Ichida (2010: 17).

was targeted, where at least two of the following boundary cues were presented: lengthening, change in head position, change in brow position, and eye blinks. A comparative study of blinks in ASL, HKSL, DSGS, and JSL found that the blink co-occurred with head nodding at the IP boundary in 66% of blinks in JSL, which was significantly different from the frequencies in the three other languages (ASL = 0%, HKSL = 3%, and DSGS = 17%). In other words, in comparison with the native signers of other sign languages, JSL native signers were found to use head nodding more frequently in a similar way to Japanese native speakers.

Tang's observation that head nods marked a syntactic/prosodic boundary aligned with the observation of Ichikawa (2011). Ichikawa conducted a comparative study with spoken Japanese to investigate the timing of JSL head nodding from a prosody perspective. In this comparative study, while referring to the same functions of head nodding as Ichida (2014), Ichikawa divided the head nods into "*concurrent* head nods" and "*successive* head nods." "Concurrent head nods" are when the timing of the head nod overlaps with the final movement of a sign at the end of the utterance and indicates a clause boundary. "Successive head nods" are when the timing of the head nod appears after the final movement of a sign in the utterance. The study found that, although almost no successive head nods were found in spoken Japanese, a relatively large number of successive head nods were observed in JSL. As successive head nods, which have conjunctive and topicalization functions, are not concurrently performed with the manual signs, the head nod may have a linguistic function. Both Japanese native speakers and JSL native signers frequently use head nodding during speech; however, there are major differences in the timing and linguistic functions of the head nodding. Therefore, it could be of interest to examine the head nodding functions in spoken Japanese.

2.2 Head nodding in spoken Japanese

Head nodding in spoken Japanese has been examined primarily in dialog settings (Maynard 1993; Onodera 2004; Kita and Ide 2007; Ichikawa 2011). Table 3 shows the observation points and head nodding functions collected from the dialog analyses of Kita and Ide (2007), Maynard (2011), and Ichikawa (2011).

Table 3 indicates that head nods in spoken Japanese utterances have a prosodic component that provides intonation, and that head nodding has the role of promoting smooth dialog when placed at syntactic endings or at the end of utterance units.

Table 3: Observation points and head nodding functions.

Previous studies	Kita and Ide (2007)	Maynard (2011)	Ichikawa (2011)
Observation points and head nodding functions	1) Facilitates the co-occurrence with grammatical units 2) Facilitates the co-occurrence of "*ne*"[5] and other particles	1) Emphasizes meaning 2) End of utterance 3) Fills utterance gaps	1) Back channeling 2) Indication of a break in the Information Transmission Unit[6] 3) Promotes response from the interlocutor

As in JSL, the head nodding in spoken Japanese functions as a prosodic component and acts as a marker. In other words, at first glance, it may seem that head movements are used in the same way. However, a major point of difference is that the head nodding in spoken Japanese has a strong paralinguistic component, as suggested by Maynard (2011), rather than distinguishing differences in meaning or conveying linguistic information in and of itself. When compared with JSL, there seem to be no strict limits on the use of head nods in spoken Japanese. Shimotani (2015) showed a silent video clip to four Japanese native speakers with no experience of studying JSL, asked them to talk to a video camera about what they saw in the video clip, and then analyzed the frequency of head nodding at the IP boundaries. It was found that there were variations between the speakers (ranging from 47% to 100%) with significant differences in the speaking style and the head nod direction. For example, some speakers nodded after first raising their heads, whereas others slightly and repetitively nodded while speaking. It was concluded that head nodding in spoken Japanese, in particular, had no strict limitations and was relatively free. However, without having any explicit instruction, hearing JSL learners gradually learn different head nodding patterns for their signed utterances.

2.3 Head nodding by JSL learners

A few studies have focused on head nodding produced by nonnative JSL signers. Takeuchi et al. (1999) compared the head nodding in JSL productions by both Deaf JSL native signers and hearing JSL learners and reported the results of an error analysis. Seven Deaf signers and 15 hearing learners with a range of 1 year

---
[5] *ne* is a common final particle of speech in Japanese conversation.
[6] "Information Transmission Unit" is defined as a "unit of chronology which conveys certain information through continuous speech (Ichikawa 2011: 157)."

or less to 6 years of experience of studying JSL were asked to memorize and reproduce a narrative story signed by a Deaf person. It was confirmed that the seven Deaf signers used 28 types of head nod, whereas only 10 of those types were observed by the hearing signers. In addition, of these 10 types, 13 of the 15 hearing signers used a head nod that involved the head moving directly downward and then returning to a neutral position, which implied that this was the easiest head nod to learn. When the expressions were deemed unnatural, it was not stated whether the errors were prosodic or syntactic errors that changed the meaning of the sentence; however, in approximately 80% of the cases, nine of the head-nod types were deemed to be erroneous, such as a head nod to show the start of a sign language story, a head nod to show a sentence break, a head nod to show the end of a story, and a head nod with a conjunctive function. According to Ichikawa's (2011) analysis, the head nods that indicated the start/end of a story and the head nods with conjunctive functions were more likely to be successive head nods that did not co-occur with the manual signs. The four head-nod types with lower error ratios co-occurred with manual signs, such as PERSON or IX-1.[7] Therefore, it was surmised that the hearing JSL learners had greater difficulties learning successive head nods than learning concurrent head nods. As stated above, successive head nods rarely occur in spoken Japanese.

Table 4 shows the findings regarding JSL and Japanese-based head nodding in the abovementioned studies.

Table 4: Summary of head nods in JSL and Japanese.

Item	JSL	Japanese
Prosodic function	Yes	Yes
Syntactic function and other linguistic components	Yes	No
Concurrent head nod	Yes	Yes
Successive head nod	Yes	Rarely
Type of head nod	28 types or more	Unclear

Although both have prosodic functions and both facilitate utterances, JSL head nods have a syntactic function that denotes meaning by their presence or absence, that is, successive head nods carry language information, such as independent connective functions, which is very different from the head nods in spoken Japanese. Although it is known that there are at least 28 types of head nods in

---

[7] IX stands for a pointing sign.

JSL, the Japanese head-nod types are unknown; therefore, further investigation is required.

Based on these previous studies and findings, the following research questions were developed.

> RQ1. Is the frequency of head nodding in hearing JSL learners similar to that in Deaf JSL native signers? (quantitative research)
>
> RQ2. Do hearing JSL learners use head nodding in the same way as Deaf JSL native signers? (qualitative research)

To answer these research questions, the head nods by hearing JSL learners and Deaf JSL native signers were compared from video material.

3 Method

3.1 Participants

The participants included four Deaf people whose native language is JSL (D-1, D-2, D-3, and D-4) and four hearing people who had started studying JSL as adults (H-1, H-2, H-3, and H-4). All those in the Deaf group were born to Deaf parents, acquired JSL as their mother tongue, and attended schools for the deaf. The Deaf group included two men and two women in their 30s and 40s. The hearing group participants, which included one man and three women ranging in age from their 20s to their 50s, had approximately 7 to 14 years of sign language study experience from taking sign language training course through private sign language classes, to informal study with Deaf friends. Of this group, all four participants regularly worked as sign language interpreters and three of them were certified sign language interpreters.

3.2 Data collection

The film called *The Pear Tree Story* (Chafe 1980) was used in this study, because it has been widely used as narrative data in linguistic research. *The Pear Tree Story* is an approximately 6-minute silent film with absolutely no speech from the characters. The participants were each shown the film and then asked to recount the story in JSL to a Deaf JSL native interlocutor who did not know the content of the story. After the JSL narration, the hearing group participants were asked to narrate the story again in Japanese to a Japanese native interlocutor who did not know the content of the story, in view of the need to confirm the meaning of the JSL expressed. When collecting data, two video cameras were used to record the narratives from the front and side of the participants.

3.3 Transcription procedure

The video-recorded narratives were transcribed and analyzed using the annotation tool, ELAN[8] (Wittenburg et al. 2006), and a Deaf collaborator, whose native language was JSL, was asked to confirm the accuracy of the transcription. First, all the manual signs were transcribed, and then, all the points where a head nod appeared were marked. In line with the definition given by Ichikawa (2011), a head nod was taken to mean a downward movement of the head to the lowest point until it moved back to a neutral position without being held in place, and the movement of the head in an upward direction before being moved downward without being held in the neutral position. Multiple continuous head nods from the repetition of the manual signs were viewed as a single nod while nodding, whereas searching for a word was excluded from the analysis. Further, the transcribed head nods were separately categorized as concurrent or successive.

The quantitative head-nod frequency analysis was conducted based on the definitions of Ichikawa (2011). A concurrent head nod was taken to be a head nod when a manual sign co-occurred with the nod, whereas a successive head nod was when the head reached the lowest position after the handshape was released or when the signing location started to shift. When the head nod occurred with the signs kept in the same location after expressing a word, it was seen to be a prosodic component, and it was judged that the sign remained in place although the meaning had finished (Brentari and Crossley 2002; Herrmann 2010; Brentari et al. 2012). When the grammatical meaning such as a classifier predicate was retained, it was judged as having a continued meaning to the manual sign and was categorized as a concurrent head nod.

The qualitative analysis of head nods required the Deaf collaborator to perform four judgment tasks. First, to select candidates for the IP boundary, the Deaf collaborator was shown the data obtained from the Deaf group and asked to mark all head nods showing major demarcations and also note if there were any major demarcations without a head nod. As in the study of Tang et al. (2010), the

---

[8] ELAN, software developed at the Max Planck Institute for Psycholinguistics, The Language Archive, Nijmegen, The Netherlands is widely used for language transcription and conversational analysis (https://archive.mpi.nl/tla/elan).

above marks were identified as the IP boundary when at least two boundary cues were presented: lengthening, change in head position, change in brow position, and eye blinks. Then, the Deaf collaborator was asked to judge the functions of the head nods appearing at the IP boundary. Finally, with a focus on the successive head nods, which rarely appeared in spoken Japanese, an investigation was made to see if any commonalities were observable in all the successive head nods in the data. After the transcription and analysis of the Deaf group, the hearing group data were shown to the Deaf collaborator, and the analysis process was repeated. Then, the head-nod expressions in each group were compared to assess the learning status of the head-nod expressions in the hearing group.

4 Results

4.1 Overall data

Table 5 shows the total duration of signing (starting with the head nod signaling the start of the narrative and ending with the sign FINISH or with the head nod signaling the end of the narrative), the total number of manual signs, the total number of head nods, the number of concurrent head nods, and the number of successive head nods for the eight participants.

Table 5: Overall data.

Participant	Total duration of signing	Total number of manual signs	Total number of head nods	Number of concurrent head nods	Number of successive head nods
D-1	2′28″	243	96/243 (.39)	56/96 (.58)	40/96 (.42)
D-2	2′06″	223	85/223 (.38)	52/85 (.61)	33/85 (.39)
D-3	4′30″	461	136/461 (.29)	89/136 (.65)	47/136 (.35)
D-4	3′12″	291	96/291 (.32)	50/96 (.52)	46/96 (.48)
H-1	3′09″	212	48/212 (.22)	27/48 (.56)	21/48 (.44)
H-2	3′14″	181	90/181 (.49)	60/90 (.67)	30/90 (.33)
H-3	2′26″	162	43/162 (.26)	28/43 (.65)	15/43 (.35)
H-4	4′06″	268	83/268 (.30)	37/83 (.45)	46/83 (.55)

The total duration of signing was between 2′06″ and 4′30″, and the total number of manual signs was between 162 and 461. Concurrent and successive head nods were observed in all data.

4.2 Frequency of head nodding

First, a comparison was made between the two groups for the frequency of head nodding against the total number of manual signs. The results are shown in Figure 1.

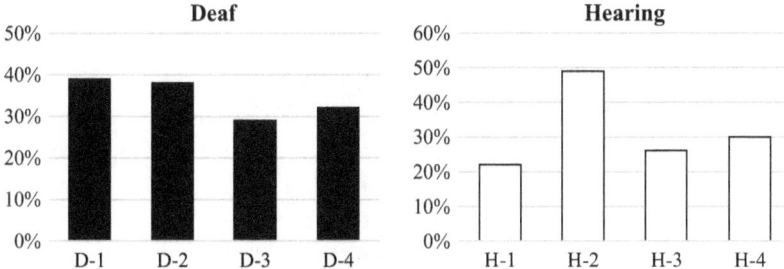

Figure 1: Frequency of head nods against the total number of manual signs.

The *t*-test found no significant differences between the Deaf and hearing groups (P = 0.80472 > 0.05), that is, the hearing group used head nods at almost the same frequency as the Deaf group. However, the observation revealed that there was greater variation in the hearing group than in the Deaf group (Deaf group STD = 0.04153 < hearing group STD = 0.10353).

Next, a comparison was made for the frequency of successive head nods against the total number of head nods. The results are shown in Figure 2.

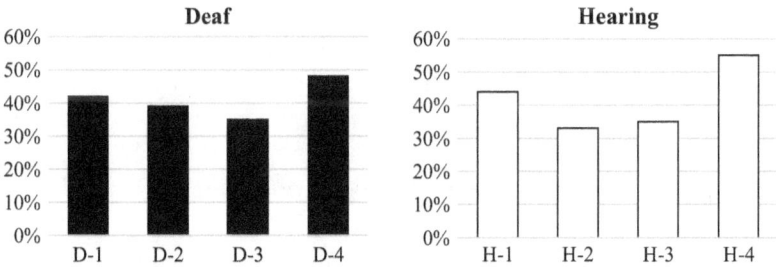

Figure 2: Frequency of successive head nods.

The *t*-test revealed no significant differences between the two groups (P = 0.96878 > 0.05). Despite the greater variations in the hearing than in the Deaf group (Deaf group STD = 0.04743 < hearing group STD = 0.08699), it was found that the successive head nods, which were rarely observed in Japanese utterances, were used by hearing signers in JSL utterances with a frequency close to that of Deaf signers.

4.3 Selection of IP boundary and prosodic components

A qualitative analysis and comparison of the head nodding were then conducted. First, the IP boundary was identified. When the Deaf collaborator marked what they believed to be the major demarcations, a total of 67 locations were extracted for the Deaf group, that is, 25 points in D-1, 9 in D-2, 17 in D-3, and 16 in D-4, and it was confirmed that there was a head nod at each point. Tang et al. (2010) reported that at least two prosodic components were observed at an IP boundary, and a similar pattern was found in these data. A minimum of two prosodic component types and a maximum of five types co-occurred at each point when a manual sign was observed, such as holding the sign or joining the hands in the middle of the torso, or where a nonmanual feature was observed, such as a blink or a change in the position of the gaze, the face, the head, or the body.

Thereafter, the IP boundary in the hearing group's data was analyzed. As there were many points where the decision was not clear to the Deaf collaborator, these points were removed from the analysis. Consequently, a total of 59 IP boundaries were found for the hearing group, that is, 8 points in H-1, 11 in H-2, 15 in H-3, and 25 in H-4, at which a head nod was observed at each point. Two to five types of prosodic components that co-occurred at each point where a sign position was held were also found in the hearing group's data. Those prosodic components included hands joined in the middle of the torso, a blink, a change in the eye gaze, and a change in the position of the head or body. The next section more closely examines the functions of these head nods.

4.4 Functions of head nodding at the IP boundary

In the data of the Deaf group, the following three functions of head nodding were determined at the IP boundary: 1) to signal a change in scene; 2) to signal the start of a role shift; and 3) to signal the end of the role shift. There were also prosodic components other than head nods, however, only the head nods and the manual sign retentions are shown by the lines in the example below.[9] Figure 3 shows that a new scene begins after the IP boundary (head nod).

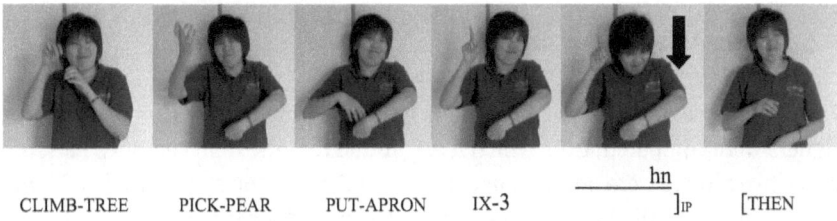

CLIMB-TREE   PICK-PEAR   PUT-APRON   IX-3   hn
                                                               ]IP   [THEN

Figure 3: Scene shifting (D-3). '(A man) climbed the tree, picked pears, put them into his apron, then...'.

In Figure 4, the beginning of the role shift is indicated by a head nod.

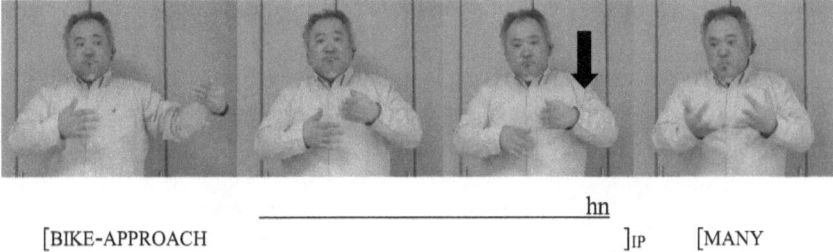

[BIKE-APPROACH   hn
                                                 ]IP   [MANY

Figure 4: Signalling the start of a role shift (D-4). 'A bike came and stopped. There are many...'.

The head nods that appear at the IP boundary have a greater range of vertical motion than those that do not appear at the IP boundary and are characterized by a downward movement that forms a gentle arch after a slight pause. Therefore, when this head-nod pattern is observed, there is a shift to a new scene, or a role shift starts or ends. Horiuchi et al. (2008) stated that successive head nods have a function of role shift ending, which was also observed in this study. The successive head nods were also found to have a function of role shift starting.

A similar pattern was found in the head nods of the hearing JSL learners, that is, they confirmed a signal to a change in scene, a start of a role shift, or an end of a role shift. Although the initial pause is omitted and the head tends to abruptly

---

[9] The following conventions are valid for all examples in this paper: sign glosses are written in small capital letters. Head nod (hn) shows the period from the start of the head movement to the end.

descend unlike Deaf signers, the hearing learners' head nods had similar functions to those used by the Deaf native signers.

4.5 Successive head nods

Finally, the use of successive head nods by the hearing learners and Deaf native signers were compared, from which it was found that the representative patterns in the two groups were not the same. First, in 163 of the 166 successive head nods expressed by the Deaf group, when the position of the head reached the lowest point, the location and handshape were transitioning to the next sign, or the signers took a pose, or lowered their hands to a neutral position in preparation for the next sign. By contrast, in 45 of the 112 successive head nods expressed by the hearing group, the handshape or signing location was retained when the position of the head reached the lowest point. On 39 occasions (approximately 35%), this was felt by the Deaf collaborator to be either unnatural or to obfuscate the meaning.

Figure 5 was signed by a Deaf native signer, and the "unnatural" examples in (3) and (4) were signed by the hearing learners. The moment where the position of the head reaches the lowest point is marked with an "x."

Figure 5: Deaf signer (D-1). 'While the man climbed the tree and picked the pears, a child on the bike . . . .

In Figure 5, successive head nods were observed at two points. At Point 1, when the head reached the lowest point, the previous sign CLIMB-TREE had already been released from its final location, and at Point 2, the handshape for the sign MIDDLE had been released and the signing location was starting to shift. As noted by Ichikawa (2011), successive head nods have their own linguistic functions, such as conjoining clauses. Therefore, successive head nods should not occur until the final sign of the IP boundary shifts to a transitionary movement. In the following examples, the hearing learners' head nods were judged to be unnatural by the Deaf collaborator:

(3) Hearing signer (H-4)

                 x   hn
[MAN   COME   ]$_{IP}$ [GOAT   PULL-GOAT
'A man came. A goat was pulled by the man.'

(4) Hearing signer (H-3)

                 x   hn
[IX-3   GOAT   ]$_{IP}$ [MAN   PULL-GOAT
'There was a goat, and a man pulled it.'

In examples (3) and (4), the head started to move downward, whereas the previous sign was maintained at its final location. The same pattern was found in 39 utterances. Those utterances included examples such as (5), where the Japanese word *de* (lit. 'and') was mouthed concurrently with the head nod.

(5) Case where a Japanese word was mouthed alongside a successive head nod (H-1)
    Head: x   hn
    Mouth: de
    Hand: CLIMB-LADDER UP   ]$_{IP}$ [PEAR   PICK-PEAR   START
'(The man) climbed the ladder and started to pick pears.'

The Deaf collaborator also observed that the hearing learners occasionally used the head nod in improper situations. In the following example (6), a head nod that resembled the one used by the native signer to indicate the shift in the scene or the beginning of the role shift occurred in an inappropriate context.

(6) Head nod thought to signal change in the scene (H-1)

                             x   hn
CALL-BOY   BOY   HAT   (hands folded)   BOY-COME
'(The boy) got another boy's attention and walked to his place.'

The Deaf collaborator expected the scene to change because of the large head nod after HAT, which was similar to the nods appearing at the IP boundary, and both hands were folded.

The following example lacks the head nod required to signal a scene change, which resulted in a shift in meaning. As shown in example (7), the English translations describe the intended meaning on the basis of what the speaker said in her Japanese narrative, followed by the meaning the Deaf collaborator interpreted.

(7) Shift in meaning due to an omitted head nod (H-2)

```
                    x   hn                    x   hn
RIDE-BIKE   IX-3   GIRL   BIKE        GIRL-RIDE-BIKE-COME
```
(Intended meaning) 'The boy was riding a bike. Then, further away, a girl came toward him on a bike.'
(Actual meaning) 'The boy was riding a bike...then he... the girl came toward him on a bike.'

If there were a head nod at the IP boundary showing a scene change after RIDE-BIKE, it would be clear that IX-3 refers to the girl, who is a new character some distance away. Because the head nod was omitted, the Deaf collaborator mistakenly interpreted IX-3 as referring to the boy and assumed that the boy was some distance away. The sign GIRL appeared immediately after IX-3, and hence, the collaborator could not follow the meaning and was perplexed.

The analysis revealed that the frequency of head nods was similar in the two groups. However, the hearing learners' head nods usage was not identical to that of the Deaf native signers.

5 Discussion and conclusion

This study investigated the degree to which JSL learners were able to acquire native-like prosodic features of JSL, the research questions for which were as follows:

> RQ1. Is the frequency of head nodding in hearing JSL learners similar to that in Deaf JSL native signers? (Quantitative research)
>
> RQ2. Do hearing JSL learners use head nodding in the same way as Deaf JSL native signers? (qualitative research)

It was clear that there were no significant quantitative differences between the two groups; however, there were significant qualitative differences.

First, there were no significant differences in the frequency of head nodding or the ratio of concurrent and successive head nods in comparison with the Deaf group. In other words, it was found that the hearing signers did use successive head nodding, which is not typically observed in Japanese utterances. Although they had not received explicit instruction, the hearing learners, all of whom had had at least 7 years of JSL study experience, were able to use their head nods at a similar frequency to the Deaf signers. The hearing learners' head nods also included native-like natural instances that co-occurred with other prosodic components, such as a blink and functioned as a signal for a change in the scene or the start/end of a role shift. However, there were cases when the head nodding was not native-like, such as when the head nodding expected at the IP boundary mistakenly appeared at other points. In other examples, the head nod at the IP boundary was omitted by the hearing learners, which resulted in a misinterpretation of the pronoun by the Deaf collaborator. These observations indicated that learning the consistent (native-like) uses of head nods at the IP boundary was not a simple task.

In addition, both groups used successive head nods with equal frequency. However, there were differences between the groups for the head nod and the connection with the manual signs. In the data obtained from the Deaf group, the head nod rarely co-occurred with the sign, whereas in the hearing group, it unnaturally co-occurred approximately 35% of the time. A successive head nod is essentially defined as a head nod that does not occur while the manual signs are being shown and is unlikely to co-occur alongside signs as a redundant prosodic component. As successive head nods inherently carry linguistic information, the handshape and location must be in a transitional movement when such head nods are used. Sign language learners may not be as alert as Deaf native signers regarding the relationships between successive head nods and the timing of the manual transition as this is not normally taught in educational settings of JSL.

In some cases, Japanese words were mouthed by the hearing learners at points that were judged to be unnatural by the Deaf collaborator. Based on Kita and Ide's (2007) study, in spoken Japanese utterances, head nodding tends to co-occur with particles; therefore, it could be speculated that the head nodding that co-occurred with the mouthing of a Japanese particle was a transfer from the head nodding rhythm in spoken Japanese, which resulted in the Deaf collaborator perceiving it as an unnatural nonnative accent. This instance of language transfer is interesting because sign language has visual modality and spoken Japanese has auditory modality. How the bimodal language contact resulted in a possible language transfer could be the focus of future research.

This study revealed the properties of head nods and the significant effects they have on the naturalness of JSL. Therefore, further research needs to assess whether the patterns found in this study are language-specific or reflect the prosodic properties shared in other sign languages worldwide. Another future research area could be to measure and numerically analyze JSL head nods using the methodology of Boyes Braem (1999). The Deaf collaborator claimed that the head nods at the IP boundary analyzed in this study had larger vertical movements than the head nods at other points and their movement often formed a gentle arch shape. If the overall movement of the head, including the head nodding at other points, can be measured and numerically converted in more detail, it may be possible to understand the prosodic rhythms of head nods more completely in JSL and more easily perform a comparison of the prosodic patterns between the JSL learners. In addition, by analyzing the data in their spoken Japanese utterances, a comparison could be made between the head nods from the same person (a hearing learner) in JSL and spoken Japanese. Furthermore, the JSL skills of all four of the hearing signers participating in this study were intermediate to high-intermediate, i.e., not beginners. By expanding the participant sample to include beginner JSL learners, it may be possible to discover the stage-by-stage processes and the order in which the hearing signers learn JSL head nodding. The "subtle" prosodic properties of sign languages are not easily detectable by hearing learners' eyes. However, our research revealed that they crucially affect the naturalness of their signed utterances, as judged by Deaf native signers. Further research on the prosody of sign languages could lead to the development of better teaching materials and methods.

Appendix: A history of teaching environment of Japanese Sign Language

In Japan, sign language education is often aimed at training sign language interpreters. However, there are few places where JSL can be studied systematically.

In the half-century since the establishment of the first sign language study group (the *shuwa* circle) in Japan in 1963, the sign language learning environment in Japan has progressed significantly. The sign language training course of the Ministry of Health, Labour and Welfare, which began in 1970, is now provided as a communication support program for community life support services in the Services and Supports for Persons with Disabilities Act.[10] In addition to providing a deeper understanding and recognition of the lives of deaf and hard-of-hearing people and the related welfare systems, the purpose of this course is to help learn the sign language vocabulary and expression techniques essential to hold everyday conversations in sign language (Japan National Center of Sign Language Education 2014). In the textbook used in this course, references to head nodding, explanations for the need to have an awareness of nonmanual features in addition to manual features are found, which state that "various expressions can be made by changing the facial expressions, intensities and speed, even if the manual sign is the same" (Japan National Center of Sign Language Education 2014: 9) and "the tip of differentiating the representation of intensity is not only about larger or smaller manual signs; facial expressions are also important. In addition to expressing emotions, there are methods such as widening or narrowing the eyes or puffing out or sucking in the cheeks" (Japan National Center of Sign Language Education 2014: 51). However, there are no specific references to head nodding. Therefore, whether instructors provide additional explanations in the course or whether the natural input for students mostly comes from observing the model expressions of the instructors should be investigated.

In the 1990s, distinct from the abovementioned welfare activities, approaches were developed to position sign language training as second language education. Sign language was first taught in 1991 using the natural approach teaching method (NA method), which is a direct teaching method (Ichida and Kimura 1998). This teaching method is used at the College of the National Rehabilitation Center for Persons with Disabilities to train sign language interpreters. As of 2015, there were nine universities where JSL was positioned as a language course open to all undergraduate students (Matsuoka et al. 2018), most of which used the NA method of instruction (Kotani et al. 2011; Matsuoka et al. 2018). Apart from universities, courses using the NA method are held in private sign language classes. In these educational settings, there are no common textbooks such as the one used in the aforementioned sign language training course. Therefore, when several teachers were asked about how instruction was provided for head nodding, they responded that based on the theory of the NA method, the aim of instruction was tacit natural learning without any explicit explanation of the grammatical theory associated with head nodding.

---

10 A law enacted in 2013 for the comprehensive support of the daily and social lives of people with disabilities.

The resources for studying sign language independently include educational TV programs, books, dictionaries, and DVDs, most of which introduce the words and sentences vital for daily conversation and the lives of Deaf/deaf people, with almost no explanations of head nodding.

References

Boyes Braem, Penny. 1999. Rhythmic temporal patterns in the signing of deaf early and late learners of Swiss German Sign Language. *Language and Speech* 42(2–3). 177–208.

Brentari, Diane, Marie A. Nadolske & George Wolford. 2012. Can experience with co-speech gesture influence the prosody of a sign language? Sign language prosodic cues in bimodal bilinguals. *Bilingualism: Language and Cognition* 15(2). 402–412.

Brentari, Diane & Laurinda Crossley. 2002. Prosody on the hands and face: Evidence from American Sign Language. *Sign Language & Linguistics* 5(2). 105–130.

Chafe, Wallace L. 1980. *The pear stories: Cognitive, cultural, and linguistic aspect of narrative production.* Norwood, NJ: Ablex.

Herrmann, Annika 2010. The interaction of eye blinks and other prosodic cues in German Sign Language. *Sign Language & Linguistics* 13(1). 3–39.

Horiuchi, Yasuo, Ryoko Saito, Hiroko Kamesaki, Masafumi Nishida, Shingo Kuroiwa & Akira Ichikawa. 2008. *Nihon Shuwa no Setsuzokushi to Unazuki no Kankei no Bunseki* [Analysis of conjunctions and head nods in Japanese sign language]. Paper presented at the 34th Annual Conference of the Japanese Association of Sign Linguistics, Kobe, Japan, 14–15 September.

Ichikawa, Akira. 2011. *Taiwa no Kotoba no Kagaku: Prosody ga Sasaeru Communication* [The science of the language of dialogs: Prosody facilitates communication]. Tokyo: Waseda University Press.

Ichida, Yasuhiro. 2010. Introduction to Japanese Sign Language: Iconicity in language. In Makiko Hirakawa, Shunji Inagaki, Setsuko Arita, Yuko Goto Butler, Kaoru Horie, Eric Hauser, Yasuhiro Shirai & Jessika Tsubakita (eds.), *Studies in Language Science 9.* 9–32. Tokyo: Kuroshio Publishers.

Ichida, Yasuhiro. 2014. *Shuwa Gengogaku* [Sign linguistics]. Paper presented at the annual seminar for certified JSL interpreters, Saitama, Japan.

Ichida, Yasuhiro & Harumi Kimura. 1998. *Shuwa Kyoiku ni Okeru Natural Approach* [Natural Approach method on sign language teaching]. *Sign Linguistics Research* 14(2). 55–59.

Japan National Center of Sign Language Education. 2014. *Shuwa wo Manabou Shuwa de Hanasou* [Let's learn sign language and communicate in sign language]. Tokyo: Japanese Federation of the Deaf.

Kimura, Harumi & Yasuhiro Ichida. 2014. *Hajimete no Shuwa: Shoho kara Yasashiku Manaberu Shuwa no Hon* [Sign language for beginners: You can learn sign language from the scratch]. Tokyo: Seikatsu Shoin.

Kita, Sotaro & Sachiko Ide. 2007. Nodding, aizuchi, and final particles in Japanese conversation: How conversation reflects the ideology of communication and social relationships. *Journal of Pragmatics* 39(7). 1242–1254.

Kotani, Masao, Fumie Shimojo & Naoko Iizumi. 2011. *Atarashii Liberal Arts to Shiteno Nihon Shuwa. Ochanomizujoshi Daigaku ni Okeru Shuwagakunyumon Donyu no Keiken kara* [JSL in the Liberal Arts. Ochanomizu University's challenge]. *Japanese Journal of Sign Linguistics* 20. 19–38.

Matsuoka, Kazumi, Kazumi Maegawa & Natsuko Shimotani. 2018. *Daigaku ni Okeru Nihon Shuwa Class no Genjo to Kadai: Minority no Gengo to Bunka heno Rikai wo Unagasu Jugyo* [Current situation and challenges of college-level courses of Japanese sign language: Teaching the language and culture of minority community]. *Journal of Plurilingual and Multilingual Education* 6. 60–71.

Maynard, Senko K. 1993. *Kaiwa Bunseki* [Conversation analyses]. Tokyo: Kuroshio Publishers.

Maynard, Senko K. 2011. *Learning Japanese for real: A guide to grammar, use, and genres of the Nihongo world*. Honolulu: University of Hawaii Press.

Nespor, Marina & Irene Vogel. 1986. *Prosodic phonology*. Dordrecht: Foris.

Nespor, Marina & Wendy Sandler. 1999. Prosody in Israeli Sign Language. *Language and Speech* 42(2–3). 143–176.

Onodera, Noriko. O. 2004. Pragmatics & Beyond New Series. In *Japanese Discourse Markers*, 132. Amsterdam/Philadelphia: John Benjamins.

Puupponen, Anna, Tuija Wainio, Birgitta Burger & Tommi Jantunen. 2015. Head movements in Finnish Sign Language on the basis of motion capture data. A study of the form and function of nods, nodding, head thrusts, and head pulls. *Sign Language & Linguistics* 18(1). 1–45.

Sandler, Wendy. 2010. Prosody and syntax in sign languages. *Transactions of the Philological Society* 108(3). 298–328.

Shimotani, Natsuko. 2015. *Head nod as a prosodic cue in Japanese sign language and its use by native signers and non-native interpreters*. Hong Kong: The Chinese University of Hong Kong MA thesis.

Takeuchi, Kaori, Harumi Kimura, Akiko Ikeda, Yumiko Fukada & Yasuhiro Ichida. 1999. *Gakushusha no Shuwabun ni Okeru Unazuki no Error Bunseki* [Error analyses of head nods by L2 learners of JSL] 20–23. Paper presented at the 25th Annual Conference of the Japanese Association of Sign Linguistics, Nigata, Japan, 10–11, July. Saitama: Japanese Association for Sign Language Studies.

Tang, Gladys, Diane Brentari, Carolina Gonzalez & Felix Sze. 2010. Crosslinguistic variation in prosodic cues. In Diane Brentari (ed.), *Sign Languages*, 519–542. New York: Cambridge University Press.

Wilbur, Ronnie B. 2000. Phonological and prosodic layering of nonmanuals in American Sign Language. In Harlan Lane & Karen Emmorey (eds.), *The Signs of Language Revisited: Festschrift for Ursula Bellugi and Edward Klima*, 213–241. Hillsdale, NJ: Lawrence Erlbaum.

Wittenburg, Peter, Hennie Brugman, Albert Russel, Alex Klassmann & Han Sloetjes. 2006. ELAN: A professional framework for multimodality research. Paper presented at the Fifth International Conference on Language Resources and Evaluation (LREC), Genoa, Italy, 22–28.

Shiou-fen Su
Composite utterances in Taiwan Sign Language

Abstract: This paper investigates composite utterances in Taiwan Sign Language (TSL) produced from native and near-native deaf signers, native hearing signers, and fluent hearing second language learners. Composite utterances, in which description, indication, and depiction are combined together manually and non-manually, are prevalent in narratives produced by deaf signers, but only a few are produced by hearing signers, even native ones. For deaf signers, language and gesture are integrated simultaneously and it is natural for them to represent the events with both hands, conflated with manual gestures and with non-manual expressions. Their utterances are produced mostly through the composite methods of describing, indicating and depicting. For hearing signers, language and gesture are produced with different modalities in their daily spoken Mandarin conversation. In their thinking-for-signing situation, the manual channel is mainly responsible for the language part. Their utterances are produced mostly with the method of describing.

Keywords: composite utterances, grounded mental spaces and conceptual blending theory, involvement strategies, method of signaling, Taiwan Sign Language

1 Introduction

Sign languages are languages produced by hands and/or trunk or face and perceived by eyes. There are two independent hands (right hand and left hand) and two independent channels (manual and non-manual) to produce sign languages. Non-manual markers include body gestures, facial expressions, etc. Not all manual expressions are conventionalized signs. Prior to the work of Stokoe (1960), everything in sign languages was regarded as gestures. In contrast, at the time that sign languages were claimed to be real human languages, all were claimed to be linguistic, even the non-manual behaviors. But in reality, both linguistic elements and non-linguistic gestures exist and both contribute to the meaning in sign language discourse. In addition, language and gesture can be integrated simultaneously to express an even more complex meaning with one single unit. Refer to the review in Goldin-Meadow and Brentari (2017). Mental spaces and conceptual blending theory discussed by Fauconnier ([1985] 1994,

1997, 1998) and Fauconnier and Turner (1996, 1998, 2002, 2006) is adopted as a theoretical framework to account for the role of these prevalent gestural elements and for how these simultaneously integrated units are understood in narratives.

Taiwan Sign Language (hereafter, TSL), like other sign languages, is a natural human language and is a main tool for deaf people in Taiwan to communicate in their daily life (Ann 1993; Chang, Su and Tai 2005; Chen 2010; Lee 2003; Smith 1989; and others). According to Enfield (2009: 15), signs from different mediums come together into a "communicative move that incorporates multiple signs of multiple types", which he calls a *composite utterance*, in a communicative action (Puupponen 2019: 11). This paper investigates composite utterances of TSL, a visual-gestural mode of language. In particular, it is about how signers integrate manual and non-manual expressions, through composite methods of *describing*, *indicating*, and/or *depicting* (Clark 1996, 2003; Clark and Gerrig 1990), to create and blend *grounded mental spaces* (Dudis 2002, 2004; Kenden 2004; Liddell 1995, 1996, 1998, 2000a, 2003; Liddell and Metzger 1998; Liddell and Vogt-Svendsen 2007 and others).

The comparison with regard to their ability to create and blend grounded mental spaces to represent the visible world more iconically and more expressively in narratives will be done as well among TSL of native deaf signers, near-native deaf signers, native hearing signers and hearing second language learners. These hearing signers' native language is Mandarin Chinese. They produce the narratives both in Mandarin and in TSL. The analysis shows that the power of simultaneity to construct narratives more informatively and more efficiently is not prevalently represented by the native hearing signers, and these fluent second language learners.

Investigating these aspects of grammar and discourse, this paper aims to answer the following issues: (1) What are the methods of signaling in TSL? (2) How do TSL signers create grounded mental spaces through composite methods of signaling? (3) How are grounded blends exploited as involvement strategies to achieve narrative functions? (4) What are the differences of the composite utterances among signed language narratives from different background of signers?

To explore these issues, TSL narratives elicited with a wordless picturebook 'Frog, where are you?' (Mayer 1969) were analyzed. They were collected from the projects led by Professors James Tai and Jane Tsay in National Chung Cheng University since 2000. The three methods of signaling, examples of composite utterances and how they signify referents differently will be described and illustrated in section 2. Grounded spaces blends will be introduced and illustrated in section 3. Composite utterances as involvement strategies will be demonstrated in section 4, and finally the conclusion.

2 Methods of signaling

In situated human interactions, language "can be viewed as intentionally communicative action involving the specific range of semiotic resources available" (Ferrara and Hodge 2018: 1). This intentionally communicative action is composite and it integrates categorical elements and gradient ones; arbitrary symbols and motivated signals to make the meaning (Clark 2016; Cooperrider and Mesh 2021; Enfield 2009; Ferrara and Hodge 2018; Holler and Levinson 2019). According to Clark's (1996) theory of language use, three methods of signaling can be 'actioned' "during the joint creation of multimodal 'composite utterances'" (Enfield 2009): *describing, indicating* and *depicting* (Ferrara and Hodge 2018: 1). 'Describing-as,' 'indicating' and 'demonstration' are the names of these three methods which Clark (1996) proposed. Ferrara and Hodge (2018: 3) "abbreviate 'describing-as' to 'describing' and use the term 'depiction' instead of 'demonstration' to correspond with more recent signed and spoken language literatures (Clark 2016; Dingemanse 2014; Dudis 2011; Liddell 2003)". These methods differ fundamentally in how they signify referents, and they "can be used alone or in combination with others" (Ferrara and Hodge 2018: 1). With those, people perform communicative acts for anchoring to material worlds – to actual people, animals, artifacts, events, coordinating attention, and building common ground to each other (Clark 2003: 243; Cooperrider and Mesh 2021: 3).

Clark's (1996) theory of language use is based on the principles of three types of 'sign' proposed by Peirce ([1902] 1955): symbols, indices, and icons. They are signaled through different acts. Symbols are signaled through acts of description, indices are through acts of indication, and icons are through acts of depiction. Language use is therefore a system of signaling with these three different methods. The primary function of indication is to designate things, and that of depiction is to enable others to experience what it is like to perceive the things depicted (Clark 2003: 245; Clark and Gerrig 1990; Ferrara and Hodge 2018: 3–4). What they depicted can be events, states, processes, or objects. Signaling of describing is also called as 'telling without showing', producing structures that are more comparable to those found in spoken languages; signaling of depicting is also referred to as 'telling and showing', thereby producing highly iconic structures (Fay et al. 2014; Russo, Giuranna and Pizzuto 2001).

In following subsections, these three methods will be explained and illustrated.

2.1 Method of describing

Conventionalized signs in signed languages, like words in spoken languages, are symbols, functioning as the signaling of describing. Each symbol signifies a category of things. For example, the sign 'TREE' is a symbol signifying a category of trees. Symbols are conventionalized pairings of form and meaning. Even the motivated signs for the same meaning in different signed languages can be totally different in forms. For example, the sign 'TREE' in ASL is totally different from the sign in Danish Sign Language and the sign in Chinese Sign Language, although they are all iconic, motivated signs. In ASL sign 'TREE', "the hands and forearms are positioned to resemble a tree growing out of the ground; the Danish equivalent uses the hands to trace the outline of a tree's branches and trunk, top to bottom; and the Chinese sign meaning tree uses two curved hands to trace the outline of a tree trunk, from the ground up" (Taub 2001: 8).

2.2 Method of indicating

Indicating is the method of signaling referents via indices using a variety of forms (Clark 1996; Ferrara and Hodge 2018: 4). Two ways of the signaling of indicating are proposed by Clark (2003): directing-to and placing-for. 'Directing-to' is to direct addressee's attention to the referent, while 'placing-for' is to place the referent for the addressee's attention. With visual-gestural modality, signers can produce or direct signs in space meaningfully. These signs are referred to as *directional or multidirectional signs* (Fischer and Gough 1978; Friedman 1976) traditionally, and are more widely known as *agreeing verbs* in sign language literatures (see Mathur and Rathmann 2012 for an overview). Liddell (2000b, 2003) refers to and analyzes them as *indicating signs* from a different perspective. See Schembri, Cormier, and Fenlon (2018) for more updated research about these constructions.

Indices in sign languages include 'directing-to' and 'placing-for' of manual and non-manual expressions, achieved manually by index finger's pointing sign, indicating verbs and gestures, depicting classifier predicates and gestures, and non-manually by body gestures and body-part gestures and by eye-gazing, head-tilting, and face and body orienting. The forms and functions of these various expressions had been illustrated in Su (2011, 2018). This paper shows and adds some examples.

In Example (1), the presence of the referent 'bed' is represented by the 'placing-for' of a non-locative sign 'BED'. To produce non-locative signs at or toward a location is to integrate language and deictic gesture, involving simultaneous naming and pointing (Liddell 2003: 180). The meaning interpreted is determined by the encoded meaning of the sign and the context in which they are used. In this example, the sign 'BED' is produced not at the neutral space but at the 'j' location to indicate the existence of the referent 'bed' (Figure 1a). And with the left hand of the sign 'BED' perseverated, an index finger pointing sign is 'directed-to' the location 'k' (Figure 1b). And a depicting classifier predicate is 'placed-for' at the location 'k' (Figure 1c). An animate entity's presence by the side of the bed is indicated. And with the right hand of the predicate perseverated, another index finger pointing sign is 'directed-to' it (Figure 1d). And finally the sign 'CHILD' is produced. The meaning of the entity as a child is constructed.[1] In summary, a new referent 'boy' is introduced with the information of his location with respective to another referent 'bed' through two different tokens of the index finger pointing sign, a non-locative sign, a depicting classifier predicate, and a describing noun.

(1) IX:i BED:j BED-perseverated +IX:k BED-perseverated+/animate.entity/-loc:k, / animate.entity/-perseverated+IX:RH CHILD.
'There, there was a bed (here, at the right). At the center (by-side the bed), there was an entity here. This entity was a child.'

RH: a. BED:j   b. IX:k   c. /animate.entity/-loc:k   /animate.entity/-perseverated
LH: BED:j   BED-perseverated.........................   d. IX: RH

Figure 1: Illustration of Example 1.

And then the signer produces the indicating sign 'SEE' (Figure 2a) and then the non-directional sign 'VIEW' (Figure 2b). Both are produced along with the non-manual expressions. The difference between the indicating sign 'SEE' and the non-directional sign 'VIEW' is the way of 'directing-to'. The movement and location parameters of the sign 'SEE' can be changed to indicate the referent(s),

---

1 According to mental spaces and blending theory, languages themselves don't have meaning, but they have meaning potential to create spaces for blending to construct meaning. So we use the word 'construct' here for the meaning construction process.

while the location parameter of this sign 'VIEW' is fixed. It has to be produced near the eye. The indicating sign 'SEE' has the ability of 'directing-to' by itself, while the non-directional sign 'VIEW' needs the help of non-manual expressions to achieve the indicating function.

(2) SEE:dir:1...// DOG ALSO JARpro+VIEW...//
 '(the boy) took a look at ..... The dog took a look at ..., too.'

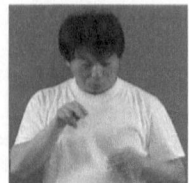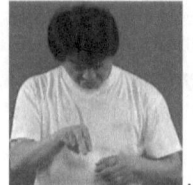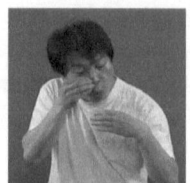

a. SEE:dir:1   b. JARpro+VIEW

Figure 2: Illustration of Example 2.

Similar to the sign 'VIEW' above, non-locative signs can also be 'placed-for' or 'directed-to' to create indices with the help of non-manual expressions. In Example (3), the non-locative sign 'DOG' is produced along with the body and head orienting to the left (Figure 3a), and the non-locative sign 'CHILD' are produced with the body orienting back to the front (Figure 3b). These signs are produced along with non-manual expressions to integrate language and deictic gestures, involving simultaneous naming and pointing. With the help of non-manual expressions, the spatial arrangement of referents is achieved.

(3) EVENING... DOG CHILD PLAY...
 'In the evening a dog and a child were playing.'

a. DOG body.head orient.L   b. CHILD

Figure 3: Illustration of Example 3.

2.3 Method of depicting

In addition to creating symbols through the method of describing and creating indices through the method of indicating, still some signs can create icons through the method of depicting. These icons partially depict meaning through perceptual resemblances (Clark 1996). They can depict the presence of referents, the size or shape of referents, the location or motion of referents, or the action of referents. They are named as *classifier predicates* (Cogill-Koez 2000; Corazza 1990; Schick 1987, 1990; Smith 1990; Supalla 2003; Valli and Lucas 1995; and others) or *verbs of motion and location* (Supalla 1978, 1982) or *depicting signs* (Liddell 2003). These signs are both iconically and spatially motivated while also exhibiting some level of conventionalization (Duncan 2005; Emmorey 2003; Ferrara and Hodge 2018: 5; and others).

Compare Example (4), Example (5) and Example (6). In Example (4), this hearing second language learner of TSL produces symbols 'HAVE', 'ONE', 'MALE', 'CHILD', 'DOG' to express the presence of referents 'boy' and 'dog'. Then she produces a non-directional sign 'FIND' (Figure 4b) to express the presence of the referent 'frog'. She prefers the method of describing.

(4) HAVE ONE MALE CHILD DOG. THEY.TWO FIND FROG.
    'There were a boy and a dog. They found a frog.'

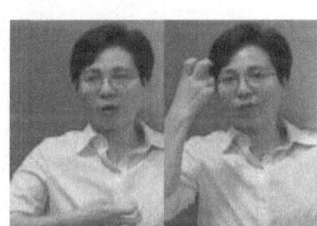

a. HAVE   b. FIND

Figure 4: Illustration of Example 4.

In contrast, the first indicating sign 'SEE' is produced 'directing-to' the 'i' location, along with non-manual expressions (Figure 5a) in Example (5). It functions as indicating the presence of the referent 'frog' in 'i' location. The manual gesture '/take.in.hand/' is produced moving from 'i' location to 'j' location (Figure 5c). The second indicating sign 'SEE' is produced 'directing-to' 'l' location, along with non-manual expressions (Figure 5d). It functions as indicating the direction of looking at the referent 'frog' in 'l' location, inside the container in this case. The direction of the indicating sign 'SEE' is determined by where the frog the deaf signer conceptually construed. These two tokens of the sign 'SEE' are examples of the 'directing-to' of indicating verbs.

(5) TSL by a near-native deaf signer
MALE CHILD . . . SEE:dir:i FROG:i. . . . Enactment:/take.in.hand.and.move/:dir:j HOME-j. . . ./container/-k+ Enactment:/put/:dir:l /container/-k+GLASS /container/-k+SEE:dir:l. . .
'A boy. . . saw a frog. . . . took (it) in hand and went back home. (He) put (it) into a glass container, and looked at (it). . ..'

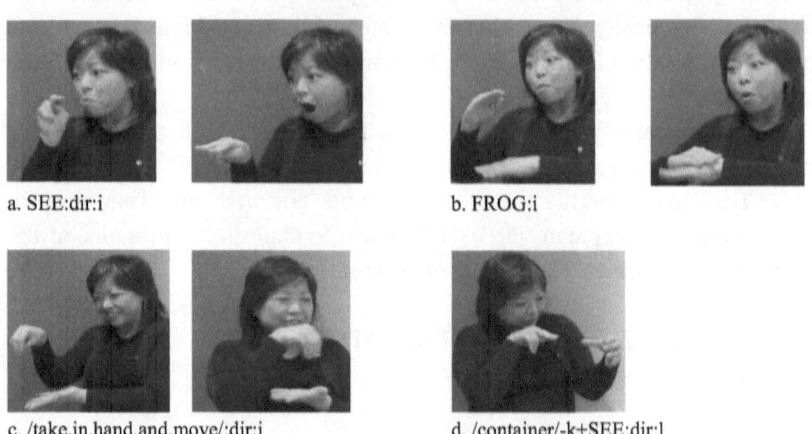

a. SEE:dir:i
b. FROG:i
c. /take.in.hand.and.move/:dir:j
d. /container/-k+SEE:dir:l

Figure 5: Illustration of Example 5.

In Example (6), the presence of the referent 'frog' is not only indicated but depicted through the method of depicting, using the handshape /布袋戲 *budaixi* 'puppet show'/ (the right handshape of Figure 6b) being placed downward in 'i' location. In addition, the presence of the referent 'boy' is indicated and depicted through the same method, using the handshape /民 *min* 'people'/ (the right handshape of Figure 6c) being placed downward in 'j' location.

(6) TSL by a near-native deaf signer
DOG DOG-perseverated+/left/, /jar/ FROG Depicting:/jar/pro+FROGpro-loc:i, MALE CHILD CHILD-perseverated+Depicting:BOYpro-loc:j
'There were a dog at left, a frog inside a jar, and a boy at right.'

a. DOG-perseverated+/left/
b. /jar/pro+FROGpro-loc:i
c. CHILD-perseverated +BOYpro-loc:j

Figure 6: Illustration of Example 6.

In addition to indicate and depict the presence of referents, the classifier predicates can also be produced to indicate and depict the motion events of referents. In Example (7), the near-native deaf signer produces the symbols 'MALE', 'THINK', 'SLEEP', 'DOG', 'SAME', etc. to express 'the boy and the dog want to sleep'. Then he produces a non-locative sign 'BED' at 'i' location (Figure 7b), and a composite icon with the handshape /民 *min* 'people'/ of both hands moving backward to the 'i' location (Figure 7c), and finally a symbol 'SLEEP' (Figure 7d). The motion event of the referents 'boy and dog' lying down on the bed is indicated and depicted with these composite symbols, indices and icons.

(7) MALE SLEEPY THINK SLEEP//
    IX DOG ALSO...// Depicting:(DOGpro+BOYpro)-move.backward(incomplete)
    BED Depicting:(DOGpro+BOYpro)-move.backward SLEEP.
    'The male was sleepy. The dog was sleepy, too. They lay on the bed to sleep.'

a. Depicting:(DOGpro+MALEpro)-move.backward(incomplete)   b. BED

c. Depicting:(DOGpro+MALEpro)-move.backward   d. SLEEP

Figure 7: Illustration of Example 7.

2.4 Composite utterances through compound methods of signaling

As we can see, these meaning-making methods of signaling differ fundamentally in how they signify referents, and they can be used alone or in combination with others (Ferrara and Hodge 2018: 1). Composite utterances through compound methods of signaling in TSL will be illustrated in this section.

Similar to the analysis in Ferrara and Hodge (2018: 8), in Example (8), the native deaf signer produces a composite utterance that both depicts and describes the boy's moving onto a rock and looking for his frog. The signer begins with an incomplete depiction, using a classifier predicate to depict the boy moving onto an as-yet un-named referent (Figure 8a). This depiction is followed by the sign 'ROCK' (i.e., a description of the object that the boy moves onto) (Figure 8c) and the tracing of the rock's shape (i.e., a depiction of the object) (Figure 8d). The signer completes his move with the similar classifier predicate to depict the boy moving onto the rock and with an enactment of head turning right and left to depict and indicate the boy's looking for his frog (simultaneously depicting the motion event and the action) (Figure 8e). In this way, the signer coordinates different acts of description, indication, and depiction to create a composite utterance recounting a moment in the boy's search for the frog. The initial incomplete classifier predicate is elaborated retrospectively through the description of the sign 'ROCK' and the depiction of the rock's shape. The second iteration of the predicate enables the signer's interactant to once again perceive what happened, but with clarified knowledge about the imagined object that the boy is moving onto.

(8) ... Depicting:/round.thing/+BOYpro-move.onto(incomplete) /round.thing/+ IX HAVE ROCK BIG Depicting:trace.rock.shape
Depicting:ROCKpro+BOYpro-move.onto
Depicting: ROCKpro+BOYpro-move.onto > Enactment: head.turn.R.and.L: search
'It had a rock, a big rock. (The boy) moved onto the rock and looked for (the frog).'

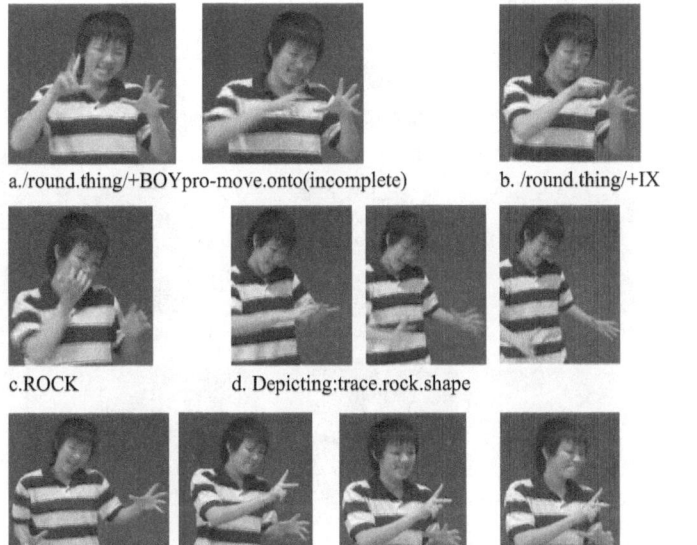

a. /round.thing/+BOYpro-move.onto(incomplete) b. /round.thing/+IX

c. ROCK d. Depicting:trace.rock.shape

e. Depicting: ROCKpro+BOYpro-move.onto > Enactment: head.turn.R.and.L: search

Figure 8: Illustration of Example 8.

In addition, after producing another character's motion and action, the owl's moving away and looking at the boy, the signer reiterates the boy's motion and action, using the similar depicting classifier predicate and the similar enactment. The difference in this case is the sign 'ROCK' and the tracing of the shape of the rock are produced first, and then the depicting classifier predicate and then the enactment. This is a more common order of the utterance of motion event with the depicting classifier predicate. That is, the Ground element of motion events is produced first, then the predicate, with the elements of Motion, Path, etc. incorporated.

The same event can be signaled differently with different methods. In the following example, the near-native deaf signer produces a composite utterance with a depicting classifier predicate and a manual gesture. The sign 'ROCK' is produced first, the method of describing (Figure 9a); and then the shape of the rock is traced, the method of depicting (Figure 9b). With the hand of tracing rock perseverated, a proform for the Figure is produced to depict the motion event that the boy is moving onto the rock (Figure 9c). In the end, an iconic gesture '/climb/' is enacted by the method of depicting (Figure 9e). The meaning of this motion event is elaborated with the Manner that the boy is 'climbing' up the rock.

(9) ROCK Depicting:trace.rock.shape Depicting:ROCKpro+Fpro-move.onto, Enactment:body.gesture:relieved, Enactment:manual.gesture:climb
'(The boy) climbed up a rock and felt relieved.'

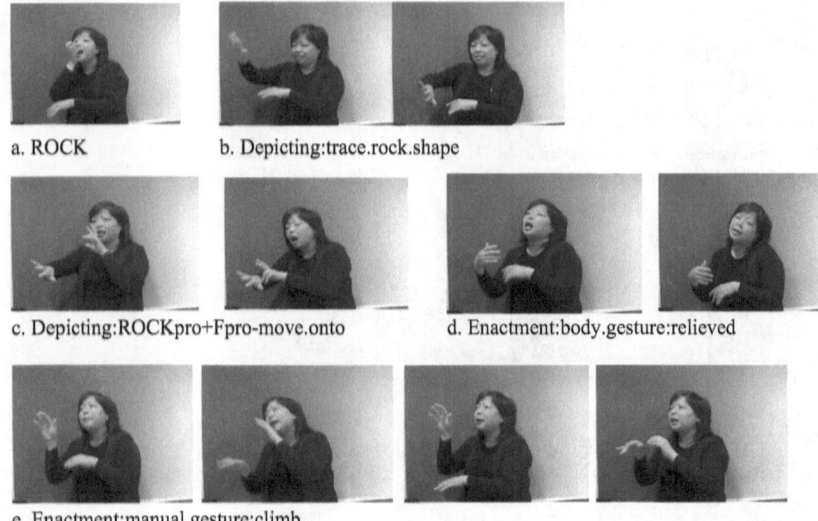

a. ROCK
b. Depicting:trace.rock.shape
c. Depicting:ROCKpro+Fpro-move.onto
d. Enactment:body.gesture:relieved
e. Enactment:manual.gesture:climb

Figure 9: Illustration of Example 9.

In the following example, the signer produces a composite utterance signaled by the methods of describing, indicating and depicting, too. The signer begins to describe the event with a sign FLY, a describing signal (Figure 10a). And a depicting classifier predicate 'OWLpro-fly.toward.signer' is followed, which both indicates and depicts a more imagistic meaning that the owl was flying toward the boy. Simultaneously, this predicate is produced with the non-manual expressions, depicting the result that the boy was frightened (Figure 10b). Then another classifier predicate is produced with the form of different handshape of both hands to represent the two characters' co-occurring events (Figure 10c). That is, the boy was running away and the owl was chasing after. Then the sign 'BE.SHOCKED' is produced along with non-manual expressions, too, depicting the character 'boy' was shocked (Figure 10d). Then the sign 'CHASE' is produced, along with non-manual expressions that indicate the boy's feeling frightened (Figure 10e).

(10) SUDDENLY OWL TREE BIRD FLY OWLpro-fly.toward.signer+facial.expression:frightened (Fpro-run+OWLpro-fly)-chase IX:chest:I BE.SHOCKED CHASE+facial.expression:frightened
'Suddenly, an owl flew out toward (the boy) from the tree and (the boy) was frightened. (The boy) ran away and (the owl) chased after. I felt shocked. (The boy) was frightened that (the owl) was chasing after (him).'

a. FLY   b. Depicting:OWLpro-move.toward+Facial.expression:frightened

c. (BOYpro-run+OWLpro-fly)-chase   d. BE.SHOCKED

e. CHASE+facial.expression:frightened

Figure 10: Illustration of Example 10.

2.5 Summary

Most utterances in sign languages are signaled not only through the method of describing. With the availability of space in deaf signed language interactions, deaf signers rely heavily on the methods of indication and depiction for meaning construction (Ferrara and Hodge 2018: 9). Words and gestures produced by hands, the manual expressions, and gestures produced by trunk and/or face, the non-manual expressions, can be integrated to create indices or icons. With the visual-gestural modality, through the method of indicating to create indices and the method of depicting to create icons, signers represent referents and make reference to them to achieve morphosyntactic and discoursive functions. In addition, events can be represented more iconically and simultaneously. That is, indices and icons can be created, in addition to symbols, to indicate and depict a more vivid discourse about the world.

According to Liddell (2003) and others, methods of indicating and depicting in signed languages, like co-speech gestures, include gestures as integrated part of language. They function not only to encode symbolic grammatical elements but also to provide essential clues in making cross-space mappings. Indices signaled through the method of indicating introduce referents as conceptually present and physically accessible and the directionality of the signaling provides access to correspond elements between spaces to construct the meaning. Icons signaled through the method of depicting, in addition, provide physical forms in real space for elements in blended spaces to inherit. These functions will be illustrated in the following sections.

3 Functions of grounded spaces blends in composite utterances

The theories about mental spaces and conceptual blending are adopted as the theoretical framework, which allows us to account for how these composite utterances are understood in narratives.

In mental space theory (Fauconnier 1994, 1997), constructing meaning of language both in production and perception depends on the existence of mental spaces. Mental spaces are conceptual packets constructed when we think and talk and with elements structured by frames and cognitive models (van Dijk 2008). Language processing can be regarded as the dynamic and constant building and blending of mental spaces.

Conceptual blending plays a fundamental role in meaning construction, too. It is an operation which constructs a partial match between two input spaces, and selectively projects from input spaces into a novel blended space, which then dynamically develops an emergent structure (Fauconnier 1997, 1998, Fauconnier and Turner 1996, 1998, 2002, 2006). Refer to the review in Birdsell (2014), too.

Applying these theories to the study of narratives, both diegesis and mimesis are useful devices to create and blend mental spaces to construct meaning. *Diegesis* conveys the contextualising information and values which provide thematic unity and coherence, and *mimesis* gives us the sense of reality (Lodge 1990: 144). Like Clark's (1996) methods of signaling, with diegesis, narrators describe things with symbols, and with mimesis, they show things with icons, as in direct quotation (Clark 2003). To show things with icons is to provide addresses or readers the sense of reality.

Like words of spoken languages, signs of signed languages serve the function of prompts or instructions. When you sign, you prompt the creation and connection of mental spaces to construct meaning. According to Fauconnier (1998), both spoken and signed languages employ grammatical devices for building spaces, such as adverbials, subject-verb combinations, conjunctions, etc. The mental spaces and the conceptual blending theory applied and extended by Liddell (1995, 1996, 1998, 2000a, 2003) and Liddell and Metzger (1998) and others is that the distinction between non-grounded blends and grounded blends is proposed. The difference between these two types of blends is that grounded blends have a grounded mental space as one of the input spaces, which is created and blended by integrating gestural elements. A grounded space is a mental space, which has perceivable element(s) in the immediate environment, where concepts are given a physical reality. Real space is one of them.

The availability of space in signed language interactions means that signers often produce descriptions, indications, and depictions simultaneously through manual and non-manual actions within composite utterances to express meanings. These meaning- making methods cannot be easily isolated or divided from each other. They must be accounted for as integrated signals. Their meanings and functions do not emerge, and are not interpreted in isolation (Ferrara and Hodge 2018: 9, Puupponen 2019: 11). According to mental space theory, these signals themselves don't carry the meaning, but instead, they have the meaning potential. They serve as prompts or instructions to connect the temporary and dynamic mental representations. What methods of indicating and depicting prompt and blend are grounded spaces blends, in which referents are conceptually present and physically accessible. Because these referents are conceptually present and physically accessible, to express their grammatical relation is usually via the method of indicating. Demonstratives, indicating verbs, depicting verbs, depicting classifier predicates and depicting gestures, all have this capability.[2] These expressive units are all combined with an act of *pointing gesture*, manually or non-manually, during discourse unfolding. They are available to encode relationships among discourse elements through the use of space. Signers will direct signs or gestures of this sort in relation to physically present or conceptually present persons or objects (Liddell 1995). That is, if the persons or objects, which are the arguments of their discourse, are present in current physical space, they direct their signs or gestures in relation to their actual locations. If they are physically non-present, then signers can set up a virtual spatial representation of the situation and they then produce or direct their signs or gestures in relation to these locations as if they were pointing at them. The virtual spatial representation includes elements such as *tokens* in token spaces and *surrogates* in surrogate spaces (Liddell 1996, 2003). These conceived-of-as-present referents can enrich narratives by providing spatial information not available in the text. As a result, addressees can make more sense of the story through 'witnessing' the event, as if it is just happening right before their eyes.

---

[2] Demonstratives in TSL include pronominal demonstratives, adnominal demonstratives, adverbial demonstratives, and identificational demonstratives. Refer to Su (2011, 2018) for the detailed illustration of those demonstratives in TSL.

In Example (11) and Example (12), the signer tells the addressee something before he really retells the story 'Frog, Where are you?'. The signer and the addressee are present in current physical space. The signer directs his signs in relation to their actual locations. Pointing to the signer means 'I', and pointing to the addressee means 'you'. Directing the sign 'TELL' from the signer himself toward the addressee means 'I tell you.' (Figure 11b), and directing the sign 'TELL' reversely means 'You tell me.' (Figure 12e).

(11) IX:signer TELL:dir:addressee IX:signer FROG WONDERFUL...
'I tell you (that) my frog is wonderful.'

a. IX:signer   b. TELL:dir:addressee

Figure 11: Illustration of Example 11.

(12) IX:addressee SELF SAY SPEAK TELL:dir:signer
'You (then think how to) say and speak by yourself (and) tell me.'

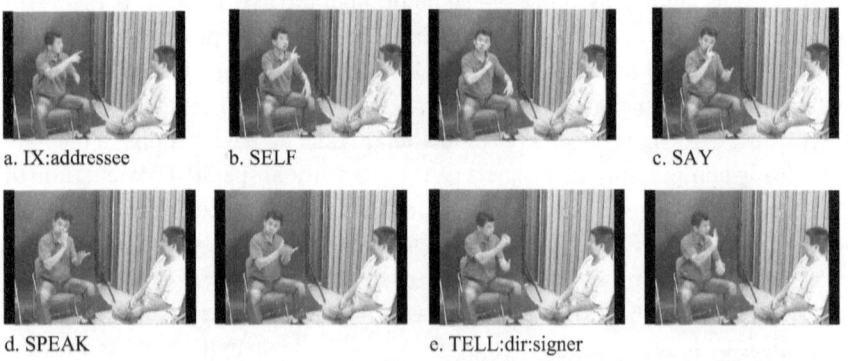

a. IX:addressee   b. SELF   c. SAY

d. SPEAK   e. TELL:dir:signer

Figure 12: Illustration of Example 12.

In contrast, in Example (13), the referents 'child', 'frog', and 'jar' are physically non-present, the signer sets up a virtual spatial representation of the situation and then produces or directs his signs or gestures in relation to these locations. The tokens for the referent 'jar' are produced in the middle of the signing space, along with the body orienting to the left (Figures 13a, 13b and 13c). The referents 'child' and 'frog' and 'the catching action' are produced relatively to the right of the signing space, along with the body orienting to the right (Figures 13d, 13e, and 13f). The put-in action is produced and directed from the relatively right to the middle of the signing space, the same place as that of the tokens for the referent 'jar' (Figure 13g).

(13) JAR(/jar/(false.start)^GLASS^Depicting:trace.jar.shape)
Anticipation.of./catch/+CHILD, LOOK.FOR, FROG /catch/ JARpro+Enactment:/put.in/
'A boy saw a frog, caught it and put it in the jar.'

(A) Body orientation to the left:

a. /jar/(false.start)   b. /jar/(false.start)-perseverated+GLASS

c. Depicting:trace.jar.shape-i+Non-manual:eyegaze.signing.hands

(B) Body orientation to the right:

d. Anticipation of /catch/ + CHILD   e. Anticipation of /catch/+ FROG

f. /catch/

Figure 13: Illustration of Example 13.

(C) Body orientation from right to left:

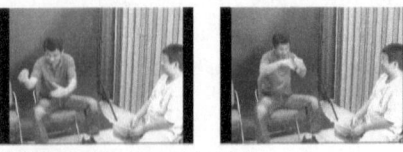

g. JARpro +Enactment:/put.in/

Figure 13 (continued).

And then all the following utterances of the child's viewing action and the frog's motion event are produced along with the same body orientation to the left (Figure 14).

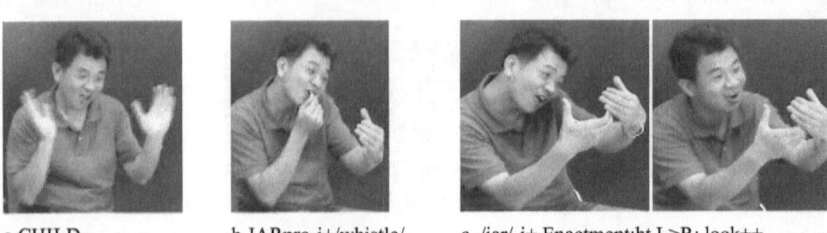

a. CHILD   b. JARpro-i+/whistle/   c. /jar/-i+ Enactment:ht.L>R: look++

Figure 14: Illustration of body orientation.

Then the signer produces the sign DOG with the face orientating relatively right again to indicate the referent shift (Figure 15a): the motion event of the character 'dog' now. When he starts to depict the motion event of the dog's moving around the jar and produces the following sign CURIOUS, the face orientation is changed back to the left again, the same conceptually construed space that the frog and the jar locate at (Figures 15b, 15c, and 15d).

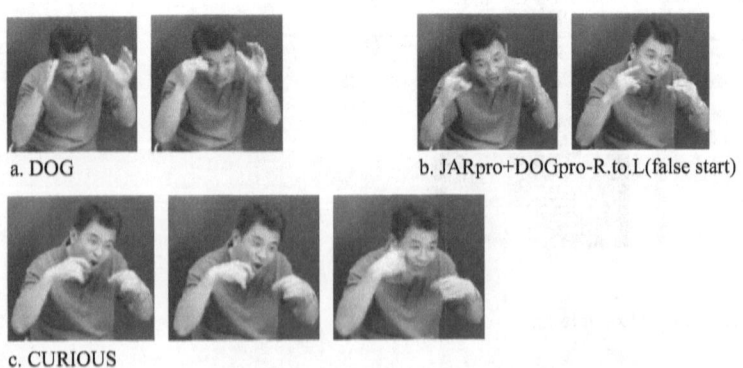

a. DOG   b. JARpro+DOGpro-R.to.L(false start)

c. CURIOUS

Figure 15: Illustration of the change of face orientation.

d. Depicting:JARpro+DOGpro-move.R.to.L.and.make.a.circle:move.around

Figure 15 (continued).

The virtual spatial representation of these conceived-of-as-present referents adds a visual component that enriches the narrative. As a result, the addressees can make more sense of the story through 'witnessing' the event, as if it is just happening right before their eyes.

Visual-gestural modality, with the potential for iconic representation (Fay et al. 2014) and for indexical/ostensive identification of referents (Meier 2002), allows signers/speakers to produce signs/gestures or direct signs/gestures at various areas of space *meaningfully*. What they create are real spaces, with perceivable elements. And the real space(s) can be blended with another input space(s) into grounded blends. Elements created in grounded blends can inherit physical forms from real spaces. The physical forms inherited from the real spaces are referents with physical reality about location, size, shape, motion, action, etc. The result is to create a *virtual demonstration*, in addition to the description (Liddell 1996, 2003).[3] During discourse unfolding, speakers/signers and addressees constantly associate the information contributed by these mental space mappings and blendings to construct the meaning.

In Example (14), two depicting classifier predicates (Figure 16a and 16c) are produced and then two depicting blends are created. In these blends, elements '|Figure|', '|Motion|', '|Path|', '|Ground|' etc. are blended out.[4] With the signs 'MALE' and 'DOG', the meaning of the element '|Figure|' of the first motion event is constructed as '|male|' (Figure 16a) and that of the element '|Figure|' of the second motion event is constructed as '|dog|' (Figure 16c).[5]

And one enactment is produced and thus one surrogate blend is created, with elements '|Agent|', '|Action|', '|Patient|', '|Ground|', etc. blended out (Figure 16b).[6]

With the symbol 'SLEEP', a cognitive model (van Dijk 2008) is evoked to describe an activity. Cognitive model is also referred to as situation model, frame,

---

[3] Similar to the idea discussed by McNeill (1992, 2005) and McNeill and Duncan (2000): While grammatical constructions symbolically *describe* events, the co-speech gestural elements constitute *demonstrations* of events.
[4] They are elements of a motion event proposed in Talmy (1985, 1991, 2000).
[5] The elements created in grounded blends will be marked by vertical brackets, like |element| (Liddell 1996, 1998, 2000a, 2003b; Liddell and Metzger 1998).
[6] They are elements of a caused motion event proposed in Talmy (2000).

or script. With the cognitive model 'sleep', even though 'bed' and 'quilt' are new information, they are not necessarily produced. This cognitive model introduces elements 'animate entity, bed, quilt', etc.

These mental spaces are under a dynamic and constant building and blending to construct the meaning of the narration. So in the end, the meaning of the elements '|Figure|', '|Motion|', '|Path|', '|Ground|' in Figure (16a) is constructed as '|male lie down on the bed|' and in Figure (16c), '|dog jump onto the bed|'. In Figure (16b), the meaning of the elements '|Agent|', '|Action|', '|Patient|', and '|Ground|' is constructed as '|male pull quilt to cover on his body|'. The final meaning constructed is 'The male lay down on the bed, pulled quilt to cover his body, and slept. The dog jumped onto the bed, and slept.'.

(14) ... MALE Depicting:MALEpro-move.backward:lie.down Enactment:manual. gesture:pull.something.to.cover.on.body SLEEP,
DOG Depicting:DOGpro-move.onto
'The boy lay down (on the bed), pulled (the quilt and covered) on his body), and slept. And the dog jumped (onto the bed and slept).'

a. Depicting:MALEpro-move.backward:lie.down

b. Enactment:manual.gesture:pull.something.to.cover.on.body

c. Depicting:DOGpro-move.onto

Figure 16: Illustration of Example 14.

Compare a TSL narrative from a native hearing signer (Example 15) to the one from the native deaf signer (Example 14). The native hearing signer prefers method of describing to express the motion and action of characters. He produces the signs 'GO' and 'SLEEP' to express the motion and action of boy and dog (Figure 17). In contrast, the deaf signer prefers a composite method of describing, indicating and depicting. In addition to the sign 'SLEEP', she produces a depicting classifier predicate to depict the boy's motion and action of moving and lying down (on the bed) (Figure 16a). And she produces a depicting gesture to depict the action of pulling quilt to cover (Figure 16b). In the end, she also produces another classifier predicate to indicate and depict the dog's motion of jumping (on the bed) (Figure 16c).

(15) EVENING IX:L MALE CHILD GO SLEEP//
DOG ALSO GO SLEEP//

a. GO

b. SLEEP

Figure 17: Illustration of Example 15.

The sleeping event of the characters 'boy and dog' can be signaled simultaneously, too. In Example (16), the deaf signer produces a symbol 'BED', then a classifier predicate with the form of handshape /民 *min* 'people'/ of both hands (Figure 18), and finally the symbol 'SLEEP'. In this utterance, the event of the characters 'boy and dog' sleeping together on the bed is indicated and depicted with the depicting classifier predicate.

(16) GO(false.start) IMMEDIATELY BED Depicting:(BOYpro+DOGpro)-move.
backward:lie.back SLEEP-B
'... immediately (boy and dog) lay back on the bed and sleep.'

Depicting: (BOYpro+DOGpro)-move.backward:lie.back

Figure 18: Illustration of Example 16.

We also compare these TSL narratives with those produced by the hearing second language learners. In Example (17), the hearing signer produces the lexicalized symbol 'ACCOMPANY' to express the event that the boy and dog sleep together. (Figure 19)

(17) EVENING MALE CHILD DOG ACCOMPANY SLEEP-A++
'In the evening, the boy and the dog went together to sleep.'

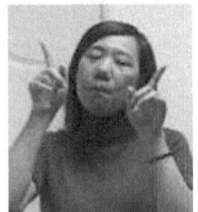 

ACCOMPANY

Figure 19: Illustration of Example 17.

Narratives from most deaf signers create a more vivid scene because their narratives have more physical forms inherited from the real spaces, which can be created by the depicting classifier predicates and the depicting gestures. We will illustrate this more in the following section.

4 Composite utterances function as involvement strategies

To make sense of the reality of narratives, story tellers usually employ *evaluative strategies* (Bamberg and Damrad-Frye 1991; Küntay and Nakamura 2004;

Labov 1972; Labov and Waletzky 1967; Nakamura 2009) or *involvement strategies* (Tannen 1986, [1989] 2007) to create the scene encouraging audiences/addressees to take an active role. These strategies can be lexical, structural, or paralinguistic (Reilly 2001; Reilly, Bates and Marchman 1998).

Repetition, constructed dialogues and images and details are prevalently employed as involvement strategies in spoken narratives,. They include: to provide additional (background) information or one's attitudes or feelings to the event; to become the character to create the scene; to deliberately conceal or adeptly reveal the main point of event at appropriate moments to achieve suspenseful or surprising effects (Labov 1972; Labov and Waletzky 1967).[7] All of these aim to engage addressee to take the viewpoint of the narrator or the character and be the observer standing inside the scene, taking inside perspective.

Producing constructed dialogues is one involvement strategy. When a story teller produces a direct quote within a narrative, he or she is illustrating or demonstrating (see Clark and Gerrig 1990) the speech of a character within the story, often producing the intonation and facial expression of that character. The narrator "takes on the perspective" of that character during the quotation. In sign languages, a narrator can also take on the perspective of a character while describing the character's actions (rather than quoting the character's words). When describing the actions of a character, narrators often portray the facial expression, eye gaze, and head movements of the character performing the action they describe. In this sense, the storyteller demonstrates aspects of the action from the attitudinal or affective perspective of that character. Sign linguists refer to both direct quotation and what we are calling "reported action" as examples of referential shift or role shift (e.g., Emmorey and Reilly 1998: 81; Engberg-Pedersen 1993; Padden 1988). They are also referred to as *constructed actions* (Liddell and Metzger 1998; Metzger 1995; Quinto-Pozos 2007; Quinto-Pozos and Mehta 2010; Roy [1989] 2000, Winston 1991, 1993, 1994, 1995; and others). In addition to constructing what the character acts, the role-playing by signers includes constructing what the character thinks, feels, says, etc. Note that the term 'constructed actions' can be used as a general term, including *constructed actions, constructed thoughts, constructed emotions and constructed dialogues*, the various behaviors that signers perform when serving as the characters (Metzger 1995).

Creating images and details is another involvement strategy. They can be created by *qualifying* modifiers (Rijkhoff 2002, 2008a, 2008b) such as adjectives and relative clauses, the method of describing. They can be created by the combination of the methods of describing, indicating, and depicting as well. That means

---

7 Refer to Su (2011, 2018) for the illustration of these strategies.

co-speech gestures can be integrated to complement messages that linguistic elements convey or don't convey. With deictic gestures providing indices about location of referents and with iconic/metaphoric gestures providing icons about kind/class, quality or quantity of referents, additional imagistic information can be indicated or depicted. Using these methods of signaling to create indices or icons can trigger the cross-space mapping in addition to encoding symbolic grammatical units. And these cross-space mappings create grounded spaces blends.

Like spoken languages integrating with co-speech gestures, the most important device to achieve these in sign languages is to integrate signs with gestures, manually and non-manually, to create grounded spaces blends. Through blending, referents and events can be made conceptually present with physical reality. With physical reality to create scene, involvement can be achieved more strongly because addressees are encouraged to take an active role in constructing meaning.

Functions of grounded spaces blends in TSL have been illustrated in Su (2011, 2018). These include the introduction of conceptually present referents with physical reality, the indication of grammatical relations deictically, and the creation of the vivid images achieving functions of narrative. This paper aims to illustrate more examples, especially with the comparison to those by hearing native signers and hearing second language learners.

4.1 Introduction of conceptually present referents with physical reality

As discussed in section 2, method of indicating includes 'directing-to' and 'placing-for'. Through indications, referents are given physical location in grounded spaces. The following examples illustrate how these two ways of indicating are employed to set up tokens in token spaces or surrogates in surrogate spaces, similar to the analysis in Liddell (1995, 2003).

In Example (18), the signer produces the symbols 'FROG', 'WHITE', 'WATER', through the method of description, and produces the icons, through the method of depicting, with the form of 'tracing the shape of a container' (Figure 20a) and the form of 'depicting an entity inside the container' (Figure 20b). Producing signs integrating with gestures can create tokens that give referents with physical reality. In this case, a *token* |frog| inside another *token*, the |white water container| (Figure 20b), is set up. These symbols and icons create three-dimensional *tokens* through associating the linguistic meaning of the sign with the respective spaces. And these signing spaces are *token spaces*. The result of these associations is to create elements conceptually present with physical location.

(18) . . .FROG AT WHITE WATER Depicting:trace.container.shape FROG Depicting:JARpro+FROGpro-in
'. . . the frog is in the white water container (jar).'

a. Depicting:trace.container.shape   b. Depicting:JARpro+FROGpro-in

Figure 20: Illustration of Example 18.

Then the signer produces an index with the form of 'the pointing of index finger to the right', through the method of indicating, and the symbols 'SMALL', 'CHILD', 'DOG', the method of describing. And then he produces an icon with the form of the handshape /民 *min* 'people'/ of both hands at 'j' location, integrating with the non-manual expressions of the form of the head tilting left (Figure 21e). This composite icon creates a grounded mental space to set up a *token* '|boy and dog|' locating on both sides and another grounded mental space to set up a surrogate '|boy and dog|' looking downward. And with the right hand of the icon perseverated, another icon with the symbol 'VIEW' integrating with the non-manual expressions of the form of the head tilting right and eyes looking downward is produced (Figure 21f). This composite icon creates the same surrogate '|boy and dog|' looking downward. The meaning is confirmed with the symbol 'VIEW'. These signs and manual gestures and non-manual expressions create three-dimensional *tokens* and *surrogates* through associating the linguistic meaning of the signs with the respective spaces. These signing spaces are *token spaces,* and surrogate spaces, respectively. The result of these associations is to create elements conceptually present with physical reality. In addition to being created conceptually present with physical location, the token |boy and dog| inherits physical form 'handshape /布袋戲 *budaixi* 'puppet show'/' of both hands, created by the depicting classifier predicate '(CHILDpro+DOGpro)- on.both.sides'.

(19) IX:R SMALL CHILD DOG Depicting:(CHILDpro+DOGpro)- on.both.sides+-Enactment:head.tilt.L:look.atDepicting:(CHILDpro+DOGpro)-on.both.sides-perseverated+VIEW
'That little child and dog is on both sides looking at and viewing (the frog).'

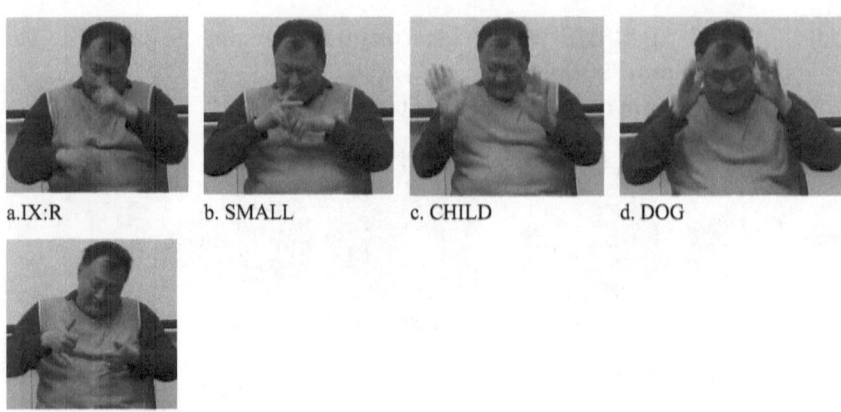

a. IX:R b. SMALL c. CHILD d. DOG

e. Depicting:(CHILDpro+DOGpro)-on.both.sides+Enactment:head.tilt.L

f. Depicting:(CHILDpro+DOGpro)-on.both.sides-perseverated+VIEW

Figure 21: Illustration of Example 19.

Compare this example above with the example below, the signer of Example (20) establishes the relative locations of characters by a gesture and two depicting classifier predicates. Producing the sign 'DOG' and the gesture '/left/' instructs the mental spaces' cognitive mechanism of blending to create a token |dog| at the location 'left' in a token space. Producing the gesture '/jar/', the sign 'FROG' and a depicting classifier predicate '/jar/pro+FROGpro-loc:i' (Figure 22b) instructs the cognitive mechanism of the depicting blending to create tokens '|frog|', '|jar|' and a virtual demonstration of '|frog| locating in the |jar|'. Also producing the sign 'CHILD' and another classifier predicate 'BOYpro-loc:j' (Figure 22c) instructs the cognitive mechanism of another depicting blending to create the token '|boy|' and a virtual demonstration of '|boy|'s locating at 'the relative right''. In addition to being created conceptually present with physical location, the token '|frog|' inherits physical form 'handshape /布袋戲 *budaixi* 'puppet show'/' and the token '|jar|' inherits the physical form 'handshape /同 *tong* 'together'/' from first grounded real space, created by the depicting classifier predicate '/jar/pro+FROGpro-loc:i' (Figure 22b). And the token '|boy|' inherits the physical form 'handshape /民 *min* 'people'/' from second grounded real space, created by another depicting classifier predicate 'BOYpro-loc:j' (Figure 22c).

(20) TSL produced by a near-native signer
DOGDOG-perseverated+/left/, /jar/FROGDepicting:/jar/pro+FROGpro-loc:i, MALE CHILD CHILD-perseverated+Depicting:BOYpro-loc:j, TOGETHER SEE: fm:j:dir:i FROG, Enactment:/frog-look.upward/
'There is a dog at left, a frog inside a jar, and a boy at right. They together are looking at the frog, and (the frog) is looking upward, too.'

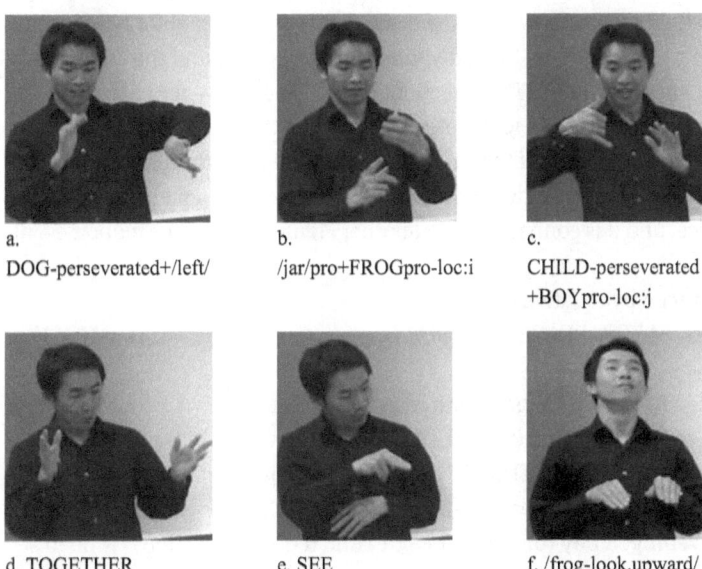

a. DOG-perseverated+/left/
b. /jar/pro+FROGpro-loc:i
c. CHILD-perseverated +BOYpro-loc:j
d. TOGETHER
e. SEE
f. /frog-look.upward/

Figure 22: Illustration of Example 20.

Both TSL deaf narratives above blend and create conceptually present referents by integrating linguistic elements and gestures, manual or non-manual, simultaneously. The spatial relations in TSL are depicted and indicated like a reality.

4.2 Indication of grammatical relations deictically

In addition, comparing the TSL narratives by the near-native signers (Example 19 and Example 20) to the one produced by the native signer (Example 21), the same scene can be expressed by integrating a depicting classifier predicate and a constructed action simultaneously (Figure 23e). In Example (21), two referents are set up spatially. The signer produces the symbols 'MALE', 'CHILD', along with the non-manual expression 'eyes gazing at the signing right hand' to set up a *token* '|boy|' at the right side (Figure 23a). And then she produces an index with the form of 'the pointing of index finger to the left' and the sign 'DOG', integrating with another index with the form of non-manual expression 'the head-tilt to the left' to set up another *token* '|dog|' at the left side (Figure 23b and Figure 23c). After the tokens are established, a classifier predicate of motion is employed to depict the movement of the referents. This classifier predicate is composed of two Figure proforms, with the form of the handshape '/布袋戲 *budaixi* 'puppet show'/' of both hands, *directing* from both sides toward the center, where the third character '|frog|' is conceptually located (Figure 23d). The classifier predicate evokes a *semantic space*. The semantic space represents the meanings encoded by the individual word or gesture and the subject-verb construction (Langacker 1987). The directionality of "Fpro-move.to.center from the 'right' side" provides the access to the element '|boy|' in the 'right' token space, and it is connected with one Figure of this motion event; while the directionality of "Fpro-move.to.center from the 'left' side" provides the access to the element '|dog|' in the 'left' token space, and it is connected with another Figure of this same motion event.

(21) TSL produced by a native signer
EVENING SLEEP^PLACE BOY(MALE$_{RH.and.gaze.R}$^CHILD$_{gaze.front}$) AND IX:L DOG$_{head\ tilt.L.and.gaze.front}$
Depicting:(BOYpro+DOGpro)-both.move.to.center
(BOYpro+DOGpro)- perseverated + Enactment:head.tilt.L.then.R: look.at, IX:down INSIDE GLASS TURNIP Depicting:trace.jar.shape IX:down INSIDE FROG Enactment:body.gesture+head.turn.R.then.L:look.toward.R.then.L
'In the evening, a boy (on the right side) and a dog (on the left) came to see a frog inside a jar (and simultaneously the frog) looked up toward its right (at the dog) and up toward its left (at the boy).'

a. MALE$_{RH.and.gaze.R}$

b. IX:L

c. DOG$_{head\ tilt.L.and.gaze.front}$

d. Depicting:(BOYpro+DOGpro)-both.move.to.center

Figure 23: Illustration of Example 21.

 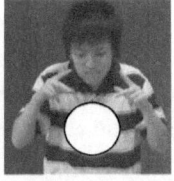

e. (BOYpro+DOGpro)-perseverated + Enactment:head.tilt.left.then.right: look.at

f. Enactment:body.gesture+head.turn.R.then.L:look.toward.R.then.L

Figure 23 (continued).

And then the signer, with the classifier predicate perseverated, *directs* her head tilting left and then right and *directs* her eyes gazing downward where the third character is located (Figure 23e). The directionality of these non-manual expressions provides the access to the elements '|boy (on the right side)|' and '|dog (on the left side)|' to connect to the Figure of the action event. And it also provides the access to the third element to connect to the Ground of the action event. The third element is the '|frog|', introduced by the following clause and created as conceptually present with physical reality through the second constructed action. The grammatical relation that the first constructed action indicates is the subject '|boy and dog|' looking at the object '|frog|' (Figure 23e). The relations and semantic roles between discourse referents are indicated by the direction of the head movement or the orientation of the face in enacting movements. These enacting movements have both iconic and indexical functions, similar to the analysis in Puupponen (2019: 13–14) and Schembri, Cormier and Fenlon (2018).

Second constructed action (Figure 23f) prompts another surrogate blending, creating a conceptually present referent '|frog|' with the physical reality. The directionality of the upward to the right and then to the left of this constructed action provides the access to the element '|frog|' to connect to the Figure of this action event and provides the access to the element '|dog|' and the element '|boy|', at |frog|'s both sides, to connect to the Ground of this action event. The grammatical relation indicated is that the subject '|frog|' looked at the object '|dog|' and at the object '|boy|'.

Without explicitly mentioning the direct object of these two predicate-like expressive units, their meanings can be still understood. In the first surrogate blend, the meaning is constructed as '|boy and dog|, the signer playing the role of the characters, are looking downward at the |frog|' (Figure 23e). In the second surrogate blend, the meaning is constructed as '|frog|, the signer playing the role of the character, is looking upward at the |dog| and at the |boy|' (Figure 23f).

In addition to demonstrating the viewing actions, the relative location of boy, dog and frog is also depicted and indicated by these simultaneous constructions with the two independent articulators and the two-channel system (manual and non-manual). These simultaneous expressions that depict and indicate the activities and the spatial relations at the same time are more efficient and more informative, similar to the study in Perniss (2007). By using classifier predicates and constructed actions simultaneously "to show exactly what happens in what manner and in what spatial relationship, storytellers are able to create a vivid picture" of the story for the interactants to 'witness' the event (Rayman 1999: 65).

The meaning of these constructed actions above (Figure 23e and 23f) is confirmed when the signer produces the signs 'VIEW' (Figure 24) and 'FINISH' in the following utterance (Example 22).

(22) VIEW FINISH, MALE . . . .
 'Finishing the viewing, the boy . . . .'

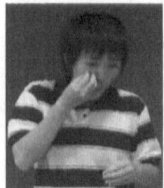
VIEW

Figure 24: Illustration of Example 22.

The use of space in sign languages is often characterized as a means of keeping track of referents. However, this is not the primary function of the blend. Its primary function is to provide a real-time partial demonstration of the event being described (Liddell 2003: 154–157). With this real-time partial demonstration of the event, the addressee is encouraged to become the observer, able to watch '|boy and dog| look downward at |frog| and simultaneously |frog| look up to the right and to the left at |boy| and |dog|'. This adds visual components that enriches the story.

We also compare these TSL narratives with those produced by the hearing people. One of them is native and the others are second language learners. Investigating the data, simultaneous constructions are not so prevalent in TSL from these hearing signers. Example (23) is one of the few. The same as the examples from the native and near-native deaf signers, this second language learner of TSL demonstrates the scene with the spatial establishment of the referents through non-manual expressions (Figure 25a, 25b). And she employs her both hands to conflate the co-occurring actions of these two characters with indicating signs (Figure 25c). But different from the narratives by these deaf signers, there are only a few physical forms inherited from the real space, created by non-manual expressions in this narrative. Narratives from native or near-native deaf signers create a more vivid scene because their narratives have more physical forms inherited from the real spaces, which are created by the depicting classifier predicates and depicting (body) gestures, in addition to non-manual expressions.

(23) CHILD+/body.ori/:R DOG+/body.ori/:L (SEE+SEE) GLASS trace.jar.shape IX:down FROG
    'A boy and a dog see a frog in a jar.'

a. CHILD+/body.ori/:R   b. DOG+/body.ori/:L   c. (SEE+SEE)

Figure 25: Illustration of Example 23.

Compare TSL narratives from the near-native deaf signer (Example 20) to the one from a native hearing signer (Example 24). The native hearing signer prefers method of describing to express the existence and location of characters. He produces the sign HAVE to express the existence of boy, dog, and frog. And he produces signs AT and INSIDE to express the location of the frog (Figures 26b and 26f). In contrast, the deaf signer (Example 20) prefers a composite method of describing, indicating and depicting. He produces the depicting classifier predicate to express the existence and location of the frog (Figure 22b). And he produces another classifier predicate to express the existence and location of the boy (Figure 22c). In the end, he also produces a body gesture to indicate and depict the frog's action of looking upward (Figure 22f).

(24) IX:L HOUSE HOUSEpro+IX:circling HOUSEpro+HAVE ONE MALE CHILD IX:L DOG HAVE ONE FROG// FROG AT Depicting:trace.container.shape(false.start)   Depicting:trace.container.shape(false.start)-perseverated+GLASS Depicting:trace.container.shape INSIDE//

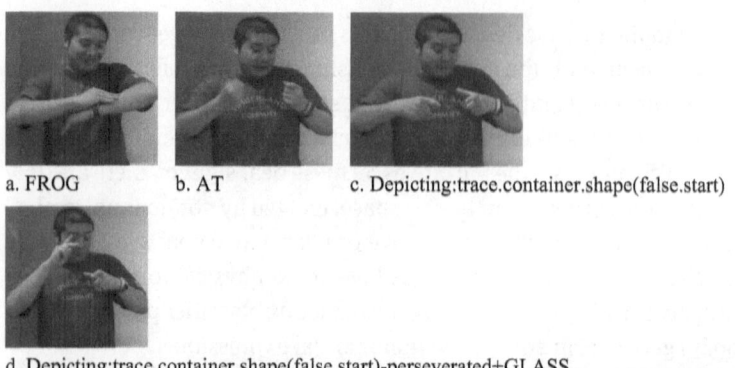

a. FROG   b. AT   c. Depicting:trace.container.shape(false.start)

d. Depicting:trace.container.shape(false.start)-perseverated+GLASS

e. Depicting:trace.container.shape   f. INSIDE

Figure 26: Illustration of Example 24.

In sum, through the composite method of signaling which integrates signs and gestures, manually or non-manually, not only physical location can be given to referents in grounded spaces, physical reality about size, shape, action or motion can be given to referents, too. Most hearing signers, even the native ones, prefer the method of describing and thus their narratives are less vivid and less iconic than those from deaf signers, who prefer the composite method of describing, indicating and depicting.

4.3 Creation of images and details

This section will illustrate more on one of the involvement strategies: creating images and details to make vivid of the narrative and hence achieve interpersonal involvement.

There are various ways to encode one of the climaxes in retelling the story 'Frog, Where are you?' (Mayer 1969): the caused motion event that 'the deer carries the boy away to the river'. In Example (25A), the hearing second language learner of TSL uses a symbol 'CARRY' (Figure 27), a conventionalized sign through the method of description. In Example (25B), the near-native TSL deaf signer uses a symbol integrated with an index through the methods of description and indication 'CARRY:dir:i' and with an icon through the method of depiction

'/face gesture: 'with effort'/' (Figure 28). And in Example (25C), the native TSL deaf signer produces a classifier predicate, an icon signaled through the method of depiction. The classifier predicate is produced with the left handshape /布袋戲 budaixi 'puppet show'/, representing the Ground proform 'boy' of the motion event and with the right handshape /守 shou 'wait'/, representing the Figure proform 'deer' of the motion event. And this Figure proform is incorporated with the elements 'Motion/Path' with the meaning of 'directing toward right', and the element 'Manner' with the meaning of 'moving up and down' (Figure 29a). The method of indication creates indices and the method of depiction creates icons. Both create real spaces. The physical forms inherited from the real spaces created in Example (25B) include the referent |deer| moving with some kind of |manner: with effort| toward the |direction: right| (Figure 28). The physical forms inherited from the real space created by the depicting classifier predicate in Example (25C) include the referent |boy|, with the image |handshape: 布袋戲 budaixi 'puppet show'|, locating at the |deer|, with the image |handshape: 守shou 'wait'|, and the |deer| moving toward the |direction: right| with some kind of |manner: up and down| (Figure 29a). The classifier predicate creates a more vivid, iconic scene for the audiences to make more sense of the story and hence achieve the interpersonal involvement much strongly.

(25) A. TSL narrative by a hearing second language learner
DEER TELL CHILD. . . CARRY GO
'The deer told the child. . . and carried him to go . . .'

CARRY   (similar to the citation form)

Figure 27: Illustration of Example 25A.

B. TSL narrative by a near-native deaf signer
IX:R DEER . . .IX:chest CARRY IX:L(you) GO:dir:R IX:R(there)+/ mouthing: hao bu hao 'how about'/,
'The deer (said): ". . .How about I carry you to go there?"
DEER CARRY:dir:R+/face and mouth gesture:mm 'with effort'/ THROW. . .
'The deer was carrying (him) and threw (him). . .'

CARRY:dir:R+/face and mouth gesture: mm 'with effort'/

Figure 28: Illustration of Example 25B.

C. TSL narrative by a native deaf signer
IX:L DEER ANGRY. BOTHER:dir:chest. /run/. MALE CHILD (DEERpro+BOYpro-loc)+DEERpro-move:dir:R+/move:up.and.down/
'The deer was angry. Why bothered me!! (The deer) started to run!! The boy was located at the deer and was being carried away up and down.'

 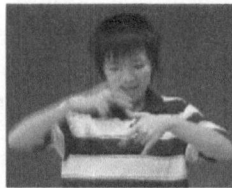 

a. (DEERpro+BOYpro-loc)+DEERpro-move:dir:R+/move:up.and.down/

b. (DEERpro+BOYpro-on)+DEERpro-move:dir:R + /tongue.protruding.out/

Figure 29: Illustration of Example 25C.

And in the end of the classifier predicate, the signer integrates a mouth gesture /th: tongue protruding/ to express her attitude or feeling about this event (Figure 29b). The meaning can be constructed as 'it is awful/unfortunate that. . .'. With this information provided additionally, the addressee will shift to take the viewpoint of the narrator and become more engaged in this story by empathizing with the story's characters. It will be like to stand in front of the event to 'witness' what have happened, the inside perspective being taken.

Let's explore more the functions of non-manual expressions and the modulation of manual parameters of expressive units. The functions of the precise path demonstrating, the internal details encoding and the inside perspective indicating for the engagement/encouragement of perspective shift are proposed.

In Figure 30, both signers produce motion events with classifier predicates and the movement speed of the classifier predicates is deliberately modulated slowly, along with the eyes gazing at the moving hand.

a. WINDOWpro+DOGpro-fall.fm: slow.motion+/eye.gaze:moving.hand/

b. /beehive/pro-i+BEEpro-many.go.fm:slow.motion+/eye.gaze:moving.hand/

Figure 30: Illustration of the motion events and the non-manual expressions.

Supalla (1978) observes that signers would manipulate their hands through space slowly and with much deliberation, as if they were attempting to outline the precise path of moving object (Bahan and Supalla 1995: 179). But employing the global movement of the moving hand is good enough to depict the path of motion events, why bothers to employ the eye-gaze behavior and the slowly deliberate modulation of movement speed?

During narrating story or experience, one can engage addressees or readers to take the viewpoint of narrator or character. English *the* is one device that narrators use when they aim to engage readers to empathize with, or adopt the viewpoint of, the narrator or the story character (Epstein 2002). Similar function can be achieved by gestures incorporated with linguistic elements in TSL. In Figure 30, the accompanying modulations of manual and non-manual expressions, functioning like gestures, signal additionally the important narrative functions. They are employed to attract addressees' attention to the event. The deliberate modulation of the movement pattern, including the slowness of speed and the elaboration of manner, is to encode the process in detail, similar to employing a long-lasting and complex gesture accompanying the speech in the progressive aspect to reflect increased focus on the internal details of an event discussed in Duncan (2003), McNeill (2003), and Parrill, Bergen and Lichtenstein (2013). And the nonmanual eye-gaze behavior functions like the narrator taking the O-VPT (observer viewpoint) and standing in front of the event to engage/encourage addressees to take *inside perspective* to feel like they were in front of the scene and 'witnessed' the event in person.

These modulations aim for achieving 'interpersonal involvement', like spoken language using qualifying modifiers such as adjectives, adverbials or relative clauses to provide details and create images and scenes (Tannen 2007). When you 'witness' in person the event happening, it makes more sense to you. They are also referred to as evaluative functions of narrative proposed by Labov (1972) and Labov and Waletzky (1967).

Example (26) illustrates a further evidence of this function. In this example, instead of describing the quantity of baby frogs with a number sign or a quantifier MANY, the deaf signer produces numerals ONE, TWO, . . ., FIVE step by step at different places to encode the finding process in detail (Figure 31). These numerals are non-locative signs (Liddell 2003) but are 'placed-for' *spatially* and *sequentially*, signaled through not only the method of description but also the method of indication, to demonstrate the detailed process of the finding event. She produces the numerals 'ONE' to 'FIVE' at different locations and signs the numerals 'ONE, TWO, THREE, FIVE' again, instead of signing the quantifier 'MANY', to indicate the precise process that the baby frogs kept appearing. This composite utterance involves simultaneous naming and pointing that create grounded blends in which elements are given physical locations and physical process of subsequent appearance.

(26) SEE:dir.front.down+/eye.gaze/:front.down+/mouth.opening/ COUPLE, AGAIN CHILD ONE-i> TWO-j> THREE-k> FOUR-l> FIVE-m CHILD ONE> TWO> THREE> FIVE
'(The boy) saw a (frog) couple, and also one baby frog, two (second), three (third), four (fourth), five (fifth).'

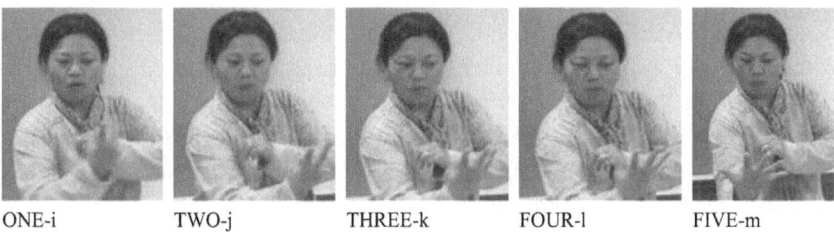

| ONE-i | TWO-j | THREE-k | FOUR-l | FIVE-m |

Figure 31: Illustration of Example 26.

Moreover, the signer in this example becomes the character 'boy' of the story through integrating the indicating verb 'SEE' with the facial expressions. She produces the indicating sign 'SEE' 'directing-to' front downward, along with eyes gazing front downward and with mouth opening. And then she produces the signs 'COUPLE' and 'CHILD', two describing signals. Producing the signs 'COUPLE', 'CHILD', and the indicating sign 'SEE', along with the non-manual expressions instructs the cognitive mechanism of the surrogate blending. The directionality of this indicating sign and these non-manual expressions provides the access to the elements '|boy and dog|' to connect to the Figure of the event and the access to the elements '|couple frogs and baby frogs|' to connect to the Ground. These conceptually present referents are created with physical reality. And through this blending, referents are given physical location in grounded spaces. This seems to present the reality for engaging addressees to take the C-VPT (character viewpoint) to participate in as if they were in the scene to 'witness' what happened right in front of them. They will feel like they see in person one baby frog (|frog| in 'i' location), then the second one (|frog| in 'j' location), the third one (|frog| in 'k' location), etc. (Figure 32). The addressees can integrate the meaning encoded by the naming and the meaning demonstrated by the grounded blends to produce a richer message that will make more sense of the story by themselves. Hence the interpersonal involvement will be achieved much strongly.

The scene the character sees is like this:

	**	frog	-i**				
	|frog|-i			**|frog|-j**	
	|frog|-i		**|frog|-k**	|frog|-j	
	|frog|-i	**|frog|-l**	|frog|-k	|frog|-j	
|frog|-m	|frog|-i	|frog|-l	|frog|-k	|frog|-j	

Figure 32: Illustration of the scene the character would see.

These strategies above are seldom found in TSL narratives by hearing signers. In Example (27), the hearing second language learner produces the symbols 'HAVE'

(Figure 33a), 'FATHER' and 'MOTHER' to express the presence of the characters 'father frog' and 'mother frog'. And then she produces the symbols 'AGAIN', 'GIVE. BIRTH', 'MANY' and 'CHILD' to express the presence of the characters 'many baby frogs' (Figures 33b, 33c, 33d, and 33e). The hearing signer prefers to describe the event with lexicalized signs while the deaf signer above produces a visual demonstration of the event (Example 26).

(27) HAVE... FATHER MOTHER, AGAIN GIVE.BIRTH MANY CHILD
'There are father and mother (frogs), and besides give birth to many children (frogs).'

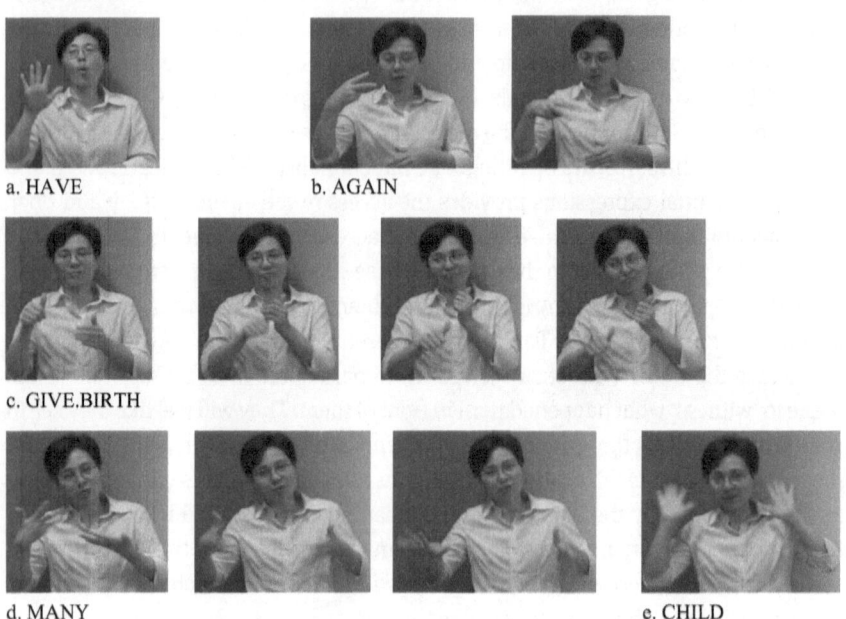

a. HAVE   b. AGAIN

c. GIVE.BIRTH

d. MANY   e. CHILD

Figure 33: Illustration of Example 27.

Compare this example above to the example by another deaf signer below, the sign 'GIVE.BIRTH' by this deaf signer is produced repeatedly three times with a mouth gesture '/mouth:bobobo/', which repeats opening mouth three times, depicting that the frog is giving birth to a lot of babies (Figure 34). This non-manual expression is similar to the analysis of mouth actions in Woll (2001, 2009) and Sandler (2009). They are analyzed as one kind of iconic gestures. Their function is to provide certain sensational image to complement/embellish what manual expressions may have already conveyed or not (Su 2011, 2018). In summary, the deaf signer produces a composite utterance signaled by the composite method of description and depiction, while the hearing signer prefers to describe the event with lexicalized signs. The deaf signer creates a more vivid narrative than the one from the hearing signer.

GIVE.BIRTH++++/mouth:bobobo/ (verb sign + gesture)

Figure 34: Illustration of the non-manual expressions.

The similar mouth action is found in another part of narratives by another deaf signer. In Example (28), the signer begins to produce the describing signals 'FROG', 'ONE' and a manual gesture '/catch/' is followed, which expresses an event that someone is catching a frog. And the utterances continue. In the end a depicting classifier predicate is produced with a mouth gesture '/mouth:bobo/', which repeats opening mouth two times, depicting that the frog is crawling and jumping again and again in the jar (Figure 35d).

(28) FROG ONE FROG /catch/, . . .
      CHILD . . . /jar/+ Enactment:head.tilt.left.and.right:look.at++ JARpro+/
      whistle/ JAR+ Enactment:head.tilt.right:look.at
      Depicting:JARpro+FROGpro-move.up.and.down+/mouth gesture: bobo/
      '(A boy) caught a frog. . . . The child whistled and looked and looked at the
      frog crawling and jumping in the jar.'

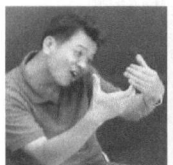

a. CHILD   b. JARpro+/whistle/   c. JAR+ Enactment:ht.L>R

d. Depicting:JARpro+FROGpro-move.up.and.down+/mouth: bobo/

Figure 35: Illustration of Example 28.

In the following example, the signer produces three tokens for the referent 'frog' to make sure the addressee understands it. Then the sign 'VIEW' is produced simultaneously with the proform for the referent 'jar', along with the non-manual expression 'head tilting to the right' (Figure 36d). This composite utterance is to describe, indicate and depict that the child is viewing the frog in the jar. In the end, the similar depicting classifier predicate 'JARpro+FROGpro-move.up.and. down' is produced. Again, the signer employs repetition, constructed actions, and images and details as involvement strategies. Through these, the grounded mental spaces are blended out, creating conceptually present referents '|child|', '|jar|', '|frog|', etc. with physical reality. The meaning of the enactment 'JAR+Enactment:head.tilt.left.and.right' above (Figure 35c) is confirmed, with the sign VIEW, the method of describing. That is the boy's being looking at the frog crawling and jumping in the jar.

(29) /frog/-c FROG-a /frog/-b UNDERSTAND^^
  FROG-a /frog/-b JARpro+FROGpro-move(false start) JARpro+VIEW
  JARpro+FROGpro-move.up.and.down
  'The boy viewed the frog crawling and jumping in the jar.'

a. /frog/-c   b. FROG-a   c. /frog/-b   d. JARpro+VIEW

Figure 36: Illustration of Example 29.

4.4 Summary

In sign language, the use of space and the availability and the partitionability (Dudis 2004) of two-channel system and two independent articulators make possible the simultaneous representation of independent meaningful elements.

With mouth gestures integrated, manner can be elaborated by adverbials (Anderson and Reilly 1998, Liddell 1980), and additional sensational images can be provided by iconic gestures (Sandler 2009) to complement what manual actions have conveyed or haven't conveyed. With facial expressions and body or body-part gestures integrated, another type of grounded blends, the surrogate blends, will be created. Through these multiple, simultaneous blends, more visible elements with rich and vivid depictions are made accessible for addressees to make more sense of the story (Dudis 2002, 2004; Liddell 2000a, 2003).

In sum, the simultaneous integration of non-manual expressions and depicting classifier predicates, with manner elaboration and precise path provided, allowing more precision in the encoding of spatial information with least effort, is the most efficient and informative device in sign language to achieve evaluative functions of narrative. Although they are *non-prototypical alignments* of the use of classifier forms and signing viewpoint, in which the manual expressions represent event from the O-VPT (observer viewpoint) and the non-manual expressions, the C-VPT (character viewpoint), they will be prevalently produced as involvement strategies especially in the *orientation* or *climax* parts of narratives. This kind of non-prototypical alignments had been addressed in Aarons and Morgan (2003), Dudis (2002), Liddell (2000a), and Perniss (2007).

5 Conclusions

This paper examines composite utterances in TSL. These composite utterances, with high degree of iconicity and simultaneity, convey the more informative and efficient messages that make more vivid sense of story. In particular, the depicting classifier predicates integrated with non-manual actions are the most prevalent simultaneous constructions because they can simultaneously integrate the most informative messages with least effort, in which lots of distinct visible elements can be created with physical forms inherited through the blending of grounded spaces.

With visual-gestural modality, resources to create indices and icons are readily available for not only deaf native and near-native signers, but also hearing native and second language learners. But these strategies are not prevalently and appropriately used in TSL produced by all signers. Deaf native and most deaf near-native signers did, while hearing native signers and hearing second language learners did not. These differences can be accounted for by the fact that native deaf and near-native deaf signers have to tell stories face-to-face, as reported in the rich story-telling culture of the deaf (Ladd 2003). However, the thinking-for-signing of native hearing signers and hearing second language learners when producing TSL narratives is similar to the thinking-for-speaking (Slobin 1996) of them when producing Mandarin. Even when producing TSL, they use method of description more and result in their narratives being less iconic and less vivid than those produced by most native and near-native deaf signers.

References

Aarons, Debra & Ruth Morgan. 2003. Classifier predicates and the creation of multiple perspectives in South African Sign Language. *Sign Language Studies* 3(2). 125–156.

Anderson, Diane E. & Judy S. Reilly. 1998. PAH! The acquisition of adverbials in ASL. *Sign Language and Linguistics* 1(2). 117–142.

Ann, Jean. 1993. *A linguistic investigation of the relationship between physiology and handshape*. Arizona: University of Arizona dissertation.

Bahan, Benjamin J. & Samuel J. Supalla. 1995. Line segmentation and narrative structure: A study of eyegaze behavior in American Sign Language. In Karen Emmorey & Judy Reilly (eds.), *Language, Gesture, and Space*, 171–191. Hillsdale, NJ: Lawrence Erlbaum Associates.

Bamberg, Michael & Robin Damrad-Frye. 1991. On the ability to provide evaluative comments: Further explorations of children's narrative competencies. *Journal of Child Language* 18(3). 689–709.

Birdsell, Brian. 2014. Fauconnier's theory of mental spaces and conceptual blending. In Jeannette Littlemore & John R. Taylor (eds.), *The Bloomsbury Companion to Cognitive Linguistics*, 72–90. London/New York: Bloomsbury.

Chang, Jung-hsing, Shiou-fen Su, & James H-Y. Tai. 2005. Classifier predicates reanalyzed, with special reference to Taiwan Sign Language. *Language and Linguistics* 6(2). 247–278.

Clark, Herbert H. 1996. *Using Language*. Cambridge: Cambridge University Press.

Clark, Herbert H. 2003. Pointing and placing. In Sotaro Kita (ed.), *Pointing: Where Language, Culture, and Cognition Meet*, 243–268. Mahwah, NJ: Lawrence Erlbaum Associates.

Clark, Herbert H. 2016. Depicting as a method of communication. *Psychological Review* 123. 324–347. doi: 10.1037/rev0000026

Clark, Herbert H. & Richard Gerrig. 1990. Quotations as demonstrations. *Language* 66(4). 764–805.

Cogill-Koez, Dorothea. 2000. Signed language classifier predicates: Linguistic structures or schematic visual representation? *Sign Language and Linguistics* 3(2). 153–207.

Cooperrider, Kensy & Kate Mesh. 2021. Pointing in gesture and sign. In A. Morgenstern & S. Goldin-Meadow (eds.), *Gesture in language: Development across the lifespan*, 3–17. Berlin: De Gruyter Mouton; Washington, DC: American Psychological Association.

Corazza, Serena. 1990. The morphology of classifier handshapes in Italian Sign Language (LIS). In Ceil Lucas (ed.), *Sign Language Research: Theoretical Issues*, 71–82. Washington, D.C.: Gallaudet University Press.

Dingemanse, M. 2014. Making new ideophones in Siwu: creative depiction in conversation. *Pragmatics and Society* 5. 384–405. doi: 10.1075/ps.5.3.04din

Dudis, Paul. 2002. Grounded blend maintenance as a discourse strategy. In Ceil Lucas (ed.), *Turn-taking, Fingerspelling and Contact in Signed Languages*, 53–72. Washington, D.C.: Gallaudet University Press.

Dudis, Paul. 2004. Body partitioning and real-space blends. *Cognitive Linguistics* 15(2). 223–238.

Dudis, Paul. 2011. The body in scene depictions. In Cynthia B. Roy (ed.), *Discourse in Signed Languages*, 3–45. Washington, DC: Gallaudet University Press.

Duncan, Susan. 2003. Gesture in language: Issues for sign language research. In Karen Emmorey (ed.), *Perspectives on Classifier Constructions in Sign Languages*, 259–268. Mahwah, NJ: Lawrence Erlbaum Associates.

Emmorey, Karen & Judy Reilly. 1998. The development of quotation and reported action: conveying perspective in ASL. In Eve Clark (ed.), *Proceedings of the Twenty-night Annual Stanford Child Language Research Forum*, 81–90. CSLI publications: Stanford, CA.

Enfield, Nick J. 2009. *The anatomy of meaning*. Cambridge, UK: Cambridge University Press. doi: https://doi.org/10.1017/CBO9780511576737

Engberg-Pedersen, Elisabeth. 1993. *Space in Danish Sign Language: The Semantics and Morphosyntax of the Use of Space in a Visual Language*. Hamburg: Signum Press.

Epstein, Richard. 2002. The definite article, accessibility, and the construction of discourse referents. *Cognitive Linguistics* 12(4). 333–378.

Fauconnier, Gilles. [1985] 1994. *Mental Spaces: Aspects of Meaning Construction in Natural Language*. New York: Cambridge University Press.

Fauconnier, Gilles. 1997. *Mappings in Thought and Language*. New York: Cambridge University Press.

Fauconnier, Gilles. 1998. Mental spaces, language modalities, and conceptual integration. In Michael Tomasello (ed.), *The New Psychology of Language: Cognitive and Functional Approaches to Language Structure*, 251–280. Mahwah, NJ: Lawrence Erlbaum.

Fauconnier, Gilles & Mark Turner. 1996. Blending as a central process in grammar. In Adele Goldberg (ed.), *Conceptual Structure, Discourse and Language*, 113–130. Stanford, CA: CSLI.

Fauconnier, Gilles & Mark Turner. 1998. Conceptual integration networks. *Cognitive Science* 22(2). 133–187.

Fauconnier, Gilles & Mark Turner. 2002. *The Way We Think: Conceptual Blending and the Mind's Hidden Complexities*. New York: Basic Books.

Fauconnier, Gilles & Mark Turner. 2006. Mental spaces: Conceptual integration networks. In Dirk Geeraerts (ed.), *Cognitive Linguistics: Basic Readings*, 303–372. Berlin: Walter de Gruyter.

Fay, Nicolas, Casey J. Lister, T. Mark Ellison, & Susan Goldin-Meadow. 2014. Creating a communication system from scratch: Gesture beats vocalization hands down. *Frontiers in Psychology (Language Sciences, Language by Hand and by Mouth Research Topic)* 5. 1–12.

Ferrara, Lindsay & Gabrielle Hodge. 2018. Language as description, indication, and depiction. *Frontiers in Psychology* 9. 1–15.

Fischer, Susan & Bonnie Gough. 1978. Verbs in American Sign Language. *Sign Language Studies* 18. 17–48.

Friedman, Lynn A. 1976. The manifestation of subject, object and topic in ASL. In Charles N. Li (ed.), *Subject and Topic*, 127–148. New York: Academic Press.

Goldin-Meadow, Susan & Diane Brentari. 2017. Gesture, sign, and language: The coming of age of sign language and gesture studies. *Cambridge Core in Behavioral and Brain Sciences* 40(e46). 1–60.

Holler, Judith & Steven C. Levinson. 2019. Multimodal language processing in human communication. *Trends in Cognitive Sciences* 23(8). 639–652.

Kendon, Adam. 2004. *Gesture: Visible Action as Utterance*. Cambridge: Cambridge University Press.

Küntay, Aylin C. & Keiko Nakamura. 2004. Linguistic strategies serving evaluative functions: A comparison between Japanese and Turish narratives. In Sven Strömqvist & Ludo Verhoeven (eds.), *Relating Events in Narrative. Vol. II: Typological and Contextual Perspectives*, 329–358. Mahwah, NJ: Lawrence Erlbaum Associates.

Labov, William. 1972. *Language in the Inner City*. Philadelphia: University of Pennsylvania Press.

Labov, William & Joshua Waletsky. 1967. Narrative analysis. In J. Helm (ed.), *Essays on the Verbal and Visual Arts (Proceedings of the 1966 Spring Meeting of the American Ethnological Society)*, 12–44. Seattle: University of Washington Press.

Ladd, Paddy. 2003. *Understanding Deaf Culture: In Search of Deafhood*. Clevedon: Multilingual Matters.

Langacker, Ronald W. 1987. *Foundations of cognitive grammar. Vol. I: Theoretical prerequisites*. Standford, CA: Standford University Press.

Lee, Hsin-Hsien. 2003. *Analyzing Handshape Changes in Taiwan Sign Language*. Taiwan, R.O.C.: National Chung Cheng University MA thesis.

Liddell, Scott K. 1980. *American Sign Language Syntax*. The Hague: Mouton.

Liddell, Scott K. 1995. Real, surrogate, and token space: grammatical consequences in ASL. In Karen Emmorey & Judy S. Reilly (eds.), *Language, Gesture and Space*, 19–41. Mahwah, NJ: Lawrence Erlbaum Associates, Publishers.

Liddell, Scott K. 1996. Spatial representations in discourse: comparing spoken and signed language. *Lingua* 98. 145–167.

Liddell, Scott K. 1998. Grounded blends, gestures, and conceptual shifts. *Cognitive Linguistics* 9(3). 283–314.

Liddell, Scott K. 2000a. Blended spaces and deixis in sign language discourse. In David McNeill (ed.), *Language and Gesture*, 331–357. Cambridge: Cambridge University Press.

Liddell, Scott K. 2000b. Indicating verbs and pronouns: Pointing away from agreement. In Karen Emmorey & Harlan L. Lane (eds.), *The signs of Language Revisited: An Anthology to Honor Ursula Bellugi & Edward Klima*, 303–320. Mahwah, NJ: Erlbaum.

Liddell, Scott K. 2003. *Grammar, gesture, and meaning in American Sign Language*. Cambridge: Cambridge University Press.

Liddell, Scott K. & Melanie Metzger. 1998. Gesture in sign language discourse. *Journal of Pragmatics* 30. 657–697.

Liddell, Scott & Marit Vogt-Svendsen. 2007. Constructing spatial conceptualizations from limited input: Evidence from Norwegian Sign Language. In Susan D. Duncan, Justine Cassell, & Elena T. Levy (eds.), *Gesture and the Dynamic Dimension of Language: Essays in Honor of David McNeill* (Gesture Studies), 173–194. Amsterdam, Philadelphia: John Benjamins. doi: https://doi.org/10.1075/gs.1.17lid

Lodge, David 1990. Narration with words. In Horace Barlow, Colin Blakemore & Miranda Weston-Smith (eds.), *Images and Understanding*, 141–53. Cambridge: Cambridge University Press.

Mathur, Gaurav & Christian Rathmann. 2012. Verb agreement. In Roland Pfau, Markus Steinbach & Bencie Woll (eds.), *Sign Language*, 136–157. Berlin, Boston: De Gruyter Mouton. doi: https://doi.org/10.1515/9783110261325.136.

Mayer, Mercer. 1969. *Frog, where are you?* New York: Dial Press.

McNeill, David. 1992. *Hand and Mind: What Gestures Reveal about Thought*. Chicago: University of Chicago Press.

McNeill, David. 2003. Aspects of aspect. *Gesture* 3(1). 1–17.

McNeill, David. 2005. *Gesture and Thought*. Chicago: University of Chicago Press.

McNeill, David & Susan Duncan. 2000. Growth points in thinking-for-speaking. In David McNeill (ed.), *Language and Gesture*, 141–161. Cambridge: Cambridge University Press.

Meier, Richard P. 2002. Why different, why the same? Explaining effects and non-effects of modality upon linguistic structure in sign and speech. In Richard P. Meier, Kearsy

Cormier, & David Quinto-Pozos (eds.), *Modality and Structure in Sgned and Spoken Languages*, 1–26. Cambridge: Cambridge University Press.

Metzger, Melanie. 1995. Constructed dialogue and constructed action in American Sign Language. In Ceil Lucas (ed.), *Sociolinguistics in Deaf Communities*, 255–271. Washington, D.C.: Gallaudet University Press.

Nakamura, Keiko. 2009. Language and affect: Japanese children's use of evaluative expressions in narratives. In Elena Lieven & Jiansheng Guo (eds.), *Crosslinguistic Approaches to the Study of Language: Research in the Tradition of Dan Isaac Slobin*, 225–240. New York/London: Psychology Press.

Padden, Carol A. 1988. *Interaction of Morphology and Syntax in American Sign Language*. New York: Garland.

Parrill, Fey, Benjamin K. Bergen & Patricia V. Lichtenstein. 2013. Grammatical aspect, gesture, and conceptualization: Using co-speech gesture to reveal event representations. *Cognitive Linguistics* 24(1). 135–158.

Perniss, Pamela M. 2007. Achieving spatial coherence in German Sign Language narratives: The use of classifiers and perspective. *Lingua* 117. 1315–1338.

Peirce, Charles S. 1955 [1902]. Logic and Semiotic: Theory of Signs. In J. Buchler (ed.), *Philosophical Writings*, 98–119. New York: Dover.

Puupponen, Anna. 2019. Towards understanding nonmanuality: A semiotic treatment of signers' head movements. *Glossa: a journal of general linguistics* 4(1). 1–39. doi: https://doi.org/10.5334/gjgl.709

Quinto-Pozos, David. 2007. Can constructed action be considered obligatory? *Lingua* 117(7). 1285–1314.

Quinto-Pozos, David & Sarika Mehta. 2010. Register variation in mimetic gestural complements to signed language. *Journal of Pragmatics* 42(3). 557–584.

Rayman, Jennifer. 1999. Story telling in the visual mode: A comparison of ASL and English. In Elisebath Winston (ed.), *Storytelling and Conversation: Discourse in Deaf Communities*, 59–82. Washington D.C.: Gallaudet University Press.

Reilly, Judy S. 2001. From affect to language: A cross-linguistic study of narratives. In Ludo Verhoeven & Sven Strömqvist (eds.), *Narrative Development in a Multilingual Context*, 399–418. Amsterdam: John Benjamins.

Reilly, Judy, Elizabeth Bates & Virginia Marchman. 1998. Narrative discourse in children with early focal brain injury. In M. Dennis (ed.), *Brain and Language* 61(3). 335–375 (special issue on discourse in children with anomalous brain development or acquired brain injury).

Rijkhoff, Jan N. M. 2002. *The Noun Phrase*. Oxford/New York: Oxford University Press.

Rijkhoff, Jan N. M. 2008a. Layers, levels and contexts in Functional Discourse Grammar. In Jan Rijkhoff & Daniel García Velasco (eds.), *The Noun Phrase in Functional Discourse Grammar*, 63–115. Berlin/New York: Mouton de Gruyter.

Rijkhoff, Jan N. M. 2008b. Descriptive and discourse-referential modifiers in a layered model of the noun phrase. *Linguistics* 46(4). 789–829.

Roy, Cynthia B. 2000[1989]. Features of discourse in an American Sign Language lecture. In Ceil Lucas (ed.), *The Sociolinguistics of the Deaf Community*, 231–251. San Diego: Academic Press. The same paper in *Linguistics of American Sign Language: An introduction* (3rd edition).

Russo, Tommaso, Rosaria Giuranna & Elena Pizzuto. 2001. Italian Sign Language (LIS) Poetry: Iconic Properties and Structural Regularities. Sign Language Studies 2(1 Fall). 84–102.

Sandler, Wendy. 2009. Symbiotic symbolization by hand and mouth in sign language. *Semiotica* 174(1). 241–275.

Schembri, Adam, Kearsy Cormier & Jordan Fenlon. 2018. Indicating verbs as typologically unique constructions: Reconsidering verb 'agreement' in sign languages. *Glossa: a journal of general linguistics* 3(1). 89. 1–40. doi: https://doi.org/10.5334/gjgl.468

Schick, Brenda S. 1987. *The Acquisition of Classifier Predicates in American Sign Language*. West Lafayette, Indiana: Purdue University dissertation.

Schick, Brenda S. 1990. The effects of morphosyntactic structure on the acquisition of classifier predicates in ASL. In Ceil Lucas (ed.), *Sign Language Research: Theoretical Issues*, 358–374. Washington D.C.: Gallaudet University Press.

Slobin, Dan I. 1996a. From "thought and language" to "thinking for speaking". In John J. Gumperz & Stephen C. Levinson (eds.), *Rethinking Linguistic Relativity*, 70–96. Cambridge: Cambridge University Press.

Smith, Wayne H. 1989. *The Morphological Characteristics of Verbs in Taiwan Sign Language*. Bloomington: Indiana University dissertation.

Stokoe, William C. 1960. Sign language structure: An outline of the communication systems of the American deaf. *Studies in Linguistics*, Occasional Papers, 8. Silver Spring, MD: Linstok Press.

Su, Shiou-fen. 2011. *Modality effects in grammar and discourse in Taiwan Sign Language*. Taiwan, R.O.C.: National Chung Cheng University dissertation.

Su, Shiou-fen. 2018. *Modality effects in grammar and discourse in Taiwan Sign Language*. Golden Light Academic Publishing.

Supalla, Ted. 1978. Morphology of verbs of motion and location. In F. Caccamise & D. Hicks (eds.), *Proceedings of the Second National Symposium on Sign Language Research and Teaching*, 27–45. Silver Spring, MD: National Association of the Deaf.

Supalla, Ted. 1982. *Structure and acquisition of verbs of motion and location in American Sign Language*. San Diego: University of California dissertation.

Supalla, Ted. 2003. Revisiting Visual Analogy in ASL Classifier Predicates. In Karen Emmorey (ed.), *Perspectives on Classifier Constructions in Sign Languages*, 249–258. New York: Psychology Press.

Talmy, Leonard. 1985. Lexicalization patterns: Semantic structure in lexical forms. In T. Shopen (ed.), *Language Typology and Lexical Description: Vol. 3. Grammatical Categories and the Lexicon*, 36–149. Cambridge: Cambridge University Press.

Talmy, Leonard. 1991. Path to realization: A typology of event conflation. *Proceedings of the Berkeley Linguistics Society* 17. 480–519.

Talmy, Leonard. 2000. *Toward a Cognitive Semantics: Vol. II: Typology and Process in Concept Structuring*. Cambridge, MA: MIT Press.

Tannen, Deborah. 1986. Introducing constructed dialogue in Greek and American conversational and literary narrative. In Florian Coulmas (ed.), *Direct and Indirect Speech*, 311–332. Berlin: Mouton.

Tannen, Deborah. [1989] 2007. *Talking Voices: Repetition, Dialogue, and Imagery in Conversational Discourse*, 2nd edn. Washington, D.C.: Georgetown University.

Taub, Sarah. 2001. *Language from the Body: Iconicity and Metaphor in American Sign Language*. Cambridge: Cambridge University Press.

Valli, Clayton & Ceil Lucas. 1995. *Linguistics of American Sign Language: A Resource Text for ASL Users*. 2nd edn. Washington, D.C.: Gallaudet University Press.

van Dijk, Teun A. 2008. *Discourse and Context. A Sociocognitive Approach.* Cambridge: Cambridge University Press. doi:10.1017/CBO9780511481499

Winston, Elizabeth A. 1991. Spatial referencing and cohesion in an American Sign Language text. *Sign Language Studies* 73. 397–409.

Winston, Elizabeth A. 1993. *Spatial mapping in comparative discourse frames in an ASL lecture.* Washington, D.C.: Georgetown University dissertation.

Winston, Elizabeth A. 1994. Space and reference in American Sign Language. In Barbara Johnstone (ed.), *Repetition in Discourse: Interdisciplinary Perspectives*, 99–113. Norwood, N.J.: Ablex.

Winston, Elizabeth A. 1995. Spatial mapping in comparative discourse frames. In Karen Emmorey & Judy Reilly (eds.), *Language, Gesture and Space*, 87–114. Hillsdale, NJ: Lawrence Erlbaum Associates.

Theresia Hofer
Time and timelines in Tibetan Sign Language (TSL) interactions in Lhasa

Abstract: This chapter explores and analyses expressions of time in the Tibetan Sign Language (TSL) as used in Lhasa. Sign languages use metaphors of space to talk about time, as well as literally and physically express time in space, something linguists have described in terms of 'timelines' (for example horizontal, sagittal or deictic timelines). This chapter complements linguistic and anthropological research with what I call the TSL 'vertical semi-elliptical timeline', in which both past and future are placed behind the signer's body and the past is expressed upwardly and the future downwardly. Among the world's documented signed and spoken languages and their co-speech gestures, this is an anthropologically interesting and typologically rare placement of time in space, especially that of the future in TSL behind the body and downwards. Following a dual methodological and theoretical approach from anthropology and linguistics, the chapter describes this articulation of time in TSL and explores how it fits with broader conceptions and patterns of time and space in Tibet and the Himalayas, in particular, broader meanings associated with the vertical dimension. The chapter also argues that the TSL vertical semi-elliptical timeline transcends the strictly-speaking 'body-anchored' timeline described by sign linguists. While it takes the body as a key referent, the vertical semi-elliptical timeline of TSL sits at the interface of the body and the wider cosmos and socio-cultural environment of Tibet.

Keywords: Tibetan Sign Language, Lhasa, time, timelines, space, body, cosmology, verticality, anthropology

---

Acknowledgements: I gratefully acknowledge the time and efforts of the research participants during my fieldwork and the colleagues who enabled it, as well as the valuable feedback to earlier drafts of his chapter, in particular by Lauren Reed, Anna Sehnalova, and the two anonymous reviewers. This research was funded by the Wellcome Trust [Grant 104523]. For the purpose of Open Access and to fulfill the requirements of the grant, the author has applied a CC BY-NC-ND public copyright license to any Author Accepted Manuscript version arising from this submission. I am also thankful for the financial and logistical support for the fieldwork and the writing up to the University of Bristol and Wolfson College at the University of Oxford; to Kazumi Matsuoka, Marie Coppola and Onno Crasborn for their outstanding support in turbulent times; and to Thea Vidnes for copy editing the chapter and Mike Ronsky for creating the map and graphics.

ට Open Access. © 2023 the author, published by De Gruyter. [CC BY-NC-ND] This work is licensed under the Creative Commons Attribution-NonCommercial-NoDerivatives 4.0 International License.
https://doi.org/10.1515/9781501510243-011

1 Introduction

Time is expressed and understood in vastly different ways around the world (Gell 1992). Time may be considered cyclically (as in many European conceptions and representations of four seasons), as polar opposites (day and night), or perhaps as a linear flow. Different domains of life, such as agriculture or medicine, as well as all languages, have developed diverse ways to understand and express time. It is important not to portray these alternatives as mutually exclusive, as they often co-exist and without there being a single synoptic system (Zeitlyn 2020).

It has further been argued that linguistic phenomena can offer a unique lens on the topic of time in different societies (Nagano 1998). Spoken languages are well studied in this regard and the sheer diversity of ways that languages encode time and by extension cosmologies is staggering. Despite this diversity, there is widespread agreement among linguists that metaphors of *space* are found across most languages of the world to express time (Klein 2010), even if this is not entirely universal (Sinha et al. 2011). So far the expression of time in sign languages has not as extensively been described compared to spoken languages, even though they are particularly interesting, as signers not only use metaphors of space to talk about time. They literally and physically express time in space, thus making the otherwise often abstract notion of time a highly visible, spatial phenomenon.

In the absence of most sign languages having grammatical tenses through the inflection of verbs (Velupillai 2012: 223–224), sign linguists study the expression of time through time adverbials and other lexical and morphological aspects (Pfau, Steinbach, and Woll 2012). One of these is the placement, or the movement, of time-related lexical items and/or verbs in space along what sign linguists call "timelines". Timelines are established in the space around the signer. Studies and graphic representations of timelines include Engberg-Pedersen's (1993) five timelines of Danish Sign Language (including the common "deictic timeline" that runs from behind the signer's dominant-hand shoulder to the place of maximal extension forward to describe past present and future), Klima and Bellugi on American Sign Language (ASL) (1979: 82), Sutton-Spence and Woll for British Sign Language (BSL) (1999) and Zeshan on Indo Pakistani Sign Language (2000), among others. In many European sign languages, as well as for example in Japanese Sign Language (JSL, Matsuoka 2015), a key deictic timeline tends to place the past behind the signer and the present and future in front of the signer, also known as a 'sagittal timeline' (Pfau, Steinbach, and Woll 2012: 190).

To this, so-called 'celestial timelines' have been added, where signers display and/or point – either metaphorically or using "absolute points" (Levinson 2003) – to the movement of the sun and/or the moon (de Vos 2012a, Yano and Matsuoka

2018). This type of timeline is mostly a feature of so-called 'rural' or 'village sign languages', which, in contrast to national sign languages that have developed by and large within urban deaf communities, are "indigenous sign languages [that are] typically shared between deaf and hearing individuals, thus facilitating a high degree of integration between deaf and hearing individuals" (Zeshan and de Vos 2012: 2). As the name already suggests, rural or village sign languages arose mostly in rural areas and in the Global South, in settings with a higher than usual incidence of deafness. In such languages, the sagittal timeline is by and large not present, or at least not as prominent. Indeed, among some such languages, like in Kata Kolok, a sign language of Bali, timelines do not exist and there are no separate signs for past vs future (De Vos 2012a: 219–228). This language has other distinctions instead, for example using the sign PIDAN to mark the 'non-present' (De Vos 2012b: 217).

Through describing and analysing expressions of time in Tibetan Sign Language (TSL) interactions in contemporary Lhasa, this chapter complements the long-standing field of research on time in sign linguistics with a rare timeline found in TSL, one that I call a 'vertical semi-elliptic timeline'. Here, both past and future are placed behind the signer's body and the past is expressed upwardly and the future downwardly. This chapter therefore offers a novel contribution to the systematic and comparative study of sign languages, also known as sign language typology, as well as to the anthropological study of time and of linguistic diversity in Tibet and the Himalayas (Roche and Suzuki 2019, Tournadre 2014). It places (linguistic) aspects of time in TSL, in a broad and comparative context based on published regional anthropological research, including expressions of time and space in songs and rituals, spoken languages, and wider cosmology. Following this dual methodological and theoretical approach, I argue that it would be too limiting to understand the TSL vertical semi-elliptical timeline as a strictly speaking 'deictic' or 'body-anchored' timeline.

2 Background

2.1 Timelines in sign languages – body use and space

A typical body-anchored timeline found in many sign languages is the sagittal timeline, one "that runs along a signer's sagittal axis, and is split at the signer's centre, such that the area behind the signer represents the past, and the front of the signer represents the future" (de Vos 2012a: 15). It is said to be parallel to the floor, and prominently used to refer to the 'past' and 'future' in relation to the ego[1] at present. It may be used at a discourse and at a lexical level. In discourse, the relative position of signs mapped onto the spatial axis reflects the temporal relationship between events (de Vos 2012a: 15). On a lexical level items placed on this timeline are either marked with a time aspect, or they are morphologically imbued with aspects of the sagittal timeline. The sagittal timeline has been described for many European sign languages, and linguists consider it to be typologically the most prevalent timeline worldwide (e.g. Meir and Sandler 2008). Most sign languages, however, feature more than one timeline, the most common ones (in addition to the sagittal one) being 'vertical' and 'horizontal' timelines (Figure 1). In addition, many nuances to these common trajectories have been described. For example, among the four timelines and one timeplane in Danish Sign Language (DSL), both the 'deictic' and the 'mixed' timeline that have ego as their centre (Engberg-Pedersen 1993: 80) can be considered sagittal. In general, all of these three timelines are considered to be 'body-anchored timelines'.

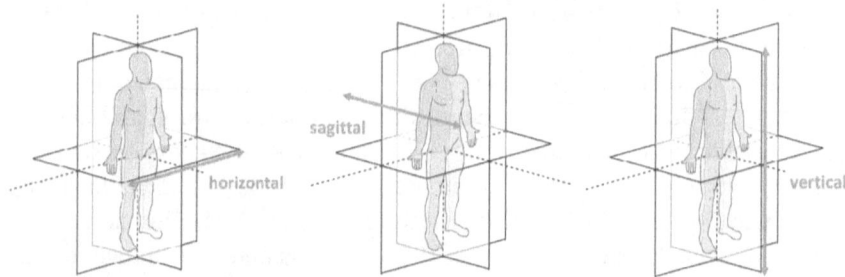

Figure 1: Graphic depictions of the 'horizontal', 'sagittal' and 'vertical' timelines (Creative Commons Licence, via Wikimedia).

In contrast, there are some (signed) languages that do not have such defined timelines. This includes spoken Yucatan Mayan and Yucatan Mayan Sign Language (Le Guen 2012), Enga Sign Language (Kendon 1980), Kata Kolok (de Vos 2012a) and Kalige Sign Language of Papua New Guinea (Reed 2019). Both Kata Kolok and Enga Sign Language for instance make a key distinction between 'present' and 'not present', which can be read as an expression of a different social and cultural emphasis and value system.

Another finding is that some sign languages, such as Miyakubo Sign Language,[2] have more than one lexical marker for 'future'. Concepts in the future,

---

[1] Ego in (sign) linguistics refers to the signer herself or himself.
[2] Miyakubo Sign Language is a shared sign language on Ehime-Oshima in south-western Japan.

such as 'tomorrow' can be expressed by using the sign THINK, SLEEP or, just as well, by signing FOLLOWING (Yano and Matsuoka 2018). FOLLOWING is also used to express "two (or more) years from now" and is particularly interesting as it is signed by placing the dominant hand on the ipsilateral side of the signer's hip (Yano and Matsuoka 2018: 654). One may be tempted to think that this indicates the space behind the signer's body to refer to the future, but as the authors explain this is not the case. FOLLOWING is not signed behind the body but rather is "possibly derived from the shape of the stern of a fishing boat... when two boats move forming a row, the latter boat follows the stern of the other boat" and so is "not related to the use of space to indicate time" (Yano and Matsuoka 2018: 657). TSL also has several lexical items to reference future, as will be explored below.

Instead of the typologically prevalent sagittal timeline, TSL uses at least three timelines: a vertical semi-elliptical timeline, which rises up the front of the body and arches towards the back for 'past', then passing down the front of the body, where present events are located, then arching towards the back of the lower body for future events; a horizontal TSL timeline on the frontal plane with past to the left and future to the right; and lastly, a circular timeline that is associated with the recurrence of the days of the week. The vertical semi-elliptical timeline is notable and seemingly unique, as the past is placed upwards and backwards and the future *downwards* and *behind* the lower body. It is situated on the dominant side of the signer's body, at about shoulder plane. Rather than a strict 'line', it forms a vertical semi-ellipse (Figure 2).

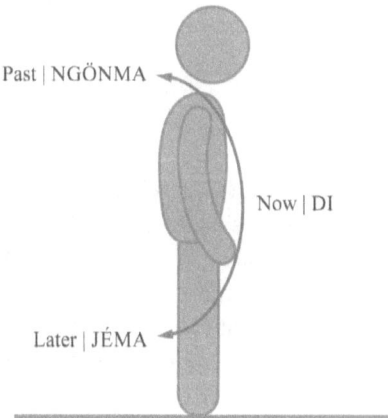

Figure 2: The TSL vertical semi-elliptical timeline to express the aspect of present, past and future.

The placement of concepts of the future and of future events *downwards* and *behind* the body is noteworthy and rare, even when compared to unusual expressions of time across the spectrum of signed and spoken languages and associated co-speech gesture. For instance, in spoken Aymara, with support from data on co-speech gesture, it has been demonstrated that the future is also behind ego, while the past is in front of ego, as an "unusual culture-specific cognitive pattern" (Núñez and Sweetser 2006). In Aymara, the basic word for 'front' (*nayra*, 'eye/front/sight') is also a basic expression meaning 'past', and the basic word for 'back' (*qhipa*, 'back/behind') is a basic expression for 'future'. Here the common European sagittal timeline seems to be reversed.

The placement of the future in TSL both *behind* the body and *downwards* and *without* a counterpart of the past on the opposite spectrum of a sagittal timeline does therefore appear to be unique. In TSL, in several ways lexical expressions of time go against the grain of spatial expressions of time in other languages, even when taking into account the well-known importance of verticality principles in Tibetan spoken languages, cultures and the historical myths of Central Tibetans (whose first king descended on a rope from heaven, before it was cut). How is this unusual timeline in TSL created and used? How does it relate and compare to other timelines in TSL? And how can we explain the TSL vertical semi-elliptic timeline in a broader socio-cultural and historical context?

Before turning to these questions and the wider socio-linguistic, environmental and cosmological context within which TSL time expressions occur, a few words about the historical and socio-linguistic situation of TSL and about my research methods.

2.2 Historical and socio-linguistic situation of Tibetan Sign Language

TSL does not fit neatly into either the 'national' or the 'rural' or 'village' type of common sign language classifications (Zeshan and de Vos 2012). TSL is atypical in being entirely formed and used outside of a Deaf School context (the root of many now national sign languages), but is not a shared 'rural' or 'village' sign language either. It emerged in the largely urban context of Lhasa and within a deaf community coming together as a result of rapid urbanisation from the late 1990s onwards. It also benefitted from support of an international NGO during the first decade of the new millennium. And, importantly, when TSL started to become formalised during this time and in this urban setting, signers drew consciously and extensively on gestural repertoires derived from deaf Tibetans living in rural areas, and the multi-modal interactions with close family members, neighbours and the wider community in both rural and urban areas. This communication includes the use of gestures/signs (*lak da* [*lag brda'*]) and what in TSL is known as RANG SHUK LAK DA (*rang shuk kyi lak da* [*rang shugs kyis lag brda'*]), which I translate as "spontaneous sign" (Hofer 2019).[3] This involves forms of communications that are socially and linguistically distinct from, if also at times overlapping with, what colleagues have referred to as "co-speech gesture" or "home sign" (e.g. Kendon 2004, McNeill 1992, Goldin-Meadow 2003), or "natural sign" with regard to Nepal (Green 2014). TSL can be thus described as an indigenous yet recently emerging and at the same time endangered sign language. It is listed with the acronym 'lsn' in *Ethnologue* (Eberhard, Simons, and Charles 2020).[4]

The number of TSL users can be estimated at several hundred deaf signers in the Tibet Autonomous Region (TAR), mostly in the regional capital city of Lhasa as well as some in Shigatse, the second largest town in the TAR (see map in Figure 3). This group comprises at present mainly deaf Tibetans between the ages of 35 to 45 (Hofer 2017a, 2020).[5] As elsewhere and due to varying social and

---

[3] There is no agreed or widespread written form for sign languages in general, and this is the case for TSL as well. I will therefore follow one of the international conventions in sign linguistics of writing signed languages by capitalizing each lexical item. Whenever I refer to lexical TSL items that are found in dictionaries, in particular the *Standard TSL Dictionary* (2011), I will capitalise what would be the closest Tibetan translation of that sign, but not necessarily following the suggested glosses found in the *Standard TSL Dictionary*. For example, TSL sign with the Tibetan meaning *nga dro* [*snga dro*] ('morning') will be rendered as NGADRO. By doing so, I do not imply a strict equivalence between the written or spoken and the signed terms.

To denote morphemes underlying a TSL term, I will use small caps, for example DI or NGÖN-MA. In writing Tibetan and TSL concepts, I will use the THL phonetics converter of the Tibetan script. General Tibetan terms will also be written in phonetics, following the THL 2010 Online Tool for Phonetic Conversion, and they are *italicised* (e.g. *nga dro*). This is only done for TSL signs. The form of written Tibetan referred to here is Modern Standard Tibetan, and the spoken form as defined and used in Tournadre and Dorje (2003). For Chinese, I use pinyin transliteration and indicate Chinese terms with the use of 'Ch.'.

When based on notes I took during fieldwork I paraphrase my interlocutors' signing into written text (for example an explanation of a term) then I use "*italics within quotation marks*" (e.g. "*I am not sure why this was no longer used*"). When I translate signing from video or very detailed notes on particular signs, either directly into English or into Lhasa Tibetan and then English, I use "quotation marks but no italics" (e.g. "we always use this sign for morning").

[4] In *Ethnologue* every listed language is required to be given a unique, standard code. The code 'tsl' was already taken by Ts'ün-Lao, a language of northern Vietnam. One of the still available unique identifier was 'lsn', and it was chosen as abbreviation for 'Lhasa sign'.

[5] Younger deaf Tibetan signers display a tendency towards relying mainly on Chinese Sign Language (CSL) due to having attended a local deaf school (established in 2000, which relies heavily on oral Chinese, sign-supported Chinese, as well as some CSL) and which has resulted in social

political reasons, only a small proportion of the estimated several thousand deaf Tibetans in Lhasa (population 600.000 residents)[6] use a form of sign language.

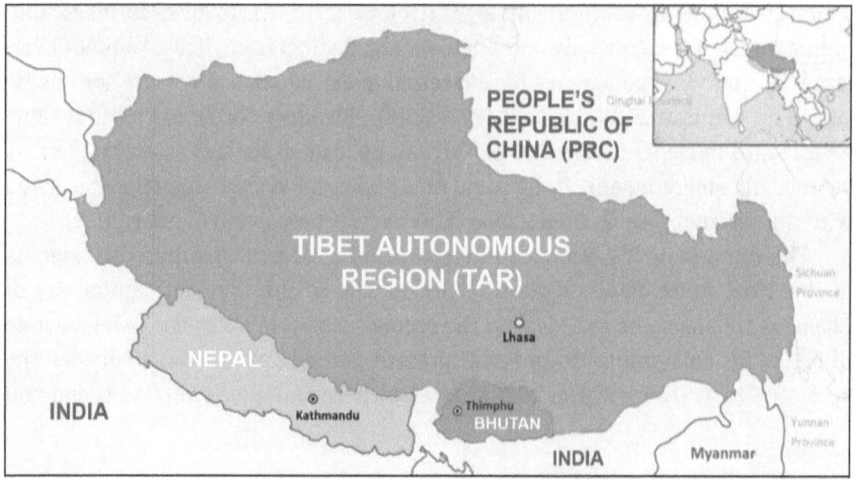

Figure 3: Map of the Tibet Autonomous Region (TAR) and Lhasa within the People's Republic of China.

Alongside the several hundred TSL-dominant deaf signers in Lhasa, there is a similarly-sized group of Tibetans, mostly under the age of 35, who rely on a local variety of Chinese Sign Language (CSL).[7] These signers are mainly the graduates of the local state-run Deaf School (known as the Lhasa Special School) established in Lhasa in the year 2000. The school uses CSL, or the Lhasa variety CSL in some instances of class-room teaching, next to oral instruction and the use of sign-supported Chinese. LhCSL is the main form communication between the deaf students and between them and their deaf teachers. The TSL-dominant signers on the other hand were too old to join the Lhasa Special School when it was established, but could also not complete their studies in the existing, regular schools, with some not entering formal education at all.

Contact between the graduates of the Lhasa Special School using CSL or LhCSL and the TSL-dominant signers has increased steadily since 2012. As a

---

networks also after graduating from the school, using mainly CSL or a local form thereof, which I call Lhasa variety of CSL (LhCSL).
6 Much statistical information and population figures are contested with regard to the actual Lhasa population and their ethnic make-up.
7 See Huang and Gu (2014) and Yang (2015) for definitions and history of CSL.

result, TSL-dominant signers are increasingly shifting towards the use of CSL and LhCSL, with a marked increase of language contact and codeswitching taking place (Hofer 2020).

2.3 Methods

This chapter draws on four months of anthropological and linguistic fieldwork with TSL signers in Lhasa, carried out between 2014 and 2017. During the fieldwork period I undertook participant observation, filmed semi-structured interviews and carried out "linguistic autobiography interviews" (Pavlenko 2007). The data used here consists of documented natural conversations between TSL signers and between TSL signers and myself, recorded using either video, photography or notes, and is what I will refer to when I write about 'TSL interactions' in this chapter. Overall twenty-five TSL-dominant deaf signers were a part of my research; in addition to these, I have also talked and carried out work with signers who use CSL, or Lhasa variety of Chinese Sign Language (LhCSL). I also accessed time-related expressions in video recordings made for the content of a TSL video database, as well as photos, drawings and descriptions, published in TSL language materials.[8] My analysis benefits from and is influenced by over 17 years of research and personal engagement in Tibet and the Himalayas as well as my position as a hearing CODA ('child of a deaf adult') and late learner of sign language.

For reasons of research ethics and to maintain the anonymity of research participants, the images in this chapter are drawn from published, secondary materials, notably the *Standard Tibetan Sign Language Dictionary* (2011) – from now on referred to as the *Standard TSL Dictionary* (TDA 2011). The *Standard TSL Dictionary* is a topic-based record of the citation forms of approximately 1,400 TSL signs in total, each with tri-lingual glosses in Tibetan, Chinese and English, bookended by a useful introduction in Tibetan, Chinese and English and a Tibetan and a Chinese alphabetical list of all entries. It is the result of several years of collaboration and

---

[8] This chapter is part of a research project funded by the Wellcome Trust, Grant 104523, about the lives and signing practices of deaf Tibetans in contemporary Lhasa, capital of the Tibet Autonomous Region (TAR). I refer to the research participants as signers, or TSL signers, given that sign language is their preferred communication mode. In line with recent trends (e.g. Kusters and Friedner 2016), I use deaf with a lowercase "d" as a more encompassing category than "Deaf" or "d/Deaf", which highlight socio-cultural identity and/or the mixed nature of audiological and socio-cultural conditions, but are not as such linguistically or culturally marked among my research participants.

co-production between deaf Tibetan signers and members of the Tibet Deaf Association (TDA), as well as hearing and deaf Chinese and international sign language consultants. It was published by the official, government licensed TAR People's Press in Lhasa, and is the largest collection of TSL signs in the public domain so far.[9] The *Standard TSL Dictionary* contains overall 45 time-related lexical items.

3 Time and time reckoning in Tibetan Sign Language – the state of the art and metaphors of space

Heng, Ling and Drokar's 2013 article, 'Time, Metaphor and Metonymy in Tibetan Sign Language', published in Chinese in an academic journal of a Minority University in the People's Republic of China (PRC), makes an important contribution to understanding spatial metaphors as well as metonymy in the expression of time in TSL. Due to the place and language of the publication, its findings have to date been relatively unavailable to the international scholarly community and its English language academic journals and books. It is therefore not only worth restating the article's findings to provide non-Chinese readers with access to what the authors (one of them a competent TSL signer from Lhasa) wrote, but it is also important as a basis for my own description and analysis of time and the three TSL timelines discussed below.[10] Heng, Ling, and Drokar investigated lexical items used to express time in TSL, which they analysed within a wider framework of spatial metaphors for time and metonymy used in expressing time in other signed and spoken language. Here I will summarise only their findings in relation to the spatial metaphors of time in TSL.

The authors state that TSL "always uses the past as being 'up' and future 'down'", and "that for the future they use the left, and for the past use the right as a second way" (Heng, Ling, and Drokar 2013: 160). They go on to explain that "there is less use of front and back" and that "signers use space for time, in ways similar to how Tibetans understand directions" (Ibid.). In other words, the authors propose that TSL expressions of time do not feature a classic, sagittal timeline.

---

9 Most video-based documentations of TSL are not freely or publicly accessible.
10 Although for aforementioned reasons of anonymity I cannot name them directly, I would here like to convey special thanks to a colleague for their help in translating this academic article from Chinese into English.

In the section titled 'The model of time recognition and metonymy', Heng Ling, and Drokar highlight that TSL has 30 lexical items to express the past 'on the top' and the 'future at the bottom', listing such expressions, including yesterday and tomorrow, last year and next year, last month and next month. They claim all of these lexical items make pronounced use of back and up, for past and back and down, for future events, but *not one* uses, or points to the front and the back of the body. Among their examples for this seemingly more pronounced use of the vertical axis in TSL "time-space metonymy" of past and future, they also name the signs for weekdays in TSL, which are pointing to parts of the face and successively are placed downwards from the start of the week on Sunday on the top of the head, to the end of the week, or Saturday at the bottom of the face, as part of this pattern.

Contrastingly, TSL signs for the times of the day (morning is to the right, mid-day at the centre and evening to the left) are shown as patterned horizontally. Here the 'future' is to the left and the 'past' to the right. The authors explain this by Tibetans having been for a long time agriculturists and as such having acute awareness of the position of the sun.

Although Heng, Ling, and Drokar state "that there is a huge gap between the Chinese Sign Language and Tibetan Sign Language" (2013: 161), they hold that in terms of "physical understanding", TSL and CSL use of metonymy and metaphors of time have more similarities than differences.

My own description and analysis of expressions of time and timelines will complement and, in some cases, correct the article's findings in three main ways: firstly, I complement the use of entries of the *Standard TSL Dictionary* with analysis of signed TSL interactions and good quality images; secondly, I offer more detail (in some cases including etymology) about the different lexical signs and their placement in space which leads to a revision of some of Heng, Ling, and Drokar's classification of verticality and horizontality; and third, my analysis is contextualised within anthropological considerations of time, cosmology and environment in Tibetan and Himalayan societies to more fully explain the typologically rare vertical semi-elliptical timeline.

* * *

In the coming section, Section 4, I provide an original description of lexical items represented on a vertical semi-elliptical time-axis (mainly using three signs of temporal deixis) and consider the wider cultural and linguistic milieu of Tibetan signers in which verticality plays a key role. This section contains three sections, offering a description and etymology for the TSL signs SAKOR ('week'), DAWA ('month') and LO ('year'). Section 5 then discusses the TSL horizontal timeline associated with 'a day' and 'times of the day'. Following on, Section 6 considers the TSL circular timeline that is associated with the days of the week and the sign SAKOR ('week'). I also make reference to time-related expressions in TSL, which cut across divisions of verticality, horizontality and circularity, for example with signs used in space and expressing time in diagonal or other kinds of movements. The chapter ends with a concluding section, Section 7, where I summarise the chapter's key findings, in particular with regard to the typologically rare vertical semi-elliptical timeline, and explain how it fits with broader conceptions and patterns of time and space in Tibet, in particular, in the vertical dimension. It argues that the rare vertical semi-elliptic timeline in TSL should therefore not be considered merely as body-referential or 'body-anchored', but rather as sitting at the intersections of the body and the broader socio-cultural environment TSL signers find themselves in.

4 The vertical semi-elliptical timeline in TSL: Future and past behind the body

Which signs of the time-related lexicon are placed on a vertical timeline in TSL? And where exactly? Furthermore, what is added by the placement of lexical items also *behind* the body and in particular of future-related items *downwards* and *behind* the body?

Although I will use the term timeline following the trend in earlier work on this topic, more precisely we should think of the TSL vertical timeline as a 'standing', i.e. vertical, semi-ellipse as shown in Figure 2. Signs placed on or above the upper and backwards parts of the body along this vertical semi-ellipse refer to the past; those placed in front of the body and at the elliptical co-vertex point denote now and the present; and those placed or moving downwards and behind the signer's lower body (and beyond the bottom convex point), refer to the future.

4.1 Signs for 'now' and the aspect of the present – DI

The core morpheme that in TSL creates the aspect of the present is a sign I call DI. DI involves the dominant hand with its index finger extended and pointing downwards, the rest of the fingers tucked in. The spatial position of DI is in front of the signer's body at the position of the co-vertex of the vertical ellipse as represented in Figure 2 and the images in Figure 4.

For reasons I explain below, I use the term DI for this morpheme, in correlation with the Lhasa Tibetan *di / dir* [*'di / 'dir*], which means 'here' or 'this' / 'that' / 'this one'. *Di / dir* is primarily a term of spatial deixis, a demonstrative pronoun or

Figure 4: Morpheme DI to mark the aspect of the 'present' and the sign DÉRING 'today' with which it is identical (TDA 2011: 427).

adjective meaning 'here' or 'this / that / this one / that one'. It indicates the proximal position of something or somebody in relation to the speaker, in contrast to the more distant terms for 'there' and 'over there'. As adjective, *di / dir* always follows the noun or a noun phrase (Tournadre and Dorje 2003: 80). In spoken and written Tibetan, *di / dir* is only rarely used in temporal deixis – for instance, it can be used in *di kap* [*'di skabs*]: "at this time, during this period" (Goldstein 2001: 573). *Di* in this case is in the first position. In TSL, rather than the mainly spatial meaning implied by *di / dir*, DI refers only to the temporal meaning of 'now / at present', or what would be called *da / da ta / da ré* [*da / da lta / da res*] in spoken Lhasa Tibetan. Alongside the morpheme DI, TSL signers – depending on their interlocutor and personal history – will sometimes voice and/or mouth the expression *di / dir* at the same time as signing DI. This as well as the semantic content of the TSL sign, is why I choose to call this morpheme DI.

DI is exactly the same handshape and action as the mono-syllabic sign DÉRING (*dé ring* [*de ring*]) or 'today'. Morpheme DI is also used to mark other time-related lexical items apart from 'today'. For example, it is used to define 'this week', 'this month' and 'this year'. DI is, in reality, always in the second position, even though the sequence of syllables is represented in reverse in some entries in the *Standard TSL Dictionary* (for example in 'last year' as reproduced in Figure 11).

Common with many other sign languages, in TSL the so-called 'target' or 'field' [French *champs*] comes first, and what it is like is defined *afterwards*, the so-called 'figure' [French *figure*]. However Tibetan spoken language also follows this syllabic order in many cases, for example in referring to this week or this month, as 'week this' and 'month this'.[11]

---

11 In contrast 'this year', or *da lo* [*da lo*] in spoken and written Tibetan, does not follow this pattern. To sign LO DI, 'this year', is therefore an inversion of the word order of (spoken) Tibetan *da*

To mark SAKOR ('week'), DAWA ('month') and LO ('year') with an aspect of present time, they are followed by morpheme DI: SAKOR DI ('this week'), DAWA DI ('this month'), and LO DI ('this year') (Figure 5).

Figure 5: SAKOR DI 'this week' (upper left), DAWA DI 'this month' (upper right) and LO DI 'this year' (lower left) (TDA 2011: 433, 436, 424).

Figure 6: SAKOR or 'week' in TSL (TDA 2011: 433).

---

lo. Goldstein also mentioned the synonym *di lo* for *da lo*, 'this year' (1984: 310), in which case this would make the literal meaning of the sign LO DI very close to the Tibetan form *di lo*, a calque, or loan translation, of sorts, except that it does not have the same syllabic order.

SAKOR (*sa kor* [*gza 'kor*]) or 'week' in TSL is a sweeping circular movement of the dominant hand around the signer's face, with the index finger extended, in a counter clock-wise direction (Figure 6). The index finger is extended in line with the lower arm and hand (rather than at a slight angle, as compared to DI). The sign SAKOR is a sort of 'summary gesture' for the seven days of the week. For days of the week, the index finger extended as in SAKOR points to parts of the face, such as to the forehead (for Monday), the eyes (Tuesday), ears (Wednesday), nose (Thursday), mouth (Friday), chin (Saturday) then adding respectively the ordinal numbers 1 to 6 (see below, and Hofer and Sagara 2019). For Sunday, the palm of the hand faces down and touches the top of the head after which one signs number 7.[12]

To sign DAWA (*da wa* [*zla ba*], 'month'),[13] the non-dominant hand, with flat palm facing inwards, acts as 'support', representing a stable surface. The dominant hand makes a motion of 'turning over', as if turning over a page from that 'support' or surface (Figure 7).

Figure 7: DAWA or 'month' in TSL (TDA 2011: 424).

The turning direction of the imaginary page is a vertical action, from down towards up. In conversations with TSL signers it emerged that this is a sign that began to be used widely, when the Tibet Deaf Association (TDA), the organisation that ran the TSL project and which between 2000 and 2014 published Tibetan Sign language dictionaries and textbooks, also produced modern month-based desk-top and wall calendars in order to promote their work and teach TSL signs.[14] These calendars were such that one also had to turn over the pages from down

---

[12] Sunday being in addition referred to as 'day seven', follows the pattern of Chinese language for week days, Monday being 'day one' and Sunday 'day seven'.
[13] Other meanings of *da wa* in Tibetan include 'moon' and 'Monday'.
[14] For example in these calendars and to promote TSL, drawings of the TSL signs for the months were accompanied by the written Tibetan and English terms, or were drawn on the specific dates when these festivals take place. In some years extra pages were added explaining certain aspects of Tibetan culture, people and places, possibly with a more international audience in mind.

towards up.¹⁵ The sign DAWA ('month') in TSL equivalent with that for calendar. DAWA can be further qualified as a 'Tibetan month' or 'Western month', due to the dual calendrical system in Central Tibet, by adding in the first position either the sign BÖ for 'Tibetan', or CHI for 'foreign', 'outside', 'western'.

Given the likely origin of the sign DAWA are the contemporary desktop and wall calendars, as evidenced in the sign DAWA ('month') being entirely different from DAWA for 'moon' in TSL,¹⁶ I believe this also points towards the partly 'urban' roots of the language. In contrast, many other, small and rural sign languages and/or gestural systems tend to indicate something about the moon when signing months (e.g. Reed 2020: 42).

The sign LO (*lo* [*lo*]), 'year' is signed with the dominant hand, its thumb and index finger pinched, making three quick movements from the wrist, as if throwing pinches of something into the air (Figure 8).

Figure 8: LO or 'year' in TSL (TDA 2011: 424).

This gesture derives its semantic content from an activity typically performed by Tibetans at the start of the Tibetan New Year, which in Tibetan is called *lo sar* [*lo gsar*], and which tends to fall sometime in February or March of the European (Gregorian) calendar. It references the making of new year offerings known

---

15 Another possible derivation of the sign is from traditional-style Tibetan books (*pé cha* [*dpe cha*]), made up of loose long pages. These are also turned over from the bottom to the top, instead of from the right to the left, or the left to the right, as would be the case for books in many other languages or traditions. However, because more recently the traditional Tibetan-style calendars or *lo to* ([*lo tho*], almanac, or 'catalogue of the year') were already produced as European style books, and pages were turned left to right, it seems credible to me – alongside the fact that TSL signs for month and calendar are identical – that the root of the TSL signs for month and calendar derive from the modern TDA produced wall and desk top calendars and planners.

16 Also the signs for the names of the months in TSL do not reference the moon at all, but instead are phonologically close to the sign DAWA for 'month', and adding to them numbers of the months through numeral incorporation (e.g. for January, see TDA 2011: 437).

as *dro so ché mar* [*gro so phye mar*] – 'wheat/grain, flour and butter [offerings]' (Figure 9). The TSL signs TROSO CHÉMAR (a two-syllable sign) shows first the wooden container in which the offerings are kept and then the throwing – three times– of a pinch of the barley grains and/or the flour/butter mixture into the air, representing three offerings to Buddha, Sangha (the Buddhist community) and Dhamma (the teachings of Buddha).

切玛(年供盒)

qiè mǎ

(nián gòng hé)

barley used in the

New Year offering urn

Figure 9: TROSO CHÉMAR is a compound of CHÉMAR + LO (TDA 2011: 458).

The three-fold Buddhist offering marking the start of a new year in the Tibetan calendar that is found in the second position of the TSL sign TROSO CHÉMAR, is the root of what I call the morpheme LO, root of the sign LO for 'year' in TSL.

LOSAR then is the compounding of the morpheme BÖ ('Tibet'/'Tibetan') and of LO ('year') creating the meaning of the TSL sign 'Tibetan Year', or *bö kyi lo* (*sar*) [*bo kyi lo* (*gsar*)] (TDA 2011: 438).

4.2 TSL signs for the past – NGÖNMA

The core morpheme with which TSL creates the aspect of the 'past' is a morpheme that I call NGÖNMA, in reference to written and spoken Tibetan *ngön ma* [*sngon ma*] and their meanings of 'before, past, in the past, formerly, the former, beginning, formerly, in the past, previously' (Goldstein 2001). It is signed with the index finger extended and pointing to behind the signer's shoulder on their dominant side.

'Yesterday' or KHASANG (*kha sang* [*kha sang*]) with which NGÖNMA is identical, is most likely derived from NGÖNMA or 'past', with the more specific indication derived from the broader meaning through pragmatics.[17] To sign 'day before

---

[17] Pragmatics is a subfield of linguistics and semiotics that studies how context contributes to meaning.

|ཁ་སང|མདང་|
昨天 zuó tiān
yesterday

Figure 10: NGÖNMA (left side) as the temporaliser to mark the aspect of 'past' and equivalent with it, the sign KHASANG or 'yesterday' (right side) (TDA 2011: 426).

yesterday' (*khé nyin mo* [*khe'i nyin mo*]) the TSL KHÉ NYINMO is made up of signing NGÖNMA twice – but pointing to two 'points' at the back of the shoulder – with the second point further back than the first point. This creates the sense of 'two days back'.

To 'place', i.e. mark, the signs SAKOR, DAWA, and LO as 'in the past', these signs are in the first position of a compound, followed by the temporaliser NGÖNMA. In effect TSL signers sign SAKOR + NGÖNMA in SAKOR NGÖNMA ('last week'); DAWA + NGÖNMA in DAWA NGÖNMA ('last month'); LO + NGÖN MA in NANING (*na ning*, 'last year') (Figure 11).

Figure 11: SAKOR NGÖNMA 'last week' (upper left), DAWA NGÖNMA 'last month' (upper right) and NANING 'last year' (lower left, with mistaken sequence as per original publication (TDA 2011: 435, 431).

The same system applies to other signs: for instance, 'a moment ago', and for anything in the past that does not lie further back than a few years. For longer timeframes in the past, TSL users use the sign NGÖNMA NGÖNMA which means 'long, long back, in the past' and is a sort of rolling gesture using both hands, above and to the back of the signer's shoulder.

4.3 TSL signs and concept for future events – JÉMA and 'plus one, two, three sleeps'

To indicate future, the same system is applied to lexical items such as week, month and year as described above, this time followed by the temporaliser JÉMA (*jéma* [*rjes ma*], a term of temporal deixis in Tibetan, meaning 'after' or 'afterwards'. JÉMA is a sign in which the dominant hand with all fingers together swings by the side of the body at about hip height to behind the body (Figure 12).

Figure 12: SAKOR JÉMA (top) 'next week', DAWA JÉMA (middle) 'next month' and DÜ SANG (bottom) 'next year' (TDA 2011: 436, 431).

While in spoken and written Tibetan *jéma* [*rjes ma*] is mainly a temporal concept, in TSL JÉMA is both spatial and temporal. It is spatial because it points to behind the lower part of the body and it is temporal because it points to the future. That which comes 'after' here has this dual sense and function, and we find this in several Tibetan grammar terms of TSL, this time in a way where the body stands in reference to a syllable.[18]

On the other hand, *jéma* in spoken Tibetan tends *not* be used to refer to the spatial dimension of 'after', as in behind the body. However, there exists the possibility to use *jéma* in spatial deixis on occasion, when the meaning is 'behind' or 'next'.

The interesting confluence here is that the hand gesture of the sign JÉMA means 'after' in the temporal sense, i.e. 'future', but makes the gesture at the side of the body, and in such a way that it essentially points to behind the (lower) body. Perhaps, this is related etymologically to the noun *jé* [*rjes*] 'footprints' or 'tracks of animals and humans', which are also left behind the body.

* * *

An exception to the vertical semi-ellipse for many lexical items related to past, present and future is the TSL sign for "tomorrow". It does not fit the pattern of past being 'up' and future being 'down and back'. Instead one signs SANG-NYIN (*sang nyin* [*sang nyin*]) as 'sleep' + 'one' – or NYE and CHIK, depending on how many days from now, one indicates the respective number sign here instead. Although the images in the *Standard TSL Dictionary* (Figure 13) show the numbers being signed high up in the signing space, in daily TSL interactions and in my primary data the numbers are signed in front of the signer and not higher than the body.

In NANGNYIN, or in two days' time (*na nyin* [*nang nyin*]), then 'sleep' is followed by number 'two' (*nyi* [*gynis*]). The position of the number, Heng, Ling

---

18 Up to 100 specialised grammar terms of Tibetan language have been created in TSL in order to teach Tibetan grammar at the Lhasa Deaf School, even if they are not all in use (cf. Hofer and Sagli 2017). Two among them, the signs JÉJUG 'suffix' (*jé jug* [*rjes 'jug*]) and YANGJUG 'post-suffix' (*yang jug* [*yang 'jug*]) use the body as if it was a syllable or a word (*tshigs*). One then places these two signs for suffix and post-suffix in so they appear and point towards the back of the body, using either one or two fingers (i.e number one or number two, index and middle finger) for the suffix or the post suffix (instead of the full hand as in JÉMA). The hand and arm make exactly the same movement. There are other instances in TSL where the body is used as a spatial metaphor, for example it is used as a root letter when signing subscripts or super scripts using the manual alphabet or spelling Tibetan words (Hofer, 2017b).

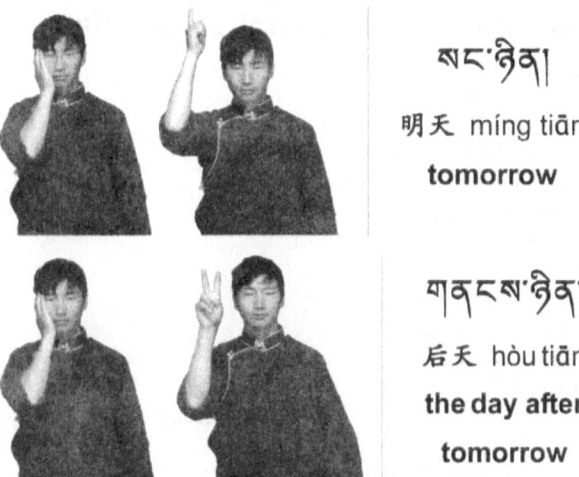

Figure 13: SANGNYIN and NANGNYIN, "tomorrow" and "day after tomorrow" (TDA 2011: 427).

and Drokar (2013) claim is signed high up so that the impression created is of the 'future' here being signed high up, rather than the more common position of 'future' being down and backwards. However, based on all the day-to-day signing interactions that I have video-recorded and researched, I would suggest that the number is usually just signed in front of the body and not higher up than the body.

* * *

The respective positions as well as directional characteristics of the signs so far discussed 'create' the vertical semi-elliptical timeline in TSL. The single-syllable sign, or the noun, to be marked by an aspect of time, are all signed in the signing space in front of the body and first. These are then followed by one of the three key terms of temporal deixis: the temporaliser for the present is signed in front of the body; the temporalisers for the past and future essentially point towards the back of the signer's body, with the past being upwards and backwards, and the future downwards and backwards. This vertical semi-elliptical timeline of TSL can be understood as a body-anchored timeline, with the physical body representing the 'middle ground' of the present, while above it and behind it is the past, meanwhile at the bottom and behind the body is the future. All this said, as Tibetans' perceptions of the body and the body's upper, middle and lower parts, are symbolically and practically intertwined with the wider environment. This is why it is worth exploring the broader context within which the TSL verticality principles occur.

4.4 Verticality principles in Tibet – historical, socio-cultural and linguistic considerations

> If the sun with its fair clouds does not shine in the east,
> The white snow mountain in the west cannot melt,
> If the white snow mountain in the west does not melt,
> The blue river water cannot run in the valley floor,
> If the blue river water dies it does not run in the river floor,
> The sandalwood tree cannot grow;
> If the sandalwood tree cannot grow,
> The cuckoo, queen of the birds, cannot alight;
> If the cuckoo, queen of the bird, does not alight,
> Tibet cannot have a good harvest.[19]
>
> Tibetan song from Dingri

This is a song from Dingri, a high altitude valley in Central Tibet, close to Mount Everest (TAR). It features within part of a chapter titled "Patterns of Place" by Ramble (1995), which explores horizontality and verticality of geographical spaces in relation to cosmology of a Tibetan-speaking region of Nepal, and not far from the Tibetan location of Dingri in the TAR. The chapter offers various perspectives on Tibetan-style ordering of the high altitude surroundings through socio-cultural and linguistic practices. Ramble's concept of "downward-bearing verticality" (1995: 151) offers significant parallels to the vertical semi-elliptical timeline found in TSL.

The aforementioned article by Heng, Ling and Drokar (2013) on metaphors and metonymy of time in TSL also searched for explanations of wider patterns of verticality in Tibet. They suggest that the Tibetan landscape with its high mountains is a key reference point for the verticality principle of the TSL vertical timeline, substantiated with reference to rivers in Tibet flowing from high up to lower down, and thus past in this way being considered higher up (2013: 161). Doubtless relevant geographic and topographic features do resonate with the TSL vertical timeline and possibly also verticality as expressed in spoken languages in the region. Nevertheless, I believe we need to consider additional and broader socio-cultural, historical and linguistic phenomena to make sense of this rare placement of time, both on the vertical timeline, but also, and in particular, the vertical semi-ellipse, and the placement of the future *downwards* and *behind* the body.

The narrative of the Tibetan song from Dingri is indeed one good example to consider in this regard. The song starts high up – with the sun, the clouds and the snow-capped mountains – and moves successively lower down to the very bottom

---

[19] Translation from Tibetan in and by Ramble 1995: 151.

of the valley, where the cuckoo alights in the sandalwood that is fed by the high altitude rivers, and where the fields of Tibetans are located and harvested. In this song, the verticality of the environment is not only culturally, but also linguistically ordered: the 'top' of the song is about the top of the mountains, and the 'bottom of the song' is about the harvest from the fields of Tibetans, located on the valley floors.

Considering the vertical axis, in his chapter Ramble (1995) discusses additional non-human orderings of the environment, and how various gods and classes of supernatural beings are also placed and ordered along a vertical axis. He argues that the position on that axis, in and of itself, is additionally relevant to fertility and the protection of various numina, rather than the inherent potentials and powers of the gods and classes of supernatural beings in and of themselves. In other words, the position within the vertical hierarchy matters.

Ramble also points out how spoken and written Tibetan language expresses vertical dimensions, notably in relation to notions of time: ". . . the concept of "upper" (*tö*) and "lower" (*smad*) are used respectively to designate the earlier and later periods of chronological sequences, such as a year, a night or a person's life-time".[20] In Tibetan it is therefore possible and common to say *lo tö* [*lo stod*] for 'the top of the year' to refer to the beginning of the year, and *lo mé* [*lo smad*] for 'bottom of the year', i.e. the end of the year (Ibid). In the same way one can say, at the top of one's life" (*tsé tö* [*tshe stod*]) and 'the bottom of one's life' (*tsé me* [*tshe smad*]), meaning the beginning and end of life. In English, by contrast, Ramble writes that the synonymy of terms such as top/beginning, earlier/above, below/later and so forth is usually reserved for written works and musical scores, rather than aspects of time more generally.

To these examples several others can be added. Not only can one say in Tibetan 'top of the year' and 'bottom of the year', one can also say the 'head of the year' (*lo go* [*lo mgo*]) and the 'tail of the year' (*lo jug* [*lo 'jug*]). This implies both temporal and spatial dimensions and the body as used in temporal and spatial orderings. In this case the head and the top of the body is associated with 'earlier' and a lower part of the body ('the tail') is associated with the bottom of the body, implying 'later on' in a temporal sense.

Also worth noting is that between the two aspects of time 'upper' and 'lower', Tibetans frequently use the term 'middle' (*bar*) to refer to the 'middle' of the year. Tibetan songs are also often divided in this tripartite way, as Ramble notes (1995). The common distinction of *tö / bar / mé* [*stod / bar / smad*] where 'upper' also means 'former / prior', and 'lower' also means 'later' comes up to name parts of

---

[20] This is also true of Thulung Rai concepts of time, discussed by Allen (1972: 93).

Tibetan books. Here 'higher' or 'top part' (*tö cha* [*stod cha*]) refers to the first part or first volume, and 'bottom part' (*mé cha* [*smad cha*] designates the second part or volume of a book. If there are three parts of a book, the middle one is called '*bar cha*', or 'middle part'. Therefore these orderings have both spatial and temporal aspects.[21]

Importantly, we need to recall that Tibetan legends trace the early Tibetans' first king to heaven, from where he descended on a heavenly rope that when cut made him the first earthly king of the (Central) Tibetans. Such accounts lend further support to the Tibetan sense of the past being 'up' and at the 'top'.

Taken altogether we can see various correlations between Tibetan ideas about spatial dimensions in cosmology and history, and how the use of metaphors of verticality to express aspects of time are found across spoken and written Tibetan (see Figure 14). TSL prominently and visibly features this verticality too. Given the wider correspondences that have just been discussed, the TSL vertical axis can therefore be understood as being more than merely 'deictic' and body-referential, or "body-anchored". It instead it sits at the intersection of the body and the wider Tibetan environment and cosmology.

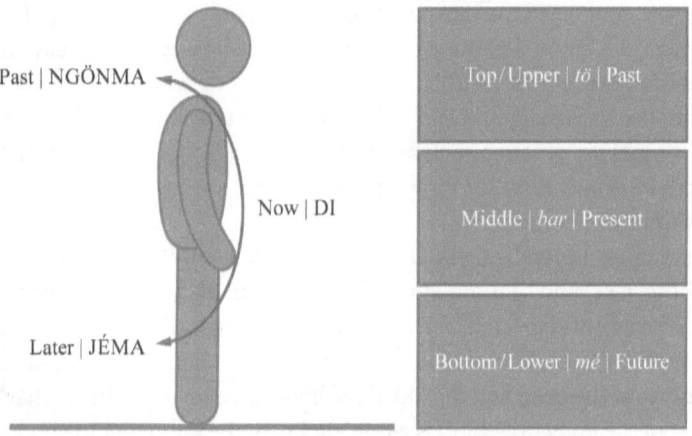

Figure 14: The TSL vertical semi-ellipse in light of common verticality principles found in Tibetan lyrics, wider cosmology, and languages in Tibet and the greater Himalayas.

---

21 'Top' (*tö*) and 'bottom' (*mé*) as purely spatial denominators abound in spoken and written Tibetan. This can be for the specifics of a place and also for whole regions, such as the western region of Tö (*stod*), but also in Kham for houses, where *to* [*mtho*] 'up' and *smad* 'down' is commonly used for 'first floor' and 'ground floor' of houses. In Central Tibet, a traditional house in villages, tend to be ordered in such a way that the 'middle' is considered the world of humans and animals, the 'top' that of deities and gods and the 'bottom' as the realms of water and earth spirits (Fjeld 2006).

While this wider cultural context can explain the importance of vertical ordering of time in TSL, it does not account for the simultaneous placement of the future behind the body. There are only very few examples of the 'future' represented behind the body, for example, in spoken Aymara and associated co-speech gestures (Núñez and Sweetser 2006), and possibly with no future in the timeline of Miyakobu Sign Language (Yano and Matsuoka 2018). To denote the future by placing signs below and behind the body is even more rare.

5 The horizontal timeline in TSL

As there are several different spatial metaphors of time found in spoken languages and several timelines in other sign languages, so also in TSL is the vertical time axis complemented by the use of other timelines. To express the concept of "one day" and certain aspects of a day, a horizontal semi-elliptic timeline is created, signed in front of the signer. Below I describe the signs for 'one day', 'morning' (usually around 10 am), 'midday' (noon and early afternoon) and 'late afternoon' (between about 15:00 to 17:00pm). In their general direction these signs are signed from right to left, deriving from east (sunrise) to west (sunset). These are not signed as absolute points (Levinson 2003), as for example in Kata Kolok (de Vos 2012a), where signers position themselves and align their pointing with the rising sun to the east or the setting sun to the west in absolute terms. However, still the origin of the sign is likely reference to sunrise to the east (the right side of the body), and the sun going down in the west (the left side of the body), albeit in an abstract way. TSL signs for 'dusk/day break' and 'night-fall' use the same horizontal elliptic plane, but their direction is reversed. TSL signs for 'early morning', 'during the day' and 'evening' follow different patterns and are described last.[22]

5.1 Times of the day in TSL using right to left directional movement

NYIMA (*nyi ma* [nyi ma], or 'day' is a movement of the dominant hand and its index finger extended (the others tucked in), all the way from the right side at horizontal level, up and towards the centre of the body and down to the left

---

[22] The TSL right to left metaphor is in contrast to the writing of Tibetan, which goes from left to right. Thus in written Tibetan , as in other scripts that follow this scheme, readers/writers tend to experience the past to be situated to the left and the future to the right.

until the horizontal plane is again reached, in one long but quick movement and clearly in an abstract way a reference to the movement of the sun over the course of a day. This can then be followed with TSL numbers to indicate the numbers of days, such as NYIMA CHIK (*chig* [*gzhigs*]) for 'one day'.

Figure 15: NYIMA 'day' and 'day time' (TDA 2011: 424).

NGADRO (*nga dro* [*snga dro*], 'morning') is signed by signing just the first half of the arc of the sign NYIMA, with the dominant hand and its index finger extended (the others tucked in), moving from the right side, up and towards the center of the body (see top of Figure 16).

NYINGUNG (*nyin gung* [*nyin dgun*], 'midday, early afternoon') is signed at the co-vertex in front of, or slightly above the head of the signer, and is a comparatively small movement of the index and middle finger in a V handshape, turning two times swiftly back and forth at about 45 to 90 degrees (see middle of Figure 16).

CHIDRO (*chi dro* [*phyi dro*], 'late afternoon') is the second half of the movement of the arc of the sign NYIMA, and references the going down of the sun. The hand with the extended index finger moves down from the center of the body to the left, back to a horizontal position (see bottom of Figure 16).

The two signs NAMLANG (*namlang* [*nam langs*], 'dawn' or 'daybreak') and MUNRUB (*munrub*, [*mun rub*], 'dusk') also make direct reference to the sun, but not in the same way as the three preceding signs for times of the day. The incorporated handshape here derives from TSL NYIMA (*nyima* [*nyi ma*], 'sun', TDA 2011: 462) and the directionality is not just from right to left.

NAMLANG ('dawn') shows the sun to rise while the handshape itself changes from slightly cupped at the bottom to fully open at the top (Figure 17, top). MUNRUB ('dusk'), exactly reverses this movement, the handshape changing from fully open to open to slightly cupped, and showing the sun to go down (Figure 17, bottom). This feature of the handshape being more or less open and cupped is similar to the way that the handshape changes depending on the time of day in a so-called 'celestial timeline', which has been described for Miyakubo Sign Language and is depicted in Yano and Matsuoka (2018: 659).

Figure 16: In TSL expressions of part of the day create the horizontal semi-elliptic timeline in front of the signer (TDA 2011: 428).

NAMLANG and MUNRUB feature the movement of the arm and the same changes of handshapes that come up in the TSL sign NYINMO or 'daytime' (*nyi mo* [*nyin mo*]). In NYINMO both hands and arms at the same time move upward and outwards, with the handshapes changing from slightly cupped at the bottom to fully open at the top of the movement (Figure 18).

TSENMO (*tsen mo* [*mtshan mo*], "evening"/ "night") reverses this movement (Figure 19).

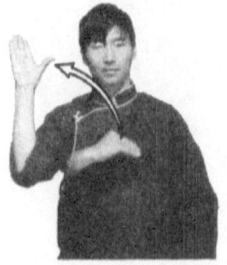

ནམ་ལངས།
天亮 tiān liàng
dawn

མུན་རུབ།
天黑 tiān hēi
toward evening

Figure 17: NAMLANG (upper image) and MUNRUB (lower image), 'dawn' and 'dusk' (TDA 2011: 429).

ཉིན་མོ།
白天 bái tiān
day

Figure 18: TSL sign NYINMO for 'daytime', (TDA 2011: 429).

མཚན་མོ།
夜晚 yè wǎn
evening

Figure 19: TSL TSENMO for 'evening' and 'night' (TDA 2011: 430).

In practice, the movement of the arms and hands often ends at just below the face and the facial expression is one in which a slight frown appears above the eyes and the eye lids are almost shut as if to indicate 'closure' of the day.

In TSL, the horizontal timeline, in front of the signer's body can be created with right-to-left movements as a reference to the movement of the sun's progression of the day. In signing late morning and late afternoon, the extended index finger is used; based on my observations, I would conclude that this is a timeline that is more 'exact' and measurable by human timekeeping, like a 'clock', where the same handshape and the extended index finger are used in TSL to tell the time. This handshape and movement is used for 'one day' and 'morning' and 'afternoon', when one cannot see a very pronounced change of light and position of the sun. During dawn in the the early morning and at dusk or nightfall, we do see a more pronounced change of light. For these time-related signs, TSL uses a second type of horizontally ordered timeline, which is created alongside a pronounced change of handshape. In contrast to the strictly directional movement from right to left which Hen, Ling, and Drokar (2013) describe, we therefore see that the movements on the TSL horizontal timeline can be bi-directional along the horizontal plane.

In spoken and written Tibetan *nyi ma* means both 'day' and 'sun'. All the signs on the the horizontal timelines described above, reference in one way or other the sun, and/or point to the position of the sun in abstract terms. The only exception to this pattern for TSl signs for parts of the day, is the TSL sign for 'early morning'.

TSL ZHOKPA (*zhok pa* [*zhogs pa*]), 'early morning' is a compound sign, that combines the morphemes NYI (*nyi* [*gnyid*], 'sleep' and NYIMA (*nyi ma* [*nyi ma*], 'sunshine' (Figure 20).

Figure 20: TSL ZHOKPA for 'early morning', (TDA 2011: 430).

In the first part of the sign the eyes are closed, and during the second the eyes open and look to the right and into the 'sun', which is signed by NYIMA ('sun'). The accompanying movement of the eyelids and the eyes add a human dimension to the so far mainly sun-referential signs for times of the day in TSL. Even though in the TSL horizontal timelines there are many common references to the sun and sunshine, none of the signs discussed here are calques, or loan translations, from spoken or written Tibetan.

6 The circular timeline and the days of the week

Heng, Ling and Drokar (2013) claim that the days of the week are another instance of the downward movement along a vertical axis – the first day of the week located at the top of the head, the last day of the week at the bottom of the face. However, when analysing the morphology and etymology of the days of the week in TSL, I have argued that the days of the week are placed as they are not due to verticality principles, but due to the first parts of the compound signs for each day being partial calques, or loan translations, from spoken Tibetan for the days for the week (Hofer and Sagara 2019). Taken together with the TSL sign SAKOR ('week'), I contend that SAKOR and the days of the week form a circular timeline.

Days of the week in spoken and written Tibetan make reference to the planets, such as the sun (e.g. *sa nyi ma* [*gza' nyi-ma*], 'sun-day'), the moon (*sa da wa* [*gza' zla-ba*], 'moon-day', *sa mig mar* [*gza' mig-dmar*] 'Mars-day' for Tuesday); modern Chinese, meanwhile, counts the days of the week, starting on Monday with 'Day One' (*xingqi yi*) to Sunday as 'Day Seven' (*xingqi er*). In speech, Lhasa Tibetans almost always use the Chinese, i.e. *xingqi yi*, 'Monday', *xingqi er*, 'Tuesday' instead of the traditional terms referring to planets (Tournadre 2003: 4, Yeshe 2008). While many sign languages mirror the spoken and written languages in their references to the planets, TSL signs for days of the week do not. Instead, in the first part of the compound signs, one points to parts of the head and face and in the second part they are formed by TSL cardinal numbers from one to seven, starting with one on Monday and ending with seven on Sunday.

The pointing to parts of the head and face in the TSL sign derives from the gestures that accompany Tibetan children's songs about the days of the week, sung in Lhasa pre-schools and during Tibetan language classes in primary school. The correlation between the name of the planets and parts of the face is made via homophones, such as '*migs*' for 'eye' which sounds like '*mig*' (mars) as in *gza' mig-dmar* for 'Tuesday', even though they have a different spelling. Instead of simply pointing to relevant parts of the face and head to refer to days of the week, TSL signers add as the second part of the compound signs the counting of the days, akin to modern Chinese ('Day One' for Monday, 'Day Two' for Tuesday, and so on), making TSL days of the week, *loan blends* that arose in the complex language contact situation in which deaf Tibetans find themselves in Lhasa (Hofer and Sagara 2019).

The Tibetan week – with the Chinese influence of consecutively numbering the days of the week – starts on Monday as 'Day 1' and moves down to Saturday, then moving up again and to the top of the head for Sunday, or 'Day 7'. It is, therefore, not a wholly downward movement nor expression of strong emphasis on verticality in Tibetan linguistic markings of time. Instead it connotes what we can call a circular timeline. The pointing to parts of the face – for each consecutive day of the week (1 to 6) – takes place on the side of the face that represents the side of the dominant hand; as already mentioned, for 'Day 7', one then moves up to the top of the head. That the origin of these TSL lexical signs is found in co-speech gestures of Tibetan children's songs (Hofer and Sagara 2019), strongly suggests that the lexical signs for days of the week in TSL are dictated by the semantics and homophony of spoken/written Tibetan rather than by a strictly spatial metaphor of time in TSL. The days of the week are not to be counted as part of a vertical timeline in TSL.

7 Conclusion

Based on linguistic and anthropological research with TSL signers and their interactions as well as language materials, this chapter has identified and described three timelines used in TSL to mark the aspect of time: a vertical semi-elliptical timeline; a horizontal semi-elliptical timeline; and a circular timeline. While vertical and horizontal timelines are also found in other sign languages, the vertical semi-elliptical timeline and, possibly, the circular timeline emerge as typologically rare among the world's documented signed and spoken languages and their co-speech gestures.

I have here focused mainly on the vertical semi-elliptical timeline as it is a prominent means of spatially ordering the aspect of time in TSL, while the circular timeline only pertains to lexical items related to a week and the days of the week. Three conclusions can be drawn for the vertical semi-elliptical timeline.

Firstly, the TSL vertical semi-elliptical timeline is unusual and noteworthy, as both past and future are located *behind* the body of the signer, at the same time as signers make use of the vertical dimension (with the past considered upwards, the future downwards, and the present directly at the front of the signer's body). In contrast, most European and also many major Asian sign languages, tend to have timelines that place the past behind the body, and the present as well as future in front of the body. Only few signed and spoken languages and co-speech gestures feature spatial metaphors of time in, where the future is placed both *downwards* and at the same time *behind* the body.

Secondly, through an exploration of broader cosmological, socio-cultural and linguistic conceptualisations commonly found in the Tibetan region and the Tibetic languages, I have explained how this particular conceptualisation of time as articulated through the vertical semi-elliptical timeline of TSL fits with broader conceptions and patternings of time and space in Tibet, in particular, in the vertical dimension. That past or earlier occurrences are expressed upward, and future and later occurrences downward, has been shown to be common among Tibetans in the Himalayan region and is attested to in a range of cultural and linguistic practices. In contrast, the future also being expressed as being behind the body has no spatial metaphors in spoken or written Tibetan (or, for example, in CSL), nor broader anthropological considerations, that I could identify. The placement of the future *behind* the body therefore remains not fully explained.

Lastly, combining linguistic description and broader anthropological analysis, I have argued that the vertical semi-elliptical timeline of TSL transcends a strictly-speaking 'body-anchored' timeline. While it takes the body as a key referent, the vertical semi-elliptical timeline of TSL sits at the interface of the body and the wider cosmos and socio-cultural environment of Tibet.

References

Allen, Nicholas. 1972. The vertical dimension of Thulung classification. *Journal of the Anthropological Society of Oxford* 3(2). 81–94.

de Vos, Connie. 2012a. *Sign-spatiality in Kata Kolok: How a village sign language in Bali inscribes its signing space*. Nijmegen: Radboud University dissertation.

de Vos, Connie. 2012b. The Kata Kolok perfective in child signing. In Connie de Vos & Ulrike Zeshan (eds.), *Sign Languages in Village Communities*, 127–152. Berlin/ Boston: De Gruyter Mouton & Ishara Press.

Eberhard, David M., Gary F. Simons, and Charles D. Fennig (eds.). 2020. *Ethnologue: Languages of the World*. Twenty-third edition. Dallas, Texas: SIL International. Online version: http://www.ethnologue.com.

Engberg-Pedersen, Elisabeth. 1993. *Space in Danish sign language: The meaning and morphosyntactic use of space in a visual language*. Hamburg: Signum-Verlag.

Fjeld, Heidi. 2006. *The rise of the polyandrous house: Marriage, kinship and social mobility in rural Tsang, Tibet*. Oslo: University of Oslo dissertation.

Gell, Alfred. 1992. *The Anthropology of Time: Cultural Constructions of Temporal Maps and Images*. Oxford: Berg.

Goldin-Meadow, Susan. 2003. *The Resilience of Language: What Gesture Creation in Deaf Children Can Tell Us about how all Children learn Language*. New York: Psychology Press.

Goldstein, Melvyn 1984. *English-Tibetan Dictionary of Modern Tibetan*. Berkeley: University of California Press.

Goldstein, Melvyn. 2001. *The New Tibetan–English Dictionary of Modern Tibetan*. Berkeley: University of California Press.

Green, Elizabeth Mara. 2014. *The nature of signs: Nepal's deaf society, local sign and the production of communicative sociality*. Berkeley: University of California dissertation.

Heng, Li, Wi Ling & Urgyen Drokar [李恒 吴铃 吾根卓嘎]. 2013. 西藏手语时间隐喻和转喻的认知研究 *(Xi zang shou yu shi jian yin yu he zhuan yu de ren zhi yan jiu)* [Time, metaphor and metonymy in Tibetan sign language]. 中央民族大学学报：哲学社会科学版 *[Journal of The Central University for Nationalities] (Human and Social Sciences Edition)* 6. 160–165.

Hofer, Theresia. 2020. 'Goat-sheep-mixed-sign' in Lhasa – deaf Tibetans' language ideologies and unimodal codeswitching in Tibetan and Chinese sign languages, Tibet Autonomous Region, China. In Annelies Kusters, Mara Green, Erin Moriarty Harrelson & Kristin Snoddon (eds.), *Sign Language Ideologies in Practice*, 81–105. Berlin/Boston: Mouton de Gruyter. doi: https://doi.org/10.1515/9781501510090-005

Hofer, Theresia. 2019 Tsampa eating, Tibetan sign language and Tibetanness. *Minpaku Newsletter* 47 (January 2019). 9–11. http://www.minpaku.ac.jp/english/research/activity/publication/periodical/newsletter

Hofer, Theresia. 2017a. Is Lhasa Tibetan sign language emerging, endangered, or both? *International Journal for the Sociology of Language* 245. 113–145.

Hofer, Theresia. 2017b. Encounters between Tibetan sign language (TSL) and the Tibetan script in contemporary Lhasa. Paper presented at the Language and Anthropology Seminars, Institute of Social and Cultural Anthropology, University of Oxford, 10 March.

Hofer, Theresia & Gry Sagli. 2017. 'Civilising' deaf people in Tibet and Inner Mongolia: Governing linguistic, ethnic and bodily difference in China. *Disability & Society* 32(4). 443–466.

Hofer Theresia & Keiko Sagara. 2019. Chinese language influences on Tibetan sign language users in Lhasa: Cardinal numbers and days of the week.' Poster presented at Theoretical Issues in Sign Language Research (TISLR) meeting, Hamburg, 26–28 September, 2019.

Huang, Wei and Dingqian Gu. 2014. Status quo of sign language. In Yuming Li & Wei Li (eds.), *Language Policies and Practices in China* (Vol. 2: Language Situation in China). Berlin/Boston: De Gruyter Mouton.

Kendon, Adam, 1980. A description of a deaf-mute sign language from the Enga province of Papua New Guinea with some comparative discussion – part I: The formational properties of Enga signs. *Semiotica* 31(1/2). 1–34.

Kendon, Adam. 2004. *Gesture: Visible Action as Utterance*. Cambridge: Cambridge University Press.

Klein, Wolfgang. 2010. How time is encoded. In Wolfgang Klein & Ping Li (eds.), *The expression of time*. Berlin/Boston: De Gruyter Mouton.

Kusters, Annelies & Michelle Friedner. 2016. Introduction – DEAF-SAME and Difference in international Deaf spaces and encounters. In Michele Friedner and Annelies Kusters (eds.), *It's a small world: International Deaf spaces and encounters*, ix–xxix. Washington DC: University of Gallaudet Press.

Le Guen, Oliver. 2012. An exploration in the domain of time: From Yucatec Maya time gestures to Yucatec Maya sign language time signs. In Ulrike Zeshan & Connie de Vos (eds.), *Sign languages in village communities: anthropological and linguistic insights*, 209–249. Berlin/Boston: De Gruyter Mouton.

Levinson, Stephen C. 2003. *Space in language and cognition: explorations in cognitive diversity*. Cambridge: Cambridge University Press.

Matsuoka, Kazumi. 2015. *Nihon shuwa de manabu shuwa gengogaku no kiso* [*The foundation of sign language linguistics with special references to Japanese sign language*]. Tokyo: Kurosio Publishers.

Meir, Iris & Wendy Sandler. 2008. *A Language in Space: The Story of Israeli Sign Language*. New York: Lawrence Erlbaum Associates.

McNeil, David. 1992. *Hand and Mind: What Gestures reveal about Thought*. Chicago/ London: University of Chicago Press.

Nagano, Yasuhiko. 1998. *Time, Language and Cognition*. Osaka: National Museum of Ethnology.

Núñez, Rafael E. & Eve Sweetser. 2006. With the future behind them: Convergent evidence from Aymara language and gesture in the cross-linguistic comparison of spatial construals of time. *Cognitive Science* 30. 401–450.

Pavlenko, Aneta. 2007. Autobiographic narratives as data in applied linguistics. *Applied Linguistics* 28(2). 163–188.

Pfau, Roland, Markus Steinbach & Bencie Woll. 2012. Tense, aspect, and modality. In Roland Pfau, Markus Steinbach & Bencie Woll (eds.), *Sign Language: An international handbook*, 186–203. Berlin/Boston: De Gruyter Mouton.

Ramble, Charles. 1995. Patterns of places. In Anne-Marie Blondeau & Ernst Steinkellner (eds.), *Reflections of the mountain: Essays in the history and social meaning of the mountain cult in Tibet and the Himalaya*, 141–153. Vienna: Verlag der Österreichischen Akademie der Wissenschaften.

Reed, Lauren W. 2019. Co-expression of past and future in a rural sign language of Papua New Guinea. Poster presentation at Theoretical Issues in Sign Language Research (TISLR) meeting, Hamburg, 26–28 September.

Reed, Lauren W. 2020. "Switching caps" – Two ways of communicating in sign in the Port Moresby deaf community, Papua New Guinea. *Asia-Pacific Language Variation* 6(1). 13–52.

Roche, Gerald & Hiroyuki Suzuki. 2018. Tibet's minority languages: diversity and endangerment. *Modern Asian Studies*. 52(2). 1227–1278. doi: 10.1093/oxfordhb/9780195390032.013.0018

Sinha, Chris, Vera Da Vilva Sinha, Jörg Zinken & Wany Sampaio. 2011. When space is not time: The social and linguistic construction of time intervals and temporal event relations in an Amazonian culture. *Language and Cognition* 3(1). 137–169. doi: 10.1515/langcog.2011.006

Sutton-Spence, Rachel & Bencie Woll. 1998. *The linguistics of British Sign Language: An introduction*. Cambridge: Cambridge University Press.

TDA (Tibet Deaf Association). 2011. *Bod kyi rgyun spyod lag brta'i tschigs mdzod* ([Dictionary of Tibetan Deaf Sign Language], Chinese title page title: *Longya shouyu zangyu cidian*, English title page title: *Standard Tibetan Sign Language Dictionary*). Lhasa: Bod ljongs mi rigs dpe skrun khang.

Tournadre, Nicolas & Sangda Dorje. 2003. *Manual of Standard Tibetan: Language and Civilization* (Introduction to Standard Tibetan [Spoken and Written]). Ithaca, New York: Snow Lion Publications.

Tournadre, Nicolas. 2014. The Tibetic languages and their classification. In Thomas Owen-Smith & Nathan Hill (eds.), *Trans-Himalayan linguistics: historical and descriptive linguistics of the Himalayan area*, 105–129. Berlin/Boston: Mouton de Gruyter.

Tournadre, Nicolas. 2003. The dynamics of Tibetan-Chinese bilingualism. *China Perspectives* 45 (January–February). 1–9.

Velupillai, Viveka. 2012. *Introduction to Linguistic Typology*. Amsterdam: John Benjamins.

Yang, Junhui. 2015. Chinese Sign Language. In Julie Bakken Jepsen, Goedele De Clerck, Sam Lutalo-Kiingi & William B. McGregor (eds.), *Sign languages of the world: A comparative handbook*, 177–194. Berlin/Boston: De Gruyter Mouton.

Yano, Uiko & Matsuoka, Kazumi. 2018. Numerals and timelines of a shared sign language in Japan: Miyakubo Sign Language on Ehime-Oshima island. *Sign Language Studies* 18(4). 640–665.

Yeshe, Kelsang. 2008. *Chinese codeswitching in modern Lhasa Tibetan: A motive-driven linguistic behaviour of Lhasa Tibetans*. Oxford: University of Oxford dissertation.

Zeitlyn, David. 2020. Haunting, Dutching, and Interference: Provocations for the Anthropology of Time. *Current Anthropology* 61(4). 495–513.

Zeshan, Ulrike. 2000. *Sign Language in Indo-Pakistan: A Description of a Signed Language*. Amsterdam: John Benjamins.

Index

Agreeing verbs 2, 72, 73, 77–79, 84, 85, 94, 95, 155, 266
Agreement 2, 40, 71–73, 77–79, 83–86, 88–89, 94, 95, 103, 109, 111, 132, 212, 312
Agreement verbs 2, 72, 73, 77–79, 84, 85, 94, 95
Allomorph 27
American Sign Language (ASL) 13, 27, 31, 52, 53, 58, 59, 65, 72, 74, 78–80, 82, 103, 107–109, 111, 112, 117, 123, 129, 138, 162, 163, 212, 232, 242, 244, 245, 266, 312
Annotation 40, 133, 172, 184–186, 190, 193, 197–199, 249
Argument structure 102–104, 109–111, 113–119, 127, 129–132

Blinks 242, 245, 250, 252, 257
Body use 313–316
Body-anchored 313, 314, 322, 331, 334, 342
Bodypart classifier 80, 103, 110, 111, 113, 115, 123–130, 132, 133

Cartography 138, 139, 142
Causative 2, 101–133
Causative alternation 2, 101–133
Classifier 2, 71–97, 103, 104, 107–133, 249, 266, 267, 269, 271–274, 277, 281, 283, 284, 287–293, 295–297, 301–303
Classifier predicates 103, 107–109, 111–113, 115, 117–122, 124, 126–127, 130, 132, 133, 249, 266, 267, 269, 271–274, 277, 281, 283, 284, 287–293, 295–297, 301–303
Classifier verbs 71–73, 79–83, 86–89, 94, 95, 118
Composite utterances 263–303
Compound 2, 14, 19, 24, 28, 31, 38, 40–53, 56, 57, 66, 186, 272–275, 327, 328, 339, 340
Concurrent head nods 245, 247, 249, 250

Constructed actions 285, 289, 291, 292, 302
Contact 9, 10, 13, 15, 22, 23, 25, 26, 29–31, 42–44, 162, 257, 318–319, 341
Co-speech gesture 162, 275, 281, 286, 316, 317, 335, 341

Data collection 8, 16–19, 22, 24, 86–94, 104, 172–175, 178–183, 186, 190–193, 198, 199, 248–249
Deaf school 10–12, 18, 38, 39, 60, 63, 113, 173, 179, 180, 190, 218, 234, 316–318, 330
Depicting 80, 86, 264–267, 269–277, 279, 281–290, 293–295, 300–303
Describing 126, 264–267, 269, 273–275, 283, 285, 287, 293, 294, 298, 299, 301, 302, 313
Diachronic change 2, 8, 31, 53
Dialect 8, 10, 11, 13, 19, 22, 25, 28, 38, 112
Distribution 10, 19, 28–30, 40, 115, 124, 187, 189–190, 193–194, 197–199, 223

ELAN 40, 113, 172, 184, 185, 189, 199, 249
Elicitation material 172, 175–183, 185, 199
Epistemic modality 137–163
Evidentials 149, 150, 157–161
Eyebrow movements 221, 242

Facial Action Coding System (FACS) 204, 219
Finnish Sign Language 244
Frozen signs 72, 78, 92, 94, 95

Gender handshapes 72, 73, 77–80, 86, 90–95
German Sign Language (DGS) 53, 81, 138, 139, 162, 163, 172, 174, 175, 177, 183, 242
Grammaticalization 2, 53, 149, 162, 204, 205, 212, 215, 221, 227, 233, 234
Grounded blends 264, 276, 281, 298, 299, 303
Grounded mental spaces 264, 277, 287, 302

Handedness 20–23
Handling classifier 71, 80, 103, 107–114, 116–121, 123, 126, 128–130, 132, 133

Handshapes 2, 15, 20, 21, 26, 27, 31, 38, 40,
    42–52, 56–61, 63–65, 71–95, 109–111,
    113–119, 122–125, 127, 129, 130, 133,
    137, 145, 146, 150, 152, 153, 155, 156, 159,
    184, 185, 198, 249, 254, 255, 257, 270,
    271, 274, 283, 287, 288, 290, 295, 323,
    336, 337, 339
Head movement 204, 205, 213, 214,
    221, 232, 233, 242, 244, 246, 253,
    285, 291
Head nods 2, 107, 162, 241–260
Hearing learners 2, 246, 254–258
Historical changes 8, 32
Historical relationship 2, 7–33
Hong Kong Sign Language (HKSL) 1, 2, 39,
    107, 108, 112, 113, 116, 120, 129, 130,
    132, 194, 203–238, 242

Iconicity 8, 12, 20, 31, 32, 41, 63, 64, 66,
    191, 303
Icons 265, 269, 271, 275–276, 286, 287, 294,
    295, 303
ID gloss 185, 186, 199
Imperatives 122, 123, 127
Indicating 9, 14, 75, 94, 120, 151, 244,
    264–270, 274, 275, 277, 283, 285–287,
    293, 294, 297, 299
Indicating signs 266–269, 293, 299
Indices 14, 15, 20, 26, 42, 43, 45, 46, 52, 61,
    71, 74, 81, 82, 84, 87, 88, 133, 146, 150,
    152, 153, 159, 186, 265–269, 271, 275,
    286, 287, 289–291, 294, 295, 303, 322,
    325–327, 330, 335, 336, 339
Inner negative polar questions
    (INPQ) 207–212, 215–217, 219–227,
    230–233, 236, 237
Intonational phrase (IP) 242, 244–246, 249,
    250, 252–258
Involvement strategies 264, 284–303
IP boundary 244–246, 249, 250, 252–258

Japanese Sign Language (JSL) 1–3, 7–33,
    65, 72, 73, 77–79, 137–163, 194,
    241–260, 312
Japanese Sign Language family 8

Kinship terms 73, 74, 79, 94
Korean Sign Language (KSL) 1–3, 7–33,
    71–97, 171–199
KSL Corpus 171–199

Lexical causative 118–119, 121, 130
Lexical database 184–186
Lexicalisation 26–28, 95, 111, 118, 121, 130
Lexicostatistics 8

Methods of signalling 2, 264–276, 286
Modal verbs 137–163
Modal verbs of epistemic state 154–157
Modal verbs of evidentiality 157–161
Modal verbs of possibility 150–154
Motivation 8, 12, 31, 56, 63, 64, 131, 163,
    178, 265, 266, 269
Mouth action 2, 151, 156, 162, 171–199,
    300, 301
Mouth gestures 144, 146, 147, 151, 156, 157,
    162, 163, 186–191, 193–199, 242, 296,
    300–302
Mouthing 42, 151, 156, 162, 186, 187, 189,
    190, 193, 194, 198, 221, 223, 225, 232,
    257, 295

Name signs 73–77, 79, 94, 175, 186
Narratives 2, 118, 180, 189, 247–250, 256,
    264, 276, 277, 281, 283–286, 289,
    292–296, 298, 299, 301, 303, 332
Negative polar questions (NPQ) 2, 203–238
Negation 2, 137–163, 177, 204–208,
    212–217, 221, 232, 233
Neutral gender 78, 90–91
Non-manual expressions 2, 137, 145, 149,
    156, 162, 163, 232, 264, 266–269, 274,
    275, 287, 289–291, 293, 297–303
Non-manual markers 204, 205, 212, 215, 227,
    228, 230, 232, 233, 263
Non-manuals 2, 84, 137, 138, 143, 145, 149,
    151, 156, 157, 159, 162, 163, 172, 186, 189,
    203–205, 208, 212, 215, 219, 221, 223,
    227–234, 263, 264, 266–269, 274, 275,
    277, 279, 286, 287, 289–294, 297–303
Non-native signers 2, 140

Numeral incorporation 12–15, 26, 30, 40, 41, 57, 59–66, 326
Numeral sign 7–33

Outer negative polar questions (ONPQ) 207–212, 215–227, 230–233, 235–237

Paradigm 2, 13, 14, 31, 48
Pear Tree Story 248
Phonological process 2, 37–66
Phonological reduction 20–23
Prosodic features 151, 242, 256
Prosodic hierarchy 242
Prosody 151, 157, 233, 241–247, 249, 252, 256–258

Quasi modals 141, 142

Resultatives 113, 120, 121

Seoul 11, 12, 17–19, 22, 87, 172, 174, 179, 185, 190, 198, 199
Shanghai Sign Language (SHSL) 1, 3, 37–66, 234
Sociolinguistic variation 10
South Korean Sign Language (SKSL) 3, 7–33

Studio setup 183–184, 199
Successive head nods 245, 247, 249–257
Swiss German Sign Language (DSGS) 242, 245
Symbols 265, 266, 269, 271, 275, 276, 281, 283, 284, 286, 287, 289, 294, 299, 300

Taiwan Sign Language (TSL) 1, 3, 7–33, 72, 194, 263–303
Temporaliser 328, 329, 331
Tianjin Sign Language (TJSL) 2, 3, 101–133
Tibetan Sign Language (TSL) 2, 3, 311–342
Timelines 2, 22, 311–342
Times of the day 321, 335–340
True modals 141, 142

Valency 109, 111, 115, 117
Variant 10–25, 27–31, 44, 52, 104, 105, 107, 108, 111, 116, 120, 121, 123, 125, 186
Vertical semi-elliptical timeline 313, 315, 316, 321–335, 341, 342
Virtual demonstration 281, 288

Whole entity classifier 80, 81, 103, 108–114, 116, 117, 119–123, 129